PRENTICE HALL REFERENCE GUIDE TO GRAMMAR AND USAGE

Fourth Edition

Muriel Harris
PURDUE UNIVERSITY

Prentice Hall
Upper Saddle River, New Jersey 07458

Library of Congress Cataloging-in-Publication Data

HARRIS, MURIEL
    Prentice Hall reference guide to grammar and
usage/Muriel
Harris.—4th ed.
        p.   cm.
    "With exercises."
    Includes index.
    ISBN 0-13-021022-6
    1. English language—Grammar—Handbooks, manuals, etc.
    2. English language—Grammar—Problems, exercises, etc.
    3. English language—Usage—Handbooks, manuals, etc.
    4. English language—Usage—Problems, exercises, etc.
    I. Title.   II. Title: Reference guide to grammar and
    usage.
PE1112.H293   1999   99-19691
428.2—dc21   CIP

Editorial Director: Charlyce Jones Owen
Editor in Chief: Leah Jewell
Assistant Editor: Vivian Garcia
Director of Production and Manufacturing: Barbara Kittle
Senior Production Manager: Bonnie Biller
Production Editor: Joan E. Foley
Copyeditor: Kathryn Graehl
Editorial Assistant: Patricia Castiglione
Manufacturing Manager: Nick Sklitsis
Prepress and Manufacturing Buyer: Mary Ann Gloriande
Director of Marketing: Gina Sluss
Marketing Manager: Brandy Dawson
Associate Creative Design Director
    and Cover Designer: Carole Anson
Interior Design: Seventeenth Street Studios

To Sam, David, Bekki, Dan, and Hannah— As Always—and Ever

This book was designed and set in 10/11 ITC New Baskerville
by Seventeenth Street Studios. Text and covers were printed
and bound by R.R. Donnelley & Sons Company.

© 2000, 1997, 1994, 1991 by Prentice-Hall Inc.
Upper Saddle River, New Jersey 07458

Printed in the United States of America
10 9 8 7 6 5 4 3

ISBN 0-13-021022-6

Prentice-Hall International (UK) Limited, *London*
Prentice-Hall of Australia Pty. Limited, *Sydney*
Prentice-Hall Canada Inc., *Toronto*
Prentice-Hall Hispanoamericana, S.A., *Mexico*
Prentice-Hall of India Private Limited, *New Delhi*
Prentice-Hall of Japan, Inc., *Tokyo*
Pearson Education Asia Pte. Ltd., *Singapore*
Editora Prentice-Hall do Brasil, Ltda., *Rio de Janeiro*

CONTENTS

To the Instructor   xiii
Hints for Using This Book   xxii

THE WRITING PROCESS

1 Purposes and Audiences   1
   a Purpose   1
   b Topic   1
   c Thesis   2

2 Writing Processes and Strategies   3
   a Planning   3
   b Drafting   7
   c Organizing   7
   d Collaborating   8
      1 Responding to writing   8
      2 Writing together   10
   e Revising   11
   f Editing and Proofreading   12

3 Paragraphs   13
   a Unity   13
   b Coherence   14
   c Development   14
   d Introductions and Conclusions   14
   e Patterns of Organization   15

4 Argument   20
   a Writing and Reading Arguments   20
   b Considering the Audience   21
      1 Types of appeals   21
      2 Common ground   22
   c Finding a Topic   23
      1 Arguable topics   23
      2 Interesting topics   24
      3 Local and general topics   24
   d Developing Your Arguments   24
      1 Claims, support, and warrants   24
      2 Logical arguments   26
      3 Logical fallacies   27
   e Organizing Your Arguments   29

5 Writing with Computers   30
   a Planning with Computers   30
   b Drafting with Computers   31
   c Organizing with Computers   31
   d Revising with Computers   31
   e Editing and Proofreading with Computers   32

REVISING SENTENCES:
ACCURACY, CLARITY, AND VARIETY

6 Comma Splices and Fused Sentences   33
   a Comma Splices   34
   b Fused or Run-on Sentences   34

7 Subject-Verb Agreement   36
   a Singular and Plural Subjects   36
   b Buried Subjects   36
   c Compound Subjects   37
   d *Either/Or* Subjects   37
   e Clauses and Phrases as Subjects   38
   f Indefinites as Subjects   38
   g Collective Nouns and Amounts as Subjects   38
   h Plural Words as Subjects   39
   i Titles, Company Names, and Words as Subjects   39
   j Linking Verbs   39
   k *There Is/There Are/It*   40
   l *Who/Which/That* and *One of . . . Who/Which/That*
       as Subjects   40

8 Sentence Fragments   42
   a Unintentional Fragments   42
   b Intentional Fragments   44

9 Dangling and Misplaced Modifiers   45
   a Dangling Modifiers   45
   b Misplaced Modifiers   47

10 Parallel Constructions   49
   a Parallel Structure   49
   b Faulty Parallelism   50

11 Consistency (Avoiding Shifts)   52
   a Shifts in Person or Number   52
       1 Unnecessary shift in person   52
       2 Unnecessary shift in number   53
   b Shifts in Verb Tense   53
   c Shifts in Tone   53
   d Shifts in Voice   54
   e Shifts in Discourse   54

12 Faulty Predication   55

13 Coordination and Subordination 57
  a Coordination 57
    1 Appropriate coordination 57
    2 Inappropriate coordination 57
    3 Excessive coordination 58
  b Subordination 58
    1 Appropriate subordination 58
    2 Inappropriate subordination 59
    3 Excessive subordination 59

14 Sentence Clarity 61
  a Moving from Known (Old) to Unknown (New) Information 61
  b Using Positive Instead of Negative 61
  c Avoiding Double Negatives 62
  d Using Verbs Instead of Nouns 62
  e Making the Intended Subject the Sentence Subject 63
  f Using Active Instead of Passive 63

15 Transitions 64
  a Repetition of a Key Term or Phrase 64
  b Synonyms 64
  c Pronouns 64
  d Transitional Words and Phrases 65
  e Transitions in and Between Paragraphs 66
    1 Transitions between sentences in a paragraph 66
    2 Transitions between paragraphs 67

16 Sentence Variety 69
  a Combining Sentences 69
  b Adding Words 70
  c Changing Words, Phrases, and Clauses 71

PARTS OF SENTENCES
17 Verbs 73
  a Verb Phrases 74
  b Verb Forms 74
    1 *-ing* verbs 74
    2 *-ed* verbs 75
    3 *to* + verb 75
  c Verb Tense 76
    1 Present tense 77
    2 Past tense 78
    3 Future tense 78
    4 Irregular verbs 79
  d Verb Voice 83
  e Verb Mood 84
  f Modal Verbs 85

18 Nouns and Pronouns 86
  a Nouns 86
    1 Singular, plural, and collective nouns 86
    2 Noun endings 86
  b Pronouns 88
    1 Personal pronouns 88
    2 Demonstrative pronouns 88
    3 Relative pronouns 88
    4 Interrogative pronouns 89
    5 Indefinite pronouns 89
    6 Possessive pronouns 89
    7 Reflexive and intensive pronouns 90
    8 Reciprocal pronouns 90

19 Pronoun Case and Reference 91
  a Pronoun Case 91
    1 Subject case 92
    2 Object case 92
    3 Possessive case 93
    4 Pronouns in compound constructions 93
    5 *Who/whom* 94
    6 Omitted words in comparisons 95
  b Pronoun Reference 96
    1 Pronoun number 97
    2 Compound subjects 97
    3 *Who/which/that* 97
    4 Indefinite words 98
    5 Indefinite pronouns 98

20 Adjectives and Adverbs 100
  a Adjectives and Adverbs 100
  b *A/An/The* 102
  c Comparisons 104

21 Prepositions 107
  a Common Prepositions 107
  b Idiomatic Prepositions 108
  c Other Prepositions 108

22 Subjects 109

23 Phrases 111

24 Clauses 113
  a Independent Clauses 114
  b Dependent Clauses 115
    1 Adjective clauses 116
    2 Adverb clauses 116

25 Essential and Nonessential Clauses and Phrases 119
  a Essential Clauses and Phrases 119
  b Nonessential Clauses and Phrases 120

26 Sentences 122
  a Sentence Purposes 124

b Sentence Structures 124
  1 Simple sentences 124
  2 Compound sentences 124
  3 Complex sentences 125
  4 Compound-complex sentences 125

PUNCTUATION

27 Commas 127
  a Commas in Compound Sentences 128
  b Commas After Introductory Words,
    Phrases, and Clauses 130
  c Commas with Essential and Nonessential Words,
    Phrases, and Clauses 132
  d Commas in Series and Lists 134
  e Commas with Adjectives 135
  f Commas with Dates, Addresses,
    Geographical Names, and Numbers 137
    1 Commas with dates 137
    2 Commas with addresses 137
    3 Commas with geographical names 137
    4 Commas with numbers 137
  g Other Uses for Commas 138
  h Unnecessary Commas 140

28 Apostrophes 142
  a Apostrophes with Possessives 142
  b Apostrophes with Contractions 143
  c Apostrophes with Plurals 143
  d Unnecessary Apostrophes 144

29 Semicolons 147
  a Semicolons in Compound Sentences 148
  b Semicolons in a Series 149
  c Semicolons with Quotation Marks 150
  d Unnecessary Semicolons 150

30 Colons 151
  a Colons to Announce Elements at the End
    of a Sentence 151
  b Colons to Separate Independent Clauses 152
  c Colons to Announce Long Quotations 152
  d Colons in Salutations and Between Elements 152
  e Colons with Quotation Marks 152
  f Unnecessary Colons 153

31 Quotation Marks 154
  a Quotation Marks with Direct and Indirect
    Quotations 154
    1 Quotation marks with prose quotations 154
    2 Quotation marks in poetry 155
    3 Quotation marks in dialogue 155

b Quotation Marks for Minor Titles and Parts
of Wholes   156
c Quotation Marks for Words   156
d Use of Other Punctuation with Quotation Marks   156
e Unnecessary Quotation Marks   157

32 Hyphens   158
a Hyphens to Divide Words   158
b Hyphens to Form Compound Words   159
c Hyphens to Join Word Units   159
d Hyphens to Join Prefixes, Suffixes, and Letters
to a Word   160
e Hyphens to Avoid Ambiguity   160

33 End Punctuation   161
a Periods   161
1 Periods at the end of a sentence   161
2 Periods with abbreviations   161
3 Periods with quotation marks   162
b Question Marks   163
1 Question marks at the end of a sentence   163
2 Question marks in a series   163
3 Question marks to indicate doubt   163
4 Unnecessary question marks   163
c Exclamation Points   164
1 Exclamation points at the end of a sentence   164
2 Exclamation points with quotation marks   165

34 Other Punctuation   166
a Dashes   166
1 Dashes at the beginning or end of a sentence   166
2 Dashes to mark an interruption   166
3 Dashes to set off a phrase or clause with
a comma   166
b Slashes   167
1 Slashes to mark the end of a line of poetry   167
2 Slashes to indicate acceptable alternatives   168
c Parentheses   168
1 Parentheses to set off supplementary matter   169
2 Parentheses to enclose figures or letters   169
d Brackets   170
1 Brackets to add comments within a quotation   170
2 Brackets to replace parentheses within
parentheses   170
e Omitted Words/Ellipsis   171

MECHANICS AND SPELLING
35 Capitals   173
36 Abbreviations   176
a Abbreviating Numbers   176

b Abbreviating Titles   176
c Abbreviating Places   177
d Abbreviating Measurements   177
e Abbreviating Dates   177
f Abbreviating Initials Used as Names   178
g Abbreviating Latin Expressions   178
h Abbreviating Documentation   178

37 Numbers   179

38 Underlining/Italics   182
a Underlining for Titles   182
b Other Uses of Underlining   182

39 Spelling   184
a Proofreading   184
b Using Spell Checkers   185
c Some Spelling Guidelines   186
  1 *ie/ei*   186
  2 Doubling consonants   187
  3 Prefixes and suffixes   188
  4 *y* to *i*   190
d Plurals   190
e Sound-Alike Words (Homonyms)   192

STYLE AND WORD CHOICE

40 Sexist Language   195
a Alternatives to *Man*   195
b Alternative Job Titles   195
c Alternatives to the Masculine Pronoun   195

41 Unnecessary Words   197
a Conciseness   197
b Clichés   200
c Pretentious Language   201

42 Appropriate Words   201
a Standard English   201
b Colloquialisms, Slang, and Regionalisms   201
c Levels of Formality   203
d Jargon and Technical Terms   206
e General and Specific Words   206
f Concrete and Abstract Words   207
g Denotation and Connotation   208

RESEARCH

43 Finding a Topic   211
a Finding a General Topic   211
b Narrowing the Topic   211

x CONTENTS

    c Formulating a Research Question 212
    d Formulating a Thesis 212

44 Searching for Information 213
    a Locating Sources of Information 213
        1 Libraries 214
        2 Online sources 215
        3 Community sources 216
        4 Interviews and surveys 216
    b Using Search Strategies 216
        1 Starting a working bibliography 216
        2 Finding useful terms 218
        3 Using search engines 218

45 Evaluating Sources 218
    a Getting Started 219
    b Evaluating Bibliographic Citations 219
        1 Author 219
        2 Timeliness 221
        3 Publisher/producer 221
        4 Audience 221
    c Evaluating Content

46 Taking Notes 223
    a Writing Notecards 223
    b Summarizing 223
    c Paraphrasing 225
    d Quoting 227
        1 When to quote 227
        2 Types of quotations 228
        3 Capitalization of quotations 229
        4 Punctuation of quotations 229

47 Using Sources 231
    a Integrating Sources 231
    b Using Signal Words and Phrases 232
    c Avoiding Plagiarism 235
        1 Information that requires documentation 235
        2 Information that does not require documentation 236

ONLINE

48 Research Online 239
    a What Is Available on the Internet? 239
    b Finding Information on the Internet 240
    c Using Search Engines on the Web

49 Web Resources 243

50 Evaluating Internet Sources 246

51 Citing Internet Sources **248**
    a MLA Online Citation   248
    b APA Online Citation   252
    c Other Formats for Citing Online Sources   254

DOCUMENTATION

52 Documenting in MLA Style   **255**
    a In-Text Citations   256
    b Endnotes   259
    c Works Cited List   260
    d Sample MLA-Style Research Paper   273

53 Documenting in APA Style   **281**
    a In-Text Citations   281
    b Footnotes   284
    c References List   284
    d Sample APA-Style Research Paper   291

54 Documenting in Other Styles   **299**
    a *Chicago Manual of Style*   299
    b CBE (Council of Biology Editors)   306
    c Style Manuals for Various Fields   310

ESL CONCERNS

55 American Style in Writing   **313**
56 Verbs   **313**
    a Helping Verbs with Main Verbs   314
        1 Modals   314
        2 Conditionals   314
    b Two-Word (Phrasal) Verbs   315
    c Verbs with *-ing* and *to* + Verb Forms   316

57 Omitted Words   **318**
    a Verbs   318
    b Subjects and *There/It*   318

58 Repeated Words   **318**
    a Subjects   318
    b Pronouns and Adverbs   319

59 Count and Noncount Nouns   **319**
60 Adjectives and Adverbs   **321**
    a Placement   321
    b Order   322
    c *A/An/The*   323
    d *Some/Any, Much/Many, Little/Few, Less/Fewer, Enough, No*   325

61 Prepositions   326
62 Idioms   327

APPENDICES

A Document Design   329
  1 Titles   329
  2 Headings and subheadings   330
  3 Page preparation   331
  4 Spacing for punctuation   332
  5 Document design   333

B Résumés   334
  1 Sections of the résumé   334
  2 Résumé styles   338
  3 Cover letters   341
  4 Electronic job search   343

Glossary of Usage   345
Glossary of Grammatical Terms   355
Using Compare and Correct and Question and Correct   373
Compare and Correct   374
Index   386
Correction Symbols   405
Question and Correct   inside back cover

TO THE INSTRUCTOR

The new material in the fourth edition of this reference guide was added for various reasons:

- To respond to requests from users of previous editions

- To keep pace with new challenges writers encounter (such as searching online for information for research papers)

- To include new information writers need (such as guidelines for citing electronic sources, other citation formats, etc.)

- To assist writers with a wider range of strategies to use as they move through various writing processes (such as working in peer response groups)

In Part One, "The Writing Process," writers are encouraged to view the various suggestions and strategies as possibilities to try when planning, writing, and revising and to select those that are most appropriate for them. New in this part is **a section on collaboration covering both peer response and group writing projects.** The first part of that section, on *peer response,* is designed for writers who have writing center tutors available to talk with, writers who work in peer response groups in classrooms, and writers who have formed writing groups to read and respond to each other's writing. If you use that section to guide peer response groups in your classes, you may also want some feedback from the groups. For example, some instructors ask members of the peer response group to write about what happened in the response group sessions. The second part of that section on collaboration, *group writing,* offers suggestions for how to proceed when a group writes a co-authored paper. My goal when discussing collaboration and, more generally, writing processes has been to help students recognize that writers compose differently and that writers need to find out what works best for them. The suggestions and strategies encourage writers to get feedback from readers and to work collaboratively, to move away from the limited—and limiting—notion that writers work alone without hearing any comments from their readers as they compose various drafts of a paper.

In response to the growing diversity of student populations, this edition also **expands the sections relevant to students learning English as a second language.** Because some of these students may come from countries where the rhetorical values emphasized are unlike American style in writing, Chapter 55 has been added to explain preferences of American writing style that these students will need to know. As in earlier editions of this reference guide, those aspects of English grammar and usage ESL students turn to most often are collected in a separate section, though these students will also find relevant hints directed to them throughout the book.

As writing courses continue to increase their emphasis on research writing, this edition has **expanded attention to evaluating sources and integrating sources into papers.** Writers who need other formats for citing sources will find information for using the Council of Biology Editors (CBE) format, *Chicago Manual* style, and other formats. Because collecting information for research papers now includes searching the Internet and other electronic sources, **a separate part of the book now covers, in depth, information on online searching that writers will need to know, including information for citing electronic sources.** In the discussion on searching the Internet for information, writers will find greatly expanded lists of useful resources and sites to search. For the information here, I'm drawing on my experience in developing an online writer's resource, the Purdue University OWL (Online Writing Lab). Our OWL offers dozens of handouts on writing skills, links to useful resources for information (and for job searches), and links to the most widely used sites for searching the Internet. You are welcome to direct your students to our Web site at <http://owl.english.purdue.edu>.

Also new to this book is **updated help with résumés, help with cover letters, and improved formatting, which will permit greater ease of use.** Tabs have been added to assist users to reach relevant sections of the book more quickly and conveniently, and each tabbed page has both a table of contents for that section and a new list of questions that users of the book are likely to ask. The questions have corresponding references to the sections where the writer can find the answers.

Through all the editions, when writing this reference guide to grammar and usage, I've kept in mind the countless numbers of students whom I've worked with elbow to elbow as a writing lab tutor and also the stacks of papers I've read as a teacher. Included here are those points of grammar and rules I have seen students struggling with and all the suggestions, proofreading techniques, and cautionary advice about pitfalls to avoid that I've passed along to them. Drawing on the experience derived from more years than I care to count, I've emphasized topics that I know are major sources of confusion and included strategies I also know students find useful. This book is thus the result of many years of field-testing and is also a collection of hints and strategies that students have shared with me.

The book reflects my efforts to produce a reference guide that all writers can use, even when they don't know much grammatical terminology. In the Purdue Writing Lab we answer hundreds of grammar hotline calls, and we sit with hundreds more students who know the word or phrase or punctuation usage they want to check, but who don't know how to find the page or section they need in a handbook. Where possible, students should be able to actively consult a guide to grammar while they are editing their writing rather than wait passively for someone else to locate and name their errors.

To help students leap this hurdle, I've created two guides, "Question and Correct" and "Compare and Correct." In the "Question and Correct" list, students can find many of their questions with accompanying references to the sections in the book they need. But it is sometimes difficult to phrase a question, so I have also included "Compare and Correct," another means to locate the appropriate pages in the book. Here students will find examples of typical troublesome constructions that may be similar to theirs. Again, references will guide them to appropriate places in the book.

Students who have had an instructor or writing lab tutor help them identify the point of grammar or usage they want to check can use the index, the contents, and the list of correction symbols to find the appropriate page or section.

The organization of the book is also intended to help writers easily locate the information they need. **The Writing Process** reviews the concerns of all writers as they move through various stages of writing and includes discussion of argument reading and writing. **Revising Sentences: Accuracy, Clarity, and Variety** provides rules and suggestions for constructions beyond the word level. **Parts of Sentences** explains parts of speech; grammatical terms having to do with single words; and concepts about phrases, clauses, and sentence types. **Punctuation** covers guidelines for the most frequently used forms in these areas. **Mechanics and Spelling** covers mechanics, such as capitals and abbreviations, as well as proofreading, the use of spell checkers, and useful spelling rules. **Style and Word Choice** offers suggestions for avoiding sexist language, wordiness, and clichés, along with guidelines on tone and word choice. **Research** moves through the processes of finding a topic, searching for information, taking notes, and evaluating and using sources. **Online** includes information on doing research online, using Web resources, and evaluating and citing Internet resources. **Documentation** covers documenting in MLA style, in APA style, and in other styles such as *Chicago Manual* and CBE, plus resources for other styles. **ESL Concerns** includes explanations of American writing style and those aspects of English grammar most needed by students learning English as a second language. The Appendices cover other important material. Appendix A, **Document Design,** covers various aspects of paper formatting; Appendix B, **Résumés,** discusses the various parts of a résumé and includes examples

relevant to students with different work experiences, plus help with cover letters. The **Glossary of Usage** and **Glossary of Grammatical Terms** round out the handbook.

Students will find this book to be user-friendly, clear, and concise. In the boxes they'll find useful strategies and errors to avoid, and in the exercises they will learn interesting bits of information about lighter topics (such as the origins of the phrase "it's a doozy" and the increasing popularity of pigs) and about relevant, current topics (such as the problems of waste disposal). The exercises are set up so that students can practice several different types of skills: proofreading, sentence combining, and in the "pattern practice," writing their own sentences using various rules.

This version of the book is what publishers call the "fourth edition," but those of us involved with writing call these later drafts "revisions." As with other revising I do, this was an opportunity to clean up minor infelicities, to clarify some explanations, and—most important—to add new material where needed. The most major additions reflect directions writing programs have taken—to emphasize discussions of writing processes in handbooks, to focus on collecting information and citing sources in research papers, to add needed information on online searching for information, and to remain aware of the needs of the many students learning English as a second language. With these additions as well as those in the third edition, I now feel confident that the book is more inclusive both in terms of the audience it is aimed at and the types of writing assignments for which it can offer help. I'm delighted that I had this opportunity to revise.

This book, then, is a guide to writing as well as to the editing or proofreading stages of writing. As I explain in "Hints for Using This Book," editing is only one of the writing processes and is most commonly performed after writers have composed their thoughts into words on paper. My advice to students is to attend to editing at the last stages, when they are close to a final draft of a paper. But research has made us aware of how nonlinear writing processes are, and some degree of editing and polishing may occur throughout various drafts. Our job as teachers is to keep our students from thinking that editing for grammatical correctness is the heart of writing. Part One of this book, on writing processes, is intended to help with that. We also need to remind our students that reference guides are useful and necessary tools, but ultimately no book can answer all questions or include every sticky or unusual case. Having an instructor or a writing center tutor to talk to is also necessary.

Supplements Available

Among the useful supplements specific to this handbook available from Prentice Hall are the following:

■ *Practicing Grammar and Usage* (by Muriel Harris). This booklet of supplementary exercises accompanies the fourth edition of the *Prentice*

Hall Reference Guide to Grammar and Usage, matching both topics and approach. You'll find all exercises in paragraph form with answer keys at the back. These booklets can be purchased by students, or you can copy individual exercises from your free booklet as needed when you adopt the *Reference Guide.* (The pages are formatted for ease of copying.)

- *Online Handbook.* This computerized reference system is compatible with most word processing packages and permits students to access information in the *Reference Guide* as they compose on a word processor. Available in Windows, Macintosh, and IBM versions.

- *Blue Pencil* and *Blue Pencil Authoring System* (by Robert Bator and Mitsura Yamada). *Blue Pencil* is an interactive editing program that allows students to practice their writing skills by making revisions in paragraph-length passages on the computer screen. If students have trouble with a particular concept, they can request additional instruction from the program. *The Blue Pencil Authoring System,* a for-sale item for instructors, allows you to create your own exercises for the *Blue Pencil* program. Available in Macintosh and IBM versions.

In addition to the text-specific supplements, the following **Prentice Hall Resources for Composition** are available to qualifying adopters. Contact your local Prentice Hall representative for details.

- *The Research Organizer* (by Sue D. Hopke of Broward Community College). This handy booklet offers guidance on the research paper and provides space for students to record their research strategy, notes, citations, outlines, and drafts all in one place. Instructors using the *Reference Guide* may copy this supplement free of charge for their class, or students may purchase the entire booklet at a minimal cost.

- *Model Research Papers,* second edition (by Janette Lewis). This collection of nine student research papers in various fields offers models of documentation, stylistic conventions, and formal requirements for different disciplines. Instructors using the *Reference Guide* may copy this supplement free of charge for their class, or students may purchase the entire booklet at a minimal cost.

- *Prentice Hall/Simon & Schuster Transparencies for Writers* (by Duncan Carter of Portland State University). This set of 100 two- and four-color transparencies features exercises, examples, and suggestions for student writing that focus on all aspects of the writing process—from generating ideas and shaping an outline to preparing a draft and revising, editing, and documenting the final paper. These transparencies also cover grammar, punctuation, and mechanics via overlays that show how sentence and paragraph errors can be corrected most effectively.

- *World Wide Web Site:* <www.prenhall.com/harris>. This exciting Web site contains multiple-choice questions, essay questions, and appropriate Web links for additional writing help. The site provides practice in writing effective sentences and quick access to help in correcting the most common grammatical errors. Exercises are self-graded and have direct references to the handbook.

- *Diagnostic and Competency Tests.* This supplement contains objective tests that can be used for pre-, mid-, and post-course evaluation. Answers to all test items are keyed to sections of the handbook.

- *Preparing for TASP.* Designed especially for teachers whose students must take the Texas statewide tests, this guide offers valuable advice and tests to help students prepare.

- *Preparing for CLAST.* Designed for teachers whose students must take the Florida statewide tests, this guide offers valuable advice and tests to help students prepare.

- *English on the Internet: A Prentice Hall Guide 1999–2000:* Helps students navigate the journey through cyberspace. Includes links to specific English Web sites and information on how to research, evaluate, and document online sources. *Free when packaged with this handbook.*

Also available to qualified adopters:

- *ABC News/Prentice Hall Video Library: Composition, Volume 2* 0-13-149030-3.

- *Computers and Writing* (by Dawn Rodrigues of University of Texas at Brownsville).

- *Classroom Strategies* (by Wendy Bishop of Florida State University).

- *Portfolios* (by Pat Belanoff of State University of New York, Stony Brook).

- *Journals* (by Christopher C. Burnham of New Mexico State University).

- *Collaborative Learning* (by Harvey Kail of University of Maine and John Trimbur of Worcester Polytechnic Institute).

- *English as a Second Language* (by Ruth Spack of Tufts University).

- *Writing Across the Curriculum* (by Art Young of Clemson University).

- *Distance Education* (by W. Dees Stallings of University of Maryland, University College).

Student packages available:

- *Student Economy Packages.* When you adopt the *Reference Guide* and another Prentice Hall composition text, the publisher makes them available in a shrink-wrapped package at a 10 percent discount off the total price.

- *Webster's Compact School and Office Dictionary.* This brief paperback dictionary is available at only $3.00 over the price of the *Reference Guide* when the two are shrink-wrapped together.

- *Webster's New World Dictionary Third College Edition.* This full-size hardcover dictionary is available at a discounted price of $9.05 when ordered with the *Reference Guide.*

- *Writer's Helper, Version 4.0* (Microsoft® Windows and Macintosh®). Based on the notion that imaginative and well-organized writing can often be attributed to software tools, *Writer's Helper* offers a collection of 19 unique pre-writing activities and 18 revising tools to help students through the writing process. The program works seamlessly with most word processing programs. *Available for $10 when packaged with this text.*

Acknowledgments

This book first took shape in the mind of Phil Miller, president of Humanities and Social Science, as he patiently listened to all my griping about grammar handbooks. His quiet wisdom and calm persistence brought this book into existence. Lynn Greenberg Rosenfeld, senior editor, English, saw the first edition of the manuscript through many formative stages, and her level-headed good sense still pervades the book. Kate Morgan, development editor, took on the heroic task of page-by-page editing of that first edition as well as huge-scale matters of organization and content. Her refinements continue to grace the pages, though I still lay claim to any faults she did not weed out. Later editions benefited from the perspectives of Alison Reeves, senior editor, English, and the careful eye, close editing, and useful suggestions of Kara Hado, development editor. This version benefited from the wisdom and guidance of Leah Jewell, editor in chief, and Vivian Garcia, assistant editor. I've profited also from the helpful comments, corrections, and suggestions of reviewers and users—including writing center tutors—who have added their voices and insights throughout this book: Robert Dial, University of Akron; James Helvey, Davidson County Community College; Michael Williamson, Indiana University of Pennsylvania; Connie Eggers, Western Washington University; Christopher Thaiss, George Mason University; Lyle W. Morgan II, Pittsburgh State University; Joe Lostracco, Austin Community College; Joyce Powell, North Lake University; Marion Perry, Erie Community College; Carol Franks, Portland State University; Donald Fucci, Ramapo College; Vivian Brown, Laredo Junior College; Walter Beale, University of North Carolina at Greensboro; Tracy Baker, University of Alabama at Birmingham. Others who were particularly helpful as I prepared the second edition were Rebecca Innocent, Southern Mississippi University; Jami Josifek, University of California at

Irvine; and Barbara Moreland, University of Texas at Arlington. I am also glad to have this opportunity to acknowledge the help of Virginia Underwood Allen (Iowa State University) with methods of explaining grammar, and the input of tutors from the Babson College writing center, under the direction of Joel Nydahl, who offered useful additions to the questions in the "Question and Correct" guide. I'd like to thank reviewers for the third edition, including Sheila Carter-Tod, Hollins College; Mary Dunn, College of Lake County; Matthew Hearn, Valdosta State University; Will Hochman, University of Southern Colorado; Eileen Moeller, Syracuse University; Sharon Shapiro, Naugatuk Valley Community-Technical College; Neal Snidow, Butte Community College; and Nancy Wood, University of Texas at Arlington; and reviewers for the fourth edition, including Terence A. Dalrymple, Angelo State University; Cheryl Dickinson, Southern Connecticut State University; Patricia Gatlin, Langston University; Rebecca Jackson, New Mexico State University; Stephanie Satie, California State University—Northridge; and K.J. Walters, Rockland Community College. For various editions, faculty, graduate students, and writing lab tutors at Purdue University who generously shared with me their wisdom and experience about writing and writing on computers include Lori Baker, Stuart Blythe, Johndan Johnson-Eilola, Barbara L'Eplattenier, Richard Morris, Edwin Nagelhout, Michelle Sidler, and Murray Shugars. Others who have kindly contributed useful suggestions and comments include Karl Beckson, Nan Hackett, Susan Pratt, Sara Sandstrom, and Kim Way (Concordia College), John Gould (Phillips Academy), and Tamzon Wilensky (Purdue University). I also owe a large debt of gratitude to the production department staff who transformed my sheets of computer printout into visually attractive, visually informative pages. Finally, I must acknowledge the extensive amount of assistance I've gotten from student writers who over the years have patiently listened to my attempts to help them and who revised into coherent papers the endless questions, doodles, diagrams, handouts, and bits of advice I kept giving them. As for my husband, Samuel, and our children—David and Rebecca, her husband Daniel, and their daughter Hannah—I prefer to think that my appreciation for them and for what they mean to me is always evident in our lives, not on pages of books.

—*Muriel Harris*

Unique FREE online study resource . . . the *Companion Website*™

www.prenhall.com/harris

Prentice Hall's exclusive *Companion Website*™ accompanies *The Prentice Hall Reference Guide to Grammar and Usage,* fourth edition, and offers unique tools and support that make it easy for students and instructors to integrate this online study guide with the text. The site is a comprehensive resource that is organized according to the chapters within the text and features a variety of learning and teaching modules:

FOR STUDENTS:

- **Study Guide Modules** contain a variety of self-graded exercises and features designed to aid students with self-study. These modules include:
  - chapter objectives that help students organize key concepts to be learned
  - essay questions that help strengthen critical thinking skills
  - quizzes with multiple-choice, true/false, and fill-in questions that supply instant scoring and feedback on student mastery of core material
  - built-in e-mail routing option that gives students the ability to forward essay responses and graded quizzes to their instructors
- **Reference Modules** contain *Web Destinations* and *Net Search* options that provide the opportunity to expand the information presented in the text. Whether through a directory of websites relevant to the subject matter of a chapter or key-term searches that automatically insert terms from the chapter into major search engines, these reference features enable students to quickly reach related information on the Web.
- **Communication Modules** include tools such as *Live Chat* and *Message Boards* to facilitate online collaboration and communication.
- **Personalization Modules** include our enhanced **Help** feature that contains a text page for browsers and plug-ins.

FOR INSTRUCTORS:

- The **Faculty Module** includes resources for teaching. This may include lecture hints, class activities, and graphics from the text, all coordinated by chapter. This module is accessed via a password provided by your local Prentice Hall representative.
- **Syllabus Manager**™ tool provides an easy-to-follow process for creating, posting, and revising a syllabus online that is accessible from any point within the companion website. This resource allows instructors and students to communicate both inside and outside of the classroom at the click of a button.

The *Companion Website*™ makes integrating the Internet into your course exciting and easy. Join us online at the address above and enter a new world of teaching and learning possibilities and opportunities.

COMPANION WEBSITE™

HINTS
FOR
USING THIS BOOK

This handbook may look like others you've used or seen, but there are some differences in this book that will make it easier—and more helpful—for you to use:

This book assumes that you are like all other writers and that you are unlike all other writers.

■ All writers need to be aware of the various writing processes they use, but every writer is different from every other writer. So, in Part One, you'll find some suggestions for writing and for using computers to write that will be helpful for you in particular but other strategies that won't work as well for you.

■ All writers struggle with writing. Perhaps there are a few people somewhere who can sit down and dash off well-written drafts. Most of us, however, need to write and rewrite and to edit our writing before handing it on to others.

■ All writers make the final choices and decisions about their writing, but writers also benefit from interacting with others who read their writing and offer feedback. Some writers benefit from collaborating with others during the early stages of planning and drafting; other writers prefer to save such collaboration until their papers are farther along.

This handbook is designed for easy use.

■ This book is arranged so that you can look up answers to your questions without knowing the necessary grammatical terms. If you have a specific question, turn to the "Question and Correct" list inside the back cover. If you don't know what to ask but you know your sentence or paragraph just doesn't seem right, turn to the pages at the back called "Compare and Correct."(There is, of course, an index if you know the point of grammar you want to check.)

■ Most of the grammatical terms you need are explained in Part Three. Others are explained as you need them, and there is also a Glossary of Grammatical Terms at the back of the book.

- The explanations in this book are stated as concisely as possible. You won't be spending extra time reading a lot of unnecessary prose.

- The information is presented with visual aids such as charts, tables, lists, and different ink shades to help you locate what you need quickly.

- On each tabbed page are questions you would ask to use information in that section of the book.

This handbook concentrates only on the most essential points of grammar and the most frequently made errors.

- This book focuses on the questions and problems writers most frequently have.

- You won't find an exhaustive list of grammatical terms or seldom-used rules in this book. However, if you want definitions of grammatical terms such as *participle, gerund,* and so on, see the Glossary of Grammatical Terms at the back of this book.

This book offers explanations and strategies and includes hints to follow.

- Rules are explained, not just stated.

- This book offers strategies to use. Sometimes, it's easier to remember a rule and apply it; sometimes it's easier just to have a strategy to follow. For example, either you can follow the rule for spelling *desert* and *dessert* or you can try one writing center tutor's strategy: she remembers that just as she likes seconds for dessert, she uses a second *s* for *dessert.* Look for other strategies in the boxes.

- Other hints are reminders to help you avoid errors that writers frequently make.

- This book is intended to answer most questions, though you may need to consult your teacher or writing center tutor for further explanation or specific information. No book can include answers to all writing questions or to all the messy exceptions to rules of English grammar.

This book offers suggestions for how computers and online sources can help you write.

- You may be fairly comfortable with writing on computers or maybe you are at the beginning stages of word processing, but the suggestions for using computers to plan, write, revise, and edit your writing will offer new approaches that can increase the usefulness of the computer.

■ Online search tools in libraries and on the Internet are extremely helpful but can be intimidating when you first jump in. The advice in the Online section of this book should help you, but your library and your access to the Internet may make conditions somewhat different at your site. The Online section also offers help with evaluating and citing Internet sources. Some addresses for useful World Wide Web sites you can go to when searching the Internet are listed in Chapter 49, and in Appendix B on résumés, you will find a few World Wide Web sites that list job openings. There are also numerous OWLs (Online Writing Labs) with a variety of resources. You can start with the OWL I helped to develop at Purdue University. Here you will find links to most of these OWLs, as well as links to dozens of handouts on writing skills, links to sources of information, and links to sites that will search the Internet for you. To reach Purdue University's OWL, use the following Internet address: <http://www.owl.purdue.edu>.

This book offers exercises in a useful format.

■ To practice your understanding of various topics, try the exercises in each chapter.

■ You'll notice that the exercises are not lists of separate sentences. Instead, you'll be checking your understanding by working on proofreading and pattern practice skills with paragraphs. The subjects of these paragraphs are of general interest and may even add to your storehouse of minor facts with which to amaze your friends. (For example, you'll read about the magnificent old Duesenberg automobile, the Turkish origins of Santa Claus, the art of whistling, the popularity of pigs as pets, and nonimpact aerobics.)

As you can tell from this description, the goal of this book is to be a useful companion for you when you write. As you edit your papers before turning them over to your readers, you may have questions such as "Do I need a comma here?" or "Something doesn't seem right in that sentence—what's wrong?" If you don't know the grammatical terms to look up in the index, try the suggestions for using this book on page xxii. If needed, browse through the "Question and Correct" or "Compare and Correct" sections.

Some Cautionary Advice

All textbook writers would like to think that what they have written supplies all the answers and solves all the reader's problems. Their book is all that students need. That must be a great feeling, but you and I know that in the case of any reference guide to grammar and usage, such as this book, knowledge of grammar is only one aspect of writing—and not the most important one either. The writer's real task is to use writing to give shape to thoughts, to focus on topics and present them clearly and coherently. For most writers, this means moving through a variety of processes to compose, develop, and organize ideas and writing several drafts—at least—with feedback, when possible, from readers as the drafts are revised and evolve into more finished products.

In this book you'll find some useful help with these writing processes, and the most effective time to use the rules for grammar and mechanics is when you are working on final or near-final drafts, polishing them for grammatical correctness, proofing for correct punctuation and spelling, and sharpening your word choices and sentence constructions. At the earlier stages of composing, you don't want to interrupt your thought processes or the flow of the ideas evolving on the page to worry about choosing the right pronoun. There is also no point in checking the punctuation of a sentence in an early draft if it may disappear in the next draft. When you have a well-developed, well-organized topic and have done all the necessary revision, you are finally ready to concentrate on matters such as sentence correctness, word choices, punctuation, spelling, and the appearance of the page. Then, you can benefit from the portions of this book that are designed to help you edit your writing to conform to standard English. When your sentences are clearly phrased and correctly punctuated and when your words are appropriately chosen and correctly spelled, your readers can more easily understand—and appreciate—your ideas.

—*Muriel Harris*

Purposes and Audiences (purp)

1a Purpose

Writing is a powerful multipurpose tool that helps us discover and explore more fully what we are thinking so that we learn as well as express our feelings and thoughts. We write to convey information, to persuade others to believe or act in certain ways, to help ourselves and others remember, and to create works of literary merit. Through writing, we can achieve a variety of purposes:

- *Summarizing:* Stating concisely the main points of a piece of writing

- *Defining:* Explaining the meaning of a word or concept

- *Analyzing:* Breaking the topic into parts and examining how these parts work or interact

- *Persuading:* Offering convincing support for a point of view

- *Reporting:* Examining all the evidence and data on a subject and presenting an objective overview

- *Evaluating:* Setting up and explaining criteria for evaluation and then judging the quality or importance of the object being evaluated

- *Discussing/Examining:* Considering the main points, implications, and relationships to other topics

- *Interpreting:* Explaining the meaning or implications of a topic

1b Topic

The subject of a piece of writing may be a topic the writer chooses, or it may be assigned. If you are asked to choose your own topic and don't readily have something in mind, assume that an interviewer or reporter is asking you one of the following questions. Your answer might begin as suggested here:

- What is a problem you'd like to solve?

  "... is a problem, and I think we should ..."

- What is something that pleases, puzzles, irritates, or bothers you?

  "What annoys (or pleases) me is ..."

- What is something you'd like to convince others of?

  "What I want others to agree on is ..."

- What is something that seems to contradict what you read or see around you?

  "Why does ..." (or) "I've noticed that ... but ..."

- What is something you'd like to learn more about?

  "I wonder how ..."

- What is something you know about that others around you may not know?

  "I'd like to tell you about ..."

 ## 1c Thesis

After you've selected a topic to write about, you also have to decide on a comment that you'll make about it. Then, you will have a thesis. Sometimes the comment part of a thesis is developed in a writer's mind early in the writing process, and sometimes it becomes clear as the writer works through various writing processes.

Topic	Comment
Television commercials	should not insult competing brands or companies.
Effective document design	helps technical writing present complex material more clearly.

HINT Starting Questions

When you start to write, ask yourself:

- Who am I in this piece of writing? (a friend? an impartial observer? someone with knowledge to share? a writer with a viewpoint to recommend? an angry customer?)

- Who is my intended audience? (peers? a potential boss? a teacher? readers of my local newspaper? colleagues in an office? people who are likely to agree with me? or disagree? or are neutral?)

- What is the purpose of this writing? (to convince? amuse? persuade? inform?)

- What are some other conditions that will shape this writing? (the assignment, length, due date, format, evaluation criteria)

Narrowing the topic is an important stage of writing because no one can write an effective paper that is vague or promises to cover too much. Some of your answers to the questions in the previous box will help you narrow your subject. If the assigned length is three pages, you have to limit your topic more than if you are asked to write a fifteen-page paper. If your audience is not all college students but specifically college students who depend on financial aid from the government, your topic is also narrowed. Being specific is a way to limit the scope of a topic. Instead of writing a short paper about how the Internet can promote learning in high school classes, you could write about a more specific topic, such as how the World Wide Web is used in high school biology classes.

2 Writing Processes and Strategies (w pr)

As we write, we engage in a variety of actions. We plan, draft, organize, revise, edit, perhaps go back to plan some more, revise, maybe reread what we've written, reorganize, put the draft aside for a while, write, and so on. All these writing processes are part of the larger act of producing a piece of writing, and there is great variety in how writers move back and forth through these processes. Because moving through all these processes takes time, most writers (especially better ones) realize that they have to start early and that they'll be engaged in some hard work. Additional suggestions for writing process strategies to use when you are working on a computer are included in Chapter 5.

2a Planning

During the planning process, you find the material you want to include in your writing. The following useful strategies can help you find material.

- **Brainstorming** Once you have a general topic in mind, one way to start planning is to turn off the editor in your brain (that voice that rejects ideas before you've had a chance to consider or develop them) and let thoughts tumble out either in conversation or on paper. Ideas tend to generate other ideas, and a variety of thoughts will surface. Some writers need to write down whatever occurs to them so that they won't forget all the material they will later sort through. The writing may be in sentences or set down as notes and phrases, depending on which format the writer finds most useful. During a brainstorming session with a writing center tutor, one writer took the following notes as she considered whether she would support term limits for the members of the United States Congress:

  For term limits
  - Prevents one person from gaining too much power and representing only one faction of the public.
  - Keeps bringing newcomers into office so they represent different parts of the public in their district.
    - New political views
    - That means that the groups who give political donations will change.

- In the last term that person can put his or her energies into working on laws and not just on getting elected.
- Stay in office too long, maybe not doing important work?

Against term limits
- People really get to know their job and have seniority.
- Leaders (Speaker of the House ... who else? majority leader? powerful committee heads?) have to have a lot of experience to do a good job.

Some facts to find out
- How many congressional representatives stay in office a long time?
- What happens to them after long terms in office?
- Do leaders really have to have a lot of experience? (Check on role of advisors and staff.)

Freewriting   Some writers find that they produce useful material when they start writing and keep writing without stopping. The writing is "free" in that it can go in any direction that occurs to the writer as she writes. The important part of freewriting is to keep going. You can also use freewriting as a "mind dump," recording everything you know about the subject you're going to write about. One student writer began his freewriting for an assignment about analyzing a stereotype he had encountered as follows:

My dream even from when I was a child was always to be a farm manager. Back in seventh grade I remember my social studies class was having a class discussion of vocations in life. Never once did anyone talk about a profession in the line of agriculture, so when I asked, "What about farm management?" I was blasted with laughter and crude comments. The comments they made were false stereotypes that people have. People think all ag students are "countrified" or are just "farm boys." Just "hicks." Another stereotypical view is that farmers are lazy, just plant and sit around at the local coffee shop and gossip. My father's farm is very diversified. We grow mint, onions, and corn. The mint and onions keep us busy all year. Many farmers get a job in town to supplement their farm income. Farmers need to keep complicated records and take hard ag courses in college. Computers are an important part of farming today.

Listing   Some writers begin by searching their minds for what they know about the subject and listing those points on paper. That also helps to clarify what they will need to find out before they begin to write. The following list was developed by a writer working on an application to a school of veterinary medicine:

What experiences have I had with animals?
- Summer assistant in local vet's office
  - Cleaned equipment.
- Helped with animals during treatment.
- Got to know how much work is involved.
  - My own pets

– Learned to care for a variety of animals.
– Should I list my course work? high school clubs?
– Helped a cousin show her sheep.
– Had to groom two sheep.

■ **Clustering and branching** Clustering establishes the relationships between words and phrases. Begin by writing a topic in the middle of a sheet of paper and circling it. Then as related ideas come to mind, draw lines to connect these ideas to other ideas in a nonlinear way. Other ideas will become the center of their own clusters of ideas as the topic branches out. When you keep an open mind, ideas spill out on the page. You can rework them in a more orderly way by putting the main idea at the top of the page and reordering the branches. The writer who created the following cluster was exploring the topic of divorce and its effects on children.

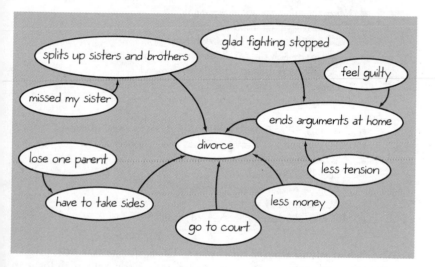

■ **Conversation/collaboration** While some writers prefer to plan by themselves, others benefit from talking with a peer response group, a writing center tutor, or a friend. Talk produces more talk, and if the listener asks questions, even more ideas can develop in the writer's mind. If you find talk useful and you are in a situation where you can't engage in conversation, try picturing yourself addressing an imaginary audience.

■ **Writer's notebook/journal** Ideas tend to float to the surface of our minds when we're engaged in other activities, such as walking to class, cooking, or taking a shower. You can capture those thoughts by recording them in a writer's notebook as soon as you can. Some good writers carry a small notebook to jot down these reminders. Others regularly keep journals, writing brief entries at least once a day. You can refer to your journal or notebook for ideas when you write.

■ **Reading** An important source of material for your writing is the reading you do. You can search out relevant information in libraries or on the Internet. You may also find connections to your topic when you read the daily newspaper, a magazine, or readings for other classes. Your writer's notebook then becomes a particularly useful place to record these connections.

■ **Outlining** Some writers benefit from producing an outline as the first stage in planning. They may or may not follow that outline, and it may change as the paper develops, but the outline is a useful planning tool. You can also use an outline after an early draft to see how your paper will be structured. The following outline was prepared for a report on how to increase donations to a local food bank for the poor:

> Show problem
> - ■ Need for food for local homeless
>   - – Present level of food needed
>   - – 2,000 per month request food
>   - – No. of homeless children increasing
>   - – Donations not keeping up with demand
>   - – Largest local donor, a restaurant, has closed
> - ■ Projections for future unemployment when auto plant closes
> Solutions
> - ■ Ask local media (newspaper, TV station) to show problem
> - ■ Send requests to local churches and synagogues
> - ■ Explore new commercial sources
>   - – Local supermarkets
>   - – College residence hall cafeterias
>   - – Restaurants
> - ■ Ask for volunteer collectors of food

■ **Who? what? when? where? how? why?** These question words, often used by journalists in gathering information for news articles, can be useful in provoking us to think more fully about a topic. *Who* or *what* might be involved or affected? *Why?* Is the location (*where?*) important? *How? What* connects the people or things involved? Try using these question words in a variety of combinations, and jot down your answers. For a paper about the effects on human skin of too much exposure to sun, the writer asked herself these questions as she gathered information:

> What damage can sun cause to human skin? Why?
> What illnesses result?
> How serious are these?
> Who is most likely to be affected?
> How can these illnesses be treated?
> How widespread is the problem?
> What are the warning signs?

- **Types of evidence** As you plan, you may find it helpful to clarify the kinds of information to be included in your paper. Will you draw primarily on personal experience gained from the direct observation of your world (what you see, hear, and read), or will you depend on reading, researching the work of others in the library, or gathering your own data from interviews or research?

- **Divide and conquer** For writing projects that seem overwhelming, you may find that making a list of the steps involved in completing the project is a useful planning strategy. Breaking the writing into groups of manageable tasks makes it easier to plunge into each one. Your list also provides a road map for how to proceed. When and how will you collect evidence? Will you go to the library tomorrow afternoon? What will you need to read before you start writing? What questions do you want to discuss with a writing center tutor?

2b Drafting

Some writers prefer to do most of their planning in their heads, and as a result, they have the general shape of a paper in mind when they start writing. Others have to write and rewrite early drafts before a working draft begins to take shape. In general, early drafts are very rough as you add, change, and rework. Some writers are ready to share their early drafts with others, to get advice, to hear how the draft sounds when read aloud by a writing center tutor, a peer response group, or themselves, and to get more ideas for revision. Other writers aren't ready to share their early drafts, and they prefer to delay reader input until a later draft. Because many good writers work collaboratively, they seek readers of their drafts before they are finished.

Writers who have time to put a draft aside for a while also find that new suggestions pop up or that something they hear or read triggers suggestions for new material to add to the draft. This is yet another reason for starting early—to allow for that "percolating" time. In addition, when you have a short period away from a draft, you gain distance so that you can be more objective about what revisions are needed. When you reread a freshly written draft, it is hard to separate what is still in your head from what is on the page, and it is even harder to see what is missing or in need of reworking.

2c Organizing

As your draft takes shape, it may follow the outline you wrote, or the outline may need to be reworked. Or you may be a writer who outlines after some drafting. At whatever stage an outline is most useful, it helps you see if the organizational structure is sound and if any sections need more material. An outline can be an informal list of major points with the minor ones listed and indented under major points. If you are using a computer, put the outline on the screen and experiment with cutting and pasting parts of the outline in different places until you see a logical flow that makes sense to you. (See Chapter 5 for more strategies for writing on computers.) If you have a large collection of evidence and notecards to organize, try color-coding the cards or sorting them according to the sections of the paper in which they will be used.

2d Collaborating

1. Responding to Writing

Most writers benefit from reader comments while we're drafting a paper. As we listen to our readers' responses, their feedback can give us a fresh perspective—a view from the outside—on how the paper is progressing. Those reader comments are only suggestions, though, and the final decisions as to how to revise in light of those comments are matters for you, the writer, to decide. There are several ways you can go about getting responses from readers of your writing, and the best time to get that feedback is before you're finished with the draft. That allows you time to make revisions based on what you hear from your readers.

Some ways you can get feedback from readers:

- **Meet with a writing-center tutor.** If you have access to a writing center, ask a tutor to act as a reader and respond to the draft. The tutor is likely to ask what your concerns are, so come prepared with questions you had about that draft as you wrote it (for example: "Does the conclusion seem sort of weak?" "Does my thesis seem clear?" "Are my examples OK?" "Does this fit the assignment?"

- **Meet with a small group of students in your class.** If your class has peer response groups or workshop days, you can meet with a small group, exchange papers, and offer reader feedback for each other. When you act as a reader, you are not only helping other writers—you are also sharpening your own critical skills. That practice in critically reading someone else's writing improves your ability to critically read your papers too. You'll begin to notice that you will more easily think of suggestions for how to revise your papers. To make small group responses helpful, you and your group can consider the following suggestions to make your time together more useful for all of you:

  Spend a few minutes comparing how you feel about hearing responses to your writing. Some writers welcome comments from readers, but others are fearful or hesitant. Once you express those feelings openly, you and your group can deal with them more honestly. And some readers are hesitant to suggest changes, either because they aren't sure how valid their own comments are or because they don't want to offend fellow students. A few minutes of discussion as to how to overcome these barriers can make the rest of the session more useful.

Come prepared with copies of your paper and some questions. Since most readers can follow along better if they are reading copies of your draft as well as listening, come prepared with enough copies to distribute to everyone. And think of some real questions you have about your draft that you want your readers to answer.

Decide on ground rules for how your group will proceed. Does your group want to have the writer read the paper aloud while readers read copies? Or would writers prefer hearing someone else read their papers? (Most writers benefit from this stage of response because they can catch little mistakes, typos, wrong words, and other problems as they listen or read and because they hear how the writing flows.) Or can each writer decide this for himself or herself? How long will the group spend on each paper? Will all the responses be oral, or do you want to write down any comments? Does your group want to draw up a uniform response sheet with itemized questions?

Decide what questions readers will respond to. A set of questions should be drawn up in advance to guide the responses. Your group can spend a few minutes working up a list before you start reading. It's important that the group decide on a list of common questions to address, and the discussion should be based on the kinds of feedback you and the other writers want. Possible questions include the following:

1. Since the first comments from readers should be positive ones, you can start by asking what the readers like about this draft. What worked well? (Writers need to know what's working well in addition to what might be revised.) What are some other strong points of this draft? (interesting topic? effective introduction? strong feelings expressed? good examples? good use of humor? effective word choice?)
2. What do you think is the main point of this paper?
3. Are there any sections that are unclear and need more explanation?
4. Does the paper fit the assignment?
5. Who is the appropriate reader or audience for this paper?
6. Are there any sections that seem out of order?
7. Are there any parts of the paper where the writing seems to digress from the topic?
8. Does the paper flow? (That is, does the paper seem to progress smoothly, or are there abrupt shifts or missing parts?)
9. What else do you want to know about the paper's topic?
10. If you had to prioritize, what is the most important revision you would suggest to the writer?

■ **Form a writing group on your own.** If writers want reader feedback but have no writing center or classroom opportunities to get that feedback, they may form writing groups. A writing group is a small group of people willing to come together on a regular basis and read each other's writing. Members can use the suggestions offered above to guide the group's format. A writing group may take on a personality of its own as members learn from each other and learn how to critique writing. Some groups that work well stay together for years.

2. Writing Together

Some writers find that their task is to write a paper as a group project with multiple authors (a common practice in the business world, where team reports are assigned). If you find yourself writing in such a group project, your group will need to set its ground rules. The first task will be to decide if all members will work on the whole paper or whether everyone will be responsible for a part.

- If each part is assigned to a different writer, your group should decide on the following:

  1. How will your group break the project into parts? A group discussion and brainstorming session can be helpful at this stage, and a final product of this session (or sessions) can be an outline.
  2. Who will do each part of the outline?
  3. Who will be assigned to put all the parts together and produce the final product?
  4. What are the deadlines by which you each submit a draft of your part to the group? (When the group meets to read drafts of separate parts, you can use the suggestions listed above to guide your discussion.)
  5. When you meet for a reading of a draft of the whole paper, how will the group decide on revisions needed to join the parts together smoothly? Should revisions be agreed to by a majority vote, or should there be a project leader who oversees the drafting of the final product?

- If the whole paper is to be co-authored, your group needs to decide how to proceed. Some steps to consider include the following:

  1. Spend time discussing your topic, refining it, and deciding on the major areas of content. This will take several meetings, and since ideas will evolve as you talk, someone needs to take notes.
  2. Try writing separate drafts. When the group comes together and reads those drafts, you may find that you can cut and paste from different writers' drafts to form a whole.
  3. Have each writer rewrite the whole that has been created. Then meet to see how the drafts have been refined. More cutting and pasting may be needed here.
  4. Have a final meeting at which the last draft is read aloud, and try to suggest any revisions still needed as the draft is read.

2e Revising

A particularly important part of writing is revising, which means re-seeing the whole and then reworking it. Because this can be difficult to do, some writers make the mistake of handing in an early draft that hasn't been adequately revised. The low grades they get are not indications of being inadequate writers but a result of handing in a paper too early in the writing process. (If you are a purchaser of computer software, think of similar problems caused when software is released too early, before the bugs are worked out. The program would have been much more successful if the developers had worked on it more before release.)

During the revision process, many writers are helped considerably by collaborative feedback from others. Writers who publish their work often get feedback and helpful advice from their editors, and scholars who submit articles and books to scholarly publications ask colleagues to read their manuscripts. Reader response can be very useful when you are revising your paper. You may have classroom opportunities for working with a response group, and you can visit your writing center to talk with a tutor who can also provide you with reader feedback. Or you might have conferences with your teacher. There are a variety of ways to get reader feedback, but it's important to remember that finally, you are the writer, and you must decide which advice to listen to and which to put aside. (See 2d for help with collaborating with your readers.)

To revise effectively, first go through all the major qualities of good writing, those aspects referred to as the higher-order concerns (HOCs) by Thomas J. Reigstad and Donald McAndrew. (The later-order concerns, or LOCs, are discussed in the section on editing.) Use the revision checklist in the box that follows to review the HOCs.

HINT **Revision Checklist (HOCs = Higher-Order Concerns)**

Purpose: What is the purpose of this paper? Do the thesis and audience fit the purpose? Have you achieved the purpose? If not, what's needed?

Thesis: Is the thesis clearly stated? Has it been narrowed sufficiently? Is it appropriate for the assignment? Can you summarize your thesis if asked? If you think of the thesis as a promise that you will discuss this statement, have you really kept all parts of that promise?

Audience: Who is the audience for this paper? Is the audience appropriate for this topic? Is it clear who the intended audience is? What assumptions have you made about the members of your audience? Did you tell them what they already know? Is that appropriate? If you are

(continued on next page)

(continued from previous page)

writing for your teacher or some expert in the field, does he or she expect you to include background material? (An essay exam or other writing in which the purpose is to evaluate the writer's knowledge should include such information even when the reader knows the material too.) Did you leave out anything your audience needs to know?

Organization: What is the central idea of each paragraph? Does that idea contribute to the thesis? Do the paragraphs progress in an organized, logical way? Are there any gaps or jumps from one part to another? Is the reader likely to get lost in any part? Do your transitions indicate when the writing moves to a new aspect of the topic?

Development: Are there places where more details or examples or specifics would help? Have you left out anything your audience needs to know? Are there details that are not relevant and should be omitted?

2f Editing and Proofreading

Editing is the fine-tuning process of writing. When you edit, you attend to what has been called the later-order concerns (LOCs), that is, details of grammar, usage, punctuation, spelling, and other mechanics that you attend to at a later stage of the paper. The most effective time to edit is when you're done revising so that you have shaped the paper and won't be making any more large-scale changes. It is far more efficient to fine-tune sentences you know will be in the final version than to edit work that might be deleted in a later draft. Yet another reason for not editing until the paper is close to completion is that you may be reluctant to delete sentences or words you have already corrected. Even if a sentence needs to be rewritten or doesn't belong in the paper, there's a natural tendency to want to leave it in because it is grammatically correct. Don't let yourself fall into that trap. Errors in grammar and usage send the wrong message to your readers about your general level of competence in using language, and such errors will cause you to get lower grades.

Proofreading is the final editing process of writing, the last check for missing words, misspellings, format requirements, and so on. If you have a list of references you consulted while writing your paper, this is the time to do a final check on the information and the format of the entries. To check your spelling, try the proofreading suggestions listed in 39a. If you use a spell checker in your word processing program, remember that spell checkers cannot flag problems with wrong forms of words such as *it's/its* or *advice/advise.* If you use a grammar checker, remember that such programs catch some but not all grammar problems and can only offer suggestions. For example, the program may highlight constructions such as *there is/there are,* but it cannot tell you whether your choice is appropriate.

HINT   **Editing and Proofreading Checklist**
(LOCs = Later-Order Concerns)

Don't try to check for everything as you edit and proofread your final draft. It's more efficient to know your typical problem areas and to use strategies for finding and correcting any errors. The boxes in this book give you numerous strategies to try. In addition, try these general suggestions:

■ Put the paper aside for a bit. It's easier to see problems when the paper is not as fresh.

■ To help your eye slow down and see each word, read the paper aloud. Try sliding a card down each line as you reread. Then, as you read aloud, your eyes and ears will both be working to help you.

■ If you tend to leave out words, point to each word as you read. Be sure that you see a written version of every word you say.

■ As you read, have a list in mind of the particular problems you tend to have when writing. Which grammatical problems have frequently been marked by teachers? Which aspects of grammar do you frequently have to check in a handbook? Here are some of the most common problems to look for in your papers:

fragments	omitted commas
subject-verb agreement	verb tenses
comma splices	spelling errors
misplaced apostrophes	run-on sentences
pronoun reference	unnecessary commas
omitted words	missing transition words

■ Keep this book close by as you edit and proofread. If you have a question and don't know which section to check, see the **"Question and Correct"** section inside the back cover of this book. If you have a written example, check the **"Compare and Correct"** section in the blue-edged pages at the back of this book to find a similar example.

3 Paragraphs (para)

Each paragraph in a paper is a group of sentences that work together to develop one idea or topic within the larger piece of writing. Effective paragraphs are unified, coherent, and developed.

 **3a Unity**

A unified paragraph focuses on one topic and does not include unnecessary or irrelevant material. To check the unity of each of your paragraphs, ask yourself what the paragraph is about. You should be able to answer in a sentence that either is implied or appears in the paragraph as the topic sentence. Any sentence not related to this topic sentence is probably a digression that doesn't belong in the paragraph.

3b Coherence

Every paragraph should be written so that each sentence flows smoothly into the next. If your ideas, sentences, and details fit together clearly, your readers can follow along easily without getting lost. To help your reader, use the suggestions in Chapter 15 for repeating key words and phrases and using synonyms, pronouns, and transitional devices between sentences and paragraphs.

3c Development

A paragraph is well developed when it covers the paragraph topic fully, using details, examples, evidence, and other specifics the reader needs as well as generalizations to bind these specifics together. You can check the development of each of your paragraphs by asking yourself what else your reader might need or want to know about that topic. Some specifics help to explain or support the more general statements, and other specifics help to make bland generalizations come alive.

3d Introductions and Conclusions

Some writers need to write their introduction before the body of the paper, and others find it easier to write their introduction after revising the body. Some writers even write the introduction last. As you draft your introduction and conclusion, consider the following points:

- **Introduction:** The purpose of the introduction is to bring the reader into the writer's world, to build interest in the subject (why should the reader read this?), and to announce the topic. Interesting details, a startling statistic, a question, an anecdote, or a surprising statement are some of the "hooks" writers can use to catch the reader's interest.

- **Conclusion:** Your paper needs a conclusion to let the reader know the end is near, much the same way as a piece of music needs a conclusion or a conversation needs a clear signal that you're about to leave or hang up. Conclusions can either look backward or forward.

  Looking Backward: If the paper has been a complex discussion, you can look back by summarizing the main points to remind the reader of what was discussed. Or you can look back to emphasize important points you don't want the reader to forget. Or, to heighten the sense of conclusion, you can come full circle by referring back to something in the introduction.

Looking Forward: If the paper is short or doesn't need a summary, you can pose a question for the reader to consider, or you can offer advice or suggest actions the reader can take based on your discussion, argument, or proposal.

3e Patterns of Organization

Paragraphs can be organized in a great variety of ways: following chronological order; moving from general to specific information or from specific to general; or following some spatial order such as top to bottom, side to side, or front to back. The patterns illustrated in the following paragraphs are ways of thinking about and organizing ideas. You can also use these patterns during planning as you think about your topic. The information about the current job market and future employment trends contained in these sample paragraphs was found during a brief search of resources on the Internet. (See Chapter 44 for a discussion about searching methods.)

- **Narration** Narratives tell stories (or parts of stories) with events usually arranged in chronological order to make a point that relates to the whole paper.

> With the rapid growth in opportunities for physical therapists, a recent graduate in this field found that her job search was a particularly pleasant experience. Offered dozens of jobs around the country, she began by deciding where she wanted to travel as well as where she might want to live. On her interview trips, she explained, "I was treated royally. Recruiters in three different cities—Atlanta, Seattle, and Tucson—paid all my expenses for on-site interviews." When she opted to stay in Seattle for some sightseeing, her hotel and food expenses were paid for two additional days. After her Seattle trip, she went to Atlanta, where recruiters offered her a particularly generous relocation package and sign-on bonus. Her experience is one more example of the fact that while job searching in many fields today is disheartening, the need for physical therapists is causing employers to compete for applicants.

- **Description** Description includes details about people, places, things, or scenes drawn from the senses: sight, sound, smell, touch, and taste.

> In the offices and laboratories of many companies, people now work in groups, sitting around a table, talking and trading ideas. Working with colleagues can be enjoyable when the group keeps its sense of humor and maintains an informal atmosphere. Bottles of flavored spring water are passed out, doughnut crumbs are scattered over reports and charts, and aging pizza boxes are stacked up along the conference room wall. But that does not mean real work isn't getting done. There is an art to group work because everyone has to learn how to work smoothly with a diversity of personalities. One worker may want to dominate the conversation or try to assert his ideas, his loud voice like a refrain above all the other noise as he insists that everyone listen to him. Another person may find that as a woman, in order to be heard she has to be more aggressive than a male

colleague might have to be. So she leans forward, elbows on the table, to insert her voice in the conversation. Early in the morning, some members of the group are trying to wake up by slurping coffee, and late in the afternoon, others want to give up and take the work home. But even with the continuous need to work on blending different people into the group, employers are finding that the results are usually better than if each employee were left alone to do his or her part of the work.

■ **Cause and effect** Cause-and-effect paragraphs trace causes or discuss effects. The paragraph may start with effects and move backward to analyze causes or start with causes and then look at the effects. The following paragraph starts with a cause, the age of the American population, and then looks at the effects of demographics on the job market:

> The growth and direction of the job market in the future is greatly affected by population trends, so government agencies such as the Bureau of Labor Statistics study population changes in order to determine where the growth in jobs will be in the next century. A major factor that influences jobs is the age of the population. Because the number of Americans over 85 will increase about four times as fast as the total population, there will be a major increase in the demand for health services. With the shift to relatively fewer children and teenagers, there will also be greater demand for products and services for older people. For example, older people with stable incomes will travel more and have more money for consumer goods, so some jobs will focus more on tending to their needs. The job market, present and future, is shaped by the age of America's population, present and future.

■ **Analogy** Use analogies to compare things that may initially seem to have little in common but that can offer fresh insights when compared.

> It's a mistake to think that the best way to look for a job is to apply for available openings. Over 75 percent of the jobs being filled every year are not on those lists. A better way of looking for a job is very much like inventing a successful item to sell in the marketplace. The "hot" best-sellers are not merely better versions of existing ones; they are totally new, previously unthought-of consumer goods or services. In the same way, the majority of the jobs being filled are not ones that existed before, and like a successful new children's toy or some new piece of electronic equipment, they did not exist because no one realized the work needed to be done. Good executives, managers, and business owners often have ideas for additional positions, but they haven't yet developed those ideas into full-blown job descriptions. Like the inventor who comes up with the concept for a new consumer product, a job seeker can land a position by asking potential employers about changing needs in their corporation and suggesting that he or she can take on those responsibilities. Finding a new need is definitely a strategy that works as well for job seekers as it does for inventors.

■ **Example and illustration** Frequently, writers discuss an idea by offering examples to support the topic sentence. Or the writer may use an illustration—which is an extended example.

Examples

According to the Bureau of Labor Statistics, America's workers will become an increasingly diverse group. While white non-Hispanic men have historically been the largest segment of the labor force—about 78 percent—that will not be true in the next century. By 2005, Hispanics will add about 6.5 million workers, an increase of 64 percent over current levels. Within the next ten years or so, African Americans, Hispanic Americans, and Asian Americans will account for roughly 35 percent of all labor force entrants. Another factor that will increase the diversity of the workplace will be the growing number of women. Although the number of women under the age of 40 entering the working world began to grow more slowly than in the past, women are expected to fill about 48 percent of all jobs by 2005. These and other groups will continue to diversify America's labor pool.

Illustration

The Bureau of Labor Statistics study of employment trends for the future reports that the fastest-growing areas for jobs will be in occupations that require higher levels of education. Office and factory automation as well as offshore production have greatly reduced the number of people needed in jobs that can be filled by high school graduates. Now, the need is for more executives, administrators, managers, and people with professional specialties—occupations that all require people with higher education. Moreover, in a complex world dominated by high-tech electronics and international markets, a high school education is no longer adequate. High school graduates will increasingly find themselves limited to the service sector, working in areas such as fast-food service, where the pay is low and there is little potential for advancement. The trend toward the need for people with higher education is expected to continue for the foreseeable future.

■ **Classification and division** Classification involves grouping or sorting items into a group or category based on unifying principles. Division starts with one item and divides it into parts.

Classification

As America moves from being a nation that produces goods to a nation that produces services, the major growth in employment will be in the service-producing industries. Included in this group, according to the Bureau of Labor Statistics, are five major categories of service employment. First, there are the service industries, which include the health services needed by a growing and aging population; all the business service industries that supply personnel for offices and for computer and data processing; the education field, which will need more teachers for more students as the population continues to grow; and also the social services areas such as child care and family services. The second major category of service-producing jobs includes those in wholesale and retail trade, spurred in part by rising incomes and the rapid increase in sales of clothing, appliances, and automobiles. Finance, insurance, and real estate make up the third major category, and government is a fourth area of service in which the number of jobs will increase. Finally, the category of transportation, communications, and public utilities will be a major area for expansion of jobs, with truck transportation accounting for 50 percent of the new jobs in this area while jobs in communications decline about 12 percent.

Division

As we look more closely at the area of marketing and sales occupations, which the Bureau of Labor Statistics defines as a growing service area, we can see that it includes a wide variety of jobs. People who work in this area sell goods and services in stores, on the phone, and by catalogs and mail order. They also purchase commodities and properties for resale, act as wholesalers for others, and scout out new stores and franchises to open. Travel agents as well as financial services counselors aim to increase consumer interest in their goods and services. Others study the market for growth trends and consumer needs or analyze sales both in the United States and abroad. Marketing and sales occupations indeed span a broad spectrum of interests, though they all have the consumer in mind.

■ **Process analysis**   A process paragraph analyzes or describes a process or the way something works. Such paragraphs can also explain how to complete some process and are ordered chronologically.

When you scout the job market, here are some steps to follow to improve your opportunities for finding the job you want. First, do not limit yourself to the jobs listed by various companies. Those lists represent only a small percentage of the jobs available, and they will draw dozens—maybe even hundreds—of applicants. Instead, draw up a list of companies you'd like to work for by browsing through their yearly reports and other materials available in a job counselor's office. Don't forget the Yellow Pages, particularly if you know the city where you want to work. Then, call the company and ask for the name of someone likely to be the hiring authority. If possible, get some name other than that of the personnel manager—that person's job is often to screen out unqualified candidates. Next, send a clear, well-focused résumé directly to that person, and don't be bashful about listing your accomplishments in terms of that company's needs. In the cover letter, state why you are the ideal person for that organization. Make your reader see why the company will be better off with you, not anyone else. Be sure to conclude the cover letter with a request for an interview and explain that you will be following up with a phone call within the next few days. At the interview, explore all the options you can, helping the other person see how you might fit in, even if there is no vacancy at the present time. You might help the person create a new position for which you'd be the best applicant. Finally, be sure to write a short letter thanking the interviewer for meeting with you.

■ **Comparison and contrast** One way to discuss two subjects is to compare them by looking at their similarities. You can also contrast them by looking at their differences. There are two options for organizing such a paragraph: (1) present first one subject and then the other, or (2) discuss both subjects at the same time, item by item.

Two Subjects, One at a Time

A government study of occupations in forestry and logging indicate that they represent two rather different areas of work. Forestry technicians compile data on the characteristics of forests, such as size, content, and condition. Generally, they are the decision makers, traveling through sections of forest to gather basic information about species of trees in the forest, disease and insect damage, seedling mortality, and conditions that may cause forest fires. One of their main responsibilities is to determine when a tract of forest is ready to be harvested. Less skilled than forest technicians are forest workers whose work includes more physical labor. They plant new tree seedlings to reforest timberland; remove diseased or undesirable trees; spray herbicides where needed; and clear away brush and debris from camp trails, roadsides, and camping areas. Like forest technicians, though, their work requires long hours out of doors in all kinds of weather.

Two Subjects, Point by Point

Many students who graduate with economics majors take one of two very different types of jobs, either as government economists or as market research analysts for large companies. Those who go to work for the government assess economic conditions in the United States and abroad and estimate the economic effects of specific changes in legislation or public policy. Marketing research analysts, on the other hand, are concerned with the design, promotion, price, and distribution of a product or service. Another area of difference is that government economists analyze data provided by government studies while marketing research analysts often design their own surveys and questionnaires or conduct interviews. But, whether they work as economists for the government or as analysts for private companies, most people in this field find that they often work under pressure of deadlines and tight schedules. In spite of the pressure, some economists and analysts combine full-time jobs with part-time or consulting work in academia or other settings.

■ **Definition** A definition of a term places it in a general class and then differentiates it from others in that class, often with the use of examples and comparisons.

Skill in problem solving is a crucial mental ability that job interviewers look for when they meet applicants, but it is not clear what this mental process is. Problem solving is an ability that assists a person in defining what the problem is and how to formulate steps to solve it. Included in this complex cognitive act are a number of characteristic mental abilities. Being flexible—remaining open to new possibilities—is a great asset in solving a problem, though a good problem solver also draws on strategies that may have worked in other settings. In addition, problem solving involves keeping the goal clearly in mind so that a person doesn't get sidetracked into exploring related problems that don't achieve the desired goal. Employers want problem solvers because having such a skill is far more valuable than having specific knowledge. Problem-solving abilities cannot be taught on the job, whereas specific knowledge often can be, and specific knowledge can become outdated, unlike the ability to solve problems.

4 Argument (arg)

Reading and writing persuasive arguments is very likely to be part of your everyday life. For example, you may have written letters to potential employers to persuade them to hire you. Perhaps you have written a business proposal to persuade your boss to implement a plan, or you've written an application to persuade some group to grant you admission to a program or give you funding. You've probably read advertisements in magazines that attempt to persuade you to buy certain products. Or maybe you have read letters from charitable organizations or political candidates persuading you to donate time or money to their causes. Even college brochures are written partly to persuade you to apply to that institution. The use of reasons as well as emotional appeals to persuade an audience is part of normal interaction with the world. People actively persuade you to believe, act on, or accept their claims, just as you want others to accept or act on your claims.

However, persuasion is not the only purpose for writing an effective argument. You might argue to justify to yourself and others what you believe and why you hold those positions. You also formulate arguments to solve problems and make decisions. The ability to argue effectively is clearly a skill everyone needs. Because argumentation is a process of researching to find support for your claims as well as a process of reasoning to explain and defend actions, beliefs, and ideas, you need to think about finding that information. (See Part Seven of this book.) You also need to consider how you present yourself as a writer to your audience, how your audience will respond to you, how you select topics to write about, and how you develop and organize your material into persuasive papers. These topics are discussed in the following sections.

4a Writing and Reading Arguments

As a writer, you have to get your readers to commit themselves to listening to you and to letting you make your case. In order to gain your reader's trust and respect, your writing should indicate that you know what you are talking about, that you are truthful, and that you are reasonable enough to consider other sides of the argument. As the reader of an argument, you need to consider the writer's credibility. For example, if you were to read an article that claims cigarette smoking is not harmful to our health and then discover that the writer works in the tobacco industry, you would question the writer's credibility. Similarly, you need to establish your own credibility with your audience.

 HINT **The Writer's Credibility**

The following suggestions will help you establish your credibility with your audience:

- **Show that your motives are reasonable and worthwhile.** Give your audience some reasonable assurance that you are arguing for a claim that is recognized as being for the general good or that shares the audience's motives. For example, are you writing an argument to a group of fellow students for more on-campus parking because you personally are having a parking problem or because you recognize that this is a problem many students are having? If you want action to solve your personal problem, you are not likely to get an attentive hearing. Why should others care about your problem? But if you help other students see that this is a widespread problem that they may have too, you are indicating that you share their motives and that you are arguing for a general good that concerns them too.

- **Avoid vague and ambiguous terms and exaggerated claims.** Vague arguments such as "everyone says" (who is "everyone"?) or "it's a huge problem" (how big is "huge"?) raise doubts about the writer's knowledge and ability to write authoritatively. Exaggerations such as "Commercialism has destroyed the meaning of Christmas" or "No one cares about the farmer's problems any more" are highly inflated opinions that weaken the writer's credibility.

4b Considering the Audience

I. Types of Appeals

You need to formulate in your mind the audience for a particular piece of persuasive writing. If you are writing to an audience that already agrees with you, you need to decide what your purpose will be. What would be accomplished if your readers already agree with you? If your audience is likely to disagree, you need to think about how to acknowledge and address reasons for disagreeing. You can use three different kinds of appeals to make your case:

- **Logical appeals** Logical reasoning is grounded in sound principles of inductive and deductive reasoning. It avoids logical fallacies and bases proofs on reality—that is, factual evidence gathered from data and events—as well as deduction, definitions, and analogies. Logical proof appeals to people's reason, understanding, and common sense.

  For example, for a paper attempting to persuade readers that a particular job training program has worked and should therefore continue to be funded, logical arguments could include data showing the number of people in the program and the success rate of their employment after being in the program. The paper could then compare those figures to data on a similar group of people who did not take part in the program.

■ **Emotional appeals** Emotional appeals arouse the audience's emotions, such as their sympathy, patriotism, pride, and other feelings based on values, beliefs, and motives. Appeals to emotions may include examples, description, and narratives.

For example, for the paper on job training programs, an effective example might be the story of a woman who was previously unemployed for a long period of time, despite intensive job seeking, but who found a good job after acquiring new skills in the program. Her testimony would appeal to the audience's sympathy and to the belief that most people want to work and will be able to do so if they could just get some help in upgrading their skills.

■ **Ethical appeals** Ethical proof appeals to the audience's impressions, opinions, and judgments about the person making the argument. That is, these appeals establish the credibility of the writer. The audience should be given proof that the writer is knowledgeable, does not distort evidence, and has some authority on the subject. To establish credibility, writers can draw on personal experience, explain their credentials for discussing the topic, and show that they are using their logical proofs appropriately.

For example, for the job training paper, the author might draw on her experience working for the program or explain that the data she is presenting comes from a highly credible source such as county or state records.

When writing arguments, consider what your audience is likely to value as evidence. You can use statistics, your experience, and research. How informed is your audience? What are the likely bases for readers' views and beliefs? What common ground can you establish with your readers so they will listen to you?

2. Common Ground

An important step in gaining a hearing from your audience is to identify the common ground you share with readers—the values, beliefs, common interests, motives, or goals where there is overlap between you and those likely to disagree with you. Without some common ground between you and the audience, there is no argument, no way to get that audience to listen to you or understand you. Think, for example, of some strong conviction you hold. If someone with an equally strong stand on the opposite side started arguing for that opposing position, are you immediately likely to listen attentively? Or would you instead start marshaling arguments for your side? For example, for a writer who firmly believes in everyone's right to own a gun, there is no common ground with equally firm advocates of gun control. Neither side is really likely to listen to the other. On the other hand, if you and your audience are in total agreement, there also is no argument. If someone who believes that higher education needs adequate funding talks to a group of faculty at his or her college, there are no points to argue. An appropriate topic for a persuasive paper will fall between these extremes and will have opposing views to consider and common ground to find.

Because the search for common ground is so important, let's examine how it might be discovered. Suppose a legislator wants to introduce a bill requiring motorcyclists to wear helmets, but the legislator knows she will be voted down because many other legislators oppose such laws that restrict people's freedom to decide these matters. One place to find some overlap would be to establish that everyone has a concern for the safety of bikers. It's also likely that everyone in the legislature will agree that bikers have a right to be on the road and that motorists often aren't sufficiently careful about avoiding them. Thus, there is general agreement (or common ground) that bikers are subject to some major hazards on the road and that everyone should be concerned about their welfare. When the legislator identifies to her audience that they share this much common ground, she is likely to get a hearing for her reasons why she wants her bill to pass.

One more example might help you to see where and how that very important common ground can be found. Suppose you are writing a proposal to the city council to spend funds beautifying one of the public playgrounds. If you believe the council is likely to turn down your proposal, you need to think about the council members' possible reasons for rejecting it. Is the city budget so tight that the council is reluctant to spend money on any projects that aren't absolutely necessary? If so, what appeals could you make in your proposal? Your opening argument could be a logical appeal, including some facts about the low cost of the beautification project. Or perhaps you could begin with an emotional appeal about the children who use the playground. What common ground do you share with the council? You and they want a well-run city that doesn't go into debt. If you acknowledge that you share those concerns and that you too don't want to put the city budget in the red, you will be more likely to get the council to listen to your proposal.

Getting ready to write a persuasive paper requires thinking about yourself as the writer and about your audience who will read your arguments. But there are other considerations as you move through this writing process. How do you find a topic? How do you find the material you want to use in the development of your arguments? How do you build sound arguments? How do you organize all this information into a paper? The following sections offer help with these important parts of the process.

4c Finding a Topic

1. Arguable Topics

Topics for persuasion are always those that can be argued, that have two or more sides that can be claimed as worth agreeing upon. For example, no one can argue that the total number of reported rapes has not increased nationally in the last fifty years, so a claim that reported rapes have gone up would not be a topic for a persuasive paper. It is simply a fact that can be checked in lists of national crime statistics. But there are multiple sides to other issues about rape. Are those numbers higher because the population has grown, because of more accurate reporting, because more rapes are being committed, or because women are more inclined to actually report such attacks? So, a persuasive paper might take a stand about the causes of the increase in reported rapes.

2. Interesting Topics

When preparing to write a persuasive paper on a topic you are free to choose, think about the wide range of matters that interest you or that are part of your life. What do you and your friends talk about? What have you been reading lately in the newspaper or in magazines? What topics have you heard about on television? What are some ongoing situations around you, that is, events that are happening or about to happen? What unresolved public or family issues concern you? What topics have you been discussing or reading about in your classes? What matters concerning yourself are unresolved and need further consideration? What event happened to you that made you stop and think? or get mad? or cheer?

3. Local and General Topics

If you start with a subject that answers any of the questions asked above, you can begin to build a paper topic either by thinking it through on a local or personal level or by enlarging your perspective beyond your local setting. For example, you might start with some new rule, guideline, or restriction on your campus, such as a new electronic device that searched you as you left the library to see if you had a book you hadn't checked out. Is that something that bothers you? Do you see it as an invasion of student privacy? or as a waste of the school's money? or as a way, finally, to stop all the library theft you know is going on in your school? These are local views of the matter, and any one might be a springboard for a paper topic in which you argue that the antitheft system is or is not a beneficial addition to the library. Or, you could move to a larger view beyond your own library or campus or city. Is this instance part of a larger issue of new technology that implies everyone should be checked for dishonest behavior? Should we accept that new library device or airport scanners as a means to safeguard our security and well-being?

4d Developing Your Arguments

I. Claims, Support, and Warrants

To develop your arguments you need to clarify what your main point or claim is, what support you are going to offer for that claim, and what warrants or unspoken assumptions are present in the argument. This system for arguments was developed by Stephen Toulmin, a modern philosopher.

Claim

A *claim* is the proposition, the assertion or thesis that is to be proved. There are three types of claims: of fact, of value, and of policy. We can find these types of claims by asking questions that identify what an argument is trying to prove:

■ Is there a **fact** the argument is trying to prove?

Did the accused person really commit that theft?
Is your college providing access for students in wheelchairs?
Is the amount of television advertising increasing in relation to the amount of programming?

■ Is there an issue of **values** in the argument?

Should schools provide sex education for children?
Should scientists be permitted total freedom to experiment with artificial insemination?
Should the beliefs of major religions be taught in school?

■ Is there an issue of **policy** in the argument?

Should legislators be allowed to hold office for an unlimited number of terms?
Should your college provide free parking for students?
Should smokers be permitted to smoke in restaurants?

Support

The *support* for an argument is the material or evidence used to convince the audience. Such support or proof may include evidence such as facts, data, examples, statistics, and the testimony of experts. Support may also include appeals to our emotions. If a claim is made that baseball is no longer the nation's favorite summer sport, then facts or data or statistics are needed to show that it once was the nation's favorite summer sport and that it has declined in popularity. If a claim is made that the U.S. Postal Service should issue commemorative stamps honoring famous American heroes of World War II, the argument might use an emotional appeal to our patriotism, asking us to remember these great people who served our country so bravely.

Warrant

The *warrant* is an underlying assumption, belief, or principle in an argument. Some warrants are made explicit, while others are left unstated. Whether or not your audience shares your assumption determines if your audience will accept or reject your argument. If you hear someone say that she didn't learn a thing in her history class because her teacher was dull, an unstated warrant is that the teacher is solely responsible for what students learn or that dull teachers cannot help students gain knowledge. In this brief argument, it may be easy to spot the warrant, but other arguments have warrants that are not as obvious. If someone argues that more police are needed to patrol the streets of inner-city neighborhoods in order to reduce illegal drug traffic, what is the warrant here? Is there more than one warrant? One assumption, or warrant, is that patrolling police are able to find and arrest drug dealers. Another assumption is that by arresting drug dealers, police can cut down the incidence of such crime. This, in turn, assumes that when some drug dealers are taken off the streets, more will not appear on the scene to take their place.

As writers develop their arguments, they have to be aware both of what warrants exist in their arguments and of what warrants exist in the audience's minds. If an audience shares the writer's warrants, the argument is likely to be more effective and convincing. If the audience does not share the writer's warrants, it will be hard to persuade the audience because the warrant is the link that connects the claim to the support and leads the audience to accept the claim. When you see a commercial that shows a well-known athlete endorsing some new pizza chain, there are several warrants or unspoken assumptions operating behind the claim that this company has good pizza and the support that the pizza is good because the athlete said so. One warrant is that this athlete is not just making a statement because she has been paid to do so. Another is that this athlete really knows what good pizza is or that her standards and tastes in pizza are the same as yours. If you accept such warrants, you are likely to be convinced that the pizza is good. The support was adequate for the argument. If not, then the athlete's statement was not adequate support, and you are not likely to be enticed to try the pizza.

Similarly, for the argument you build, you should also examine the warrants in the opposing arguments. What assumptions are left unsaid in the case made by the opposing side? Does the opposing argument rest on underlying assumptions or accepted beliefs which your readers ought to know about because they might not accept those warrants? For example, if you oppose physician-assisted suicide for the terminally ill, the opposing side may not have presented any evidence that shows that doctors always know when a patient is terminally ill. This might be a warrant in their case that doctors should be allowed to make such judgments. Would your audience accept that warrant? If not, then you make your argument stronger by calling attention to the warrant.

2. Logical Arguments

Another consideration as you build your argument is the logical direction of the argument. For the claim you make, is it appropriate to move from a statement of a general principle to logical arguments that support that generalization? If so, your argument will develop deductively. Or is it more appropriate to construct your case from particular instances or examples that build to a conclusion? If so, your argument is an inductive one.

Deductive Reasoning

When you reason deductively, you draw a conclusion from assertions (or premises). You start with a generalization or major premise and reason logically to a conclusion. The conclusion is *true* when the premises are true and is *valid* when the conclusion follows necessarily from the premises. For example, if you read an argument that starts with the generalization that all politicians spend their time seeking reelection, any conclusion that is drawn will not be true because the generalization is not universally true. An example of *invalid* deductive reasoning is the argument which proceeds to the following conclusion:

Premise: Lack of exercise causes people to be overweight.

Premise: Jillian is overweight.

Conclusion: Therefore, Jillian doesn't exercise.

In this example, it is possible that Jillian does exercise but eats fattening food that causes her to remain overweight. Thus, this is not a valid argument because the conclusion does not necessarily follow from the premise.

Inductive Reasoning

When you reason inductively, you come to conclusions on the basis of observing a number of particular instances. Using the examples you observe, you arrive at a statement of what is generally true of something or of a whole group of things. For example, if you try a certain medication a few times and find that each time you take it, it upsets your stomach, you conclude that this medication bothers you. Inductive conclusions are, however, only probable at best. A new example might prove the conclusion false, or the number of examples may not have been large enough for a reasonable conclusion to be drawn. Or, the quality of the examples might be questionable. Suppose, for example, you want to find out the most popular major on your campus, and you decide to stand outside the engineering building. You ask each student entering and leaving the building what his or her major is, and the vast majority of the students say that they are majoring in engineering. The conclusion that engineering is the most popular major on campus is not reliable because the sample does not represent the whole campus. If you moved to the agriculture building and stood there and asked the same question, it's likely you would find agriculture to be the most popular major.

3. Logical Fallacies

Letters to the editor in a newspaper, advertisements, political campaign speeches, and courtroom battles are apt to offer proofs that have not been carefully thought through. As you develop your own arguments and read the arguments of others, you need to check for mistakes in the reasoning and to see whether opposing views present support that might have errors in reasoning. It is unfortunately very easy to fall into a number of traps in thinking, some of which are described here:

HINT **Recognizing and Avoiding Fallacies**

■ **Hasty generalization:** A conclusion reached with too few examples—or examples that are not representative.

Example: Your friend complains that the phone company is a bunch of bumblers because they never send a bill that is correct.

To Avoid: Many hasty generalizations contain words such as *all, never,* and *every.* You can correct them by substituting words such as *some* and *sometimes.*

■ **Begging the question (circular reasoning):** An argument that goes around in circles, assuming that what has to be proved has already been proved.

Example: When a salesperson points out that the product she is selling is "environmentally friendly," you ask why. Her reply is that it doesn't pollute the atmosphere. Why doesn't it pollute the atmosphere? Because, she explains, it's environmentally friendly.

To Avoid: Check to see if there is no new information in the development of the argument. If the arguments go round in circles, look for some outside proof or reasoning.

■ **Doubtful cause *(post hoc, ergo propter hoc):*** A mistake in reasoning that occurs when one event happens and then another event happens. As a result, people mistakenly reason that there is a cause and effect relationship when no such relationship exists. (The Latin phrase *post hoc, ergo propter hoc* means "after this, therefore because of this.")

Example: If a school institutes a dress code and vandalism decreases the next week, it is tempting to reason that the dress code caused a decrease in vandalism, but this sequence does not prove a cause-and-effect relationship. Other factors may be at work, or incidents of vandalism might increase the next month. More conclusive evidence is needed.

To Avoid: Do not automatically assume that because one event follows another, the second event was caused by the first event. Check for a real cause-and-effect relationship, an effect that can be continually repeated with the same results.

■ **Using irrelevant proof to support a claim *(non sequitur):*** Describes a line of reasoning in which the conclusion is not a logical result of the premises. (The Latin phrase *non sequitur* means "it does not follow.")

Example: That movie was superb because it cost so much to produce.

To Avoid: The proof of a statement must be a logical step in reasoning with logical connections. In the example given here, the amount of money spent on filming a movie is not necessarily related to the movie's quality and is therefore an irrelevant proof.

■ **False analogy:** Assumes without proof that if objects or processes are similar in some ways, they are similar in other ways.

Example: If engineers can design those black boxes that survive plane crashes, they should be able to build the whole plane from that same material.

To Avoid: Check whether other major aspects of the objects or processes being compared are not similar. In the example above, the construction materials used in a huge and complex plane cannot be the same as those for the little black boxes.

- **Attack the person *(ad hominem)*:** Refers to a personal attack on someone that is intended to overthrow or dismiss the argument. (The Latin phrase *ad hominem* means "against the man.")

Example: If an economist proposes a plan for helping impoverished people, her opponent might dismiss her plan by pointing out that she's never been poor.

To Avoid: Avoid reasoning that diverts our attention from the quality of the argument to the person offering it.

- **Either . . . or:** Establishes a false either/or situation and does not allow for other possibilities or choices that may exist.

Example: Either America balances the budget, or the country will slide into another Great Depression.

To Avoid: When offered only two alternatives, look for others as well.

- **Bandwagon:** An argument that claims to be sound because a large number of people approve of it.

Example: In a political campaign, we might hear that we should vote for someone because many other people have decided this person is the best candidate.

To Avoid: Do not accept an argument just because some or even many others support it.

4e Organizing Your Arguments

The organization of an argument depends in part on how you analyze your audience. One way to begin is with the common ground you share with the audience so that your readers will be more likely to pay attention to your argument. You may wish to bring up points that favor your opponents' side of the argument early in the paper and discuss the merits of these points, or you may decide that it would be more effective to do this near the end of the paper. You can also consider other organizational patterns, such as starting with the claim followed by a discussion of the reasons. You may find a problem-and-solution pattern more appropriate. Cause and effect is yet another pattern to consider. You can either start with the cause and then trace the effects or begin with the effects and work back to the cause. You can also build your argument by establishing the criteria or standards by which to judge a claim and then showing how your claim meets these criteria. If your conclusion is one that an audience is not likely to be receptive to at first, a better organization might be to move through your points and then announce your thesis or claim after you have built some acceptance for your arguments.

5 Writing with Computers (comp)

Using word processing software on a computer is an efficient way to write. You can add, delete, revise, and move blocks of words around with great ease and speed. You will probably find your drafts easier to read as you revise. Even if you cannot type well (and many successful computer users can't), a computer can be both a convenience and an aid throughout the writing process. But remember to save your files—often—and make backup copies of your files, even when you've carefully saved them. Disks can go bad, and files can get lost.

Listed here are a number of strategies to try in all aspects of the writing process.

5a Planning with Computers

- **Freewriting and brainstorming** If freewriting or brainstorming are useful strategies for you (see 2a), do this on the computer. You can use a cut-and-paste feature to place parts of those planning notes into a draft as needed. Some writers find that they can freewrite more easily if they turn down the brightness on their computer screen so that it's dark and they cannot see what they type. You may also want to create separate files for different topics within the freewriting.

- **Writing an e-mail message** As you think about your assignment or topic, write an e-mail message to someone in your class or to a friend. Use that e-mail message to try out ideas as you would in a conversation with peer group members or a writing center tutor. Encourage the person who receives your e-mail to ask questions that help you clarify your ideas. If you want a copy of one of your messages, send it to your own e-mail address as well.

- **Planning visually** Use a draw or paint program to do some visual planning such as clustering and branching (see 2a).

- **Making an outline** Set up headings for an outline in large bold letters. Later, when you go back to fill in the subheadings and subpoints, you will be able to see the larger structure of the paper. Some word processing programs let you go back and forth between a screen showing only the headings and screens showing the detailed material within sections.

- **Keeping a journal** If keeping a journal helps you, start a journal file for each assignment and include thoughts and questions that occur to you as you work. Include a plan for how you will proceed through the assignment, and if there are stages or steps to complete, write a "to do" list. Include phrases and ideas that occur to you and that may fit into the paper with some cutting and pasting from one file to another.

- **Storing notes** As you gather material from your reading and other research sources, develop a separate file or make use of a feature in your word processing program to store those notes.

5b Drafting with Computers

- **Creating a scrap file** As you start drafting, make two separate files, one for the paper you are writing and the other for scraps—words, sentences, and paragraphs—that you discard as you draft. Use the scrap file by cutting and pasting into it anything that doesn't seem to fit in as you write. This scrap file can be a very useful storage space for materials that should be deleted from the paper you are writing now but that may be useful for other assignments. You may also want a scrap file for key words, words that come to mind and that can be useful when needed, or for phrases that may come in handy as section headings in your paper.

- **Adding notes** As you work, you may come up with a suggestion you want to consider or a question that needs to be checked, but you don't want to stop writing. You can include a reminder to yourself by writing a note on the screen in bold letters or in parentheses. Be sure to delete these notes before you submit a final draft.

- **Splitting screens** Consider this strategy if it helps you to look at information or additional writing in one file while you draft in another file. If you can view multiple files on your screen at the same time, you can look at the material in your scrap, outline, or note files. This is especially useful because you can cut, paste, and copy between files.

5c Organizing with Computers

- **Mixing up the order of paragraphs or sentences** Make a new copy of your file and then, in the new file, use the cut-and-paste feature to move paragraphs around. You may see a better organizing principle than the one you had been using. Do the same with sentences within paragraphs.

- **Checking your outline** Look again at the bold-lettered headings of the outline you made during planning (or create one now), and reassess whether your outline is adequate and well organized.

5d Revising with Computers

- **Starting at the beginning of a file** Each time you open your file, you are at the beginning of the draft. Start there and read until you come to the section where you will be working. Rereading has several advantages. It helps you get back into the flow of thought, and it permits you to re-see what you've written so that you can do some revising as you read forward.

■ **Renaming a file** Each time you open your file, save it with a new file name so that you always know which is the most recent version you've worked on. If your first draft is Draft1, the next time you open that file, save it as Draft2. Then, the next time you can save it as Draft3, and so on.

■ **Printing out hard copies to read** It may help you to look at a printed copy of your paper as you revise so that you can see the development and organization, as well as get a sense of the whole paper. If you do print out a draft of your paper, however, resist the temptation to hand in that draft because it looks neat and seems to have a finished appearance.

■ **Using page or print view to check paragraphs** Switch to the page or print view so that you can see a whole page on the screen. Do the paragraphs look about the same length? Is one noticeably shorter than the others? Does it need more development? Is there a paragraph that seems to be disproportionately long?

■ **Highlighting sentence length** Working with a copy of your main file, hit the return key after every sentence so that every sentence looks like a separate paragraph. Are all of your sentences the same length? If so, do you need variety? Do they all start the same way? Do you need to use different sentence patterns? (See Chapter 16 on sentence variety.)

5e Editing and Proofreading with Computers

■ **Using online tools** There are a number of online tools you can use while editing, such as spell checkers and grammar checkers. However, grammar checkers are often not very effective because it is hard to distinguish between appropriate and inappropriate advice they offer. Some word processing programs come with a thesaurus that is useful for looking up synonyms for words you've been using too much or for finding more specific words than the ones you have used.

■ **Changing the appearance of key features of your writing** Put active verbs in bold letters, put passive constructions in italics, use larger fonts for descriptive words, underline your thesis statement, and so on. By changing the appearance of these features, you may find that some of your writing habits need to be changed too. Perhaps you use too many passives or you don't use enough descriptive words.

■ **Editing on hard copy** It may be easier for you to print out a draft and mark that for editing changes, in addition to printing out previous drafts when revising. If you do, put marks in the margins to indicate lines where changes are to be made so that you can easily find them again.

6 Comma Splices and Fused Sentences (cs/fs)

A **comma splice** and a **fused sentence** (also called a **run-on sentence**) are punctuation problems in compound sentences. (See 26b2 on compound sentences.) There are three patterns for commas and semicolons in compound sentences:

1. Independent clause, and   independent clause.
but
for
or
nor
so
yet

2. Independent clause;   independent clause.

3. Independent clause;   however,   independent clause.
therefore,
moreover,
thus,
consequently,
(etc.)

Commas in Compound Sentences

Use a comma when you join two independent clauses (clauses that would be sentences by themselves) with any of the following seven joining words:

and   but   for   or   nor   so   yet

The game was over, **but** the crowd refused to leave.

Some variations:

■ If both independent clauses are very short, you may omit the comma.

Lucinda may come or she may stay home.

■ Some people prefer to use a semicolon when one of the independent clauses already has a comma.

Every Friday, depending on the weather, Sam likes to play tennis; but sometimes he has trouble finding a partner.

HINT   **Commas with *and***

Don't put commas before every *and* in your sentences. *And* is frequently used in ways that do not require commas.

Semicolons in Compound Sentences

If you use any connecting words other than *and, but, for, or, nor, so,* or *yet,* or if you don't use any connecting words, you'll need a semicolon.

The game was over; **however,** the crowd refused to leave.
The game was over; the crowd refused to leave.

6a Comma Splices

The **comma splice** is a punctuation error that occurs either when independent clauses are joined only by a comma and no coordinating conjunction or when a comma is used instead of a semicolon between two independent clauses.

Comma Splice: In Econ 150, students meet in small groups for an extra
hour each week,ᴀ this helps them learn from each other.
and

Comma Splice: The doctor prescribed a different medication, however,
it's not helping.
;

6b Fused or Run-on Sentences

The **fused** or **run-on sentence** is a punctuation error that occurs when there is no punctuation between independent clauses.

Fused or Run-on Sentence: I didn't know which job I wantedᴀI
couldn't decide.
, and (or) ;

There are several ways to fix comma splices, fused sentences, and run-ons:

- Add one of the seven joining words (*and, but, for, or, nor, so, yet*) (and be sure to use a comma).

- Separate the independent clauses into two sentences.

- Change the comma to a semicolon. (See 29a.)

- Make one clause dependent on another clause. (See 24b and 27b.)

Exercise 6.1: Proofreading Practice

In the following paragraph, there are some sentences that contain comma splices. Underline the sentences that contain this punctuation error, and place either a semicolon or the correct coordinating conjunction in the appropriate sentence.

(1) Office gossip no longer takes place at the water cooler. (2) Companies that are online have a new way to relay gossip, e-mail is the medium. (3) Recent court cases have made corporate executives rethink policies on transmitting e-mail and destroying old messages.

(4) Seemingly harmless conversations between colleagues have been retrieved, this information has been used in sexual harassment cases and other lawsuits. (5) A single employee can store thousands of pages of e-mail messages, however the mail is not censored or monitored. (6) Consequently, companies are eager for systems that review and spot-check e-mail. (7) Company executives are employing programs that censor e-mail and block messages containing inappropriate material, this monitoring prevents embarrassing situations. (8) CEOs understand that Big Brother has a better view since employees began hitting the Send button.

Exercise 6.2: Proofreading Practice

In the following paragraph there are some compound sentences that require commas. Add commas where they are needed.

(1) Cacao beans have been grown in the Americas for several thousand years. (2) They were considered a treasure and were cultivated by the Aztecs for centuries before the Spanish discovered them in Mexico. (3) Cocoa reached Europe even before coffee or tea and its use gradually spread from Spain and Portugal to Italy and France and north to England. (4) In 1753 the botanist Linnaeus gave the cacao plant its scientific name, *Theobroma cacao,* the food of the gods. (5) The tree is cacao, the ground bean is cocoa, and the food is chocolate but it bears no relation to coca, the source of cocaine. (6) Most cacao trees grow within ten degrees of the equator. (7) In the late nineteenth century the Portuguese took the plant to some islands off Africa and it soon became an establishment crop in the Gold Coast, Cameroon, and Nigeria, where the temperature and humidity are ideal for it.

Exercise 6.3: Pattern Practice

Combine some of the short sentences listed here (and change a few words, if you need to) so that you have five compound sentences that follow the pattern shown here. Be sure to punctuate correctly with a comma.

Independent clause, [and / but / for / or / nor / so / yet] independent clause.

There are many varieties of chocolate.
All varieties come from the same bean.
All varieties are the product of fermentation.
Once fermented, beans must be dried before being packed for shipping.
Chocolate pods cannot be gathered when they are underripe or overripe.

Chocolate pods are usually harvested very carefully by hand.
In the processing different varieties of chocolate are produced.
Dutch chocolate has the cocoa butter pressed out and alkali added.
Swiss chocolate has milk added.
Conching is the process of rolling chocolate over and over against itself.
Conching influences the flavor of chocolate.
Chocolate is loved by millions of people all over the world.
Some people are allergic to chocolate.

7 Subject-Verb Agreement (agr)

Subject-verb agreement occurs when the subject and verb endings agree in number and person.

7a Singular and Plural Subjects

The subject of every sentence is either singular or plural, and that determines the ending of the verb.

1. Singular
Singular nouns, pronouns, and nouns that cannot be counted, such as *news, time,* and *happiness* (see Chapter 59), take verbs with singular endings.

I chew.   Water drips.   Time flies.   You laugh.   The news is dull.

2. Plural
Plural nouns and pronouns take verbs with plural endings.

We know.   The cups are clean.   They stretch.   The stamps stick.

7b Buried Subjects

It is sometimes difficult to find the subject word when it is buried among many other words. In that case, disregard prepositional phrases; modifiers; *who, which,* and *that* clauses; and other surrounding words.

Almost **all** of Art's many friends who showed up at the party last night at
    (subject)
Andy's **brought** gifts.
    (verb)

[In this sentence, *Almost* is a modifier, *of Art's many friends* is a prepositional phrase, and *who showed up at the party last night at Andy's* is a *who* clause that describes *friends*.]

HINT **Subject-Verb Agreement**

For a present tense sentence, you can't have two -s endings at the same time, one on the subject and the other on the verb. Plural subject nouns have an -s at the end and so do many third person, present tense, singular verbs. So, a plural subject can't have a singular verb, and a singular subject can't have a plural verb.

Chimes ring.   The boy jumps.

HINT **Finding the Subject and Verb**

1. It's easier to find the verb first because the verb is the word or words that change when you change the time of the sentence, from present to past or past to present.

Matt **walks** to class.   Yesterday Matt **walked** to class.
(verb)   *(verb)*

Tomorrow, Matt **will walk** to class.
(verb)

2. Eliminate phrases starting with the following words because they are normally not part of the subject:

including	along with	together with
accompanied by	in addition to	as well as
except	with	no less than

Everyone in our family, including my sister, **has taken** piano lessons.
(subject)   *(verb)*

7c Compound Subjects

Subjects joined by *and* take a plural verb (X *and* Y = more than one, plural).

The **dog** and the **squirrel** are running around the tree.

The **company** and its **subsidiary** manufacture auto parts.

Sometimes, though, the words joined by *and* act together as a unit and are thought of as one thing. If so, use a singular verb.

Peanut butter and jelly is a popular filling for sandwiches.

7d Either/Or Subjects

When the subject words are joined by *either . . . or, neither . . . nor,* or *not only . . . but,* the verb agrees with the closest subject word.

Either **Alice** or her **children** are going to bed early.

Neither the **choir** nor the (director) is ready for the performance.

Not only the **clouds** but also the (snow) was gray that day.

7e Clauses and Phrases as Subjects

When a whole clause or phrase is the subject, use a singular verb.

(What I want to know) is why I can't try the test again.

(Saving money) is difficult to do.

(To live happily) seems like a worthwhile goal.

However, if the verb is a form of *be* and the noun afterward (the complement) is plural, the verb has to be plural.

What we saw <u>were</u> pictures of the experiment. [What we saw = pictures]

7f Indefinites as Subjects

Indefinite words with singular meanings such as *each, every,* and *any* take a singular verb when (1) they are the subject word or (2) they precede the subject word.

Each <u>has</u> her own preference.

Each **book** <u>is checked in</u> by the librarian.

However, when indefinite words such as *none, some, most,* or *all* are the subject, the number of the verb depends on the meaning of the subject.

Some of the book <u>is</u> difficult to follow.   [The subject of the sentence here is a portion of the book and is therefore thought of as a single unit and has a singular verb.]

Some of us <u>are</u> leaving now.   [The subject of this sentence is several people and is therefore thought of as a plural subject with a plural verb.]

All she wants <u>is</u> to be left alone.

All my sweaters <u>are</u> in that drawer.

7g Collective Nouns and Amounts as Subjects

Collective nouns are nouns that refer to a group or a collection (such as *team, family, committee,* and *group*). When a collective noun is the subject and refers to the group acting as a whole group or single unit, the verb is singular.

Our **family** has just bought a new car.

In most cases, a collective noun refers to the group acting together as a unit, but occasionally the collective noun refers to members acting individually. In that case, the verb is plural.

The **committee** are unhappy with each other's decisions.

[The subject here is thought of as different people, not a single unit.]

When the subject names an amount, the verb is singular.

Twenty-five **cents** is cheap.   Four **bushels** is enough.
More than 125 **miles** is too far.   Six **dollars** is the price.

7h Plural Words as Subjects

Some words that have an -s plural ending, such as *civics, mathematics, measles, news,* and *economics,* are thought of as a single unit and take a singular verb.

Physics is fascinating.   The **news** is disheartening.
Measles is unpleasant.   Modern **economics** shows contradictions.

Some words, such as those in the following list, are treated as plural and take a plural verb, even though they refer to one thing. (In many cases, there are two parts to these things.)

Jeans are fashionable.   **Eyeglasses** are inexpensive.
Pants cover his tan.   **Shears** cut cloth.
Scissors cut paper.   **Thanks** are not necessary.
Clippers trim hedges.   **Riches** are his dream.

7i Titles, Company Names, and Words as Subjects

For titles of written works, names of companies, and words used as terms, use singular verbs.

All the King's Men is the book assigned for this week.
General Foods is hiring people for its new plant.
"Cheers" is a word he often says when leaving.

7j Linking Verbs

Linking verbs agree with the subject rather than the word that follows (the complement).

Her **problem** is frequent injuries.

Short **stories** are my favorite reading matter.

7k There Is/There Are/It

The verb depends on the complement that follows the verb.

There is an excellent old movie on TV tonight.

There are too many old movies on TV.

However, *it* as the subject always takes the singular verb, regardless of what follows.

It was the bears in the park that knocked over the garbage cans.

7l Who, Which, That, and One of . . . Who/Which/That as Subjects

When *who, which,* and *that* are used as subjects, the verb agrees with the previous word they refer to (the antecedent).

They are the students **who** study hard.

He is the student **who** studies the hardest.

In the phrase *one of those who* (or *which* or *that*), it is necessary to decide whether the *who, which,* or *that* refers only to the one or to the whole group. Only then can you decide whether the verb is singular or plural.

Rena is one of those shoppers who buy only things that are on sale.

one of those shoppers who buy

[In this case, Rena is part of a large group, shoppers who buy only things that are on sale, and acts like others in that group. Therefore, *who* takes a plural verb because it refers to shoppers.]

The *American Dictionary* is one of the dictionaries on the shelf that includes Latin words.

one . . . that includes

[In this case the *American Dictionary*, while part of the group of dictionaries on the shelf, is specifically one that includes Latin words. The other dictionaries may or may not. Therefore, *that* refers back to that *one* dictionary and takes a singular verb.]

Exercise 7.1: Proofreading Practice

In the following paragraph, choose the correct verb that agrees with the subject.

How children's drawings develop (1. is, are) a fascinating subject. For example, a two-year-old and sometimes even a three-year-old (2. does not, do not) create any recognizable forms when scribbling, and most of the children recently studied by a child psychologist (3. seem, seems) not to be be aware of the notion that a line stands for the edge of an object. Typically, by the age of three, children's spontaneous scribbles along with their attempts at drawing a picture (4. become, becomes) more obviously pictorial. When a child has drawn a recognizable shape, either the child or some nearby adult (5. attempt, attempts) to label the shape with a name. By the age of three or four, there (6. is, are) attempts to draw images of a human, images that look like a tadpole and consist of a circle and two lines for legs. Psychologists, especially those who (7. study, studies) the development of people's concepts of reality (8. conclude, concludes) that young children's tadpole-like drawings (9. is, are) a result of inadequate recall of what people look like. However, Layton Peale is one of a number of psychologists who (10. insist, insists) that young children do have adequate recall but (11. isn't, aren't) interested in realism because they prefer simplicity. Once the desire for realism (12. set, sets) in, it leads to the more complex drawings done by older children.

Exercise 7.2: Pattern Practice

Using the following patterns for correct subject-verb agreement, write two sentences of your own.

Pattern A: Compound subject joined by *and* with a plural verb

The whole flower exhibit and each display in it were carefully planned for months.

Pattern B: An amount as a subject with a singular verb.

Ten dollars is a small price to pay for that.

Pattern C: A title, company name, or word with a singular verb.

The Mysteries of the Universe is a new educational TV series.

Pattern D: An item that is a single unit but is thought of as plural (such as pants, scissors, and jeans) with a plural verb

The scissors need sharpening.

Pattern E: Plural words (such as *physics, economics,* and *measles*) with a singular verb

The news of the election results is being broadcast live from the election board office.

Pattern F: *Either . . . or, neither . . . nor,* or *not only . . . but*—with a verb that agrees with the nearest subject

Either Todd or his friends are capable of handling that job.

Pattern G: A whole clause as the subject with a singular verb

Whatever the finance committee decides to do about the subject is acceptable to the rest of us.

Pattern H: A *who, what,* or *that* clause with a verb that agrees with the correct antecedent

Psycho is one of those movies that shock viewers no matter how many times they watch reruns.

8 Sentence Fragments (frag)

A **sentence fragment** is an incomplete sentence.

To recognize a fragment, consider the basic requirements of a sentence:

- A sentence is a group of words with at least one independent clause (see 24a).

  After buying some useful software for her computer, <u>Elena splurged on</u>
  (independent clause)

  <u>several computer games to play.</u>

- A clause has at least one subject and a complete verb, plus an object or complement if needed. (See Chapter 22.)

  During the evening, the <u>mosquitoes</u> <u>avoided</u> the <u>campfire</u>.
                       (subject)   *(verb)*   *(object)*

8a Unintentional Fragments

- **The fragment without a subject or verb** This type of fragment lacks a subject or verb.

  Fragment: The week spent on the beach just relaxing and soaking up the sun.

  [Week is probably the intended subject here, but it has no verb.]

  Revised: The <u>week</u> spent on the beach just relaxing and soaking up the
             (subject)

          sun <u>was</u> the best vacation I had in years.
          (verb)

  Fragment: She selected a current news item as the topic of her essay. Then wondered if her choice was wise.

HINT   **Finding Fragments**

1. When you proofread for fragments, be sure that each word group has both a subject and a complete verb. Remember that *-ing* words are not complete verbs because they need a helping verb. (See 17b.)

2. To find subjects and predicates in sentences with one-word verbs, make up a *who* or *what* question about the sentence. The predicate is all the words from the sentence used in the *who* or *what* question, and the subject is the rest.

  My grandmother lived in a house built by her father.

  [Who lived in a house built by her father?]

  Predicate: lived in a house built by her father

  Subject: My grandmother

[The second of these two word groups is a fragment because it has no subject for the verb *wondered*.]

Revised: She selected a current news item as the topic of her essay. Then <u>she</u> <u>wondered</u> if her choice was wise.
(*subject*) (*verb*)

■ **The fragment caused by a misplaced period** Most fragments are caused by detaching a phrase or dependent clause from the sentence to which it belongs. A period has been put in the wrong place, often because the writer thinks a sentence has gotten too long and needs a period. Such fragments can be corrected by removing the period between the independent clause and the fragment.

Ever since fifth grade I have participated in one or more team sports,
beginning
~~Beginning~~ with the typical grammar school sports of basketball and volleyball.

[The second word group is a detached phrase that belongs to the sentence preceding it.]

Travelers to Europe should consider visiting in the spring or fall,
because
~~Because~~ airfares and hotels are often cheaper then.

[The second word group is a dependent clause that was detached from the sentence before it.]

HINT **Proofreading for Fragments**

1. To proofread for fragments caused by misplaced periods, read your paper backward, from the last sentence to the first. You will be able to notice the fragment more easily when you hear it without the sentence to which it belongs. Most, but not all, fragments occur **after** the main clause.

2. To find dependent clauses separated from the main clause, look for the marker word typically found at the beginning of the dependent clause. (See 24b.2.) If it is standing alone with no independent clause, attach it to the independent clause that completes the meaning. Typical marker words that begin dependent clauses are the following:

after	because	since	what
although	before	though	when
as	even though	unless	whether
as if	if	until	while

Fragment: Denise had breakfast at the doughnut shop near Hafter Hall,
after
~~After~~ she went to her 8 A.M. biology class.

(*continued on next page*)

(continued from previous page)

3. Another way to identify a dependent clause is to be sure that it is not an independent clause that answers a yes/no question.

They often spend Sunday afternoons watching football games on TV.

Do they often spend Sunday afternoons watching football games on TV?

[This question yields a yes/no answer and is therefore an independent clause.]

Because they often spend Sunday afternoons watching football games on TV.

Do because they often spend Sunday afternoons watching football games on TV?

[This is not a reasonable question and is not, therefore, an independent clause.]

8b Intentional Fragments

Writers occasionally write an intentional fragment for its effect on the reader. Intended fragments should be used only when the rest of the writing clearly indicates that the writer could have written a whole sentence but preferred a fragment. In the following three sentences the second word group is an intended fragment. Do you like the effect it produces?

Fragment: Jessica walked quietly into the room, unnoticed by the rest of the group. *Not that she wanted it that way.* She simply didn't know how to make an effective entrance.

Exercise 8.1: Proofreading Practice

In these paragraphs there are both complete sentences and fragments. Read through the passage and underline the fragments.

(1) If you've ever doubted your child's identity, advanced technology makes it easy and affordable to set your mind at ease. (2) DNA testing, a procedure that determines genetic relationships, is now available to the average person. (3) For a fee of around $500. (4) Previously, DNA testing was used in criminal cases and in custody disputes involving celebrities. (5) When large sums of money were at stake. (6) Now the average person can find out if a child is in fact his or her biological offspring.

(7) The procedure is fast and easy. (8) The parent and child need to provide a sample from the inside of the cheek. (9) With a cotton swab collecting the tissue that is needed. (10) The sample is then sent to the lab, and an answer can be had within ten days. (11) In some areas, the sample can be sent through the mail. (12) Instead of being given at the lab.

(13) Advanced technology requires responsibility and caution. (14) Especially when a family's happiness is at stake. (15) Many people feel that DNA testing has caused the breakdown of otherwise happy families. (16) Ethical issues involved in the testing. (17) Doctors have been urging labs that offer the testing to encourage counseling for the people involved. (18) Discovering that your child is not your own is a very complex issue. (19) And not a matter to be taken lightly.

Exercise 8.2: Pattern Practice

Read the following paragraph and note the pattern of dependent and independent clauses (see Chapter 24) in each sentence. Practice by following those patterns to write your own sentences, and check to see that you have not written any fragments. As a guide to help you, the first sentence has been done. For your own sentences, you may wish to write about some modern convenience you particularly like (or dislike) or some modern convenience you wish someone would invent.

Sample answer:

Pattern: Independent clause + dependent clause

Sample Sentence: Those hot-air dryers in public restrooms are a Grade A nuisance because it's impossible to dry your face without messing up your hair.

(1) The communications industry has made billions of dollars because Americans love instant gratification. (2) The average American can be heard talking on a cellular phone in the oddest of places, including the stall of a public restroom. (3) A high school student carries a cellular phone, and her most noticeable fashion accessory is a beeper. (4) When a friend calls another friend, she may be subjected to "call waiting" and put on hold. (5) The telephone company offers many instant-gratification services such as call forwarding, conference calling, and voice mail. (6) Because many people have become distracted while talking and driving, law-enforcement agents have given more tickets related to cell phone use in the past year than in the previous three years combined.

9 Dangling and Misplaced Modifiers (dm)

9a Dangling Modifiers

A **dangling modifier** is a word or word group that refers to (or modifies) a word or phrase that has not been clearly stated in the sentence. When an introductory phrase does not name the doer of the action, the phrase then refers to (or modifies) the subject of the independent clause that follows.

Having finished the assignment, Jill turned on the TV.

[*Jill*, the subject of the independent clause, is the doer of the action in the introductory phrase.]

However, when the intended subject (or doer of the action) of the introductory phrase is not stated, the result is a dangling modifier.

Having finished the assignment, the TV was turned on.

[This sentence says that the TV finished the homework. Since it is unlikely that TV sets can get our work done, the introductory phrase has no logical or appropriate word to refer to. Sentences with dangling modifiers say one thing while the writer means another.]

Characteristics of dangling modifiers:

- They most frequently occur at the beginning of sentences but can also appear at the end.
- They often have an *-ing* verb or a *to* + verb phrase near the start of the phrase.

Dangling Modifier: After getting a degree in education, more experience in the classroom is needed to be a good teacher.

Revised: After getting a degree in education, Sylvia needed more experience in the classroom to be a good teacher.

Dangling Modifier: To work as a lifeguard, practice in CPR is required.

Revised: To work as a lifeguard, you are required to have practice in CPR.

There are two strategies for revising dangling modifiers:

1. Name the doer of the action in the dangling phrase.

Dangling Modifier: Without knowing the guest's name, it was difficult for Maria to introduce him to her husband.

Revised: Because Maria did not know the guest's name, it was difficult to introduce him to her husband.

2. Name the appropriate or logical doer of the action as the subject of the independent clause.

Dangling Modifier: Having arrived late for practice, a written excuse was needed.

Revised: <u>Having arrived</u> late for practice, the (team member) needed a written excuse.

Exercise 9.1: Proofreading Practice

In the following paragraph there are several dangling modifiers. Identify them by underlining them.

According to some anthropologists, the fastball may be millions of years older than the beginning of baseball. To prove this point, prehistoric toolmaking sites, such as Olduvai Gorge in Tanzania, are offered as evidence. These sites are littered with smooth, roundish stones not suitable for flaking into tools. Suspecting that the stones might have been used as weapons, anthropologists have speculated that these stones were thrown at enemies and animals being hunted. Searching for other evidence, historical accounts of primitive peoples have been combed for stories of rock throwing. Here early adventurers are described as being caught by rocks thrown hard and fast. Used in combat, museums have collections of these "handstones." So stone throwing may have been a major form of defense and a tool for hunting. Being an impulse that still has to be curbed, parents still find themselves teaching their children not to throw stones.

Exercise 9.2: Pattern Practice

Using the patterns of the sample sentences given here, sentences in which the modifiers do not dangle, write your own sentences. The first sentence is done as an example.

1. After realizing there were no familiar faces at the party, Josh returned home to watch television.

Sentence in the Same Pattern
While cleaning the house, Mona looked for her lost ring.

2. To finish the New York City Marathon, runners must train on a daily basis before the race.
3. Unlike high school, college offers independence and freedom.
4. Rather than fail the test, Carla decided to stay home and study.
5. The party was a blast, having plenty of food and good music.

9b Misplaced Modifiers

A **misplaced modifier** is a word or word group placed so far away from what it refers to (or modifies) that the reader may be confused. Modifiers should be placed as closely as possible to the words they modify in order to keep the meaning clear.

Misplaced Modifier: The assembly line workers were told that they had been fired by the personnel director.

[Were the workers told by the personnel director that they had been fired, or were they told by someone else that the personnel director had fired them?]

Revised: The assembly line workers were told by the personnel director that they had been fired.

Misplaced modifiers are often the source of comedians' humor, as in the classic often used by Groucho Marx and others:

The other day I shot an elephant in my pajamas. How he got in my pajamas I'll never know.

Single-word modifiers should be placed immediately before the words they modify. Note the difference in meaning in these two sentences:

I earned nearly $30. [The amount was almost $30, but not quite.]

I nearly earned $30. [I almost had the opportunity to earn $30, but it didn't work out.]

HINT   **Misplaced Modifiers**

Some one-word modifiers that may get misplaced.

almost	hardly	merely	only
even	just	nearly	simply

Exercise 9.3: Proofreading Practice

In these sentences there are some misplaced modifiers or unclear modifiers. Underline them and indicate a more appropriate place in the sentence by drawing an arrow to that place.

After finishing a huge dinner, he <u>only</u> ate a few cherries for dessert.

(1) The man who was carrying the sack of groceries with an umbrella walked carefully to his car. (2) He only bought a small amount of food for his lunch because he was going to leave town that afternoon. (3) He whistled to his huge black dog opening the car door and set the groceries in the trunk. (4) The dog jumped into the trunk happily with the groceries.

Exercise 9.4: Pattern Practice

Choose one of the one-word modifiers listed in the box above, and use the word in several places in a series of sentences to create different meanings. Write out the meaning of each sentence.

Example (using the word *almost*)

Almost everyone in the office earned a $500 bonus last year. [Most of the people earned a $500 bonus, but a few people did not.]

Everyone in the office **almost** earned a $500 bonus last year. [There was almost a chance to earn a bonus, but it didn't work out. Therefore, no one earned a bonus.]

Everyone in the office earned **almost** a $500 bonus last year. [Everyone earned a bonus, but it was less than $500.]

10 Parallel Constructions (//)

10a Parallel Structure

Parallel structure is the use of the same grammatical form or structure for equal ideas in a list or comparison. The balance of equal elements in a sentence helps to show the relationship between ideas. Often the equal elements repeat words or sounds.

Parallel: The instructor carefully explained <u>how to start the engine</u> and
(1)

<u>how to shift gears</u>.
(2)

[1 and 2 are parallel phrases in that both start with *how to:*

■ <u>how to</u> start the engine

■ <u>how to</u> shift gears]

Parallel: <u>Getting the model airplane off the ground</u> was even harder than
(1)

<u>building it from a kit</u>.
(2)

[1 and 2 are parallel phrases that begin with *-ing* verb forms:

■ <u>Getting</u> the model airplane off the ground

■ <u>building</u> it from a kit]

Parallel: She often went to the aquarium <u>to watch the fish</u>, <u>to enjoy the</u>
(1)   *(2)*

<u>solitude</u>, and <u>to escape from her roommate</u>.
(3)

[1, 2, and 3 are parallel phrases that begin with *to* + verb.]

Parallelism is needed in the following:

■ Items in a series or list

Parallel: Items often overlooked when camping include the following:

    I. All <u>medications</u> normally taken on a daily basis

    2. <u>Books</u> to read during leisure time

    3. <u>Quinine tablets</u> to purify water

    [parallelism with a series of nouns in a list]

Parallel: The three most important skills for that job are

- <u>being</u> able to adapt to new requirements
- <u>knowing</u> appropriate computer languages
- <u>keeping</u> lines of communication open

    [parallelism with *-ing* verbs]

- *Both . . . as/either . . . or/whether . . . or/neither . . . nor/not . . . but/not only . . . but also* (correlative conjunctions)

Parallel: **Both** <u>by the way</u> he dressed **and** <u>by his attempts</u> at humor, it was clear that he wanted to make a good impression.

    [parallelism with *by the . . .* phrases]

- *And, but, or, nor, yet* (coordinating conjunctions)

Parallel: Job opportunities are <u>increasing</u> in the health fields **but** <u>decreasing</u> in many areas of engineering.

    [parallelism using *-ing* verbs]

- Comparisons using *than* or *as*

Parallel: The mayor noted that it was easier <u>to agree</u> to the new budget **than** <u>to attempt</u> to veto it.

    [parallelism in a comparison with *to* + verb]

10b Faulty Parallelism

Nonparallel structure (or **faulty parallelism**) occurs when like items are not in the same grammatical form or structure.

                                     eliminating

Many companies are <u>reducing</u> their labor force as well as ~~eliminate~~ some
                   (1)   *(2)*

employee benefits.

When the investigator took over, he started his inquiry by <u>calling</u> the
                                                      (1)
                      requesting
witnesses back and ~~requested~~ that they repeat their stories.
                 (2)

The article looked at <u>future uses of computers</u> and ~~what~~ <u>their role</u>
                              (1)   *(2)*

~~will be~~ in the next century.

HINT **Proofing for Parallel Structure**

I. As you proofread, **listen** to the sound when you are linking or comparing similar elements. Do they balance by sounding alike? Parallelism often adds emphasis by the repetition of similar sounds.

2. As you proofread, **visualize** similar elements in a list. Check to see that the elements begin in the same way.

Isaiah wondered whether it was better <u>to tell</u> his girlfriend that he forgot or <u>if</u> he should make up some excuse.

[Isaiah wondered whether it was better

- <u>to tell</u> his girlfriend that he forgot

(or)

- <u>if</u> he should make up some excuse]

Revised: Isaiah wondered whether it was better <u>to tell</u> his girlfriend that he forgot or <u>to make up</u> some excuse.]

Exercise 10.1: Proofreading Practice

In this paragraph, underline the parallel elements in each sentence.

One of the great American cars was the J-series Duesenberg. The cars were created by Fred and August Duesenberg, two brothers from Iowa who began by making bicycles and who then gained fame by building racing cars. Determined to build an American car that would earn respect for its excellent quality and its high performance, the Duesenbergs completed the first Model J in 1928. The car was an awesome machine described as having a 265-horsepower engine and a top speed of 120 mph. Special features of the car were its four-wheel hydraulic brakes and extensive quantities of lightweight aluminum castings. The masterpiece was the Duesenberg SJ, reputed to have a 320-horsepower engine and to accelerate from zero to 100 mph in 17 seconds.

Exercise 10.2: Pattern Practice

Using these sentences as patterns for parallel structures, write your own sentences using the same patterns. You may want to write about some favorite vehicle of your own, such as a car or bike.

1. A common practice among early Duesenberg owners was to buy a bare chassis and to ship it to a coach builder, who would turn the chassis into a dazzling roadster, cabriolet, or dual-cowl phaeton.
2. Duesenbergs that were originally purchased for six thousand dollars or so and that are now being auctioned off for more than a million dollars are still considered to be superb examples of engineering brilliance.
3. After the Duesenberg first appeared on the market and people realized its excellence, the phrase "It's a doozy" became part of American slang.

II Consistency (Avoiding Shifts) (shft)

Consistency in writing involves using the same (1) pronoun person and number, (2) verb tense, (3) tone, (4) voice, and (5) indirect or direct form of discourse.

IIa Shifts in Person or Number

Avoid shifts between first, second, and third person pronouns, and between singular and plural. The following table shows three "persons" in English pronouns:

PRONOUN PERSON		
	Singular	**Plural**
First person (the person or persons speaking)	I, me	we, us
Second person (the person or persons spoken to)	you	you
Third person (the person or persons spoken about)	he, she, it	they, them

Some readers view first or second person writing as too personal or informal and suggest that writers use third person for formal or academic writing. Second person, however, is appropriate for giving instructions or helping readers follow a process.

First, (you) open the hood of the car and check the water level in the battery.

[The pronoun *you* can be used or omitted.]

First person is appropriate for a narrative about your own actions and for essays that explore your personal feelings and emotions. Some teachers encourage writers to use first person to develop a sense of their own voice in writing.

1. Unnecessary Shift in Person
Once you have chosen to use first, second, or third person, shift only with a good reason.

                                          he or she does
In a <u>person's</u> life, the most important thing ~~you do~~ is to decide on a
    (3rd)   *(2nd)*

type of job.

[This is an unnecessary shift from third to second person.]

2. Unnecessary Shift in Number

To avoid pronoun inconsistency, don't shift unnecessarily in number from singular to plural (or from plural to singular).

> Working women face
> ~~The working woman faces~~ many challenges to advancement in a career.
>   *(sing.)*

> When <u>they</u> marry and have children, <u>they</u> may need to take a leave of
>   *(pl.)*   *(pl.)*

> absence and stay home for several months.

[The writer uses the singular noun *woman* in the first sentence but then shifts to the plural pronoun *they* in the second sentence.]

11b Shifts in Verb Tense

Because verb tenses indicate time, keep writing in the same time (past, present, or future) unless the logic of what you are writing about requires a switch.

Narrative writing can be in the past or present, with time switching if needed. Explanatory writing (exposition) that expresses general truth is usually kept in present time, though history is written in past time.

Necessary Shift: Many people today <u>remember</u> very little about the Vietnam War except the filmed scenes of fighting they <u>watched</u> on television news at the time.

[The verb *remember* reports a general truth in the present, and the verb *watched* reports past events.]

Unnecessary Shift: While we <u>were watching</u> the last game of the World Series, the picture suddenly <u>gets</u> fuzzy.

[The verb phrase *were watching* reports a past event, and there is no reason to shift to the present tense verb *gets*.]

Revised: While we <u>were watching</u> the last game of the World Series, the picture suddenly <u>got</u> fuzzy.

11c Shifts in Tone

Once you choose a formal or informal tone for a paper, keep that tone consistent in your word choices. A sudden intrusion of a very formal word or phrase in an informal narrative or the use of slang or informal words in a formal report or essay indicates the writer's loss of control over tone.

> The job of the welfare worker is to assist in a family's struggle to obtain
>   children's
> funds for the ~~kids'~~ food and clothing.

[The use of the informal word *kids'* is a shift in tone in this formal sentence.]

11d Shifts in Voice

Don't shift unnecessarily between active and passive voice in a sentence. (See 17d for a review of active and passive verbs.)

Active: He <u>insisted</u> that he was able to perform the magic trick.

Passive: The magic trick <u>was not considered</u> to be difficult by him.

He <u>insisted</u> that he was able to perform the magic trick, which ~~was not~~ *he did not*

~~considered~~ to be difficult ~~by him~~. *consider*

When choosing between passive and active, remember that many readers prefer active voice verbs because they are clearer, more direct, and more concise. The active voice also forces us to think about who the doer of the action is. For example, in the following sentence the writer uses passive rather than considering who the doer is:

Many arguments are offered against abortion. [By whom?]

But there are occasions to use passive:

■ When the doer of the action is not important or is not known

The pep rally was held before the game.
For the tournament game, more than five thousand tickets were sold.

■ When you want to focus on the action, not the doer

The records were destroyed.

■ When you want to avoid blaming, giving credit, or taking responsibility

The candidate conceded that the election was lost.

■ When you want a tone of objectivity or wish to exclude yourself

The experiment was performed successfully.
It was noted that the results confirmed our hypothesis.

11e Shifts in Discourse

When you repeat the exact words that someone says, you are using **direct discourse,** and when you change a few of the words in order to report them indirectly, you are using **indirect discourse.** Mixing direct and indirect discourse results in unnecessary shifting, a problem that causes lack of parallel structure as well.

Direct Discourse: The instructor said, "Your reports are due at the beginning of next week. Be sure to include your bibliography."

Indirect Discourse: The instructor said that our reports are due at the beginning of next week and that we should be sure to include our bibliographies.

Unnecessary Shifting: The instructor said that our reports are due at the beginning of next week and be sure to include your bibliography.

[This sentence also mixes together a statement and a command, two different moods. For more on mood, see 17e.]

Exercise 11.1: Proofreading Practice

As you read the following paragraph, proofread for consistency and correct any unnecessary shifts. Underline the inconsistent word and write a more consistent form. You may also want to omit some words or phrases.

Many people think that recycling material is a recent trend. However, during World War II more than 43 percent of America's newsprint was recycled, and the average person saved bacon grease and other meat fat, which they returned to local collection centers. What you would do is to pour leftover fat and other greasy gunk from frying pans and pots into tin cans. Today, despite the fact that many trendy people are into recycling, only about 10 percent of Americans' waste is actually recycled. The problem is not to get us to save bottles and cans but to convince industry to use recycled materials. There is a concern expressed by manufacturers that they would be using materials of uneven quality and will face undependable delivery. If the manufacturer would wake up and smell the coffee, they would see the advantages for the country and bigger profits could be made by them.

12 Faulty Predication (pred)

Faulty predication occurs when the subject and the rest of the clause (the *predicate*) don't make sense together.

Faulty Predicate: The <u>reason</u> for her sudden success <u>proved</u> that she was talented.

[In this sentence the subject, *reason,* cannot logically prove "that she was talented."]

Revised: Her sudden success proved that she was talented.

Faulty predication often occurs with forms of the verb *to be* because this verb sets up an equation in which the terms on either side of the verb should be equivalent.

Subject		Predicate
2×2	=	4
2×2	is	4
Dr. Streeter	is	our family doctor.

Faulty Predication: Success is when you have your own swimming pool.

[The concept of success involves much more than having a swimming pool. Having a pool can be one example or a result of success, but it is not the equivalent of success.]

Revised: One sign of success is having your own swimming pool.

HINT   **Faulty Predication**

Faulty predication often occurs in sentences with the following constructions:

    is when . . .   is why . . .   is where . . .   is because . . .

It is best to avoid these constructions in academic writing.

                                                              that
Faulty Predication: The reason I didn't show up is ~~because~~ I overslept.

Exercise 12.1: Proofreading Practice

Rewrite the following examples of faulty predication so that they are correct sentences.

1. Relaxation is when you grab a bowl of popcorn, put your feet up, and watch football on television for two hours.
2. Computer science is where you learn how to program computers.
3. One of the most common ways to improve your math is getting a tutor.
4. The next agenda item we want to look at is to find out the cost of purchasing decorations.
5. His job consisted mainly of repetitious assembly line tasks.

Exercise 12.2: Pattern Practice

The patterns of the following five sentences avoid faulty predication. Practice these patterns by completing the second sentence in each set. Be sure to use the same pattern even though your subject matter will be different.

1. A good science fiction movie is one that has an exciting plot and realistic special effects.

   A good _____ is _____.

2. His job as a receptionist is to direct people to the right office.

   His job as a _____ is _____.

3. One sign of her excellent memory is her ability to remember the punch lines of all the jokes she hears.

One sign of her _____ is _____.

4. The reason I didn't buy those boots is that they are overpriced.

The reason _____ is that _____.

5. Stage fright is a kind of apprehension accompanied by a dry mouth, sweaty hands, and a fluttery stomach.

_____ is _____.

13 Coordination and Subordination

13a Coordination (coord)

When an independent clause is added to another independent clause to form a sentence, both clauses are described as **coordinate** because they are equally important and have the same emphasis.

1. Appropriate Coordination

Independent clauses are joined together by coordinators and appropriate punctuation (see Chapters 6, 24a, and 27a). Two types of words join coordinate clauses.

- **Coordinating conjunctions** (the seven coordinating words used after a comma) are:

| and | but | for | or | nor | so | yet |

- **Conjunctive adverbs** (coordinating words used after a semicolon) include:

| consequently | otherwise | however | thus |
| furthermore | therefore | moreover | nevertheless |

The following sentences illustrate appropriate coordination because they join two clauses of equal importance and emphasis.

Kathy is doing well as a real estate broker, and she hopes to become wealthy before she is thirty-five.

Some people take vitamin C tablets for colds; however, other people prefer aspirin.

2. Inappropriate Coordination

Inappropriate coordination occurs when two clauses that are either unequal in importance or have little or no connection with each other are joined together as independent clauses. Inappropriate coordination can be corrected by making one clause dependent on the other. However, if there is little connection between the clauses, they may not belong in the same sentence or paragraph.

Inappropriate Coordination: Winter in Texas can be very mild, and snow often falls in New England during the autumn.

[The connection between these two clauses is very weak; they don't belong together unless the writer can show more connection.]

Inappropriate Coordination: Jim was ill, and he went to the doctor.
Revised: Because Jim was ill, he went to the doctor.

[In this case the first clause can be shown to depend on the second clause.]

3. Excessive Coordination

Excessive coordination occurs when too many equal clauses are strung together with coordinators. As a result, a sentence can ramble on and become tiresome or monotonous. Excessive coordination can be corrected by breaking the sentence into smaller ones or by making the appropriate clauses into dependent ones.

Excessive Coordination: Kirsten is an exchange student from Holland, and she is visiting the United States for the first time, so she decided to drive through the Southwest during vacation.

Revised: Kirsten, an exchange student from Holland visiting the United States for the first time, decided to drive through the Southwest during vacation.

13b Subordination (sub)

When one clause has less emphasis or is less important in a sentence, it is **subordinate** to or dependent on the other clause.

I. Appropriate Subordination

The relationship of a dependent or subordinate clause to a main clause is shown by the marker word that begins the subordinate clause. (See 24b and 26b.) Some common marker words (called *subordinating conjunctions*) are:

after	before	unless
although	if	until
as	once	when
as though	since	whether
because	though	while

Although I like snow, I enjoy Florida vacations in winter.

Mr. Stratman, <u>who never missed a football game</u>, was one of the team's greatest supporters.

The house <u>that she grew up in</u> was torn down.

2. Inappropriate Subordination

Inappropriate subordination occurs when the more important clause is placed in the subordinate or dependent position and has less emphasis.

Inappropriate Subordination: A career <u>that combines a lot of interaction with people and opportunities to use my creative talents</u> is my goal.

Revised: My career goal is to combine a lot of interaction with people and opportunities to use my creative talents.

3. Excessive Subordination

Excessive subordination occurs when a sentence has a string of clauses subordinate to each other. As a result, readers have difficulty following the confusing chain of ideas dependent on each other. To revise excessive subordination, place the string of dependent clauses in separate sentences with independent clauses.

Excessive Subordination: These computer software companies should inform their employees about advancements and promotions with the company because they will lose them if they don't compete for their services since the employees can easily find jobs elsewhere.

Revised: These computer software companies should inform their employees about advancements and promotions with the company. If these companies don't compete for the services of their employees, the companies will lose them because the employees can easily find jobs elsewhere.

Exercise 13.1: Proofreading Practice

In the following paragraph there are some sentences with inappropriate coordination and subordination. Rewrite these sentences so that the paragraph has appropriate coordination and subordination.

(1) Most people think of pigs as providers of ham, bacon, and pork chops, and they think of pigs as dirty, smelly, lazy, stupid, mean, and stubborn, but there's more to pigs than this bad press they've had, so we should stop and reevaluate what we think of pigs. (2) President Harry Truman once said that no man should be allowed to be president who does not understand hogs because this lack of understanding indicates inadequate appreciation of a useful farm animal. (3) Some people are discovering that pigs make excellent pets. (4) In fact, pigs have been favorite characters in children's fiction, and many people fondly

remember Porky Pig and Miss Piggy, the Muppet creation, as well as the heroic pig named Wilbur in E. B. White's *Charlotte's Web*. (5) Now there are clubs for those who keep pigs as pets, and they are not just on farms where they have long been favorites as pets for farm children, who are likely to be fond of animals. (6) People with pigs as pets report that their pigs are curious, friendly little animals that are quite clean despite the "dirty as a pig" saying, though they are also not very athletic and have a sweet tooth. (7) Pigs can be interesting pets and are useful farm animals to raise.

Exercise 13.2: Pattern Practice

To practice using subordination and coordination appropriately, use these suggested patterns in your own sentences. You can build your sentences from the short sentences offered here.

1. Coordination: Join independent clauses with any of the following words (or others listed on previous pages).

, and	, but	, or
; moreover,	; however,	; therefore,

2. Subordination: Subordinate dependent clauses to independent clauses by using any of the following words (or others listed on previous pages) at the beginning of the dependent clause.

after	once	when
although	since	whether
as	that	which
because	though	while
before	unless	who
if	until	whose

You can use these clauses to build your paragraph:

Plastic used to be considered a cheap, shoddy material.
Now plastic is taking the place of traditional materials.
Cars are made of plastic.
Boats, airplanes, cameras, fishing rods, watches, suitcases, toothpaste tubes, and plates are made of plastic.
Plastic has replaced the glass in eyeglasses.
Plastic has replaced the wood in tennis rackets.
Plastic has replaced cotton and wool in our clothing.
Plastic seems new.
Plastic has been with us for a long time.
Amber is a natural form of plastic.
Celluloid is a nearly natural plastic.
Celluloid was developed in 1868 as a substitute for ivory in billiard balls.
Celluloid proved to be too flammable.
New types of plastic have mushroomed.
The use of plastics has steadily increased.
By the mid-1970s plastic had become the nation's most widely used material.

14 Sentence Clarity (clar)

The suggestions offered in this section will improve the clarity of your sentences. These suggestions are based on what is known about how to help readers follow along more easily and understand sentence content more fully.

14a Moving from Known (Old) to Unknown (New) Information

To help readers understand your writing, begin your sentences with something that is generally known or familiar before you introduce new or unfamiliar material later in the sentence. Then, when that new material is known, it becomes familiar, or "old," and you can go on to introduce more new material. Note how these sentences move from familiar (or old) information to new:

Familiar ⟶ Unfamiliar:

Every semester, after final exams are over, I'm always faced with the problem of what to do with lecture notes. These old notebooks might be useful some day, but they just keep piling up on my bookcase. Some day, it will collapse under the weight of information I might never need.

This example is not as clear:

Unfamiliar ⟵ Familiar:

Second-rate entertainment is my categorization of most movies I've seen lately, but occasionally, there are some with worthwhile themes. In the Southwest, the mysterious and rapid disappearance of an Indian culture is the topic of a recent movie I saw that I would say has a worthwhile theme.

You probably found these sentences hard to read because the familiar information comes after the new information.

14b Using Positive Instead of Negative

Use the positive (or affirmative) instead of the negative because negative statements are harder for people to understand.

Unclear Negative: Less attention is paid to commercials that lack human interest stories.

Revised: People pay more attention to commercials with human interest stories.

14c Avoiding Double Negatives

Use only one negative at a time in your sentences. Using more than one negative word creates a double negative, which is grammatically incorrect and leaves the reader with the impression that the writer isn't very literate. Some double negatives are also hard to understand.

Double Negative: He did not have no money.

Revised: He had no money.   (or)   He did not have any money.

Double Negative: I don't think he didn't have no money left after he paid for his dinner.

[This sentence is particularly hard to understand because it uses both a double negative and negatives instead of positives.]

Revised: I think he had some money left after he paid for his dinner.

HINT   **Double Negatives**

1. Watch out for contractions with negatives in them. If you use the following contractions, do not use any other negatives in your sentence.

aren't	don't	wasn't
couldn't	hadn't	weren't
didn't	hasn't	won't
doesn't	isn't	wouldn't

any
She doesn't want ~~no~~ more riders in the car.

2. Watch out for other negative words:

hardly	no place	nothing
neither	nobody	nowhere
no one	none	scarcely

any
They hardly had ~~no~~ popcorn left.

14d Using Verbs Instead of Nouns

Try to use verbs if possible rather than noun forms. Actions expressed as verbs are more easily understood than actions named as nouns.

Unnecessary Noun Form: The decision was made to adjourn.

Revised: They decided to adjourn.

Some Noun Forms	Verbs to Use Instead
The determination of . . .	They determine . . .
The approval of . . .	They approve . . .
The preparation of . . .	They prepare . . .
The discovery of . . .	They discover . . .
The analysis of . . .	They analyze . . .

14e Making the Intended Subject the Sentence Subject

Be sure that the real subject or the doer of the action in the verb is the grammatical subject of the sentence. Sometimes the real subject of a sentence can get buried in prepositional phrases or other less noticeable places.

Subject Buried in a Prepositional Phrase:

For real music lovers, <u>it is</u> preferable to hear a live concert instead of a tape.

[The grammatical subject here is *it*, which is not the real subject of this sentence.]

A revision brings the real subject out of the prepositional phrase. The following example shows one possibility:

Revised: <u>Music lovers prefer</u> to hear a live concert instead of a tape.

Real Subject Buried in the Sentence:

<u>It seems</u> like ordering from catalogs is something that Chris does too much.

If the real subject, *Chris*, becomes the sentence subject, the entire sentence becomes more clear.

Revised: <u>Chris seems</u> to order too much from catalogs.

14f Using Active Instead of Passive

The active verb (see 17d) is often easier to understand than the passive because the active voice explains who is "doing" the action.

Active: The committee <u>decided</u> to postpone the vote.
                                (active)

Not as clear: The decision that <u>was reached</u> by the committee was to
                                            (passive)

postpone the vote.

Exercise 14.1: Proofreading Practice

The following paragraph has numerous problems with clarity. Each sentence in the paragraph could be revised by using one or more of the suggestions in this chapter. List the section numbers of all the suggestions that could be followed to improve each of these sentences.

(1) Little attention was paid to Y2K until the time when analysts began to think about how the year 2000 would affect computers.

(2) The panic that was caused by Y2K revolved around the idea that systems won't hardly work right when the year turned from 1999 to 2000. (3) The 00 would be understood by the computer to be 1900 and could cause major chaos. (4) The majority of the problem was expected to affect bank accounts, telephone service, utilities, and food supply. (5) It seemed that crashing computers is something that most experts expected. (6) The discovery of this problem actually took place more than fifty years ago, but nobody didn't want to address something that was fifty years in the future. (7) Consequently, companies raced against the clock to rid their systems of the Y2K problem.

Exercise 14.2: Pattern Practice

Look back through this chapter at the patterns for the changes you suggested in Exercise 14.1. Use those patterns to revise the paragraph above so that it is clearer.

15 Transitions (trans)

Transitions are words and phrases that build bridges between sentences, parts of sentences, and paragraphs. These bridges show relationships and help to blend sentences together smoothly. Several types of transitions are illustrated here.

15a Repetition of a Key Term or Phrase

Among the recent food fads sweeping America is the interest in **exotic foods**. While not everyone can agree on what **exotic foods** are, most of us like the idea of trying something new and different.

15b Synonyms

Since the repetition of a key word or phrase can become boring, use a synonym (a word or phrase having essentially the same meaning) to add variety while not repeating.

One food Americans are not inclined to try is **brains.** A Gallup Poll found that 41 percent of the people who responded said they would never try **brains.** Three years later, the percentage of those who wouldn't touch **gray matter** had risen to 49 percent.

15c Pronouns

Pronouns such as *he, she, it, we,* and *they* are useful devices when you want to refer back to something mentioned previously. Similarly, *this, that, these,* and *those* can be used as links.

In addition to brains, there are many other foods that <u>Americans</u> now find
(1)

more distasteful than <u>they</u> did several years ago. For example, more people
(1)

now say they would never eat <u>liver, rabbit, pig's feet, or beef kidneys</u> than
(2)

said so three years ago. Even restaurant workers who are exposed to <u>these</u>
(2)

delicacies aren't always wild about <u>them.</u>
(2)

15d Transitional Words and Phrases

English has a huge storehouse of words and phrases that cue the reader
to relationships between sentences. Without these cues the reader may
be momentarily puzzled or unsure of how sentences relate to each
other. For example, read these two sentences:

> John is very tall. He does not play basketball.

If it took you a moment to see the connection, try reading the same
two sentences with a transitional word added:

> John is very tall. However, he does not play basketball.

The word *however* signals that the second sentence contradicts or con-
trasts with the first sentence. Read the following:

> The state government was determined not to raise taxes. Therefore, . . .

As soon as you reached the word *therefore*, you knew that some conse-
quence or result would follow.

The transitions listed in the following table are grouped according to
the categories of relationships they show:

TRANSITIONS	
Adding	and, besides, in addition, also, too, moreover, fur-ther, furthermore, next, first, second, third, finally, last, again, and then, likewise, similarly
Comparing	similarly, likewise, in like manner, at the same time, in the same way
Contrasting	but, yet, however, still, nevertheless, on the other hand, on the contrary, in contrast, conversely, in another sense, instead, rather, notwithstanding, though, whereas, after all, although
Emphasizing	indeed, in fact, above all, add to this, and also, even more, in any event, in other words, that is, obviously

(continued on next page)

TRANSITIONS *(continued from previous page)*

Ending	after all, finally, in sum, for these reasons
Giving examples	for example, for instance, to illustrate, that is, namely, specifically
Pointing to cause and effect, proof, conclusions	thus, therefore, consequently, because of this, hence, as a result, then, so, accordingly
Showing place or direction	over, above, inside, next to, underneath, to the left, to the right, just behind, beyond, in the distance
Showing time	meanwhile, soon, later, afterward, now, in the past, then, next, before, during, while, finally, after this, at last, since then, presently, temporarily, after a short time, at the same time, in the meantime
Summarizing	to sum up, in brief, on the whole, as has been noted, in conclusion, that is, finally, as has been said, in general, to recapitulate, to conclude, in other words

HINT *And* and *But* as Transitions

In this list you'll notice words such as *and* and *but*, which some people prefer not to use to begin sentences. Others think these are useful words to achieve variety and smooth transitions between sentences.

Although jet lag is a nuisance for travelers, it can be a disaster for flight crews. **But** flight crews can reduce the effects of jet lag by modifying their sleep patterns. **And** airlines are beginning to recognize the need for in-flight naps.

15e Transitions in and Between Paragraphs

I. Transitions Between Sentences in a Paragraph

Your paragraphs are more easily understood when you show how every sentence in the paragraph is connected to the whole. To signal the connections, use **repetition, synonyms, pronouns,** and **transitional words and phrases.** In the following example, these connections are highlighted.

 = repetition   = pronouns

 = synonyms   = transitional words and phrases

While drilling into Greenland's layers of ice, scientists recently pulled up evidence from the last ice age showing that the island's climate underwent extreme shifts within a year or two. This unexpected finding is based on evidence from ice cores that the climate often shifted from glacial to warmer weather in just a few years. In addition, other evidence indicates that the annual amount of snow accumulation also changed abruptly at the same time. As the climate went from cold to warm, the amount of snowfall jumped abruptly by as much as 100 percent. This change happened because more snow falls during warmer periods when the atmosphere holds more water. From this evidence, scientists therefore conclude that warming and cooling of the earth may be able to occur much faster than had been previously thought.

2. Transitions Between Paragraphs

As you start a new paragraph, you should also show the link to previous paragraphs, and an effective place to do this is in the first sentence of the new paragraph. Use the following strategies for including transitions between paragraphs:

■ **Use repetition as a hook.** One way to make a connection is to reach back to the previous paragraph, referring to an element from there in the beginning of your next paragraph. Some writers think of this as using a hook. They "hook" an element from above and bring it down—through the use of repetition—to the next paragraph, providing a connecting thread of ideas.

Suppose your paper discusses the changing role of women in combat. In a paragraph on the history of women's roles in warfare, you conclude with the example of Harriet Tubman, an African American who led scouting raids into enemy territory during the Civil War. In the next paragraph you want to move to new roles for women in modern combat. Your opening sentence can "hook" the older use of women as scouts and tie that to their new role as pilots in the Persian Gulf War.

While a few women served in more limited roles as <u>scouts</u> in previous
("hook" to previous paragraph)
wars, in the Persian Gulf War women took on more extensive roles as pilots flying supplies, troops, and ammunition into combat zones.

■ **Use transitional words to show direction.** Because every paragraph advances your paper forward, the first sentence can be used to point your readers in the direction of your whole essay. Think of the first sentence of every paragraph as being like a road map, indicating to your readers where they are headed.

For example, suppose your next paragraph in a paper on campaign reform presents a second reason in your argument against allowing large personal contributions to political candidates. Use a transitional word to show that you are building a list of arguments:

<u>Another reason</u> political candidates should not receive large personal contributions is . . .

[The underlined words show that the writer is adding another element.]

Or suppose that your next paragraph is going to acknowledge that there are also arguments for the opposing side in this topic. You would then be going in the opposite direction or contrasting one side against the other.

<u>Not everyone, however,</u> is in favor of making personal contributions to candidates illegal. Those who want to continue the practice argue that . . .

[The underlined words signal a turn in the opposite direction.]

Exercise 15.1: Proofreading Practice

To practice recognizing different types of transitions, read the following paragraph and underline the transitions. Categorize them by putting the appropriate numbers near the words you mark, using these numbers:

1. Repetition of key term or phrase
2. Synonyms
3. Pronouns
4. Transitional words or phrases

The largest ocean liner of its time set sail for New York in April 1912. This now-famous ship, the Titanic, never finished its voyage. It hit an enormous iceberg halfway through the trip and caused the 2,227 passengers to head for the lifeboats. Then, within hours, the mammoth vessel plunged beneath the icy Atlantic Ocean. Next, the Titanic broke in two and fell to the bottom of the ocean. It was seen by explorers only from a distance and was untouched until 1986, when a team of researchers entered the boat and explored it. Eventually, a small piece of steel brought back from one of the expeditions was examined to determine whether this material played a part in the sinking of the ship. Later, researchers tried raising a portion of the ship from the bottom of the ocean, but it was too heavy and fell underneath the water once again. In time, the ship itself will disintegrate, but the fascination with the Titanic will remain.

Exercise 15.2: Proofreading Practice

Below, the connections or transitional links are missing in paragraph 1, but they are added in paragraph 2. Paragraph 3, like paragraph 1, needs transi-

tions. Use the types of transitional links described in Chapter 15 and illustrated in paragraph 2 to revise paragraph 3. Your revisions will be paragraph 4.

Paragraph 1

I like autumn. Autumn is a sad time of year. The leaves turn to brilliant yellow and red. The weather is mild. I can't help thinking ahead to the coming of winter. Winter will bring snowstorms, slippery roads, and icy fingers. In winter the wind chill factor can make it dangerous to be outside. I find winter unpleasant. In the autumn I can't help thinking ahead to winter's arrival. I am sad when I think that winter is coming.

Paragraph 2

Although I like autumn, it is also a sad time of year. Of course, the leaves turn to brilliant yellow and red, and the weather is mild. Still, I can't help thinking ahead to the coming of winter with its snowstorms, slippery roads, and icy fingers. Moreover, in winter the wind chill factor can make it dangerous to be outside. Because I find these things unpleasant, in the autumn I can't help thinking ahead to winter's arrival. Truly, I am sad when I think that winter is coming.

Paragraph 3

Caring for houseplants requires some basic knowledge about plants. The plant should be watered. The plant's leaves should be cleaned. The spring and summer bring a special time of growth. The plant can be fertilized then. The plant can be repotted. The diameter of the new pot should be only two inches larger than the pot the plant is presently in. Some plants can be put outside in summer. Some plants cannot be put outside. If you are familiar with basic requirements for houseplants, you will have healthy plants.

16 Sentence Variety (var)

Sentences with the same word order and length produce the kind of monotony that is boring to readers. To make your sentences more interesting, add variety by making some longer than others and by finding alternatives to starting every sentence with the subject and verb.

16a Combining Sentences

- You can combine two sentences (or independent clauses) into one longer sentence.

  Doonesbury cartoons laugh at contemporary politicians, but the victims of the satire probably don't read the cartoon strip.

- You can combine the subjects of two independent clauses in one sentence when the verb applies to both clauses.

> **HINT** **Joining Independent Clauses**
>
> To join an independent clause to another with *and, but, for, or, nor, so,* or *yet,* use a comma. Use a semicolon if you do not use connecting words or if you use other connecting words such as *therefore* and *however.*

Original: During the flood, the Wabash River overflowed its banks. At the same time, Wildcat Creek did the same.

Revised: During the flood, both the Wabash River and Wildcat Creek overflowed their banks.

■ You can join two predicates when they have the same subject.

Original: Ken often spends Sunday afternoons watching football on TV. He spends Monday evenings the same way.

Revised: Ken often spends both Sunday afternoons and Monday evenings watching football on TV.

16b Adding Words

■ You can add a description, a definition, or other information about a noun after the noun.

Dr. Lewis , our family dentist, recently moved to Florida.

I plan to visit New York , a city with a wide variety of ethnic restaurants .

Professor Nguyen , is a political science teacher , ~~She~~ gives lectures in the community on current events.

■ You can add a *who, which,* or *what* clause after a noun or turn another sentence into a *who, which,* or *what* clause.

Ed , who takes his job very seriously, always arrives at his desk at 7:55 A.M.

The experiment failed because of Murphy's law , which ~~This law~~ states that buttered bread always falls buttered side down.

■ Sometimes, you can delete the *who, which, what* words, as in the following example:

The National Football League, ~~which is~~ popular with TV fans, is older than the American Football League.

■ You can add phrases and clauses at the beginning of the sentence. For example, you can begin with a prepositional phrase. Some prepositions you might use include the following:

In . . .	Because of . . .	On . . .
At . . .	In addition to . . .	From . . .
For . . .	Under . . .	Between . . .

In addition to soup and salad, she ordered bread sticks and coffee.

From an advertiser's point of view, commercials are more important than the TV programs.

- You can begin with infinitives (*to* + verb) or with phrases that start with *-ing* and *-ed* verbs.

To attract attention, the hijackers ordered the plane to fly to Africa.

Tired of hearing her dog whining, she finally opened the door and let the cold, wet pooch in the house.

- You can add transitional words (see Chapter 15) at the beginning of sentences.

However, I don't want to make a decision too quickly.

In addition, the new model for that sports car will have a turbo boost.

- You can begin with dependent clauses by starting these clauses with dependent markers such as the following:

after . . .	because . . .	since . . .	when . . .
although . . .	if . . .	until . . .	while . . .

After the parade was over, the floats were quickly taken apart.

When spring comes, I'll have to start searching for a summer job.

16c Changing Words, Phrases, and Clauses

- You can move adjectives after the *is* verb to the front of the sentence so that they describe the subject noun.

Original: The homecoming queen was surprised and teary-eyed. She waved enthusiastically to the crowd.

Revised: Surprised and teary-eyed, the homecoming queen waved enthusiastically to the crowd.

- You can expand your subject to a phrase or clause.

Hunting is his favorite sport.

Hunting grouse is his favorite sport.

To hunt grouse in the early morning mists is to really enjoy the sport.

Whoever has hunted grouse in the early morning mists knows the real joys of the sport.

That grouse hunting is enjoyable is evident from the number of people addicted to the sport.

- You can change a sentence to a dependent clause (see 24b) or put it before or after the independent clause.

Because he   , he
~~He~~ overslept yesterday morning and missed class⁄ ~~He~~ did not hear the announcement of the exam.

Although *, scientists*
America is overly dependent on foreign oil, ~~Scientists~~ have not yet found enough alternative sources of energy.

Exercise 16.1: Pattern Practice

Below, paragraph 1 (which you will probably find very choppy and boring) is composed of sentences in a very similar pattern. Paragraph 2, a revision of paragraph 1, follows the strategies for achieving variety that are described in this chapter. As you read through paragraph 2, identify the various strategies used to achieve sentence variety. Use those and other strategies described in this chapter to revise paragraph 3, which (like paragraph 1) is composed of sentences in a very similar pattern.

Paragraph 1

(1) Whistling is a complex art. (1) It involves your lips, teeth, tongue, jaw, rib cage, abdomen, and lungs. (3) It occasionally also involves your hands and fingers. (4) Whistling sounds are produced by the vibration of air through a resonating chamber. (5) This resonating chamber is created by your mouth or hands. (6) One factor is particularly crucial. (7) This factor is the type of space produced in your mouth by your tongue. (8) Whistling is usually thought of as a means of entertainment. (9) It can also be a means of communication. (10) Some people include whistling as part of their language. (11) Others use whistling to carry messages over long distances.

Paragraph 2 (Revision of Paragraph 1)

(1) Whistling is a complex art that involves your lips, teeth, tongue, jaw, rib cage, abdomen, and lungs, and occasionally your hands and fingers. (2) Whistling sounds are produced by the vibration of air through a resonating chamber, created by your mouth or hands. (3) One particularly crucial factor is the type of space produced in your mouth by your tongue. (4) Although whistling is usually thought of as a means of entertainment, it can also be a means of communication. (5) Some people include whistling as part of their language, and others use whistling to carry messages over long distances.

Paragraph 3

Scientists neglect whistling. Amateurs and hobbyists do not neglect it. There are whistling contests all over the United States. Accomplished whistlers whistle classical music, opera, jazz, Broadway show tunes, polkas, and even rock and roll at these contests. People whistle very differently. Some people pucker their lips. Other people use their throat, hands, or fingers to produce whistling sounds. These whistling sounds resemble the flute. Whistling has several advantages. One advantage is that it is a happy sound. Whistlers never lose their instrument. Their instrument doesn't need to be cleaned or repaired. Their instrument costs nothing. It is easily transported. Learning how to whistle is hard to explain. Whistling is something you pick up either at a young age or not at all.

17 Verbs (v)

A **verb** is a word or group of words that expresses action, shows a state of existence, or links the subject (usually the doer of the action) to the rest of the sentence. The first step in distinguishing complete sentences from incomplete ones is recognizing the verb. Many sentences have more than one verb, but they must have at least one. Verbs provide several kinds of essential information in a sentence:

■ Some verbs express action.

Tonya **jogs** every day.

I **see** my face in the mirror.

■ Some verbs (called linking verbs) indicate that a subject exists or link the subject (the who or what) and the rest of the sentence together.

She **feels** sad.

The shark **is** hungry.

■ Verbs indicate time.

They **went** home.   [past time]

The semester **will end** in May.   [future time]

■ Verbs indicate number.

Matt always **orders** anchovy pizza.
[singular—only one doer of the action, Matt]

Qun and Medhi always **order** sausage pizza.
[plural—two doers of the action, Qun and Medhi]

■ Verbs indicate the person for the subject (the who or what, usually the doer of the action).

First person: *I* or *we*
I **love** to cook.

Second person: *you*
You **love** to cook.

Third person: *he, she, it, they*
He **loves** to cook.

HINT   **Finding the Verb**

You can find the verb (or part of it, when the verb has more than one word) by changing the time expressed in the sentence (from the present to the past, from the past to the future, and so on). In the following examples the word that changes is the verb, and the sentence expresses something about the past or present because of the verb form.

Present	Past
Tamar **jogs** every day.	Tamar **jogged** every day.
I **see** my face in the mirror.	I **saw** my face in the mirror.
She **feels** sad.	She **felt** sad.
The shark **is** hungry.	The shark **was** hungry.

17a Verb Phrases

A **verb phrase** is several words working together as a verb.

He **has gone** home.

I **am enjoying** my vacation.

They **should have attended** the movie with me.

17b Verb Forms

Verb forms are words that are not complete verbs in themselves and may be part of a verb phrase or may appear elsewhere in the sentence.

I. *-ing* Verbs

Forms of the verb that end in *-ing*, called *gerunds*, are never complete verbs by themselves. To be part of the verb phrase, the *-ing* form needs a helping verb and is then part of a progressive tense verb (see 17c). The *-ing* form may also be used alone elsewhere in the sentence.

The computer program **is working** smoothly.

[*Working* is a verb form because it is only a part of the verb phrase. *Is working* is the whole verb phrase because of the helping verb *is*.]

Feeling guilty is one of his favorite pastimes.

[*Feeling* is part of the subject. It is a verb form but not a verb.]

Everyone enjoys **laughing.**

[*Laughing* is the direct object of the verb. (The direct object completes the meaning or receives the action of the verb.) *Laughing* is a verb form but not a verb.]

HINT   **Fragments**

Some incomplete sentences, called *fragments,* are caused by using only an *-ing* verb form with no helper.

                                                    is showing **(or)** shows
Harlan, with his fast track record yesterday, ~~showing~~ all the practice and effort of the last three months.

[This is not a complete sentence because *showing* is not a complete verb.]

For more information on fragments, see Chapter 8.

2. *-ed* Verbs

To show past tense, most verbs have an *-ed* or *-d* added to the base form. (The base form is the main entry in the dictionary.) With no helping verb, the *-ed* or *-d* form is the simple past tense. When the *-ed* form has a helping verb such as *has* or *had,* it is part of one of the perfect tenses (see 17c). The *-ed* or *-d* form can also be used alone elsewhere in the sentence.

She **has jumped** farther than any other contestant so far.

[*Jumped* is part of the verb phrase, and *has jumped* is the complete verb phrase.]

I read that chapter, the one **added** to last week's assignment.

[*Added* is not part of the verb phrase.]

3. *to* + Verb

Another verb form, called the *infinitive,* has *to* added to the base form. This infinitive form is used with certain verbs (see 56c).

I was supposed **to give** her the ticket.
[*Was supposed to give* is the whole verb phrase.]

To forgive is easier than **to forget.**
[*To forgive* and *to forget* are not part of the verb phrase.]

Exercise 17.1: Proofreading Practice

To practice your ability to identify verbs, verb phrases, and verb forms, underline the verbs and verb phrases in the following sentences. Circle the verb forms both in verb phrases and elsewhere in the sentence. As an example, the first sentence is already marked. Remember, many sentences have more than one verb or verb phrase.

Remember to ask yourself the following questions:

■ *To find a verb or verb phrase:* Which word or group of words expresses action, shows a state of existence, or links the subject, the doer of the action, to the rest of the sentence?

- *To find a verb form:* Which words end in -*ing* or -*ed* or have *to* + verb? Which of these are not complete verbs in themselves?

(1) For a long time psychologists have(wondered)what memories are and where they are(stored)in the human brain. (2) Because it is the basis of human intellect, memory has been studied intensely. (3) According to one psychologist, memory is an umbrella term for a whole range of processes that occur in our brains. (4) In particular, psychologists have identified two types of memory. (5) One type is called declarative memory, and it includes memories of facts such as names, places, dates, and even baseball scores. (6) It is called declarative because we use it to declare things. (7) For example, a person can declare his or her favorite food is fried bean sprouts. (8) The other type is called procedural memory. (9) It is the type of memory acquired by repetitive practice or conditioning, and it includes skills such as riding a bike or typing. (10) We need both types of memory in our daily living because we need facts and we use a variety of skills.

Exercise 17.2: Pattern Practice

The following paragraph is in the present tense. Change it to the past tense by underlining the verbs and writing the past tense verb above the word that is changed. As an example, the first sentence is already marked.

studied
(1) To learn more about memory, a psychologist <u>studies</u> visual memory by watching monkeys. (2) To do this, he uses a game that requires the monkey to pick up a block in order to find the food in a pail underneath. (3) After a brief delay the monkey again sees the old block on top of a pail and also sees a new block with a pail underneath it. (4) The new block now covers a pail with bananas in it. (5) The monkey quickly learns each time to pick up the new block in order to find food. (6) This demonstrates that the monkey remembers what the old block looks like and also what distinguishes the new block. (7) The psychologist concludes that visual memory is at work.

17c Verb Tense

Verb tense indicates the time of the verb: past, present, or future.

The four tenses for the past, present, and future are as follows:

- Simple
- Progressive: *be* + -*ing* form of the verb
- Perfect: *have*
  had + the -*ed* form of the verb
  shall
- Perfect progressive: *have*
  had + *been* + -*ing* form of the verb

The following table shows verb forms:

VERB FORMS			
	Present	**Past**	**Future**
Simple:	I walk.	I walked.	I will walk.
Progressive:	I am walking.	I was walking.	I will be walking.
Perfect:	I have walked.	I had walked.	I will have walked.
Perfect progressive:	I have been walking.	I had been walking.	I will have been walking.

I. Present Tense

Simple Present

- Present action or condition: She **counts** the votes. They **are** happy.
- General truth: States **defend** their rights.
- Habitual action: He **drinks** orange juice for breakfast.
- Future time: The plane **arrives** at 10 P.M. tonight.
- Literary or timeless truth: Shakespeare **uses** humor effectively.

Form: This is the form found in the dictionary and is often called the base form. For third person singular subjects (*he, she, it*), add an *-s* or *-es*.

I, you, we, they **walk.** I, you, we, they **push.**
He, she, it **walks.** He, she, it **pushes.**

HINT   **Meaning of Present Tense Verbs**

Students learning English as a second language may have difficulty in deciding when American culture determines that something is a general, literary, or timeless truth and should be expressed in simple present tense. If so, a teacher or writing center tutor can help.

Present Progressive

- Activity in progress, not finished, or continued: The committee **is studying** that proposal.

Form: This form has two parts: *is* (or) *are* + *-ing* form of the verb.

We **are going.**   He **is singing.**

Present Perfect

- Action that was completed in the past or began in the past and leads up to and includes the present: The company **has sold** that product since January.
- Habitual or continued action started in the past and continuing into the present: She **has** not **smoked** a cigarette for three years.

Form: Use *have* (or) *has* + *-ed* form of regular verbs (called the *past participle*).

I **have eaten.**   He **has** not **called.**

Present Perfect Progressive

■ Action that began in the past, continues to the present, and may continue into the future: They **have been considering** that purchase for three months.

Form: Use *have* (or) *has* + *been* + *-ing* form of the verb.

He **has been running.**   They **have been meeting.**

2. Past Tense

Simple Past

■ Completed action: We **visited** the museum during the summer.

■ Completed condition: It **was** cloudy yesterday.

Form: Add *-ed* for regular verbs. For other forms, see the list of irregular verbs in this section.

I **walked.**   They **awoke.**

Past Progressive

■ Past action that took place over a period of time: They **were driving** through the desert when the sandstorm hit.

■ Past action that was interrupted by another action: The engine **was running** when he left the car.

Form: Use *was* (or) *were* + *-ing* form of the verb.

She **was singing.**   We **were running.**

Past Perfect

■ Action or event completed before another event in the past: When the meeting began, she **had** already **left** the building.

Form: Use *had* + *-ed* form of the verb (past participle).

He **had** already **reviewed** the list when Mary came in.

Past Perfect Progressive

■ Ongoing condition in the past that has ended: The diplomat **had been planning** to visit when his government was overthrown.

Form: Use *had* + *-ing* form of the verb.

They **had been looking.**   She **had been speaking.**

3. Future Tense

Simple Future

■ Actions or events in the future: The recycling center **will open** next week.

Form: Use *shall* (or) *will* + base form of the verb. (In American English, *will* is commonly used for all persons, but in British English, *shall* is often used for the first person.)

I **will choose.**   They **will enter.**

Future Progressive

■ Future action that will continue for some time: I **will be expecting** your call.

Form: Use *will* or *shall* + *be* + *-ing* form of the verb.

He **will be studying.**   They **will be driving.**

Future Perfect

■ Actions that will be completed by or before a specified time in the future: By Thursday, we **will have organized** the whole filing cabinet.

Form: Use *will* (or) *shall* + *have* + *-ed* form of the verb (past participle).

They **will have walked.**   We **will have finished.**

Future Perfect Progressive

■ Ongoing actions or conditions until a specific time in the future: In June we **will have been renting** this apartment for a year.

Form: Use *will* (or) *shall* + *have* + *been* + *-ing* form of the verb.

They **will have been paying.**   She **will have been traveling.**

4. Irregular Verbs

The most often used irregular verbs have the forms shown in the following table:

IRREGULAR VERB FORMS				
	Present		**Past**	
Verb	*Singular*	*Plural*	*Singular*	*Plural*
to be	I am	we are	I was	we were
	you are	you are	you were	you were
	he, she, it is	they are	he, she, it was	they were
to have	I have	we have	I had	we had
	you have	you have	you had	you had
	he, she, it has	they have	he, she, it had	they had
to do	I do	we do	I did	we did
	you do	you do	you did	you did
	he, she, it does	they do	he, she, it did	they did

IRREGULAR VERBS

Base (or Present)	Past	Past Participle
arise	arose	arisen
awake	awoke	awoken
be	was, were	been
beat	beat	beaten
become	became	become
begin	began	begun
bend	bent	bent
bet	bet	bet
bind	bound	bound
bite	bit	bitten (or) bit
bleed	bled	bled
blow	blew	blown
break	broke	broken
bring	brought	brought
build	built	built
burst	burst	burst
buy	bought	bought
cast	cast	cast
catch	caught	caught
choose	chose	chosen
cling	clung	clung
come	came	come
cost	cost	cost
creep	crept	crept
cut	cut	cut
deal	dealt	dealt
dig	dug	dug
dive	dived (or) dove	dived
do	did	done
draw	drew	drawn
drink	drank	drunk
drive	drove	driven
eat	ate	eaten
fall	fell	fallen
feed	fed	fed
feel	felt	felt
fight	fought	fought
find	found	found
fling	flung	flung
fly	flew	flown
forbid	forbade	forbidden
forget	forgot	forgotten
forgive	forgave	forgiven
freeze	froze	frozen
get	got	gotten
give	gave	given
go	went	gone

Base (or Present)	Past	Past Participle
grind	ground	ground
grow	grew	grown
hang	hung	hung
have	had	had
hear	heard	heard
hide	hid	hidden
hit	hit	hit
hold	held	held
hurt	hurt	hurt
keep	kept	kept
know	knew	known
lay	laid	laid
lead	led	led
leave	left	left
lend	lent	lent
let	let	let
lie	lay	lain
lose	lost	lost
make	made	made
mean	meant	meant
meet	met	met
mistake	mistook	mistaken
pay	paid	paid
prove	proved	proved (or) proven
put	put	put
quit	quit	quit
read	read	read
ride	rode	ridden
ring	rang	rung
rise	rose	risen
run	ran	run
say	said	said
see	saw	seen
seek	sought	sought
sell	sold	sold
send	sent	sent
set	set	set
shake	shook	shaken
shed	shed	shed
shine	shone	shone
shoot	shot	shot
shrink	shrank	shrunk
shut	shut	shut
sing	sang	sung
sink	sank (or) sunk	sunk
sit	sat	sat
sleep	slept	slept

(continued on next page)

IRREGULAR VERBS *(continued from previous page)*

Base (or Present)	Past	Past Participle
slide	slid	slid
speak	spoke	spoken
spend	spent	spent
spin	spun	spun
split	split	split
spread	spread	spread
spring	sprang	sprung
stand	stood	stood
steal	stole	stolen
stick	stuck	stuck
sting	stung	stung
stink	stank	stunk
strike	struck	struck
swear	swore	sworn
sweep	swept	swept
swim	swam	swum
swing	swung	swung
take	took	taken
teach	taught	taught
tear	tore	torn
tell	told	told
think	thought	thought
throw	threw	thrown
understand	understood	understood
wake	woke	waken
wear	wore	worn
weep	wept	wept
win	won	won
wind	wound	wound
wring	wrung	wrung
write	wrote	written

Exercise 17.3: Proofreading Practice

In the following paragraph, choose the correct verbs from the options given in parentheses. Remember that the time expressed in the verb has to agree with the meaning of the sentence.

The way children (1. learn, will learn) to draw seems simple. But studies show that when given some kind of marker, young children (2. have begun, will begin, begin) by scribbling on any available surface. At first, these children's drawings (3. are, should be, had been) simple, clumsy, and unrealistic, but gradually the drawings (4. have become, should become, become) more realistic. One researcher who (5. will study, could study, has studied) the drawings of one- and two-year-olds concludes that their early scrawls (6. are representing, may represent, had represented) gestures and motions. For example, the researcher notes that one two-year-old child who was observed (7. took, has taken, had taken) a marker and (8. is hopping, hopped, had hopped) it around on the paper, leaving a mark with each imprint and explaining as he drew that the rabbit (9. was going, had gone, could have gone) hop-hop. The researcher (10. had concluded, has concluded, concludes) that the child was symbolizing the rabbit's motion, not its size, shape, or color. Someone who (11. had seen, sees, might see) only dots on a page (12. would not see, has not seen, had not seen) a rabbit and (13. should conclude, would conclude, had concluded) that the child's attempts to draw a rabbit (14. have failed, had failed, failed).

Exercise 17.4: Pattern Practice

The following paragraph is written in present tense. At the beginning of the paragraph, add the words, Last year, *and rewrite the rest of the paragraph so that it is in past tense. To do so, change all the underlined verbs to past tense.*

St. John's wort <u>is</u> one of the new herbal supplements advertised in magazines and news reports as an alternative remedy for treating anxiety and depression. This herb <u>has</u> been around for hundreds of years, since before the dawn of antidepressants. Many depressed people <u>take</u> medications such as Prozac, but research <u>reveals</u> that herbal treatments are also effective. A person who <u>experiences</u> anxiety or depression may <u>benefit</u> more from an herbal remedy rather than from a drug that <u>causes</u> side effects. Antidepressants often <u>cause</u> side effects such as weight gain, lack of interest in sex, and insomnia. Herbal remedies such as St. John's wort may <u>have</u> no side effects. Many people who <u>have</u> tried this remedy <u>say</u> that they <u>enjoy</u> life more and <u>are</u> anxiety-free. Experimenting with an herbal remedy <u>is</u> not harmless, however; like a drug, an herbal remedy <u>is</u> capable of causing permanent damage.

17d Verb Voice

Verb voice tells whether the verb is in the active or passive voice. In the active voice, the subject performs the action of the verb. In the passive voice, the subject receives the action. The doer of the action in the passive voice may either appear in a "by the . . ." phrase or be omitted.

Active: The dog **bit** the boy.

Passive: The boy **was bitten** by the dog.   [The subject of this sentence is the boy, but he was not doing the action of biting.]

HINT   **Passive Voice**

In the passive voice the verb phrase always includes a form of the *to be* verb, such as *is, are, was, is being,* and so on. Also, if the doer of the action is named, it is in a "by the . . ." phrase.

17e Verb Mood

The **mood** of a verb tells whether it expresses a fact or opinion (**indicative**); expresses a command, a request, or advice (**imperative**); or expresses a doubt, a wish, a recommendation, or something contrary to fact (**subjunctive**).

■ **Indicative** Verbs in the indicative (or declarative) mood express a fact or opinion and have their subjects stated in the sentence.

He **needs** a computer to print out his résumé.

The environmentalists and loggers **could** not **reach** any agreement.

■ **Imperative** Verbs in the imperative mood express a command, make a request, or offer advice. The subject word is not included because the subject is understood to be the reader (you).

Open that window, please.

Watch your step!

Next, **put** the wheel on the frame.

■ **Subjunctive** In the subjunctive mood, verbs express a doubt, a wish, a recommendation, or something contrary to fact. In the subjunctive, present tense verbs stay in the simple base form and do not indicate the number and person of the subject.

It is important that she **be** (not *is*) here by 9 P.M.

The form requires that a passport photo **accompany** (not *accompanies*) the application.

For past subjunctive, the same form as simple past is used; however, for the verb *be, were* is used for all persons and numbers.

I wish she **had arrived** on time.

If I **were** (not *was*) him, I'd sell that car immediately.

If land **were** (not *was*) cheaper there, they could buy a farm.

Exercise 17.5: Proofreading Practice

In the following paragraph, underline verb phrases in each sentence and indicate the voice of the verb by writing "active" or "passive." Ask yourself the following questions:

■ Is the subject receiving any action? If so, it's passive. If not, it's active.

■ Is there a doer named in the "by the . . . " phrase? If so, it's passive.

The mood of most of the verbs is factual (declarative). If you find any verb that states something contrary to fact (subjunctive), write "subjunctive." If you spot a command (imperative), write "imperative."

(1) Fun and unique training programs await this year's college graduates. (2) Interactive computer simulations are the newest method for training the Nintendo generation. (3) The realization by corporate

trainers that new employees in the 21 to 30 age group performed best when interacting with a computer or video game led to the invention of these special training programs. (4) Designers were informed that it is important for an employee to be comfortable when new material and methods are being presented. (5) "Play the game and learn the trade" is the motto of many companies recruiting young college graduates. (6) The transformation brought about by interactive training systems is just beginning.

Exercise 17.6: Sentence Practice

Combine the short sentences in the following paragraph into longer ones. Underline all the verb phrases in your revised sentences, and label them as active or passive. Try to use mostly active verbs, but you will find that some passive verbs are also useful.

Corporate Gameware is a new company. It was founded by Marc Prensky. He noticed that younger employees performed well using interactive games. He thought they could learn skills through this method. Some skills are customer relations, company policies, and troubleshooting client problems. It is a better option than reading a training manual. Some business schools have adopted this idea. The military also uses interactive software. Studies show this approach is working. Employees like this method. Training an employee takes less time. They are better trained. There is less turnaround of staff. They feel confident. They like coming to work.

17f Modal Verbs

Modals are helping verbs that express ability, a request, or an attitude, such as interest, expectation, possibility, or obligation. The following table shows some common modal verbs:

COMMON MODAL VERBS	
Verb	**Use**
shall, should	Express intent to do something, advisability: You **should** try to exercise more often.
will, would	Express strong intent: I **will** return those books to the library tomorrow.
can, could	Express capability, possibility, request: I **can** lend you my tape of that concert.
may, might	Express possibility or permission, request: She **may** buy a new computer.
must, ought to	Express obligation or need: I **ought to** fill the gas tank before we drive into town.

18 Nouns and Pronouns

18a Nouns (n)

A **noun** is a word that names a person, place, thing, or idea. The following words are nouns:

Marilyn Monroe	Des Moines	peace
Henri	light bulb	justice
forest	pictures	French

(For proper and common nouns, see Chapter 35.)

1. Singular, Plural, and Collective Nouns

A **singular noun** refers to one person, place, or thing and is the form you would look up in the dictionary.

A **plural noun** is the form that refers to more than one person, place, or thing.

A **collective noun** refers to a group acting as a unit, such as a committee, a herd, or a jury.

Exceptions: Some nouns do not fall in these categories because they refer to abstract or general concepts that cannot be counted and do not have plural forms. Examples are *homework, peace, furniture,* and *knowledge.* (See Chapter 59.)

Singular Nouns	Plural Nouns	Collective Nouns
box	boxes	family
child	children	senate

2. Noun Endings

Nouns have endings that show plural and possession. (See Chapter 28 on apostrophes and 39d on the spelling of plurals.)

PLURALS		
	Singular	**Plural**
-s or -es	one cup	many cups
	a box	two boxes
Changed form	one child	three children
	one man	some men
-f or -fe → v + -es	one half	two halves
	the leaf	the leaves
Other forms	one ox	a pair of oxen
	the medium	all the media
No change	a deer	several deer
	one sheep	two sheep

HINT **Noun Plurals**

1. The *-s* noun ending can be either the plural marker or the possessive *-s* marker. Don't make the mistake of putting an apostrophe in plural nouns.

There was a sale on potato ~~chip's~~. *chips*

2. Some writers do not use—or hear—plural forms in their speech, but standard English requires plural endings in writing. If you tend to omit written plurals, proofread your last drafts. To help your eye see the end of the word, point to the noun with your pen or finger to be sure that you see the plural ending. Some writers need repeated practice to notice the missing plural endings.

3. Although the *-s* marks the plural at the end of many nouns, it is also the ending for singular verbs with *he, she, it,* or a singular noun as the subject.

He walk**s**.

The shoe fit**s**.

An *-s* ending may be needed either at the end of the noun for a plural or at the end of the verb for a singular form. Therefore, both the subject and the verb cannot have an *-s* marker at the end.

Possession

The possessive form shows ownership or a close relationship. This is clear when we write "Mary's hat" because Mary owns or possesses the hat, but the possessive is less apparent when we write "journey's end" or "yesterday's news." It is more helpful to think about the "of" relationship between two nouns that exists in the possessive form.

Mary's hat   two days' time

the hat of Mary   time of two days

The possessive marker is either an *'s* or *'*. When the plural *-s* or *-es* is added to the noun, only an apostrophe is added after the plural. For singular nouns ending in *-s*, such as *grass*, the *-s* after the apostrophe is optional. It can be added if it doesn't make pronouncing the word more difficult. (See 28a.)

Singular	Plural
Miriam's hat	the girls' hats
the glass's edge	all the glasses' edges
James's story (or) James' story	
Aldez' zip code	
[Adding an *'s* would make the pronunciation difficult.]	

> **HINT**   **Apostrophes**
>
> Everything to the left of the apostrophe is the word and its plural. A proof-reading strategy is to check the order of what is written. First, write the word; then add any plural markers; and finally, add the possessive markers afterward.
>
> | | Word | Plural | Possessive Marker |
> |---|---|---|---|
> | girls' gloves = | girl | s | ' |
> | baby's toe = | baby | | 's |

18b Pronouns (pr)

A **pronoun** takes the place of a noun. If we had only nouns and no pronouns in English, we would have to write the following sentences:

Lee lost Lee's car keys.

When Michael went to the library, Michael found some useful references for Michael's paper.

1. Personal Pronouns
Personal pronouns refer to people or things.

Subject Case	Object Case	Possessive Case	
I	me	my	mine
you	you	your	yours
he	him	his	his
she	her	her	hers
it	it	its	its
we	us	our	ours
they	them	their	theirs

2. Demonstrative Pronouns
Demonstrative pronouns refer to things.

this	**This** cup of coffee is mine.
that	He needs **that** software program.
these	Can I exchange **these** tapes?
those	No one ordered **those** soft drinks.

3. Relative Pronouns
Relative pronouns show the relationship of a dependent clause (see 24b) to a noun in the sentence.

that	He knew **that** it was too soon to expect results.
which	They took the television set, **which** was broken, to the dump.
who	Mrs. Bloom is the friend **who** helped me.
whom	That manager, **whom** I respected, was promoted.
what	Everyone wondered **what** the loud noise was.

Sometimes relative pronouns can be omitted when they are understood.

> This isn't the sandwich **that** I ordered.
> This isn't the sandwich I ordered.

4. Interrogative Pronouns

Interrogative pronouns are used in questions.

who	**Who** wrote that screenplay?
whose	**Whose** jacket is this?
whom	**Whom** do you wish to talk to?
which	**Which** movie do you want to see?
what	**What** will they do now?

5. Indefinite Pronouns

Indefinite pronouns make indefinite reference to nouns.

anyone/anybody	The notice said that **anyone** could apply.
some	May I have **some**?
everyone/everybody	She was delighted that **everybody** showed up.
everything	That dog ate **everything** on the table.
nothing	There is **nothing** he can't fix.
one	Please give me **one**.
someone/somebody	Would **somebody** show me how this works?

 Indefinite Pronouns

Indefinite pronouns are usually singular and require a singular verb.

Everyone is going to the game.

However, some indefinite pronouns, such as *both, few,* and *many,* require a plural verb. Other indefinite pronouns, such as *all, any, more, most, none,* and *some,* may be either singular or plural, depending on the meaning of the sentence.

Singular: Some of my homework is done.

[Here *some* refers to a portion or a part of the homework. Because a "portion" or a "part" is thought of as a single entity, the verb is singular.]

Plural: Some of these plates are chipped.

[Here some refers to at least several plates. Because *several* is thought of as plural, the verb is plural.]

Singular: All the coffee is brewed.

Plural: All the customers are pleased.

6. Possessive Pronouns

Possessive pronouns do not take an apostrophe.

its nose   [not *it's* nose]
that dog of **hers**   [not that dog of *her's*]
the house is **theirs**   [not the house is *theirs'*]

Some writers confuse the possessive pronouns with contractions.

It's a warm day = **It is** a warm day.
There's a shooting star = **There is** a shooting star.

(See Chapter 28 on apostrophes.)

7. Reflexive Pronouns
Reflexive pronouns, which end in *-self* or *-selves,* intensify the nouns they refer back to.

myself	I covered **myself** in sunscreen.
yourself	Please help **yourself.**
itself	The pig stuffed **itself** with feed.
themselves	They allowed **themselves** enough time to eat.

8. Reciprocal Pronouns
Reciprocal pronouns refer back to individual parts of plural terms.

each other	They congratulated **each other.**
one another	The group helped **one another** to prepare.

Exercise 18.1: Proofreading Practice

Read the following paragraph; underline all the -s and -es endings that mark plural nouns, and circle all the 's, s', and ' possessive markers.

It is a sad fact of life that what some people call the "everyday courtesies of life" are disappearing faster than finger bowls and engineers' slide rules. People in movie theaters carry on loud conversations, older people on buses rarely have anyone get up and offer them a seat, and few shoppers bother to offer thanks to a helpful salesperson. Some people say that courteous ways seem to have lingered longer in small towns than in big cities and that some regions—notably the South—cling more than others to some remaining signs of polite behavior. But more often we hear complaints that courtesy is declining, dying, or dead. Says one New York executive: "There's no such thing as umbrella courtesy. Everybody's umbrella is aimed at eye level." And a store owner in another city says that short-tempered waiters in restaurants and impatient salesclerks in stores make her feel as if she's bothering them by asking for service. Common courtesy may be a thing of the past.

Exercise 18.2: Proofreading Practice

In the following paragraph there are some missing -s and -es plural noun endings and missing possessive markers. Add any that are missing.

Among the people who are most aware of the current lack of everyday politeness are airline flight attendant and newspaper advice columnist. Says one flight attendant: "Courtesy is almost zero. People think you're supposed to carry all their bag on and off the flight, even when you have dozen of other passenger to attend to." One syndicated advice columnist notes that courtesy is so rare these day that when someone is kind, helpful, or generous, it is an event worth writing about to an advice columnist. Some teacher blame televisions poor example, especially the many rude detective who shove people around, bang down all those door, and yell in peoples face. Too many of our current movie hero are not particularly gallant, thoughtful, or polite. As a psychologist recently noted, it is hard to explain to children what good manner are when they don't see such behavior on their television or movie screen.

Exercise 18.3: Pattern Practice

In the following paragraph there are many singular nouns. When it is appropriate, change the singular nouns to plural, add the appropriate noun endings, and change any other words or word endings that need to be altered.

The foreign tourist who travels in the United States often notices that the American is not as polite as a person from another country. The tourist from Europe, who is used to a more formal manner, is particularly offended by the American who immediately calls the tourist by his or her first name. Impoliteness in the United States extends even to an object. An English businessperson noted that in America a public sign issues a command: "No Smoking" or "Do Not Enter." In England such a sign would be less commanding: "No Smoking Please" or "Please Do Not Enter." An American can also be rude without meaning to be. As a Japanese visitor noticed, the nurse who led him into the doctor's office said, "Come in here." In Japan, the visitor noted, a nurse would say, "Please follow me." The foreign tourist, unfortunately, has a variety of such stories to take back to his or her country.

Exercise 18.4: Pattern Practice

Write a sentence using each of the nouns and pronouns listed here. Make the noun plural if it can be used in the plural.

1. laughter	6. liberty	11. these
2. machine	7. ice	12. whose
3. chair	8. engineering	13. itself
4. homework	9. key	14. anyone
5. book	10. telephone	15. its

19 Pronoun Case and Reference

19a Pronoun Case (ca)

Pronoun case refers to the form of the pronoun needed in a sentence. The following table shows the pronoun cases:

PRONOUN CASES

	Subject		Object		Possessive	
	Singular	*Plural*	*Singular*	*Plural*	*Singular*	*Plural*
First person	I	we	me	us	my, mine	our, ours
Second person	you	you	you	you	your, yours	your, yours
Third person	he	they	him	them	his	their, theirs
	she	they	her	them	her, hers	their, theirs
	it	they	it	them	it, its	their, theirs

1. Subject Case

Subject case of pronouns is used when pronouns are subjects or are used after linking verbs such as *is*.

> **She** won the lottery.   [*She* is the subject case pronoun.]

> Who's there? It is **I.**   [In the second sentence *I* is the subject case pronoun that comes after the linking verb *is.*]

2. Object Case

Object case of pronouns is used when pronouns are objects of verbs (receive the action of the verb).

> I hugged **her.**   [object of the verb]

> Seeing Dan and **me**, she **waved.**   [object of the verb]

■ **As indirect object** When pronouns are indirect objects of verbs (explain for whom or to whom something is done), use the object case.

> I gave **her** the glass.   [indirect object]

The indirect object can often be changed to a *to + object pronoun* phrase.

> I gave the glass **to her.**

■ **As object of prepositions** Use the object case when pronouns are used as objects of prepositions (complete the meaning of the preposition).

> Al gave the money to **them.**   [object of the preposition]

HINT   **Pronoun Case**

I. Remember that *between, except,* and *with* are prepositions and take the object case.

me
between you and +

her
except Alexi and ~~she~~

him me
with ~~he~~ and +

2. Don't use *them* as a pointing pronoun in place of *these* or *those*. Use *them* only as the object by itself.

those
He liked ~~them~~ socks.   (or)   He liked them.

3. Possessive Case

Possessive case refers to pronouns used as possessives.

Is this **her** hat?   (or)   Is this **hers**?

We gave **him** our pens.   (or)   We gave him **ours.**

HINT   **Possessive Pronouns**

I. Possessive case pronouns never take apostrophes.

its
The insect spread ~~it's~~ wings.

2. Use possessive case before *-ing* verb forms.

his
The crowd cheered ~~him~~ making a three-point basket.

4. Pronouns in Compound Constructions

To find the right case when your sentence has two pronouns or a noun and a pronoun, temporarily eliminate the noun or one of the pronouns as you read it to yourself. You'll hear the case that is needed.

he
John and ~~him~~ went to the store.

[If *John* is eliminated, the sentence would be "*Him* went to the store." It's easier to notice the wrong pronoun case this way.]

When in doubt as to which pronoun case to use, some writers mistakenly choose the subject case because it sounds more formal or "correct."

me
Mrs. Wagner gave the tickets to **Lutecia** and ~~I.~~

[Once again, try the strategy of dropping the noun, *Lutecia*. You'll be able to hear that the sentence sounds wrong. ("Mrs. Wagner gave the tickets to *I*.") Because *to* is a preposition, the noun or pronoun that follows is the object of the preposition and should be in the object case.]

When a pronoun and noun are used together, use the same strategy of dropping the noun to hear whether the case of the pronoun sounds wrong.

We
~~Us~~ **players** gave the coach a rousing cheer.

[When you drop the noun *players,* the original sentence would be "Us gave the coach a rousing cheer." The pronoun is the subject of the sentence and needs the subject case, the pronoun *we.*]

us
The lecturer told ~~we~~ **students** to quiet down.

[When you drop the noun *students,* the original sentence would be "The lecturer told we to quiet down." Instead, the sentence needs the pronoun in the object case, *us,* because it is the object of the verb.]

I
The newest members of the club, **Mahendi** and ~~me~~, were asked to pay our dues promptly.

[Since the phrase *Mahendi and me* explains the noun *members,* which is the subject of the sentence, the subject case of the pronoun, *I,* is needed.]

me
The usher had to find programs for the latecomers, **Mahendi** and ~~I~~.

[The phrase *Mahendi and I* explains the noun *latecomers,* the object of the preposition *for.* Thus, the pronoun has to be *me,* the object case.]

5. Who/Whom

In informal speech some people may not distinguish between *who* and *whom.* But for formal writing, the cases are as follows:

Subject	Object	Possessive
who	whom	whose
whoever	whomever	

Subject Case: Who is going to the concert tonight?

[*Who* is the subject of the sentence.]

Object Case: To **whom** should I give this ticket?

[*Whom* is the object of the preposition *to.*]

Possessive Case: No one was sure **whose** voice that was.

[When *who* introduces a dependent clause after a preposition, use the subject case.]

Give this to **whoever** wants it.

HINT   *Who* and *Whom*

If you aren't sure whether to use *who* or *whom,* turn a question into a state-ment or rearrange the order of the phrase:

Question: (Who, whom) are you looking for?

Statement: You are looking for **whom.**
(object of the preposition)

Sentence: She is someone **(who, whom)** I know well.

Rearranged Order: I know **whom** well.
(direct object)

6. Omitted Words in Comparisons

In comparisons using *than* and *as,* choose the correct pronoun case by recalling the words that are omitted.

He is taller than **(I, me).**
[The omitted words here are "am tall."]

He is taller than **I** (am tall).

Our cat likes my sister more than **(I, me).**
[The omitted words here are "it likes."]

Our cat likes my sister more than (it likes) **me.**

Exercise 19.1: Proofreading Practice

In the following paragraph there are some errors in pronoun case. Underline the incorrect pronoun forms, and write the correct form for the underlined word.

Have you ever wondered how people in the entertainment industry choose what you and me will see on television, read in books, and hear on tapes and CDs? Some producers and publishers say that the executives in their companies and them rely on instinct and an ability to forecast trends in taste. But we consumers cannot be relied on to be consistent from one month to the next. So, market researchers constantly seek our opinions. For example, they ask we moviegoers to preview movies and to fill out questionnaires. Reactions from we and our friends are then stud-ied closely. Sometimes, the market researchers merely forecast from pre-vious experience what you and me are likely to prefer. Still, some movies fail for reasons that the market researchers cannot understand. When that happens, who does the movie studio blame? The producer will say that the director and him or her did all they could but that the leading actor failed to attract an audience. Sometimes, though, us moviegoers simply get tired of some types of movies and want more variety.

Exercise 19.2: Pattern Practice

Using the patterns given here, write a similar sentence of your own for each pattern.

Pattern A: A sentence with an object case pronoun after the preposition *between, except,* or *with*

> Everyone was able to hear the bird call **except her.**

Pattern B: A sentence with a compound object that includes a pronoun in the object case.

> The newspaper article listed Arthur and **him** as the winners of the contest.

Pattern C: A sentence with a comparison that includes a subject case pronoun

> Everyone in the room was dressed more warmly than **I.**

Pattern D: A sentence with a comparison that includes an object case pronoun

> The bird was more frightened of the dog than **me.**

Pattern E: A sentence with a compound subject that includes a subject case pronoun

> During the festival the announcer and **she** took turns thanking all the people who had helped to organize the events.

19b Pronoun Reference (ref)

Pronoun reference is the relationship between the pronoun and the noun (antecedent) for which it is substituting. Pronouns substitute for nouns. To help your reader see this relationship clearly, remember the following rules:

■ Pronouns should indicate to which nouns they are referring.

■ Pronouns should be reasonably close to their nouns.

> **Unclear Reference:** Gina told Michelle that **she** took **her** bike to the library.

[Did Gina take Michelle's bike or her own bike to the library?]

> **Revised:** When Gina took Michelle's bike to the library, she told Michelle she was borrowing it.

Be sure your pronoun refers to a noun that has been mentioned on the page and not merely implied. Also, watch out for the vague *they* that doesn't refer to any specific group or the vague *this* or *it* that doesn't refer back to any specific word or phrase.

the screenwriters and producers
In Hollywood ~~they~~ don't know what the American public really wants in movies.

[Who are the *they* referred to here?]

When the town board inquired about the cost of the next political

the politicians
campaign, the board was assured that ~~they~~ would pay for **their** own campaigns.

[To whom do *they* and *their* refer? Most likely *they* refers to the politicians who will be campaigning, but "politician" is only inferred.]

Martina worked in a national forest last summer, and ~~this~~ may be her career choice.
serving as a forest ranger

[What does *this* refer to? Because no word or phrase in the first part of the sentence refers to the pronoun, the revised version has one of several possible answers.]

1. Pronoun Number

For collective nouns, such as *group, committee,* and *family,* use either a singular or plural pronoun, depending on whether the group acts as a unit or acts separately as many individuals within the unit.

The committee reached **its** decision before the end of the meeting.

[Here the committee acted as a unit.]

The committee relied on **their** own consciences to reach a decision.

[Here everyone relied separately on his or her own conscience.]

Remember to be consistent in pronoun number. Don't shift from singular to plural or plural to singular.

After **someone** studies violin for a few months, **she** may decide to try the piano. Then, ~~they~~ can compare and decide which instrument ~~they~~ like better.
she ... *she* s

2. Compound Subjects

Compound subjects with *and* take the plural pronoun.

The **table** and **chair** were delivered promptly, but **they** were not the style I had ordered.

For compound subjects with *or* or *nor,* the pronoun agrees with the subject word closer to it.

The restaurant offered either regular **patrons** or each new **customer** a free cup of coffee with **his** or **her** dinner.

Neither this **house** nor the **others** had **their** shutters closed.

3. Who/Which/That

When *who, which,* or *that* begins a dependent clause, use the word as follows:

■ *Who* is used for people (and sometimes animals).

He is a person **who** can help you.

■ *Which* is used most often for nonessential clauses, though some writers also use it for essential clauses (see Chapter 25).

The catalogue, **which** I sent for last month, had some unusual merchandise.

[The *which* clause here is nonessential.]

■ *That* is used most often for essential clauses.

When I finished the book **that** she lent me, I was able to write my paper.

[The *that* clause here is essential.]

4. Indefinite Words

Indefinite words such as *any* and *each* usually take the singular pronoun.

Each of the boys handed in **his** uniform.

5. Indefinite Pronouns

He was traditionally used to refer to indefinite pronouns ending in *-body* and *-one*.

Everyone brought **his** own pen and paper.

Use the following strategies to avoid the exclusive use of the masculine pronoun when the reference is to both males and females (a practice seen by many people as sexist; see Chapter 40 on sexist language):

■ Use both the masculine and feminine pronoun.

Everyone has **his** or **her** coat.　[Some people view this as very wordy.]

■ Switch to the plural subject and pronoun.

All the people have **their** coats.

■ Use the plural pronoun.

Everyone has **their** coat.　[Some people view this as incorrect. Others, such as the National Council of Teachers of English, accept this as a way to avoid sexist language.]

■ Use *a, an,* or *the* if the meaning remains clear.

Everyone has **a** coat.

Exercise 19.3: Proofreading Practice

Each pronoun in the following paragraph should clearly and correctly refer back to a noun in the sentence in which it appears. Rewrite the sentences that have a problem with the pronoun's reference and clarity.

(1) More than one million children will be home schooled in the United States next year. (2) Parents who educate their children at home do so because home schooling is good for them. (3) Many parents believe that each child is an individual, and their educational needs are best met by them. (4) A mother who home schools him claims it has brought the family closer and increased his self-confidence. (5) Other parents believe the public education system in this

country is in need of repair, and they need to do something about it. (6) Some states have made it very easy for a parent to start educating them at home. (7) In Montana, a parent may remove their child from school simply by registering with the superintendent. (8) This is a cause for concern among educators. (9) Many school districts are in favor of a formal system of accountability for them when they take their children out. (10) Consequently, the increase in home school-ing will require a comprehensive study of the best method to monitor their achievement.

Exercise 19.4: Proofreading Practice

In the following paragraph, there are some pronoun reference problems. Under-line all pronouns that do not clearly refer back to nouns, and write clearer or more appropriate nouns or pronouns for the underlined words. You may find that you will need to change some other words as well.

They have been saying for years that prevention is the most effective defense against cancer. The four major killers are breast, prostate, colon, and lung cancers, and the United States has more of them than any other country. It is now the responsibility of every person to edu-cate themselves about cancer prevention. For example, some fats are said to be good for the prevention of cancer, and some fats are known to be dangerous. These are flaxseed and olive oils, as opposed to coconut and corn oils. Furthermore, vegetables like broccoli and toma-toes have cancer-fighting chemicals that they recommend. Exercise is also a factor in the fight against cancer because an obese person places themselves at a higher risk for the disease. Through education and awareness, we can fight cancer.

Exercise 19.5: Pattern Practice

Using the patterns shown here, write a sentence of your own with pronouns that correctly and clearly refer back to the noun.

Example: Everyone should put his or her jacket in the closet upon arriving at school.

Sentence using the same pattern (indefinite pronoun):
Anybody can purchase his or her book at the sale price.

1. The girl and the boy walked arm in arm, and they seemed to be in love. (Compound subject)

2. All the people in the theater ate their popcorn. (Indefinite pronoun)

3. He is a person who can do almost anything. (Who, which, that)

4. After a student graduates from high school, she may wish to travel abroad for the summer before heading to college. (Pronoun number)

5. Each of the girls wore her favorite dress to the prom. (Indefinite words)

20 Adjectives and Adverbs (ad)

20a Adjectives and Adverbs

Adjectives and **adverbs** describe or add information about other words in a sentence. To distinguish adjectives from adverbs, locate the words they describe or modify. Adjectives modify nouns and pronouns. Adverbs modify verbs, verb forms, adjectives, and other adverbs.

Adjectives modifying nouns and pronouns:

red	house	It	was **beautiful.**
(adjective)	*(noun)*	*(pronoun)*	*(adjective)*
cheerful	smile	They	were **loud.**
(adjective)	*(noun)*	*(pronoun)*	*(adjective)*

Adverbs modifying verbs, verb forms, adjectives, and other adverbs:

danced	**gracefully**	ran **very**	**quickly**
(verb)	*(adverb)*	*(verb) (adverb)*	*(adverb)*
very	tall	had **barely**	moved
(adverb)	*(adjective)*	*(adverb)*	*(verb form)*

Many adverbs end in *-ly:*

Adjective	Adverb
rapid	rapidly
nice	nicely
happy	happily

But the *-ly* ending isn't a sure test for adverbs because some nouns have an *-ly* ending for the adjective form (*ghost* and *ghostly*), and some adverbs do not end in *-ly* (*very, fast, far*). To be sure, check your dictionary to see whether the word is listed as an adjective or adverb.

To use adjectives and adverbs correctly:

- Use *-ed* adjectives (the *-ed* form of verbs, past participles) to describe nouns. Be sure to include the *-ed* ending.

  used clothing   painted houses   experienced driver

- Use adjectives following linking verbs such as *appear, seem, taste, feel,* and *look.*

  The sofa seemed comfortable.   [sofa = comfortable]

  The water tastes salty.   [water = salty]

Some verbs can be either linking or action verbs depending on the meaning. Note the two different meanings of the verb *looked:*

The cat looked sleepy. [cat = sleepy]

The cat looked eagerly at the canary. [In this sentence the cat is performing the action of looking.]

- Use adverbs to modify verbs.

He ran ~~quick~~ quickly. The glass broke ~~sudden~~ suddenly. She sang ~~sweet~~ sweetly.

- Be sure to distinguish between the following adjectives and adverbs:

Adjective	Adverb
sure	surely
real	really
good	well
bad	badly

She ~~sure~~ surely likes to dance. The car runs ~~bad~~ badly. He sings ~~good~~ well.

HINT **Using *Well***

Well can also be an adjective when it refers to good health.

Despite her surgery, she looks well. [she = well]

- When you use adverbs such as so, such, and too, be sure to complete the phrase or clause.

Hailey was so tired ^ that she left the office early.

Malley's is such a popular restaurant ^ that reservations are recommended.

Tran's problem was that he was too proud ^ to ask for help.

Exercise 20.1: Proofreading Practice

The following paragraph has some errors in adverb and adjective forms. Rewrite the paragraph so that all the adjectives and adverbs are correct. Underline the words you have changed.

What will life be like for the child born in the United States in the year 2000? Inform historians have diligent researched what will sure be in store for these youngsters. First, it is expected that children born in the year 2000 will live twice as long as those born in 1900. They will enjoy an affluenter lifestyle and better health than their baby-boomer grandparents. Convenient, children will be able to eat broccoli Jell-O instead of the actual despise vegetable. They will join an enormous inflated population of 275 million people, with the majority living in California, Texas, and Florida. Larger homes will be squeezed onto smaller lots, and an abundance of homes will be for sale as baby boomers begin to retire. The more academic inclined person born in the year 2000 will have to pay $320,000 for a year at Harvard. There will not be a real big change in methods of child rearing. Parents will struggle with the same child-rearing dilemmas that consumed the latter part of the 20th century. In fact, a child is a child and faces the same challenges no matter what year he or she is born. The new millennium promises to be an excite time to live!

Exercise 20.2: Pattern Practice

Using the patterns given here, write a sentence of your own for each pattern.

Pattern A: Sentence with an *-ed* adjective modifying a noun

The **fertilized** plant grew quickly on my windowsill.

Pattern B: Sentence with an adverb modifying another adverb

The sound echoed **very** clearly.

Pattern C: Sentence with the adverb *so, such,* or *too* that is complete

It was **such** a long concert that I was tempted to leave during intermission.

Pattern D: An *-ed* adjective after a linking verb

The old man seemed **pleased** when the child said hello.

Pattern E: Sentence with the adverb *well*

With some coaching, the game-show contestant answered the questions very **well.**

Pattern F: Sentence with the adverb *badly*

As the horse cleared the hurdle, it got caught on a bar, fell, and hurt its back leg **badly.**

20b A, An, The

> **A, an,** and **the** precede nouns. The choice between *a* and *an* is determined by the word that follows it.

■ Use *a* when the word starts with a consonant sound.

a book	a horse	a very big house
a one-inch pipe	a youth	a PTA parent
a union	[Use *a* when the *u* sounds like the *y* in *you.*]	

HINT   Using A

A is used before consonant **sounds**, not just consonants. In the phrase *a one-syllable word*, the word *one* starts with a "wah" sound, which is a consonant sound. Similarly, in the phrase *a union*, the word *union* starts with a "you" sound.

■ Use *an* when the word following it starts with a vowel or an unsounded *h* (as in *honor, hour,* and *honest*).

an egg   an hour   an onion
an ancient coin   an eagle   an idea
an SOS signal   [the *S* here is sounded as "es"]

HINT   **Using An**

Formerly, *an* was used before unaccented syllables beginning with *h,* as in the following:

   an historian   an hotel   an habitual offender

However, this is becoming less frequent, and *a* is now considered acceptable, as in the following:

   a historian   a hotel   a habitual offender

Exercise 20.3: Proofreading Practice

Read the following paragraph and underline any errors in the use of a *or* an. *Circle* a *or* an *when it is used correctly.*

Maintaining a clear complexion, salvaging a unusually bad semester, and decorating a dorm room are among the topics treated in one of the magazine world's fastest-growing segments, magazines for college students. This market is fueled by advertisers eager to reach a untapped market of twelve to thirteen million college students with an large disposable income and a earning potential of many billions of dollars after graduation. Most college magazines are quarterlies, distributed free at a campus newsstand or by direct mail as an insert in the college paper. While profits are high, there is some criticism that these magazines are merely a advertising vehicle and do not focus on substantive issues, such as taking a close look at student loan programs or attempting a honest appraisal of racism on campus.

Exercise 20.4: Pattern Practice

Write a sentence using the suggested nouns and also using a, an, *or* the *before these nouns.*

Example: egg, piece of toast, cup

Sentence: For breakfast, I ordered an egg, a piece of toast, and a cup of coffee.

1. used car, salesperson, helpful
2. train, hour, Alaska
3. yeast, bread, oven, cookbook
4. A's, F's (as letter grades in a college course), grade book
5. old barn, young chickens, wire fence

20c Comparisons

Adverbs and adjectives are often used to show comparison, and the degree of comparison is indicated in their forms. In comparisons, most adjectives and adverbs add -er and -est as endings or combine with the words *more* and *most* or *less* and *least*.

Positive form is used when no comparison is made.

a **large** box   an **acceptable** offer

Comparative form is used when two things are being compared (with -er, more, or less).

the **larger** of the two boxes

the **more** (or **less**) **acceptable** of the two offers

Superlative form is used when three or more things are being compared (with -est, most, or least).

the **largest** of the six boxes

the **most** (or **least**) **acceptable** of all the offers

ADJECTIVES AND ADVERBS IN COMPARISON

Positive	Comparative	Superlative
(for one; uses the base form)	*(for two; uses -er, more, or less)*	*(for three or more; uses -est, most, or least)*
tall	taller	tallest
pretty	prettier	prettiest
cheerful	more cheerful	most cheerful
selfish	less selfish	least selfish

Curtis is **tall.**

Curtis is **taller** than Rachel.

Curtis is the **tallest** player on the team.

IRREGULAR FORMS OF COMPARISON

Positive	Comparative	Superlative
(for one)	*(for two)*	*(for three or more)*
good	better	best
well	better	best
little	less	least
some	more	most
much	more	most
many	more	most
bad, badly	worse	worst

Some guidelines for choosing between -er and -est or more and most (or less and least) are as follows:

■ With one-syllable words, the *-er* and *-est* endings are commonly used.

| quick | quicker | quickest |

■ With two-syllable words, some adjectives take *-er* and *-est,* and some use *more* and *most* (or *less* and *least*). Check the dictionary to be sure.

| happy | happier | happiest |
| thoughtful | more thoughtful | least thoughtful |

■ For adverbs, *more* and *most* or *less* and *least* are commonly used.

| smoothly | more smoothly | least smoothly |

■ For words with three or more syllables, use *more* and *most* or *less* and *least.*

| generous | more generous | least generous |

HINT   Comparisons

1. Be sure to avoid double comparisons in which both the *-er* and *more* (or *-est* and *most*) are used.

the ~~most~~ farthest   ~~more~~ quicker

2. Be sure to complete your comparisons by using all the needed words.

driving down
Driving down Hill Street is slower than ᴧWestern Avenue.

[The act of driving down one street is being compared to the act of driving down another street. The streets themselves are not being compared.]

it is in
The weather here is as warm as ᴧPhoenix.

those of
The results of the second medical test were more puzzling than ᴧthe first test.

3. Remember to choose the correct pronoun case in comparisons with omitted words. (See 19a.)

Terry jumps higher than **I** (do).

Terry likes Julie more than (he likes) **me.**

Exercise 20.5: Proofreading Practice

In the following paragraph there are a number of errors in the words used to show comparisons. Revise the paragraph to correct these errors.

(a) A new sport, already popular in Canada and sweeping across the United States, is indoor box lacrosse. (2) It is more faster, furiouser, and often a more brutal version of the field game of lacrosse. (3) Box lacrosse is indeed an exciting game, as it is more speedy and more rougher than ice hockey but requires the kind of teamwork needed in basketball. (4) Scores for box lacrosse are more high than those for field lacrosse because the indoor game has a more smaller playing area with the most opportunities for scoring. (5) The team in box lacrosse is also more smaller than field lacrosse; there are only six people on a side in the indoor game and ten people on conventional field lacrosse teams. (6) In addition, box lacrosse is played on artificial turf in ice-hockey rinks, and the sticks are more short and more thinner than conventional field lacrosse sticks. (7) Almost anything goes in this rough-and-tumble indoor sport.

Exercise 20.6: Pattern Practice

Listed here is some information to use in sentences of your own. Try to include as many comparisons as you can in your sentence.

Example: Write a sentence comparing the cost of the items listed here. Use the word *expensive* in your sentence.

bananas: $0.25/pound

apples $0.49/pound

pears $0.60/pound

Sample Sentence: At the First Street Fruit Market, apples are more expensive than bananas, but bananas are less expensive than pears, which are the most expensive of these three fruits.

1. Write a sentence of your own about the magazines described here, and use the word *interesting*.

   Today's Trends is very dull.

   Home Magazine is somewhat interesting.

   Now! is very interesting.

2. Write a sentence of your own about the ages of the three teenagers described here, and use the words *old* and *young*.

   Chip is thirteen years old.

   Michelle is fifteen years old.

   Ethan is eighteen years old.

3. Write a sentence of your own about the movies described here, and use the word *scary*.

   Terror at Night is not a very scary movie.

   Teen Horror is a somewhat scary movie.

   Night of the Avengers is a very scary movie.

4. Write a sentence of your own about the car engines described here, and use the word *powerful*.

The Hyundai engine is not very powerful.

The Ford engine is fairly powerful.

The Ferrari engine is very powerful.

5. Write a sentence of your own about the professors described here, and use the word *clear*.

Professor Tischler's lectures are not very clear.

Professor Liu's lectures are somewhat clear.

Professor Gottner's lectures are very clear.

21 | Prepositions (prep)

Prepositions connect nouns and pronouns to another word or words in a sentence.

They left **in** the morning.

[The preposition *in* connects *morning* with the verb *left*.]

21a Common Prepositions

The following is a list of common prepositions:

about	despite	out
above	down	out of
according to	during	outside
across	except	over
after	except for	past
against	excepting	regarding
along	for	round
along with	from	since
among	in	through
apart from	in addition to	throughout
around	in case of	till
as	inside	to
at	in spite of	toward
because of	instead of	under
before	into	underneath
behind	like	unlike
below	near	until
beneath	next	up
beside	of	upon
between	off	up to
beyond	on	with
by	onto	within
concerning	on top of	without

21b Idiomatic Prepositions

If choosing the right preposition is difficult, look up the word it is used with (not the preposition) in the dictionary. The following combinations can be troublesome:

Wrong	Revised
apologize about	apologize for
bored of	bored with
capable to	capable of
concerned to, on	concerned about, over, with
in search for	in search of
independent from	independent of
interested about	interested in, by
outlook of life	outlook on life
puzzled on	puzzled at, by
similar with	similar to

21c Other Prepositions

Selecting other prepositions can also be difficult. See the Glossary of Usage at the back of this book for help with the following combinations:

among, between	different from, different than
compared to, compared with	off (*not* off of)
could have (*not* could of)	should have (*not* should of)

HINT **Using Prepositions**

In formal writing, avoid putting a preposition at the end of a sentence, if possible.

Informal: This is the argument he disagreed **with.**

Formal: This is the argument **with** which he disagreed.

Some prepositions, however, cannot be rearranged.

He wants to go **in.**

The mayor was well thought **of.**

The results may not be worth worrying **about.**

Exercise 21.1: Proofreading Practice

In the following paragraph, underline the prepositions that are incorrectly used, and then write in the correct words.

The next time you are stuck with traffic, look toward the sky. You might be puzzled on the birds flying south for the winter. The management of human traffic could of been solved hundreds of years ago if we had patterned our behavior on migratory birds. Researchers interested about migration have noted that, thanks to the flocking system, birds do not crash into each other or go astray. This theory was published to *Physical Review* about four years ago. The theory refers of the behavior of gases and liquids and the idea that a bird flock behaves like a liquid being poured into a glass. If one drop of liquid or one bird deviates from the course, the rest remains intact. Researchers hope this information will help engineers to design spaces that allow people to flow smoothly among one area to the next and avoid bottlenecks upon the road. Within the future, when you "flock" on the beach, spare a thought to those feathered friends.

Exercise 21.2: Pattern Practice

In the following sentences, supply appropriate prepositions in the blanks.

(1) It has been proved that people's outlook _____ life can help them live longer. (2) A person who is bored _____ living tends to contract illnesses more often than a person who looks forward _____ every new day. (3) Someone who is always expecting the worst and is overly concerned _____ the negatives in life is more likely to become depressed. (4) All people are capable _____ living life _____ the fullest. (5) Don't spend your days in search _____ the answers to all of life's questions. (6) It is better to look forward to each new day _____ a challenge.

22 Subjects (sub)

A **subject** is the word or words that indicate who or what is doing the action of active verbs. The subject of a passive verb is acted upon by the verb.

 HINT   **Finding the Subject**

To find the subject, first look for the verb (see Chapter 17), and then ask *who* or *what* is doing the action for active verbs. Ask *who* or *what* is acted on for passive verbs.

Annie worked as an underpaid lifeguard last summer.

1. Locate the verb: *worked* (active).
2. Ask: Who or what *worked?*
3. The answer is "Annie worked," so *Annie* is the subject.

Annie was paid less than minimum wage by the swimming pool manager.

1. Locate the verb: *was paid* (passive).
2. Ask: Who or what *was paid?*
3. The answer is "Annie was paid," so *Annie* is the subject.

There are several complications to remember when finding subjects:

■ Some subjects have more than one word.

Juan and Quo realized that despite being roommates, they really liked each other.

1. Who *realized?* Juan and Quo.
2. The subject is *Juan and Quo.*

That roommates occasionally disagree is well known.

1. What *is* well known? That roommates occasionally disagree.
2. The subject is *That roommates occasionally disagree.*

■ Some subjects may be buried among describing words before and after the subject word.

The major **problem** with today's parents is their tendency to avoid being like their parents.

Almost **all** of his recordings are now available on compact disks.

Too many **farmers** in that area of the state planted soybeans last year.

■ Subjects in commands are not expressed in words because the person being addressed is the reader (*you*). "Turn the page" really means that you, the reader, should turn the page.

Close the door.   [Who is being told to close the door? You are.]

Mix the eggs thoroughly before adding milk.   [Who is being told to mix the eggs? You are.]

■ Most subjects come before the verb, but some come in the middle of or after the verb. For questions, the subject comes in the middle of or after the verb.

When is the **band** going to start?

Are **they** here yet?

■ For sentences that begin with *there is, there are,* or *it is,* the subject comes after the verb.

There is a buzzing **sound** in my left ear.

Now there are buzzing **sounds** in both ears.

It is **one** of those medical mysteries, I guess.

■ For verbs in the passive voice, the doer of the action is expressed in a phrase beginning with *by,* and the subject receives the action. When we are not interested in who is doing the action or when it is obvious who did it, the *by* phrase is omitted.

The ball was hit by the boy.   (or)   The ball was hit.

The experiment was performed by several assistants.   (or)
The experiment was performed.

Exercise 22.1: Proofreading Practice

Underline the subjects of all the verbs in the following sentences. Remember, it's easier to start by finding the verb and then asking who? *or* what? *As an example, the first sentence is already marked.*

(1) <u>Humans</u> are unique in preferring to use the right hand. (2) Among other animals, each individual favors one hand or another, but in every species other than humans, the split between the right and left hand is even. (3) Only humans seem to favor the right hand. (4) Even in studies of prehistoric people, anthropologists have found this preference. (5) For example, in ancient drawings over five thousand years old, most people are shown using their right hands. (6) This evidence suggests that handedness is not a matter of cultural pressures but perhaps of some genetic difference. (7) Although left-handedness seems to run in families, it is not clear how hand preference is passed from one generation to the next.

Exercise 22.2: Pattern Practice

In each blank, write a subject word or words that could fit the sentence. Try to add a word or phrase describing the subject.

(1) <u>Greedy credit card companies</u> have found new targets to plunge into debt. (2) These _____ have begun issuing credit cards to college students with little money and no credit history. (3) _____ are now walking around campus with the ability to accumulate thousands of dollars of debt. (4) Worst of all, _____ usually do not know about the cards until their children's bills arrive. (5) Some _____ have begun screening credit applications from college students more stringently. (6) _____ have found that it is difficult to squeeze blood from a stone, so they might as well not issue cards to college students.

23 Phrases (phr)

> A **phrase** is a group of related words without a subject and complete verb. The words in phrases act as the subject or verb in a sentence, or they can add information to other parts of the sentence.

Note how the related words in these phrases work together to offer information:

<u>A major earthquake</u> hit the area last night.

[This phrase is the subject of the sentence.]

<u>Listening to music</u> is one form of relaxation.

[This phrase is the subject of the sentence.]

Dr. Prada, <u>a famous brain surgeon</u>, will be on television this evening.

[This phrase tells us more about the subject, Dr. Prada.]

The bike <u>leaning on its side</u> fell over during the rainstorm.

[This phrase also tells us more about the subject.]

They <u>may have been eating</u> when I called.

[This phrase is the verb phrase.]

He always walks <u>with his toes pointed out</u>.

[This phrase gives added information about the verb.]

Her favorite pastime is <u>visiting museums</u>.

[This phrase comes after a linking verb and completes the subject.]

Jenny looks like Crazy Edna, <u>a second cousin of mine</u>.

[This phrase gives added information about another element in the sentence.]

Exercise 23.1: Proofreading Practice

In the following paragraph, some of the phrases have been underlined. Each one of those underlined phrases performs one of the six functions listed. Identify the function of the phrase by writing the appropriate number near the phrase. The first sentence has been done as an example.

1. The phrase acts as the subject.
2. It tells something more about the subject.
3. It acts as the verb.
4. It tells something more about the verb.
5. It completes the subject of a linking verb.
6. It tells something more about another element in the
   sentence.

(1) <u>Finding a place for our garbage</u> is a problem as old as human
     1

beings. (2) On the Pacific coast there are <u>large, round shell mounds</u> where for centuries Indians <u>had been discarding</u> the bones and clam-shells that constituted their garbage. (3) When people gathered together <u>in cities</u>, they hauled their waste to the outskirts of town or dumped it <u>into nearby rivers</u>. (4) In the United States the first munic-ipal refuse system was instituted in Philadelphia, <u>a well-organized city</u>. (5) Here slaves were forced to wade <u>into the Delaware River</u> and toss bales of trash into the current. (6) Eventually <u>this dumping into rivers</u> was outlawed, and people looked for new solutions to the garbage prob-lem. (7) Municipal dump sites, <u>unused plots of land far away from houses</u>, were <u>a frequent answer</u>. (8) But the number of landfill sites <u>is decreasing</u> as many dumps are closed because of health hazards or because of cost. (9) America, <u>a land of throwaway containers and fancy packaging</u>, clearly faces a garbage problem, <u>a problem without any obvious answers</u>.

Exercise 23.2: Pattern Practice

In each of the following sentences, one of the phrases has been underlined. Describe the function of that phrase, and then make up your own sentence that has a phrase performing the same function. The first sentence has been done as an example.

1. American <u>is facing</u> a garbage crisis that gets worse each year.
   (verb phrase)

2. In 1960 <u>the average American</u> sent 2.2 pounds of trash to the dump each day, but now it's 5.1 pounds a day.

3. We need new dump sites, but they are <u>hard to find</u> because no one wants a landfill next door.

4. Some cities, <u>the ones without potential new landfill space</u>, have given up looking for nearby sites.

5. These cities <u>have started</u> a new practice, exporting their garbage to other states.

6. For example, in Ohio, trash arrives <u>from New Jersey</u>.

7. Exporting garbage is an answer, <u>a temporary one</u>, until other states start refusing to accept someone else's trash.

24 Clauses (cl)

A **clause** is a group of related words that (unlike a phrase) has both a subject and a complete verb. A sentence may have one or more clauses.

■ A sentence with one clause:

Some <u>students</u> <u>see</u> themselves working in office environments and
    (subject) *(verb)*

wearing formal business clothes.

■ A sentence with two clauses:

Although <u>it</u> <u>becomes</u> expensive to buy a wardrobe of
    (subject 1) *(verb 1)*

business clothes, such <u>people</u> <u>enjoy</u> the daily opportunities
                (subject 2) *(verb 2)*

to dress well.

■ A sentence with one clause embedded in the middle of another clause:

<u>Students</u>   <u>who</u>   <u>seek</u> well-paying jobs often <u>think</u> of careers in
(subject 1) *(subject 2)* *(verb 2)*   *(verb 1)*

business and finance.

24a Independent Clauses (in cl)

An **independent clause** can stand alone as a complete sentence because it doesn't depend on anything else to complete the thought. An independent clause has the following characteristics:

■ It has a complete verb and subject.

<u>No one</u> <u>could understand</u> the message written on the blackboard.
(subject) *(complete verb)*

■ It expresses a complete thought and can stand alone as a sentence.

He never wanted to lend me any of his cassette tapes.

■ Two different groups of connecting words can be used at the beginning of an independent clause:

1. *And, but, for, or, nor, so, yet* (coordinating conjunctions)

Detasseling corn is exhausting work, **but** she needed the money.

(For use of the comma with these connectors, see 27a.)

2. *Therefore, moreover, thus, consequently,* etc. (conjunctive adverbs)

Detasseling corn is exhausting work; **however,** she needed the money.

(For the use of the semicolon with these connectors, see Chapter 6 and 29a.)

■ An independent clause can be combined with a dependent clause or with another independent clause to form a sentence (see Chapter 26):

1. An independent clause can be its own sentence.

The popularity of some cartoon characters lasts for years.

2. Two independent clauses can form one sentence.

Mickey Mouse, Donald Duck, and Bugs Bunny are perennial favorites, but other once-popular characters such as Jiggs and Maggie have disappeared.

3. An independent clause can be joined with a dependent clause.

Since Garfield the cat and Peanuts have become great favorites, perhaps they will last for several generations like Mickey Mouse.

Exercise 24.1: Proofreading Practice

In the following paragraph, there are groups of underlined words that are numbered. Identify each group as a phrase or a clause. The first sentence has been done as an example.

(1) For years strange noises, <u>which would start in June and last until</u>
                                            (clause)

September, filled the air around the waters of Richardson Bay, <u>an inlet</u>
<u>of water near Sausalito, California.</u> (2) The noise was heard in the
(phrase)

houseboats, <u>especially those with fiberglass hulls,</u> moored along the
southwestern shore of the bay. (3) <u>The noise was usually described as a</u>
<u>deep hum like an electric foghorn or an airplane motor.</u> (4) The noise,
<u>which would start in late evening,</u> would stop by morning, <u>ruining peo-</u>
<u>ple's sleep.</u> (5) <u>During the summer of 1984 the hum was unusually loud</u>
<u>and stirred investigations.</u> (6) Originally, suspicion centered on a nearby
sewage plant, <u>which was suspected of dumping sewage at night when no</u>
<u>one would notice.</u> (7) Some others thought there were <u>secret Navy</u>
<u>experiments going on.</u> (8) An acoustical engineer, <u>studying the mys-</u>
<u>tery sound for months,</u> kept thinking he would find the answer, <u>but he</u>
<u>didn't.</u> (9) Finally, a marine ecologist identified the source of the hum
as the sound of the plainfin midshipman, <u>a fish also known as the</u>
<u>singing toad.</u> (10) <u>The male's singing</u> was the sound everyone heard, he
said, <u>though some people still suspect the sewage plant.</u>

Exercise 24.2: Pattern Practice

In this paragraph on visual pollution, notice the patterns of clauses that are
present.

1. Some sentences have one clause.
2. Some have two clauses separated by punctuation.
3. Some have one clause in the middle of another.

Each sentence in the paragraph follows one of these patterns. Identify that pat-
tern by its number, and then write your own paragraph of five or more sen-
tences. Identify the pattern of clauses in each of your sentences by using these
same numbers. As a subject for your paragraph, you may want to describe
other types of pollution, such as noise pollution caused by dual-exhaust cars,
air pollution caused by cigarette smoke or overpowering perfumes, or visual
pollution caused by litter.

(1) One type of pollution that the government has tried to eliminate
is the visual pollution of billboards along our highways. (2) In 1965
Congress passed the Highway Beautification Act to outlaw those ugly
signs, but the act didn't work. (3) While the federal government paid
for the removal of 2,235 old billboards in 1983, the billboard industry
was busy putting up 18,000 new signs in the same year. (4) Since then
the situation has gotten worse. (5) The 1965 act had all kinds of loop-
holes; however, the real problem is a requirement in the act to pay billboard companies for removing the signs. (6) Since some communities
don't have the funds for this, too many old signs are still standing,
along with all the new ones going up.

24b Dependent Clauses (dep cl)

A **dependent clause** cannot stand alone as a complete sentence because it depends on another clause in the sentence to
complete the thought.

Finding Dependent Clauses

1. Dependent clauses have adverbs at the beginning of the clause.(See the explanation of adverb clauses in 24b.2.)

2. Say the dependent clause aloud, and you'll hear that you need to add more information.

"When I got up this morning . . ." [Are you waiting for more information?]

3. To locate dependent clauses punctuated as sentences, try proofreading your papers backward from the last sentence to the first.

There are two kinds of dependent clauses: adjective and adverb clauses.

1. Adjective Clauses (*who/which/that* clauses)

An **adjective clause** gives additional information about a noun or pronoun in the sentence and starts with one of the following words: *who, which, that, whose, whom.*

The singer, **who used to play lead guitar**, now lets the other band members play while she sings.

The group tried a concert tour, **which was a financial disaster.**

The rumor **that the poor ticket sales were due to mismanagement** never appeared in print.

2. Adverb Clauses (*because/if/when* clauses)

An **adverb clause** gives more information about other verbs, adjectives, or adverbs in a sentence or another clause. Adverb clauses start with adverbs such as the following common ones:

after	before	though	when
although	even if	unless	whenever
as	even though	until	whether
as if	if	what	while
because	since	whatever	

Finding Adverb Clauses

You can recognize adverb clauses by these marker words at the beginning. Because of the meaning of these words, they create the need for another clause to complete the thought. Think of the relationship as follows:

After X, Y. [*After* X happens, Y happens.]

Because X, Y. [*Because* X happens, Y happens.]

> **If** X, Y. [*If* X happens, Y will happen.]
>
> **After** I eat lunch tomorrow . . . [*What* will happen?]
>
> After I eat lunch tomorrow, I will call you.
>
> **Because** it was so dark out . . . [What happened?]
>
> Because it was so dark out, she tripped on the steps.
>
> **If** I win the lottery . . . [What will happen?]
>
> If I win the lottery, I'll quit my job and retire.
>
> **When** it began to rain . . . [What happened?]
>
> When it began to rain, the game was canceled.

Dependent clauses may appear at the beginning of a sentence, before the independent clause, or at the end of the sentence, where they are harder to recognize.

I will call you **after I eat lunch tomorrow.**

She tripped on the steps **because it was so dark out.**

The game was canceled **when it began to rain.**

HINT   **Punctuating Dependent Clauses**

To punctuate dependent clauses:

■ When the adverb clause appears at the beginning of a sentence, it is followed by a comma.

■ When the adverb clause follows an independent clause, no punctuation is needed before the adverb clause. (See 27b.)

Until gas prices are cheaper, I will buy only compact cars.
[adverb clause first]

I will buy only compact cars **until gas prices are cheaper.**
[adverb clause last]

Exercise 24.3: Proofreading Practice

Identify the dependent clauses in the following paragraph by underlining them and labeling them as either adjective or adverb clauses.

(1) The tiny lichen is an amazing plant. (2) It can survive in an incredibly difficult environment because it can do things no other plant can do. (3) The lichen, which can anchor itself on a bare rock by etching the rock's surface with powerful acids, grows into the pits that it burns out. (4) Because lichens grow in cold climates above the tree line, they are frozen or covered by snow most of the year. (5) Unlike the cactus in

the desert, the lichen has no way of retaining moisture. (6) Because of this, the sun dries lichens into waterless crusts during the day. (7) When there is a drought, lichens may dry out completely for several months. (8) Even under ideal conditions their total daily growing period may last only for an hour or two while they are still wet with morning dew. (9) The lichen, which may take twenty-five years to grow to a diameter of one inch, can live for several thousand years. (10) These amazing plants are able to live in all sorts of difficult places, but not in cities because the pollution may kill them.

Exercise 24.4: Pattern Practice

Write your own paragraph with sentences that include dependent clauses. As in Exercise 24.3, identify the dependent clauses by underlining them and labeling them as either adjective or adverb clauses. If possible, use the sentences in Exercise 24.3 as patterns. As a subject for your paragraph, you may wish to describe an animal, a person, or another plant like the lichen that manages to survive under difficult conditions.

Exercise 24.5: Proofreading Practice

Identify the independent clauses in this paragraph by underlining them. If an independent clause is interrupted by a dependent clause, put parentheses around the dependent clause. The first sentence has been done as an example.

Kwanzaa, (which is an African American holiday celebrated from December 26 through January 1), did not originate in any one of the 55 African countries. When the festival was first introduced in 1966, it was designed as a ritual to welcome the first harvests to the home. Dr. Maulana Karenga, who created the festival, was responding to the commercialism of Christmas. Similar to Hanukkah, Kwanzaa uses candles as symbols of the holiday. The seven principles that the candles represent are unity, self-determination, responsibility, cooperative economics, purpose, creativity, and faith. The seven candles, which are red, black, and green, remind participants of the seven principles and the colors in flags of African liberation movements. Gifts are exchanged, and on December 31, participants celebrate with a banquet reflecting the cuisine of various African countries. Kwanzaa has become an important American celebration.

Exercise 24.6: Pattern Practice

Read the following paragraph, and identify the sentence patterns by the kinds of clauses in each sentence. Choose the most appropriate of the following numbers, and write that number in the space after the number of the sentence.

1. Independent clause as its own sentence
2. Two independent clauses joined into one sentence
3. One independent clause with a dependent clause
4. Two independent clauses and a dependent clause

The first sentence has been done as an example. Write your own paragraph using these sentence patterns. You may want to write about another technolog-

ical advance that involves a question of ethics such as cloning or selective abortion.

(1) _3_ While the World Wide Web has provided new opportunities for information retrieval, it has also provided a network for criminals to lure potential victims. (2) ___ Chat rooms, which are sites enabling a conversation between strangers, are proving to be dangerous areas for some vulnerable people. (3) ___ In several documented cases, pedophiles have used these chat rooms to arrange meetings with children. (4) ___ Concerned law-enforcement officers, working through the Internet, pose as children and arrange to meet suspects in order to arrest them. (5) ___ This work is extremely difficult, and it requires a great deal of patience. (6) ___ First, the undercover officer must scan the chat rooms searching for pedophiles. (7) ___ Apparently, these child molesters use common ploys, which the officers are trained to recognize, to lure victims. (8) ___ When the team spots a suspect on the Internet, the operation swings into action, and usually within one hour the undercover agent has an arranged meeting time and place. (9) ___ Many criminals have been caught, and some have been successfully prosecuted, thanks to this method. (10) ___ Parents are urged to monitor children's Internet activity.

25 Essential and Nonessential Clauses and Phrases

25a Essential Clauses and Phrases (es)

An **essential clause** or **phrase** (also called a *restrictive, or necessary,* clause or phrase) appears after a noun and is essential in the sentence to complete the meaning. An essential clause or phrase cannot be moved to another sentence or omitted because the meaning of the sentence would change.

Compare the meaning of the following two sentences with and without the clause after the noun *people:*

People <u>who can speak more than one language</u> are multilingual.

People are multilingual.

[The second sentence seems odd because not all people are multilingual. The *who* clause in the sentence above is essential because we need it to understand the meaning.]

Please repair all the windows <u>that are broken</u>.

[If the *that* clause is taken out, the sentence is a request to repair all the windows, not just those that are broken. Since the meaning of the sentence is changed when the *that* clause is removed, the *that* clause is essential to the sentence.]

Sylvester Stallone's movie <u>*Rambo II*</u> will be on TV tonight.

[The movie title *Rambo II* is necessary because Sylvester Stallone has appeared in many movies. If the phrase *Rambo II* is taken out of the sentence, it then says that Stallone's only movie will be on TV.]

> **HINT** **Essential Clauses**
>
> 1. Essential clauses and phrases are not set off by commas.
>
> 2. Clauses starting with *that* are almost always essential.

25b Nonessential Clauses and Phrases (non es)

A **nonessential clause** or **phrase** (also called a *nonrestrictive* or *unnecessary* clause or phrase) adds extra information but can be removed from a sentence without disturbing the meaning. The information can be put in another sentence.

Compare the following two sentences to see if the primary meaning of the sentence remains the same after the clause is removed:

My cousin Jim, <u>who lives in Denver</u>, is coming for a visit over Thanksgiving vacation.

My cousin Jim is coming for a visit over Thanksgiving vacation.

[The *who* clause is nonessential because it adds information about where Jim lives but is not necessary. The assumption here is that the writer has only one cousin named Jim. If the writer had two cousins named Jim, one who lives in Denver and another in St. Louis, then *who lives in Denver* would be necessary.]

Sandwich Supreme, <u>one of the first of a new chain of gourmet sandwich shops</u>, serves six different types of cheese sandwiches with a choice of three different types of bread.

[If the phrase describing Sandwich Supreme as a part of a chain of gourmet shops is removed from the sentence, the meaning of the main clause remains intact. The phrase is therefore not essential.]

Rambo II, <u>starring Sylvester Stallone</u>, will be on TV tonight.

[In this sentence, the phrase noting who stars in the movie can be removed because it merely adds information about the name of one of the actors. Compare this sentence with the example of *Rambo II* as an essential clause in 25a.]

> **HINT** **Nonessential Clauses**
>
> Nonessential clauses and phrases are set off by a pair of commas when they appear within a sentence. Only one comma is needed when they appear at the end of a sentence. (See 27c.)

> The compact disk, <u>a revolutionary advance in high-fidelity recording</u>, has made records obsolete.
>
> [Here the nonessential phrase appears in the middle of the sentence and needs two commas.]
>
> Consumers are spending millions of dollars now on compact disks, <u>a revolutionary advance in high-fidelity recording</u>.
>
> [Here the nonessential phrase appears at the end of the sentence and needs only one comma.]

Some sentences will be punctuated differently depending on the meaning.

Phil's son <u>Steve</u> is playing in the soccer match.

[This sentence states that Phil has more than one son, and the son named Steve is playing in the soccer match.]

Phil's son, <u>Steve</u>, is playing in the soccer match.

[This sentence states that Phil has only one son, and an extra bit of information is that his name is Steve.]

The bank offered loans to the farmers, <u>who were going to plant soybeans</u>.

[This sentence states that all farmers received loans.]

The bank offered loans to the farmers <u>who were going to plant soybeans</u>.

[This sentence states that the bank offered loans only to the farmers planting soybeans, not to those planting other crops.]

Exercise 25.1: Proofreading Practice

In the following paragraph there are underlined phrases. Identify these as either essential or nonessential phrases by writing an E (for essential) or N (for non-essential) near each underlined phrase.

(1) Art fraud, <u>a widespread problem</u>, is probably as old as art itself. (2) Fourteenth-century Italian stonecarvers <u>who wanted to deceive their buyers</u> copied Greek and Roman statues and then purposely chipped their works so they could peddle them as antiquities. (3) Today forgers, <u>who have become specialists in different kinds of fraud</u>, produce piles of moderately priced prints, paintings, statues, and pottery. (4) The people <u>whom they defraud</u> are usually beginning or less knowledgeable collectors. (5) These people, <u>who usually can afford to spend only a few thousand dollars at most for a work of art</u>, have not developed a skilled eye for detecting fraud.

Exercise 25.2: Proofreading Practice

In the following paragraph there are some underlined clauses and phrases, both essential and nonessential. Practice using clauses and phrases like these in your writing by composing your own sentences in the same patterns as the following sentences. As your topic, you may want to describe another common kind of fraud or deception that exists today.

(1) Thomas Hoving, <u>the former director of the Metropolitan Museum of Art</u>, estimates that 40 percent of the art <u>that is on the market today</u> is fake. (2) However, much of this fraudulent art is not detected because even buyers <u>who suspect fraud</u> find it difficult to prove that the seller knowingly unloaded a fake on them. (3) Thus collectors <u>who get stuck with dubious pieces of art</u> usually don't go to court. (4) Instead, they attempt to return the piece to the person <u>from whom they bought it</u>. (5) If that isn't possible, some collectors, <u>particularly the less honest ones</u>, pass the piece of art on to another unsuspecting buyer.

26 Sentences (sent)

A **sentence** is a group of words that has at least one independent clause and expresses a relatively complete thought. The following characteristics of sentences help to distinguish them from fragments:

- Although sentences are said to express "a complete thought," sentences normally occur in the context of other sentences that explain more fully. A sentence may therefore seem to need more information because it will refer to other sentences.

  He was able to do it.

  [This is a complete sentence because it is an independent clause. We don't know who "he" is or what "he" was able to do, but when this sentence appears with others, more explanation will make the meaning clear.]

- Sentences can start with any word.

  1. *And* and *but* are connecting words that can start an independent clause.

     But the dog did not bark.

     [This sentence may not seem "complete" because it needs a context of other sentences to explain the whole situation.]

  2. *Because, since,* and other markers that begin adverbial clauses can open a sentence as long as an independent clause follows.

     Because she did not lock her bike, it was stolen.

     [dependent clause first, then an independent clause]

  3. Dependent clauses and phrases can start a sentence as subjects.

That it was hot did not bother the athletes.

[dependent clause as subject]

4. Transitional words and phrases, such as *first, to sum up,* and *meanwhile,* can begin a sentence.

Next, she lifted the window.

[We don't know what "she" did first, but again, the context of other sentences will help.]

- Sentences can have pronouns as subjects.

He was proud of his accomplishments.

- Sentences don't have to have any specified length. They can have only a few or many words.

Go away!   [short complete sentence]

Whenever it is time to put away my winter clothing after a long, cold winter season, I always have a deep feeling of relief as if I am forcing the cold air to stay away until next year.   [long complete sentence]

- The complete verb in a sentence may be in a contraction.

He's here.   **That's** enough.

[The verb, *is,* is less obvious because it is contracted.]

- Punctuation errors and other problems in a sentence may occur, but these errors do not make a sentence a fragment.

The current interest in healthful foods has not diminished the sale of fast food, high-fat hamburgers and hot dogs continue to sell well.

[This sentence is incorrectly punctuated with a comma, but it is still a sentence. See 6a.]

HINT   **Sentence Punctuation Patterns**

To punctuate a sentence, remember these patterns:

A. [Independent clause] [.]

B. [Independent clause] , and [independent clause] [.]
, but
, for
, or
, nor
, so
, yet

C. [Independent clause] [;] [independent clause] [.]

(continued on next page)

(continued from previous page)

D. [Independent clause] ; therefore, [independent clause] [.]

   ; moreover,

   ; consequently,

   ; thus,

   (and so on)

E. [Dependent clause] [,] [independent clause] [.]

F. [Independent clause] [dependent clause] [.]

G. [First part of an independent clause] [,] [nonessential] [,] [rest of the clause] [.]

H. [First part of an independent clause] [essential] [rest of the clause] [.]

For a more complete explanation of sentence punctuation, see Chapters 27 and 29.

26a Sentence Purposes

Sentences can be described by their purpose:

- Making a statement (declarative): The divorce rate is increasing.
- Asking a question (interrogative): Is anyone home?
- Giving a command (imperative): Put that book on the table.
- Expressing strong feeling (exclamatory): That's an amazing feat!

26b Sentence Structures

Sentences can be described by their structure.

1. Simple Sentences

Simple sentences have one independent clause.

[Independent clause]
Doctors are concerned about the rising death rate from asthma.

2. Compound Sentences

Compound sentences have two or more independent clauses.

[Independent clause] + [independent clause]
Doctors and researchers are concerned about the rising death rate from asthma, but they don't know the reason for it.

3. Complex Sentences

Complex sentences have at least one independent clause and at least one dependent clause (in any order).

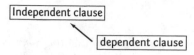

Doctors and researchers are concerned about the rising death rate from asthma because it is a common, treatable illness.

4. Compound-Complex Sentences

Compound-complex sentences have at least two independent clauses and at least one dependent clause (in any order).

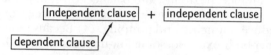

Doctors and researchers are concerned about the rising death rate from asthma because it is a common, treatable illness, but they don't know the reason for the 23 percent increase in the last five years.

Exercise 26.1: Proofreading Practice

Identify each of the numbered groups of words in the paragraph below with the appropriate letter(s) from this group:

I	=	*incomplete sentence*
S	=	*simple sentence*
CP	=	*compound sentence*
CX	=	*complex sentence*
CP-CX	=	*compound-complex sentence*

(1) When we have a romantic relationship with another person, we want to know how the other person feels about us. (2) But, as psychologists have found out from their studies, we rarely resort to asking about the other person's feelings. (3) Some people do this, but most people tend to use indirect means. (4) Such as asking a third person's opinion or using some more indirect means of inquiry. (5) A recent study of college students confirmed the tendency among students to use indirect means; moreover, in the study two psychologists learned students' most-often-used indirect tactic, which was to make the other person choose between alternatives, for example, asking the other person to choose their relationship over something else such as an opportunity to go off for a weekend of skiing. (6) Another way described by the students was testing the other person's limits of endurance in terms of behavior. (7) For example, the student would do something just to see if the other person would put up with it. (8) Yet another kind of testing of relationships was trying to make the other person jealous, and about one-third of the students being studied cited this as a kind of test of the other person's love. (9) The psychologists, who were also looking for instances of people who directly

ask the other person about their feelings, found very few examples. (10) Asking the other person directly was reported to be a very difficult thing to do.

Exercise 26.2: Pattern Practice

Practice the sentence patterns in the following paragraph by writing your own simple, compound, complex, and compound-complex sentences. Follow the patterns used by these sentences. For your subject matter, you may write about a form of exercise you prefer.

(1) Many people who have suffered the sprains and aches of aerobic exercising now prefer an alternative form called low-impact aerobics. (2) This involves ways to exercise without causing stress to the body, and it requires strength, endurance, flexibility, and balance. (3) Low-impact exercises involve larger arm motions and leg motions that keep one foot on the floor to reduce bouncing and jumping. (4) Because some people want more upper-body exercise, some low-impact routines also include the use of wrist weights. (5) Low-impact aerobics may not deliver the same aerobic benefit as traditional programs, but for those who want to avoid injury or cannot follow the more strenuous routines, it is a good choice. (6) However, for both traditional aerobics and the low-impact variety, the main cause of injury is still bad shoes, bad floors, bad stretches, and bad instruction.

27 Commas (,)

Commas are signals to help readers understand the meaning of written sentences. In the same way as our voices convey meaning by pausing or changing in pitch, commas indicate pauses to help readers understand writing. Thus, the sound of your sentences may help to indicate where commas are needed. But sound isn't always a dependable guide because not every voice pause occurs where a comma is needed and not every comma needs a voice pause. The rules in this section, along with some clues you get from pauses in your voice, will indicate where you'll need commas.

COMMAS AND SEMICOLONS IN SENTENCES

For simple sentences, use pattern 1.
For compound sentences, use patterns 2, 3, and 4.
For complex sentences, use patterns 5, 6, and 7.

1. | Independent clause | | . |

2. | Independent clause | | , | **coordinating conjunction:** | independent clause | | . |
   and   nor
   but   so
   for   yet
   or

3. | Independent clause | | ; | | independent clause | | . |

4. | Independent clause | | ; | **independent clause marker:** | independent clause | | . |
   however,
   nevertheless,
   therefore,
   consequently,
   (etc.)

5. **Dependent marker:** | dependent clause | | , |
   | independent clause | | . |
   Because
   Since
   If
   When
   While
   After
   (etc.)

(continued on next page)

COMMAS AND SEMICOLONS IN SENTENCES *(continued)*

6. | Independent clause | **dependent marker:** | dependent clause | . |

because
since
if
when
while
after
(etc.)

7. Subject | dependent clause | verb/predicate.

(Use commas before and after the dependent clause if it is nonessential.)

27a Commas in Compound Sentences

There are three ways to join independent clauses together into a compound sentence.

1. Use the comma with one of the seven coordinating conjunctions:

and	for	nor	yet
but	or	so	

_____ (clause) _____ , **and** _____ (clause) _____ .

The television program was dull, <u>but</u> the commercials were entertaining.

After the storm, they collected seashells along the beach, <u>and</u> everyone found some interesting specimens, <u>but</u> the conservationists asked them not to take the shells home.

Exception: A comma may be omitted if the two independent clauses are short and there is no danger of misreading.

We were tired so we stopped the game.

She smiled and we all smiled back.

HINT   **How to Remember Coordinating Conjunctions**

To remember the seven coordinating conjunctions, think of the phrase **"fan boys"**:

for	**a**nd	**n**or	
but	**o**r	**y**et	**s**o

---

2. Join independent clauses with a semicolon and a connecting word such as the following:

however,	therefore,	consequently,
thus,	moreover,	then,

_____ (clause) _____; **thus,** _____ (clause) _____.

The camping sites were all filled; however, the park ranger allowed latecomers to use empty spaces in the parking lot.

David's new sports car was designed for high-speed driving; moreover, it was also designed to be fuel efficient.

HINT   **Commas in Compound Sentences with Semicolons**

Use a comma after the connecting word.

3. Join the independent clauses with a semicolon and no joining words.

_____ (clause) _____ ; _____ (clause) _____.

Everyone in the room heard the glass shattering; no one moved until it was clear that there was no danger.

(For the errors caused by not following one of these three patterns, see Chapter 6.)

Exercise 27.1: Proofreading Practice

In the following paragraph, there are compound sentences that need commas or semicolons. Add the appropriate punctuation.

An inventor working on a "flying car" says that traveling several hundred miles by commercial airplane is a fairly inefficient way to get around. First you have to drive through traffic to the airport and then you have to park your car somewhere in order to board a plane. You fly to another crowded airport outside a city but then you have to take another automobile to your final destination in town. A more practical solution would be a personal commuter flying vehicle. The inventor, working in a company supported by several government agencies, has developed a vertical takeoff and landing vehicle that has the potential to allow everyone to take to the air. The vehicle can take off and land vertically and it travels five times faster than an automobile. The most recently developed model looks more like a car than a plane however, it operates more like a cross between a plane and a helicopter. Above 125 mph in flight, it flies like a conventional plane and below 125 mph, it maneuvers like a helicopter. It has a number of safety features, such as six engines therefore it can recover if it loses an engine while hovering close to the ground.

Exercise 27.2: Sentence Combining

Using the punctuation pattern for commas in compound sentences, combine the following short sentences into longer, compound sentences.

Remember, commas in compound sentences follow this pattern:

```
_____ (clause) _____  ┌ , and ┐ _____ (clause) _____.
                            │ but nor │
                            │ for so  │
                            └ or yet  ┘
```

1. The personal commuter flying vehicle now being designed has room for four passengers.
2. It can fly roughly 850 miles per tank of fuel at a cruising speed of 225 mph.
3. The vehicle can rise above 30,000 feet.
4. It can also hover near the ground.
5. According to the inventor, it has taken two decades of theoretical studies to design the vehicle's shape.
6. It has also taken ten years of wind-tunnel tests to achieve the aerodynamic shape.
7. Government officials foresee an entire transportation network in the future based on the personal flying vehicle.
8. There will have to be automated air traffic control systems for these vehicles.
9. The technology for controlling these vehicles already exists.
10. The technology will create electronic highways in the sky.

27b Commas After Introductory Words, Phrases, and Clauses

A comma is needed after introductory words, phrases, and clauses that come before the main clause.

Introductory Words

Yes,   No,   However,
Well,   In fact,   First,

<u>Well,</u> perhaps he meant no harm. <u>In fact,</u> he wanted to help.

Introductory Phrases

■ Long prepositional phrases (usually four words or more):

<u>In the middle of a long, dull movie,</u> I decided to get some popcorn.

<u>Due to his determination not to get a C,</u> he did all the homework.

■ Phrases with *-ing* verbals, *-ed* verbals, and *to* + verb:

<u>Having</u> finished the test before the bell rang, he left the room.

<u>Tired</u> of never having enough money, she took a second job.

<u>To get</u> a seat close to the stage, you'd better come early.

Introductory Clauses

■ Introductory dependent clauses that begin with adverbs such as the following:

After . . .	Because . . .	Until . . .
Although . . .	If . . .	When . . .
As . . .	Since . . .	While . . .

While I was eating, the cat scratched at the door.

Exception: The comma may be omitted when the introductory phrase or clause is short and there is no danger of misreading.

While eating I read the newspaper.

After they retired they moved to Mexico.

 Commas with Introductory Words

When dependent clauses come after the main clause, there is no comma.

When the telephone rang, the dog started to bark.

The dog started to bark when the telephone rang.

Use commas after introductory clauses, phrases, and words in the following cases:

- If the introduction is five or more words

- If there is a distinct voice pause after the introductory part

- If it is necessary to avoid confusion

  Possibly Confusing: As I stated the rules can be broken occasionally.

  Revised: As I stated, the rules can be broken occasionally.

When your sentence starts with an *-ing* verbal, *-ed* verbal, or *to* + verb, be sure you don't have a dangling modifier (see Chapter 9).

Exercise 27.3: Proofreading Practice

In the following paragraph, there are introductory words, phrases, and clauses that require commas. And commas where needed.

(1) A recent study showed that small cars are tailgated more than big ones. (2) Moreover the drivers of subcompact and compact cars also do more tailgating themselves. (3) In the study traffic flow at five different locations was observed, and various driving conditions were included, such as two-lane state roads, four-lane divided highways, and so on. (4) In all more than 10,000 vehicles were videotaped. (5) Although subcompact and compact cars accounted for only 38 percent of the vehicles on the tape their drivers were tailgaiting in 48 percent of the incidents observed. (6) In addition to having done all this tailgating these drivers were the victims of tailgating 47 percent of the time. (7) Midsize cars made up 31 percent of the cars on the tapes but accounted for only 20 percent of the tailgaters and 24 percent of the drivers being tailgated. (8) Having considered various reasons for this difference the researchers suggest that drivers of other cars may avoid getting close

to midsize cars because of the cars' contours. (9) Because midsize cars have more curves in their sloping backs and trunks people have more trouble seeing around them.

Exercise 27.4: Pattern Practice

The following sentences illustrate some of the rules for using introductory commas. Identify the rule by selecting the appropriate letter from the list given here, and then write your own sentence in this pattern.

Pattern A: Comma after an introductory word
Pattern B: Comma after an introductory phrase
Pattern C: Comma after an introductory clause

1. Because tailgaiting is a road hazard that is known to cause many accidents, other studies have searched for causes of tailgating.
2. For example, one study examined how people judge distances on the road.
3. Puzzled by the question of why small cars are tailgated so often, researchers studied other drivers' perceptions of how far away small cars appear to be.
4. Despite the fact that many of the people studied were generally able to guess distances accurately, they sometimes perceived small cars to be more than forty feet farther away than they actually were.
5. If drivers tend to think that small cars are really farther away than they actually are, this may explain why small cars are tailgated so often.
6. However, researchers continue to study this problem.

27c Commas with Essential and Nonessential Words, Phrases, and Clauses

Nonessential word groups (see 25b) require a pair of commas, one before the nonessential element and the other afterward (unless there is a period). Essential word groups do not have commas to set them off from the rest of the sentence.

HINT **Recognizing Essential and Nonessential Word Groups**

■ When an essential clause is removed, the meaning is too general.

Students **who cheat** harm only themselves.

[With the word group "who cheat" removed, the sentence would say that students harm themselves. That's too general and does not convey the meaning of the sentence.]

■ When a nonessential clause is removed, the meaning is the same.

The restaurant, which serves only breakfast and lunch, was closed.

[With the word group "which serves only breakfast and lunch" removed, the sentence still says that the restaurant was closed. The meaning of the main clause is the same.]

- When the word group interrupts the flow of words in the original sentence, it's a nonessential element and needs commas. Some people can hear a slight pause in their voice or a change in pitch as they begin and end a nonessential element.

- When you can move the word group around in the sentence or put it in a different sentence, it is a nonessential element.

No one, however, wanted to tell her she was wrong.

No one wanted, however, to tell her she was wrong.

However, no one wanted to tell her she was wrong.

- When the clause begins with *that,* it is always essential.

I'll return the sweater **that I borrowed** after I wear it again tonight.

That clauses following verbs that express mental action are always essential.

| I think that . . . | She believes that . . . | He dreams that . . . |
| They wish that . . . | We concluded that . . . | |

- Word groups (called appositives) following nouns that identify or explain the nouns are nonessential and need commas.

Uncle Ike, a doctor, smoked too much even though he continued to warn his patients not to smoke.   [Uncle Ike = a doctor]

The movie critic's review of *Heartland, a story about growing up in Indiana,* focused on the beauty of the scenery.

[*Heartland* = a story about growing up in Indiana]

When this word group is the last element in the sentence, keep it attached to the sentence and set it off with a comma. Some fragments are appositives that became detached from the sentence.

, a

She is a good friend. A person whom I trust and admire.

Exercise 27.5: Proofreading Practice

Some of the sentences in the following paragraph have essential and nonessential clauses, words, or phrases. Underline these elements, write N (for nonessential) or E (for essential), and add commas where they are needed.

The recently introduced television rating system is designed to provide parents with a method of monitoring the shows that children watch. The system which was introduced last year operates using a rating scale that flashes in an upper corner of the television screen. However, the parent is responsible for employing diligence when a child is viewing television programs. For example a very young child would not know what the symbols represent. An older child who knows what the symbols represent may choose to ignore them if a parent is not present. Experts agree that the system is not without faults. Many parents feel that the television industry should forgo the rating system and remove sex and violence from television shows. Proponents of the system mainly directors of television networks state that parents have the option of restricting television viewing for their children. The subject matter of television programming is not a new debate. However, the rating system adds another dimension to this topic which will continue to concern parents and the owners of television networks.

Exercise 27.6: Pattern Practice

In Exercise 27.5 there are sentences illustrating the following patterns for punctuating essential and nonessential elements in sentences. Using these patterns and the examples from the paragraph in Exercise 27.5, write your own sentences in the same pattern with correct punctuation.

Pattern A: Subject + comma + nonessential clause + comma + verb + object

Pattern B: Subject + essential clause + verb + object

Pattern C: Introductory phrase + comma + nonessential word + comma + subject + verb + object

Pattern D: Subject + verb + object + comma + nonessential phrase

27d Commas in Series and Lists

Use commas when three or more items are listed in a series.

A series of words:

Would you prefer the poster printed in yellow, blue, green, or purple?

A series of phrases:

He first spoke to Julio, then called his roommate, and finally phoned me.

A series of clauses:

She never dreamed she'd be in the movies, she hadn't even tried out for a part, and she was sure she didn't have enough talent to act.

There are some variations in using commas in lists. The comma after the last item before *and* or *or* is preferred, but it may be omitted if there is no possibility of misreading.

Americans' favorite spectator sports are football, baseball, and basketball.
[optional comma]

However, the comma before *and* cannot be omitted in sentences where terms belong together, such as *bread and butter*, or where some misreading is possible.

He talked about his college studies, art, and history.

[This sentence means that he talked about three things: his college studies, art, and history.]

He talked about his college studies, art and history.

[This sentence means that his college studies were in art and history.]

If one or more of the items in a series have commas, semicolons should be used between items.

The group included Bill Packo, the guitarist; Jim Hinders, drums; and Art Clutz, electronic keyboard.

Exercise 27.7: Proofreading Practice

In the following paragraph, there are some series of three or more items that need punctuation. Add commas where they are needed.

Imagine not being able to recognize the face of your sister your boss or your best friend from high school. Imagine looking into a mirror seeing a face and realizing that the face you see is totally unfamiliar. Though this may sound impossible, a small number of people do suffer from a neurological condition that leaves them unable to recognize familiar faces. The condition is called prosopagnosia and results from brain damage caused by infection or stroke. Many people with this problem who have been studied have normal vision reading ability and language skills. They know that a face is a face they can name its parts and they can distinguish differences between faces. But only through other clues —hearing a familiar voice remembering a specific feature like a mustache hearing a name or recalling a particular identifying mark such as an unusual scar—can the people who were studied call up memories of people they should know. Researchers studying this phenomenon have found evidence suggesting that the step leading to conscious recognition of the face by the brain is somehow being blocked.

Exercise 27.8: Pattern Practice

The following sentences all have examples of items in a series. Using these sentences as patterns, write your own sentences with correctly punctuated items in series.

1. His favorite pastimes are sleeping late on weekends, drinking too much beer, and watching game shows on television.
2. She's convinced that it's better to work hard when you're young, to save your money, and then to spend it all when you retire.
3. Do you prefer jogging shoes with leather, canvas, or mesh tops?
4. Some people try to forget their birthdays, some like to have big celebrations, and others don't have any strong preference.

27e Commas with Adjectives

Use commas to separate two or more adjectives that describe the same noun equally.

cold, dark water   happy, healthy baby

However, not all adjectives in front of a noun describe the noun equally. When they are not equal (or coordinate) adjectives, do not use commas to separate them.

six big dogs

bright green sweater   [the color of the sweater is bright green]

HINT   Using Commas with Adjectives

Can you add *and* between the adjectives? Can the adjectives be written in reverse order? If so, separate the adjectives with commas.

■ a greedy, stubborn child

[Either of the following is acceptable:]

a greedy, stubborn child   (or)   a stubborn, greedy child

■ an easy, happy smile

an easy, happy smile   (or)   a happy, easy smile

But notice the following examples, which do not describe the noun equally.

■ a white frame house [The following is not acceptable: a frame white house.]

■ two young men [The following is not acceptable: young two men.]

Exercise 27.9: Proofreading Practice

In the following paragraph, there are sentences with missing punctuation for adjectives placed before nouns. Add commas with the adjectives where they are needed and circle the commas.

Online shopping is the newest fastest way to shop! If you are a person who hates noisy crowded stores, especially during the holidays, go online to browse, comparison shop, and even bid on hard-to-find items. Among the best buys on the Internet are fine vintage wines, some clothing, CDs, books, and toys. Mail order retailers from Eddie Bauer, J. Crew, and Spiegel all have informative interesting shopping sites. The sites provide colorful realistic illustrations of merchandise along with stock availability of colors and sizes. For example, instead of running from store to store to price a white broadcloth shirt in your size, you can quickly obtain this information by checking online sites. However, buyer beware! You must know prices to be able to determine whether you are getting a fair price. Add the shipping and handling to find out whether you are getting a bargain. If the total price equals the price at your local mall, an online purchase saves you the time spent traveling to the store and waiting in line with tired cranky shoppers, only to find a tired cranky salesperson at the register. Now, you can be tired and cranky from shopping in the privacy of your own home.

Exercise 27.10: Pattern Practice

Using the patterns given here as guides, write your own phrases correctly punctuated with commas. Write two different phrases for each pattern given.

1. Twelve angry jurors (use a number and another describing word).
2. A shiny gold ring (use a color and another describing word).
3. Tall, lean man (use at least two body features).
4. Loving, compassionate eyes (use at least two emotions).
5. Solid steel shed (use a material and another describing word).

27f Commas with Dates, Addresses, Geographical Names, and Numbers

I. Commas with Dates
June 12, 1960,   (or)   12 June 1960

[No commas are needed if the day comes before the month.]

May, 1972,   (or)   May 1972

[Commas may be omitted if only the month and year are given.]

The order was shipped out on September 2, 1998, and not received until May 12, 1999.

The application deadline was 15 August 1999 with no exceptions.

2. Commas with Addresses
In a letter heading or on an envelope:

Jim Johnson, Jr.
1436 Westwood Drive
Birlingham, ID 98900

In a sentence:

You can write to Jim Johnson, Jr., 1436 Westwood Drive, Birlingham, Idaho 98900 for more information.

3. Commas with Geographical Names
Put commas after each item in a place name.

The planning committee has decided that Chicago, Illinois, will be the site for this year's conference and Washington, D.C., for next year's meeting.

4. Commas with Numbers
Separate long numbers into groups of three going from right to left. Commas with four-digit numbers are optional.

4,300,150
27,000
4,401   (or)   4401

Exercise 27.11: Proofreading Practice

Add commas in the following paragraph where they are needed.

The United States Government Printing Office has a catalog of thousands of popular books that it prints. If you'd like a copy of this catalog, write to the Superintendent of Documents United States Government Printing Office Washington DC 20402. There are books on agriculture, business and industry, careers, computers, diet and nutrition, health, history, hobbies, space exploration, and other topics. To pay for the books, you can send a check or money order, but more than 30000 customers every year set up deposit accounts with an initial deposit of at least fifty dollars. Future purchases can then be charged against this account. There are also Government Printing Office bookstores all around the country where you can browse before buying. They do not stock all 16000 titles in the inventory, but they do carry the more popular ones. For example, if you live in Birmingham, you can find the Government Printing Office bookstore in Roebuck Shopping City 9220-B Parkway East Birmingham Alabama 35206. There are other bookstores in Cleveland Ohio and Jacksonville Florida.

Exercise 27.12: Pattern Practice

Using the patterns and examples given here, write your own sentences correctly punctuated with commas. Write two different sentences for each pattern given.

Pattern A: Sentence with a date

Everyone knows that July 4, 1776, was a memorable day in American history.

Pattern B: Sentence with an address

His business address is Fontran Investments, 3902 Carroll Boulevard, Indianapolis, IN 46229.

Pattern C: Sentence with a geographical name

She enjoyed her car trip to Santa Fe, New Mexico, and plans to go again next spring.

Pattern D: Sentence with two numbers of four digits or more

The police estimated that more than 50,000 people took part in the demonstration, but the organizers of the event said they were sure that at least 100,000 had shown up.

27g Other Uses for Commas

Commas have other uses in sentences, including the following:

- To prevent misreading:

Confusing: To John Harrison had been a sort of idol.

Revised: To John, Harrison had been a sort of idol.

Confusing: On Thursday morning orders will be handled by Jim.

Revised: On Thursday, morning orders will be handled by Jim.   (or)

Revised: On Thursday morning, orders will be handled by Jim.

- To set off sharply contrasted elements at the end of a sentence:

    He was merely ignorant, not stupid.

- To set off a question:

    You're one of the senator's right-hand people, aren't you?

- To set off phrases at the end of the sentence that refer to the beginning or middle of the sentence:

    Shaundra waved enthusiastically at the departing boat, laughing happily.

- To set off direct quotations and after the first part of a quotation in a sentence:

    Becky said, "I'll see you tomorrow."

    "I was able," she explained, "to complete the job on time."

- To set off the opening greeting and closing of a letter:

    Dear David,

    Sincerely yours,

Exercise 27.13: Proofreading Practice

The following paragraph needs some punctuation. Add commas where they are needed.

There is new hope for infertile couples who want to have a child with genetic material from both parents. A New York University fertility specialist says he has developed a technique that adds an infertile woman's genetic material to a donor egg. Says one woman undergoing fertility treatments "This gives new hope to women who want a natural child." Dr. Jamie Grifo talked about the procedure, called oocyte nuclear transfer, with reporters. "The purpose of this is to give more options to infertile women" he said "but the procedure is still in the experimental phase." A pregnancy has not occurred yet, but the doctor has been given approval to complete the process on five women. Previously, a woman using a donor egg to become pregnant would have no genetic link to the child. "Now" says the doctor "a child conceived from this procedure would actually contain genetic material from three people." That the genes will come from the mother's nucleus and will determine how the child looks and acts is comforting for an infertile woman. As with all research ethical questions have been raised, but the research team maintains that this process is for infertility purposes not for cloning purposes. The process promises to be a major breakthrough in the area of infertility research.

■ **Exercise 27.14: Pattern Practice**

Using the patterns and examples given here, write your own sentences correctly punctuated with commas. Write two different sentences for each pattern given.

Pattern A: To prevent misreading

After eating, the cat stretched out near the fire and fell asleep.

[If the comma is left out, is there a possible misreading?]

Pattern B: To set off sharply contrasted elements at the end of the sentence

Everyone thought the car had stopped, not broken down.

Pattern C: To set off a question.

They were at the game, weren't they?

Pattern D: To set off a phrase at the end of a sentence that refers to the beginning or middle of the sentence

Jennie decided not to go out in the evening, preferring to enjoy the quiet in her apartment.

Pattern E: To set off direct quotations

Professor Bendini said, "Don't call me tonight to ask about your grade."

27h Unnecessary Commas

Putting in commas where they are not needed can mislead readers because unnecessary commas suggest pauses or interruptions not intended as part of the meaning. (Remember, though, that not every pause needs a comma.)

■ Don't separate a subject from its verb:

Unnecessary Comma: The eighteen-year-old in most states, is now considered an adult.

■ Don't put a comma between two verbs:

Unnecessary Comma: We laid out our music and snacks, and began to study.

■ Don't put a comma in front of every *and* or *but*.

Unnecessary Comma: We decided that we should not lend her the money, and that we should explain our decision.

[The *and* in this sentence joins two *that* clauses.]

■ Don't put a comma in front of a direct object. (Remember, clauses beginning with *that* can be direct objects.)

Unnecessary Comma: He explained to me, that he is afraid to fly on airplanes because of terrorists.

■ Don't put commas before a dependent clause when it comes after the main clause, except for extreme or strong contrast.

Unnecessary Comma: She was late, because her alarm clock was broken.

Extreme Contrast: She was still quite upset, although she did win an Oscar Award.

■ Don't put a comma after *such as* or *especially*.

Unnecessary Comma: There are several kinds of dark bread from which to choose, such as, whole wheat, rye, oatmeal, and bran bread.

Exercise 27.15: Proofreading Practice

In the following paragraph, there are some unnecessary commas. Put an X *under the commas that should be removed.*

Although the dangers of alcohol are well known, and have been widely publicized, there may be another danger that we haven't yet realized. Several controlled studies of drunken animals have indicated to researchers, that in an accident there is more swelling and hemorrhaging in the spinal cord, and in the brain, if alcohol is present in the body. To find out if this is true in humans, researchers studied the data on more than one million drivers in automobile crashes. One thing already known is, that drunks are more likely to be driving fast, and to have seat belts unfastened. Of course, their coordination is also poorer than that of sober people, so drunks are more likely to get into serious accidents. To compensate for this, researchers grouped accidents according to type, speed, and degree of vehicle deformation, and found that alcohol still appears to make people more vulnerable to injury. The conclusion of the study was, that the higher the level of alcohol in the person's body, the greater the chance of being injured or killed. In minor crashes, drunk drivers were more than four times as likely to be killed as sober ones. In average crashes, drunk drivers were more than three times as likely to be killed, and in the worst ones, drunks were almost twice as likely to die. Overall, drunks were more than twice as likely to die in an accident, because of the alcohol they drank.

Exercise 27.16: Pattern Practice

Using the sentence patterns and examples given here, write your own sentences correctly punctuated with commas. Write two different sentences for each pattern given.

Pattern A: Subject + verb + object + *and* + verb + object.

Before the test <u>Midori</u> <u>studied</u> the botany <u>notes</u> from the lectures and
  (subject) *(verb)* *(object)*

<u>reread</u> the <u>textbook</u> several times.
(verb) *(object)*

Pattern B: Independent clause + dependent clause.

<u>He decided not to live in the dorm</u> <u>because it was so expensive.</u>
  (independent clause) *(dependent clause)*

Pattern C: A sentence with a *that* clause or phrase as a direct object.

My high school physical education teacher often told me <u>that eating a good</u>
(that clause)

<u>breakfast</u> was an important part of keeping in good shape.

Pattern D: A sentence with a subject that has many words modifying it.

Almost <u>everyone</u> attending the recent meeting of the union <u>decided</u> not
   (subject)   *(verb)*

to vote for the strike.

28 Apostrophes (')

28a Apostrophes with Possessives

Use the apostrophe to show possession (see 18).

- For singular nouns, use *'s.*

the book's author   a flower's smell

- For a singular noun ending in *-s,* the *s* after the apostrophe is optional if the *s* doesn't make the pronunciation difficult.

James's car   (or)   James' car
the grass's color   (or)   the grass' color

But if adding the *s* after the apostrophe makes the pronunciation difficult, omit the *s.* This happens especially when the next word starts with *s* or *z.*

Euripides' story   [Trying to say *Euripides's story* is a bit difficult.]

- For plural nouns ending in *-s,* add only an apostrophe.

both teams' colors   six days' vacation

- For plural nouns not ending in *-s* (such as *children, men,* or *mice*), use *'s.*

the children's game   six men's coats

- For the indefinite pronoun (pronouns ending in *-body* and *-one,* such as *no one, someone,* and *everybody*), use *'s.*

no one's fault   someone's hat

- For compound words, add *'s* to the last word.

brother-in-law's job   everyone else's preference

- For joint ownership by two or more nouns, add *'s* after the last noun in the group.

Mary and Tom's house   bar and restaurant's parking lot

■ For individual ownership when several nouns are used, add 's after each noun.

Mary's and Tom's houses.   [This indicates that there are two houses, one belonging to Mary and the other to Tom.]

 Using Apostrophes

1. When you aren't sure if you need the apostrophe, turn the phrase into an "of the" phrase.

the day's effort = the effort of the day

2. Occasionally, you'll have both the "of the" phrase and the apostrophe.

the painting of Cesar's   [Without the 's this phrase would mean that Cesar was pictured in the painting as the subject.]

3. When you aren't sure whether the word is plural or not, remember this sequence:

■ First, write the word.
■ Then, write the plural.
■ Then, add the possessive apostrophe marker.

Thus, everything to the left of the apostrophe is the word and its plural, if needed.

Word (and plural)	Possessive Marker	Result
cup	's	cup's handle
cups	'	cups' handles

28b Apostrophes with Contractions

Use the apostrophe to mark the omitted letter or letters in contractions.

it's = it is   don't = do not   that's = that is
o'clock = of the clock   '79 = 1979

Jimmy's going = Jimmy is going   [very informal usage]

28c Apostrophes with Plurals

Use apostrophes to form the plurals of lowercase letters and abbreviations with periods. For capital letters, abbreviations without periods, numbers, symbols, and words used as words, the apostrophe before the -s is optional if the plural is clear. In all cases, the 's is neither italicized nor underlined.

Necessary apostrophes:

| *a*'s | B.A.'s | *A*'s |

Optional apostrophes:

9s	(or)	9's
1950s	(or)	1950's
UFOs	(or)	UFO's
ands	(or)	and's
&s	(or)	&'s

HINT   **Using Apostrophes Consistently**

Be consistent in choosing one or the other of these options.

28d Unnecessary Apostrophes

Do not use the apostrophe with possessive pronouns or with the regular plural forms of nouns. Possessive pronouns do not need apostrophes.

| his | hers | its | |
| ours | yours | theirs | whose |

Is that umbrella ~~yours'~~ *yours* or mine?   I think ~~it's~~ *its* leg is broken.

Remember, *it's* and *who's* are contractions, not possessives.

| it's = it is | **It's** a good time to clean out the closet. |
| who's = who is | **Who's** going to run for vice-president? |

Do not use the apostrophe with regular plural forms of nouns that do not show possession.

The ~~Smiths'~~ *Smiths* went to Disney World for vacation.

Exercise 28.1: Proofreading Practice

The following paragraph has some words that should show possession. Add apostrophes where they are needed.

Although teachers commonly use tests to grade their students learning, taking a test can also help students learn. Peoples memories seem to be more accurate after reading some material and taking a test than after merely reading the material with no testing. In fact, studies have shown that students who take several tests learn even more than those who take only one test after reading material. Although everyones ability to memorize material generally depends on how well the material was studied, scientists research does indicate that test taking aids memory.

The type of test is also important because multiple-choice exams help us to put facts together better while fill-in-the-blank questions promote recall of specific facts. These questions ability to test different types of learning suggests that teachers ought to include different types of tests throughout the semester.

Exercise 28.2: Pattern Practice

Using the patterns and examples given here, write your own sentences correctly punctuated with apostrophes. Write two different sentences for each pattern given.

Pattern A: Two singular nouns with 's.

If **Daniel's** car doesn't start, we can borrow **Alicia's** van.

Pattern B: A singular noun ending in -s with '

Does anyone know Mr. **Myconos'** zip code?

Pattern C: Two plural nouns ending in -s with '

Although the **girls'** coats were on sale, all the **boys'** coats were regular price.

Pattern D: A plural noun not ending in -s with 's

We helped collect money for the **Children's** Fund.

Pattern E: An indefinite pronoun with 's

I would really appreciate **someone's** help right now.

Pattern F: One compound word with 's

It was the **president-elect's** decision not to campaign on TV.

Pattern G: One example of joint ownership with 's.

The next morning he felt the **pizza and beer's** effects.

Exercise 28.3: Proofreading Practice

In the following informal paragraph, there are contractions that should be marked. Add apostrophes where they are needed.

Dance clubs used to be for dancing, but that was before moshing and crowd surfing became popular. Young adults flock to dance clubs and concerts to enter mosh pits, which are masses of flailing guys who wave their arms and slam into each other. "Its a way of communicating and having fun," says one mosher. However, theres more to this activity than meets the eye. Whats supposed to be fun has turned into a liability for club owners. Recently, a young man died from head injuries after crowd surfing during a concert. His parents sued the club owner for negligence and inability to control the crowd. The lawsuit even alleges that the bouncer pushed the young man off the stage and caused him to fall and hit his head. The owner claims that "its mosh at your own risk." In fact, many concert producers and club owners have been putting disclaimers on the back of tickets. Another owner claims, "Youre responsible for yourself out there." Some bands request that fans refrain from moshing, but others encourage this dangerous behavior. It looks as if there will continue to be a core group of moshers, but to reduce liability, club owners are hoping for a resurgence of ballroom dancing.

Exercise 28.4: Pattern Practice

Using the patterns and examples given here, write your own sentences correctly punctuated with apostrophes. Write one sentence for each pattern given.

Pattern A: A sentence with *its* and *it's*

Whenever **it's** raining out, our cat races inside the house to keep **its** fur dry.

Pattern B: A sentence with two contractions

They're quite sure they **didn't** owe us any money.

Pattern C: A sentence with *who's* and *whose*

I wonder **whose** skates those are and whether you know **who's** going with us.

Exercise 28.5: Proofreading Practice

The following paragraph needs apostrophes to mark plurals. Add the apostrophe even if it is optional.

In the 1990s, the use of standardized tests, such as the SATs for high school juniors, has come under scrutiny. Critics say that these commonly used tests do not reflect a student's ability, nor do they project a level of success in college. In the 1970s and 1980s, the SATs were the primary factor for entrance to college. A movement to consider other factors such as GPAs, activities, and the interview began after educational leaders explored the merits of alternative assessment. Alternative assessment evaluates the whole student and frowns upon ranking the number of As on a transcript and GPAs. However, the SATs are an American institution, and thousands of high school students are still subjected to this procedure each spring. Perhaps in the 2000s the SATs will be a thing of the past.

Exercise 28.6: Pattern Practice

Using the patterns and examples given here, write your own sentences correctly punctuated with apostrophes. Write a sentence for each pattern given.

Pattern A: The plural of two lowercase letter

On his new typewriter the **e's** and **c's** looked alike.

Pattern B: The plural of two abbreviations without periods

The electronics stores sold their **TVs** at a better discount than their **CDs.**

Pattern C: The plural of a number and a capital letter

There were several **3's** in her new license plate number and some **M's** too.

Pattern D: The plural of a date and a word

He dressed like a **1960s** hippie and sprinkled lots of "**far out's**" and other outdated slang in his speech.

Exercise 28.7: Proofreading Practice

Add apostrophes as needed in the following paragraph.

Mention the words *day care* to working parents, and a collective sigh can be heard. There is a shortage of reliable day-care centers in the United States, and the situation is not improving. In fact, its getting worse. The need for child-care workers and centers has increased because of the number of mothers returning to the work force. Because of the high cost of living in certain areas, many women reenter the work force after having children. For example, New York City and Los Angeles have high rates of women working outside the home. One working mother said, "Ill pay a high price to know my childs care is excellent, but I cant even find child care near my home." Many women are accepting positions in companies simply because the companies offer on-site centers for day care. Other companies offer some type of reimbursement to employees paying for child care. "The best situation," says one mother, "is to have a family member care for your child." However, women agree that this is usually not possible in this day and age. The need for affordable, reliable child care will continue to grow.

Exercise 28.8: Pattern Practice

Using the patterns and examples given here, write your own correctly punctuated sentences. Write a sentence for each pattern given.

Pattern A: A sentence with two possessive pronouns

I can never remember whether the car is **hers** or **his.**

Pattern B: A sentence with *it's* and *its*

It's never clear whether that dumb dog wants **its** ears scratched or **its** water dish filled.

Pattern C: A sentence with a plural noun that does not show possession and a plural noun that does show possession.

There are six pages of **ads** in that magazine with different **dealers'** prices.

29 Semicolons (;)

The semicolon is a stronger mark of punctuation than a comma. It is almost like a period but does not come at the end of a sentence. Semicolons are used only between closely related equal elements, that is, between independent clauses and between items in a series. See the table "Commas and Semicolons in Sentences" in Chapter 27.

29a Semicolons in Compound Sentences

Use the semicolon when joining independent clauses not joined by the seven connectors that require commas: *and, but, for, or, nor, so,* or *yet.*

Two patterns for using semicolons are the following:

- Independent clause + semicolon + independent clause

  He often watched TV reruns; she preferred to read instead.

- Independent clause + semicolon + joining word or transition + comma + independent clause

  He often watched TV reruns; however, she preferred to read instead.

Some joining words or transitional phrases must be preceded by a semicolon.

after all,	finally,	in the second place,
also,	for example,	instead,
as a result,	furthermore,	meanwhile,
at any rate,	hence,	nevertheless,
besides,	however,	on the contrary,
by the way,	in addition,	on the other hand,
consequently,	in fact,	still,
even so,	in other words,	therefore,

Variations in Compound Sentences

A semicolon can be used instead of a comma with two independent clauses joined by *and, but, for, or, nor, so,* or *yet* when one or more of the clauses has its own comma. The semicolon thus makes a clearer break between the two independent clauses.

- Independent clause with commas + semicolon + independent clause:

  Congressman Dow, who headed the investigation, leaked the story to the
  (independent clause with commas)

  press; but he would not answer questions during an interview.

A colon can be used between two independent clauses when the second clause restates the first (see Chapter 30).

Her diet was strictly vegetarian: she ate no meat, fish, poultry, or eggs.

Exercise 29.1: Proofreading Practice

In the following paragraph, there are compound sentences that need punctuation. Add semicolons and commas where they are needed.

Even before children begin school, many parents think they should take part in their children's education and help the children to develop mentally. Such parents usually consider reading to young toddlers important moreover they help the children memorize facts such as the days of the week and the numbers from one to ten. Now it is becoming clear that parents can begin helping when the children are babies. One particular type of parent communication, encouraging the baby to pay attention to new things, seems especially promising in helping babies's brains develop for example handing the baby a toy encourages the baby to notice something new. Some studies seem to indicate that this kind of activity helped children score higher on intelligence tests several years later. Parents interested in helping their babies' brain development have been encouraged by this study to point to new things in the baby's environment as part of their communication with their babies thus their children's education can begin in the crib.

Exercise 29.2: Pattern Practice

Using the patterns and examples given here, write your own sentences correctly punctuated with semicolons. Write two sentences for each pattern given.

Pattern A: Independent clause + semicolon + independent clause

I didn't know which job I wanted; I was too confused to decide.
    (independent clause)   *(independent clause)*

Pattern B: Independent clause + semicolon + joining word or transitional phrase + comma + independent clause.

Three friends recommended that movie; however, I was bored by it.
    (independent clause)   *(joining word)* *(indep. clause)*

Pattern C: Independent clause + comma + *and* (or) *but* + independent clause

               (comma)
The shirt is a little small, but he has nothing else to wear.
 (independent clause) *(joining word)*   *(independent clause)*

29b Semicolons in a Series

For clarity, use semicolons to separate a series of items in which one or more of the items contain commas. Semicolons are also preferred if items in the series are especially long.

- Items with their own commas:

Among her favorite videotapes to rent were old Cary Grant movies, such as *Arsenic and Old Lace*; any of Woody Allen's movies; and children's classics, including *The Sound of Music, Willy Wonka and the Chocolate Factory*, and *The Wizard of Oz*.

- Long items in a series:

When planning the bus schedule, they took into consideration the length of travel time between cities where stops would be made; the number of people likely to get on at each stop; and the times when the bus would arrive at major cities where connections would be made with other buses.

29c Semicolons with Quotation Marks

If a semicolon is needed, put it after the quotation marks.

Her answer to every question I asked was, "I'll have to think about that"; she clearly had no answers to offer.

29d Unnecessary Semicolons

Don't use a semicolon between unequal parts of a sentence, such as between a clause and a phrase or between an independent clause and a dependent clause. Don't use a semicolon in place of a dash, comma, or colon.

They wanted to see the government buildings in the city; especially the
(should be a comma)
courthouse and the post office.

He kept trying to improve his tennis serve; because that was the weakest
(should be no punctuation)
part of his game.

When Mike kept spinning his car wheels to get out of the sand, I realized he was really just persistent; not stupid.
(should be a dash)

The office clearly needed several more pieces of equipment; a computer,
(should be a colon)
an answering machine, and a paper shredder.

Exercise 29.3: Proofreading Practice

In the following paragraph, there are some unnecessary semicolons to delete and some necessary semicolons to add. Put an X by semicolons that are incorrect, and write in the appropriate punctuation. Add semicolons and other punctuation where needed, and replace any wrong punctuation with semicolons. Underline the added semicolons and other punctuation. Also underline the semicolons you put in to replace wrong punctuation.

In the not-too-distant future, when airline passengers board their flights, they will be able to enjoy a number of new conveniences; such as choosing their snacks and drinks from onboard vending machines, selecting movies, TV programs, or video games for screens mounted on the seat in front of them, and making hotel and car-rental reservations from an onboard computer. Such features are what aircraft designers envision within the next five years for passenger jets. Their plans, though, may not be realized until much further in the future, if ever. But the ideas reflect the airline industry's hopes. If fare wars stop and ticket prices stabilize, passengers may begin choosing different airlines on the basis of comfort, not cost; if that happens, airlines will have to be ready with new and better in-flight features. A Boeing Company executive says that "cabin environment will be a major factor;" that is, designers must make the cabin so attractive that it will offset lower fares on other airlines. The problem, however, is added weight caused by some of the suggested features; such as; computers, video screens, and more elaborate kitchens. Added weight will mean that the plane consumes more fuel; thus driving up the price of the ticket. Still, some carriers, determined to find answers, are studying ways to use the new services to generate income; particularly in the area of commercial-supported or pay-as-you-use video entertainment.

Exercise 29.4: Pattern Practice

Using the patterns and examples given here, write your own sentences correctly punctuated with semicolons. Write one sentence for each pattern given.

Pattern A: Semicolons with a series of items that have their own commas

The McDonnell Douglas Corporation's new wide-body jet, scheduled to begin service soon, is designed for greater passenger comfort and will have refrigerators to hold fresh food; aisles wide enough so that passengers, even heavyset people, can walk past a serving cart; and high-resolution video monitors for every ten rows.

Pattern B: A comma before the phrase *such as*

Other planes are being built with changes sought by passengers, such as larger overhead storage bins, handrails above the seats, and fresher air in the cabins.

Pattern C: A semicolon after the quotation marks

One airline executive says that, for now, it is "hard to justify the costs of some suggested innovations"; however, airlines must be ready to meet the challenge if more passengers start choosing their carrier on the basis of comfort.

30 Colons (:)

The colon is used in more formal writing to call attention to words that follow it.

30a Colons to Announce Elements at the End of a Sentence

Use the colon at the end of a sentence to introduce a list, an explanation (or intensification) of the sentence, or an example.

The university offers five majors in engineering: mechanical, electrical, civil, industrial, and chemical engineering.

After weeks of intensive study, there was only one thing she really wanted: a vacation.   [A dash can also be used here, though it is more informal.]

> **HINT**   **The Meaning of the Colon**
>
> Think of the colon as the equivalent of the phrase *that is.* For most elements at the end of the sentence, you could have said *that is* where the colon is needed.
>
> > When the company president decided to boost morale among the employees, the executive board announced an improvement that would please everyone: pay raises.   [: = that is]

30b Colons to Separate Independent Clauses

Use the colon instead of a semicolon to separate two independent clauses when the second amplifies or restates the first clause. Again, think of the colon as the equivalent of *that is.* An independent clause following a colon may begin with a capital or lowercase letter, although the lowercase letter is preferred.

Some say that lobbying groups exert too much influence on Congress: they can buy votes as a result of their large contributions to the right senators and representatives.

30c Colons to Announce Long Quotations

Use the colon to announce long quotations (more than one sentence) or a quotation not introduced by such words as *said, remarked,* or *stated.*

The head of the company's research department, Ms. Mann, said: "We recommended budgeting $1 million for the development of that type of software, but we were turned down. We regrouped and tried to think of a new approach to change their minds. We got nowhere."

He offered an apology to calm her down: "I'm truly sorry that we were not able to help you."

30d Colons in Salutations and Between Elements

Use the colon in the salutation of a formal or business letter, in scriptural and time references, between a title and subtitle, with proportions, between city and publisher in bibliographical format, and after an introductory label.

Dear Mayor O'Daly: 6:15 a.m.
Genesis 1:8   a scale of 4:1
"Jerusalem: A City United"   New York: Midland Books

30e Colons with Quotation Marks

If a colon is needed, put it after the closing quotation mark.

"To err is human; to repeat an error is stupid": that was my chemistry teacher's favorite saying in the lab.

30f Unnecessary Colons

Do not use the colon after a verb or a phrase like *such as* or *consisted of.*

The people who applied were: Mr. Orland, Mr. Johnson, and Ms. Lassiter.
(no punctuation needed)

She preferred a noncontact sport such as: tennis, swimming, or golf.
(no punctuation needed)

HINT **Replacing Unnecessary Colons**

When you revise for unnecessary colons, you can either omit any punctuation or add a word or phrase such as *the following* after the verb.

The committee members who voted for the amendment were the following: Mia Lungren, Sam Heffelt, and Alexander Zubrev.

Exercise 30.1: Proofreading Practice

The following paragraph needs some colons and has some correct and incorrect colons. Add colons where they should be, and put an X near incorrect colons or other incorrect punctuation. If other punctuation is needed instead, put it above the incorrect punctuation. Underline colons that are added.

When the Apollo astronauts brought back bags of moon rocks, it was expected that the rocks would provide some answers to a perennial question; the origin of the moon. Instead, the moon rocks suggested a number of new theories. One that is gaining more supporters is called: the giant impact theory. Alan Smith, a lunar scientist, offers an explanation of the giant impact theory "Recently acquired evidence suggests that the moon was born of a monstrous collision between a primordial, just-formed Earth and a protoplanet the size of Mars." This evidence comes from modeling such a collision on powerful supercomputers. The theory proposes the following sequence of events (1) as Earth was forming, it was struck a glancing blow by a projectile the size of Mars; (2) a jet of vapor then spurted out, moving so fast that some of it escaped from Earth and the rest condensed into pebble-sized rock fragments; and (3) gravitational attraction fused this cloud of pebbles into the moon. Several reasons make some scientists favor this theory, for example it dovetails with what is known about the moon's chemistry, and it explains why the moon's average composition resembles Earth's. Another lunar scientist says, "We may be close to tracking down the real answer."

Exercise 30.2: Pattern Practice

Using the patterns and examples given here, write your own sentences correctly punctuated with colons. Write one sentence for each pattern given.

Pattern A: Sentence with a list following a colon

The coffee shop offered samples of five new coffee flavors: mocha java, chocolate fudge, Swiss almond, cinnamon, and French roast.

Pattern B: Independent clause + colon + second independent clause that restates or explains the first clause

That cat has only one problem: she thinks she is a human.

Pattern C: Sentence with a quotation not introduced by words such as *said, remarked,* or *stated*

Jim clarified his views on marriage: "It should be a commitment for a life-time, not a trial run for a relationship."

3I Quotation Marks (" ")

3Ia Quotation Marks with Direct and Indirect Quotations

Use quotation marks with direct quotations of prose, poetry, and dialogue.

I. Quotation Marks with Prose Quotations

Direct quotations are the exact words said by someone or the exact words you saw in print and are recopying. Use a set of quotation marks to enclose direct quotations included in your writing.

Indirect quotations are not the exact words said by someone else but the rephrasing or summarizing of someone else's words. Do not use quotation marks for indirect quotations. (For more information, see 31c and 46d.)

If the quotation extends more than four typed or handwritten lines on a page, set the quotation off by indenting ten spaces from the left margin and double-space the quotation. Do not use quotation marks for this indented material.

■ Direct quotation of a whole sentence: Use a capital letter to start the first word of the quotation.

Mr. and Mrs. Allen, owners of a 300-acre farm, said, "We refuse to use that pesticide because it might pollute the nearby wells."

■ Direct quotation of part of a sentence: Do not use a capital letter to start the first word of the quotation.

Mr. and Mrs. Allen stated that they "refuse to use that pesticide" because of possible water pollution.

■ Indirect quotation:

According to their statement to the local papers, the Allens will not use the pesticide because of potential water pollution.

- Quotation within a quotation: Use single quotation marks (' at the beginning and ' at the end) for a quotation enclosed inside another quotation.

  The agricultural reporter for the newspaper explained, "When I talked to the Allens last week, they said, 'We refuse to use that pesticide.'"

- If you leave some words out of a quotation, use an ellipsis mark (three spaced periods) to indicate omitted words. If you need to insert something within a quotation, use a pair of brackets [ ] to enclose the addition. (See 34d.)

- Full direct quotation:

  The welfare agency representative said, "We are unable to help this family whom we would like to help because we don't have the funds to do so."

- Omitted material with ellipsis:

  The welfare agency representative said, "We are unable to help this family . . . because we don't have the funds to do so."

- Added material with brackets:

  The welfare agency representative explained that they are "unable to help this family whom [they] would like to help."

2. Quotation Marks in Poetry

When you quote a single line of poetry, write it like other short quotations. Two lines can be run into your text with a slash mark to indicate the end of the first line. Leave a space before and after the slash mark. If the quotation is three lines or longer, set it off like a longer quotation. (Some people prefer to set off two-line quotations for emphasis.) Quote the poem line by line as it appears on the original page, and do not use quotation marks. Indent ten spaces from the left margin. (For more information, see 34b.)

- Poetry quoted in your writing:

  In his poem "Mending Wall," Robert Frost says: "Something there is that doesn't love a wall, / That sends the frozen-ground-swell under it."

- Longer quotation from a poem set off from the sentence:

  In his poem "Mending Wall," Robert Frost questions the building of barriers and walls:
  > Before I built a wall I'd ask to know
  > What I was walling in or walling out,
  > And to whom I was like to give offense.

3. Quotation Marks in Dialogue

Write each person's speech, however short, as a separate paragraph. Use commas to set off *he said* or *she said*. Closely related bits of narrative can be included in the paragraph. If one person's speech goes on for several paragraphs, use quotation marks at the beginning of each paragraph but not at the end of every paragraph before the last one. To signal the end of the person's speech, use quotation marks at the end of the last paragraph. (For more information, see 46d.)

"May I help you?" the clerk asked as she approached the customer.

"No, thanks," responded the woman in a quiet voice.

"We have a special sale today on sweaters," persisted the salesperson. She continued to stand next to the customer, waiting for the woman to indicate why she was there.

"How nice for you," the customer replied as she walked out, leaving a puzzled clerk wondering what she meant.

31b Quotation Marks for Minor Titles and Parts of Wholes

Use quotation marks for titles of parts of larger works (titles of book chapters, magazine articles, and episodes of television and radio series) and for short or minor works (songs, short stories, essays, short poems, one-act plays, and other literary works that are shorter than three-act plays or book length).

For larger, complete works, see Chapter 38 on italics. Neither quotation marks nor italics are used for referring to the Bible or legal documents.

Whenever he got involved with hard work in his garden, he'd hum his favorite song, "Old Man River."

Mark Twain's short story "The Celebrated Jumping Frog of Calaveras County" helped frog-jumping contests gain their great popularity.

She wanted to memorize the first eighteen chapters of Genesis.

31c Quotation Marks for Words

Use quotation marks for words that are used as words rather than for their meaning, and for words used in special ways, such as for irony (when the writer means the opposite of what is being said). Italics (underlining) can also be used. Be consistent throughout your papers in choosing either quotation marks or italics.

Quotation marks can also be used to introduce unfamiliar or technical terms when they are used for the first time (and defined). No quotation marks are needed in later uses of the word after it has been introduced the first time.

"Neat" is a word I wish she'd omit from her vocabulary.

The three-year-old held up his "work of art" for the teacher to admire.

31d Use of Other Punctuation with Quotation Marks

Put commas and periods before the second set of quotation marks. When a reference follows the quotation, put the period after the reference. (For more information, see 46d.)

"The Politics of Hunger," a recent article in *Political Quarterly*, discussed the United Nations' use of military force to help victims of hunger.

He said, "I may forget your name, but I never remember a face."

Jenkins said, "Moshenberg's style of writing derives from his particular form of wit" (252).

Put the colon and semicolon after the quotation marks.

The critic called the movie "a potential Academy Award winner"; I thought it was a flop.

Put the dash, question mark, and exclamation point before the second set of quotation marks when these punctuation marks apply to the quotation and after the second set of quotation marks when the mark applies to the whole sentence.

He asked, "Do you need this book?"   [The quotation here is a question.]

Does Dr. Lim always say to her students, "You must work harder"? [The quotation here is a statement, but it is included in a sentence that is a question.]

31e Unnecessary Quotation Marks

Don't put quotation marks around the titles of your essays (though someone else will use quotation marks if referring to your essay), and don't use quotation marks for common nicknames, bits of humor, technical terms, and trite or well-known expressions.

The crew rowed together like "a well-oiled machine."

[No quotation marks needed.]

He decided to save his money until he could buy a "digital audio tape deck."

[No quotation marks needed.]

Exercise 31.1: Proofreading Practice

Add quotation marks where they are needed in the following paragraph, and delete any quotation marks that are incorrect, unnecessary, or inappropriately placed. Place an X by the line where quotation marks are deleted.

Remember Silverton wine coolers? Silverton, like hundreds of other products that appeared in the same year, was pulled from the shelf after it failed to gain a market. Silverton didn't seem to have any connotation as a cooler, explains G. F. Strousel, the company's vice-president in charge of sales. Every year new products appear briefly on the shelf and disappear, and established products that no longer have "customer appeal" are canceled as well. "Either way," experts say, "the signs that point to failure are the same." Companies looking to cut their losses pay attention to such signs. In a recent newspaper article titled *Over 75% of Business Ideas Are Flops,* T. M. Weir, a professor of marketing, explains that products that don't grow but maintain their percentage of the market are known as cash cows, and those that are declining in growth and in market share are called dipping dogs. Says Weir, "Marketers plot the growth and decline of products, especially of the dipping dogs, very closely." According to several sources at a New York research firm that studies new product development, "the final decision to stop making a product is a financial one." When the "red ink" flows, the product is pulled.

Exercise 31.2: Pattern Practice

Using the patterns and examples given here, write your own correctly punctuated sentences. Write two sentences for each pattern given.

Pattern A: Direct quotation with a whole sentence being quoted

The president of the university stated, "It is my fervent hope that next year there will be no tuition increase."

Pattern B: Direct quotation with a part of a sentence being quoted

The president of the university vowed that next year "there will be no tuition increase."

Pattern C: A quotation within a quotation

The announcer said, "You heard it live on this station, Coach Williams predicting that his team 'will run away with the game tomorrow.'"

Pattern D: Dialogue between two speakers

"Can you help me with the chem lab report?" Ivan's roommate asked.

"I'll try, but my notes aren't very complete," Ivan said as he ambled off to turn up the stereo.

"That's OK. They have to be better than mine."

Pattern E: Quotation marks with a minor title or a title of a part of a whole work

In his autobiography Hsao titled his first chapter "In the Beginning."

Pattern F: Quotation marks with a word used as a word

I can't believe that any grown person really says "Golly, gee whiz."

32 Hyphens (hyph)

32a Hyphens to Divide Words

Use the hyphen to indicate that the last part of a word appears on the next line. Be sure to divide words between syllables.

Check your dictionary to see how words are split into syllables. When you split words, do so in a way that is most helpful to your reader. Follow these guidelines:

- Don't divide one-syllable words.
- Don't leave one or two letters at the end of the line.
- Don't put fewer than three letters on the next line.
- Don't divide the last word in a paragraph or the last word on a page.

Wrong: She took the big package a-
part very carefully.

[If there is no room for the word on the first line and the syllable to be left at the end of the line is only one letter, put the whole word on the next line.]

Wrong: Twila was so hungry she ordered panc-
akes, eggs, and sausage.

Revised: Twila was so hungry she ordered pan-
cakes, eggs, and sausage.

[If the first syllable contains two or more letters, it can be left at the end of the line.]

32b Hyphens to Form Compound Words

Use the hyphen to form compound words. Hyphens are used in compounds of all kinds, including fractions and numbers that are spelled out, from twenty-one to ninety-nine. Because accepted usage and dictionaries vary, words forming compounds may be written separately, as one word, or connected by hyphens.

mother-in-law   thirty-six

clear-cut   two-thirds

For words in a series, use hyphens as follows:

mother-, father-, and sister-in-law

four-, five-, and six-page essays

32c Hyphens to Join Word Units

Use the hyphen to join two or more words that work together and serve as a single descriptive word before a noun. When the words come after the noun, they are usually not hyphenated. Don't use hyphens with -ly modifiers.

The office needed up-to-date scores.	(or)	The office needed scores that were up to date.
The repair involved a six-inch pipe.	(or)	The repair involved a pipe that was six inches long.

They brought along their nine-year-old son.	(or)	They brought along their son, who was nine years old.

32d Hyphens to Join Prefixes, Suffixes, and Letters to a Word

Use hyphens between words and the prefixes *self-*, *all-*, and *ex-*. For other prefixes, such as *anti-*, *non-*, *pro-*, and *co-*, use the dictionary as a guide. Use the hyphen when you add a prefix to a capitalized word (for example, *mid-August*) and when you add the suffix *-elect* to a word. In addition, use the hyphen to join single letters to words.

co-author	self-supporting
anti-abortion	president-elect
pro-American	T-shirt
D-day	all-encompassing

The hyphen is also used to avoid doubling vowels and tripling consonants.

anti-intellectual (not: antiintellectual)

bell-like (not: belllike)

32e Hyphens to Avoid Ambiguity

Use the hyphen to avoid confusion between words that are spelled alike but have different meanings.

re-creation (to make again)	vs.	recreation (fun)
re-cover (cover again)	vs.	recover (regain health)
co-op (something jointly owned)	vs.	coop (cage for fowls)

Exercise 32.1: Proofreading Exercise

Add hyphens where they are needed in the following paragraph and delete any that are incorrect. Place an X by the line where a hyphen is deleted.

For health conscious people who cringe at the thought of using a toothpaste with preserves and dyes, there are now alternative toothpastes made entirely from plants. One brand of these new, all natural toothpastes advertises that its paste includes twenty nine different herbs, root and flower-extracts, and seaweed. Some of these toothpastes have a pleasant taste and appearance, but the owner of a San Francisco health food store decided not to carry one brand because it is a reddish brown paste. "When squeezed from a tube, it resembles a fat earthworm," she explained. She prefers a brand made of propolis, the sticky stuff bees use to line their hives, and myrrh. Another brand, a black paste made of charred eggplant powder, clay, and seaweed, is favored by the hard core macrobiotic crowd. This interest in natural toothpastes may be cyclical, explains the director of an oral health institute. He recalls a gray striped, mint flavored paste from the Philippines that sought to capitalize on a spurt of interest several years ago. It was a big-seller for a few months and then disappeared.

Exercise 32.2: Pattern Practice

Using the patterns and examples given here, write your own correctly hyphenated sentences. Write one sentence for each pattern given.

Pattern A: Hyphen that splits a word at the end of a line

Pattern B: Hyphen with at least two compound words

My great-grandmother worked in a garment factory for twenty-seven years.

Pattern C: Hyphen with two words serving as a single descriptive word in front of a noun (and, if possible, the same two words after the noun)

The plastic-trimmed suitcase was promptly returned by unhappy customers who said the plastic trim fell off within several weeks.

Pattern D: Hyphen with prefixes or suffixes

The slogan on her T-shirt announced her pro-choice views.

33 End Punctuation

At the end of a sentence, use a period, a question mark, or an exclamation point.

33a Periods (.)

1. Periods at the End of a Sentence

Use the period to end sentences that are statements, mild commands, indirect questions, or polite questions where an answer is not really expected.

He's one of those people who doesn't like pets.   [statement]

Hand in your homework by noon tomorrow.   [mild command]

She asked how she could improve her golf game.   [indirect question]

Would you please let me know when the bus arrives.   [polite question]

2. Periods with Abbreviations

Use the period after most abbreviations.

Mr.	Mrs.	etc.	9 P.M.
Ms.	Ave.	A.D.	Ph.D.
R.S.V.P.	Inc.	U.S.A.	Dr.

Don't use a second period if the abbreviation is at the end of the sentence.

She studied for her R.N.

Periods are not needed after certain common abbreviations, the names of well-known companies, agencies, organizations, and the state abbreviations used by the U.S. Postal Service.

NATO   NBA   CIA   YMCA
TV   NFL   FBI   DNA
TX (and other state postal abbreviations)

3. Periods with Quotation Marks

Put periods that follow quotations inside the quotation marks.

As she said, "No one is too old to try something new."

However, if there is a reference to a source, put the period after the reference.

Hemmings states, "This is, by far, the best existing example of Renaissance art" (144).

Exercise 33.1: Proofreading Practice

Add periods where they are needed in the following paragraph. Take out any periods used incorrectly. Place an X by a line where a period is deleted.

Several years ago the nation's print and broadcast media joined with advertising agencies to launch a massive media campaign against drugs. Some, like ABC-TV, announced that they would donate prime-time T.V. spots, but CBS Inc, while agreeing to cooperate, announced its intention to continue to commit funds for campaigns for other public issues such as AIDS prevention. James R Daly, a spokesman for the anti-drug campaign, said, "We are glad to see other companies joining in to help the campaign". For example, the Kodak Co. donated the film needed for TV spots, and in Washington, DC, a group of concerned parents volunteered to do additional fund-raising. In the first two years of this media campaign, more than $500 million was raised Says Dr Harrison Rublin, a leading spokesperson for one of the fund-raising groups, "One thirty-second ad aired at 8 PM is ten times more effective than a hundred brochures on the subject".

Exercise 33.2: Pattern Practice

Using the patterns and examples given here, write your own correctly punctuated sentences. Write two sentences for each pattern given.

Pattern A: Statement (with a period at the end)

Luis started guitar lessons at the age of six.

Pattern B: Mild command (with a period at the end)

Return that pencil to me when you are done.

Pattern C: Indirect quotation (with a period at the end)

Jennifer asked the gas station attendant whether he had a wrench.

Pattern D: Polite question (with a period at the end)

Would you please send the material I am requesting as soon as possible.

Pattern E: An abbreviation with periods

He couldn't decide whether to enroll for a B.S. or a B.A. degree.

Pattern F: An abbreviation without periods

The computer shop featured IBM and Apple computers.

Pattern G: With a quotation

His father announced, "If you use the car tonight, then you pay for the gas."

Pattern H: With a quotation and a reference

According to the article, "Smokers can no longer demand rights that violate the air space of others" (Heskett 27).

33b Question Marks (?)

1. Question Marks at the End of a Sentence

Use a question mark after direct quotations but not after indirect quotations.

Direct Quotation: "Do you have another copy of this book in stock?"

Indirect Quotation: She asked the salesperson if he had another copy of the book in stock.

Use the question mark in statements that contain direct quotations.

"Did Henry ever pay back that loan?" she wondered.

Enclose the question mark inside the quotation marks only if the question mark belongs to the quotation.

Alice said, "Who's that standing by the door?"

Did Alice really say, "Get lost"?

2. Question Marks in a Series

Question marks may be used between parts of a series.

Would you prefer to eat at a restaurant? go on a picnic? cook at home?

3. Question Marks to Indicate Doubt

Question marks can be used to indicate doubt about the correctness of the preceding word, figure, date, or other piece of information.

The city was founded about 1837 (?) but did not grow significantly until about fifty years later.

4. Unnecessary Question Marks

Don't use a question mark within parentheses to indicate sarcasm. Instead, rewrite the sentence so that the meaning is clear from the use of appropriate words.

Unnecessary Question Mark: She was sure that it was her intelligence (?) that charmed him.

Revised: Although she was sure that it was her intelligence that charmed him, she was greatly mistaken.

Exercise 33.3: Proofreading Practice

In the following paragraph, add question marks where they are needed and delete any incorrect, unnecessary, or inappropriate question marks. Place an X by a question mark that should be deleted or changed.

Recent research has found that the heat can kill you? Two meteorologists exploring weather patterns for the second half of the twentieth century found that the frequency of heat waves increased substantially from 1949 (?) to 1995. The deaths of six hundred people in a 1995 Chicago heat wave prompted the researchers to examine the effects of heat on society. The main question of the researchers was whether hot and humid weather that occurs at night is dangerous? Subsequently, the team did find that prolonged periods of hot weather that last through several nights have the most profound effects on people, especially the elderly. A nursing home administrator asked the researchers, "What precautions should be taken when the heat is extreme." These knowledgeable (?) researchers responded, "Extreme summer heat affects people's health more than other types of severe weather. The elderly should drink plenty of fluids and remain indoors during the hottest part of the day?" With proper precautions, the deaths of countless people from extreme heat can be avoided.

Exercise 33.4: Pattern Practice

Using the patterns and examples given here, write your own correctly punctuated sentences. Write two sentences for each pattern given.

Pattern A: Sentence with a question mark

Which way should I turn this knob?

Pattern B: Statement with a direct question

"Can you speak French?" he asked.

Pattern C: Quotation with question mark inside the quotation marks

Jeff kept demanding, "Did she really ask my name?"

Pattern D: Quotation with the question mark outside the quotation marks

Why did the coach say, "No more practice this week"?

Pattern E: Question mark to indicate doubt about a piece of information

The cavalry unit had about 1,000 (?) horses before the battle.

33c Exclamation Points (!)

1. Exclamation Points at the End of a Sentence

Use an exclamation mark after strong commands; statements said with great emphasis; interjections; and sentences intended to express surprise, disbelief, or strong feeling.

What a magnificent surprise!

I am not guilty!

Definitely!

Don't overuse the exclamation mark, and don't combine it with other end punctuation as shown here:

Wow! What a party! There was even a live band!

I won $500!

Is he for real?!

2. Exclamation Points with Quotation Marks
Enclose the exclamation mark inside quotation marks only if it belongs to the quotation.

He burst into the room and yelled, "We are surrounded!"

In the middle of the meeting Maude quietly explained, "My committee has already vetoed this motion"!

Exercise 33.5: Proofreading Practice

Add exclamation marks where they are needed in the following paragraph, and delete any that are incorrect, unnecessary, or inappropriate. Place an X by a line where an exclamation mark is deleted.

At the end of winter, when gardeners are depressed from the long months indoors, plant catalogs start flooding the mail! With their large type the catalogs blare out their news to hungry gardeners. "Amazing!!" "Fantastic!!!" "Incredible!!!!" The covers always belong to some enormous new strain of tomatoes. "Bigger than Beefsteaks" or "Too Big to Fit on This Page"! they yell. Even the blueberries are monsters. "Blueberries as big as quarters!" the catalogs promise. All you do, according to these enticing catalogs, is "Plant 'em and stand back!?!" On a gloomy February afternoon, many would-be gardeners are probably ready to believe that this year they too can have "asparagus thicker than a person's thumb"!!!

Exercise 33.6: Pattern Practice

Using the patterns and examples given here, write your own correctly punctuated sentences. Write one sentence for each pattern given.

Pattern A: Sentence with an exclamation mark

This is the happiest day of my life!

Pattern B: Quotation with an exclamation mark enclosed

After the ballots were counted, Dan yelled, "I won!"

Pattern C: Quotation with an exclamation mark outside

Every time we try to study, Bob always says, "Let's go out instead"!

34 Other Punctuation

34a Dashes (dash)

Dashes, considered somewhat informal, can add emphasis and clarity. But they shouldn't be overused, especially as substitutes for commas or colons. When you are typing, use two hyphens to indicate the dash. Do not leave a space before or after the hyphens. For handwritten papers, draw a dash as an unbroken line, at least twice as long as a hyphen.

1. Dashes at the Beginning or End of a Sentence

Use the dash at the beginning or end of the sentence to set off added explanation or illustration and to add emphasis or clarity. If the added explanation is of less importance than the rest of the sentence, use parentheses.

Fame, fortune, and a Ferrari—these were his goals in life.

[When dashes are used this way at the beginning of a sentence, they tend to come after a series of items that are explained in the rest of the sentence, which usually then begins with *these, all,* or *none.*]

Her acting gave an extra touch of humor to the play—an added sparkle.

2. Dashes to Mark an Interruption

Use the dash as an interrupter to mark a sudden break in thought, an abrupt change or surprise, or a deliberate pause and to show in a dialogue that the speaker has been interrupted.

According to her way of looking at things—but not mine—this was a worthwhile cause.

The small child stood there happily sniffing a handful of flowers—all the roses from my garden.

Of course Everett was willing to work hard to get good grades—but not too hard.

Sherri announced, "I'm going to clean up this room so that—"
"Oh no, you don't," yelled her little brother.

3. Dashes to Set Off a Phrase or Clause with a Comma

When a phrase or clause already has commas within it, you can use dashes to set off the whole word group.

Hildy always finds interesting little restaurants—such as Lettuce Eat, that health-food place, and Ho Ming's Pizza Parlor—to take us to after a concert.

Exercise 34.1: Proofreading Practice

Add dashes where they are needed in the following paragraph.

If you love to shop for clothes but hate fitting rooms, there is a new invention that can eliminate trying on clothing in stores. Surprisingly, scientific researchers not tailors have developed a body scanner that measures a person's body. Going to stores to try on clothes could be an outdated practice; you could do it all at home. The body scanner is shaped like a photo booth and contains infrared lights that measure more than 300,000 points on the body. This invention, which is really an electronic tailor, is in the development stage. The team expects that the scanner will be ready for use soon but not in the next year. Potential customers such as the leading London fashion designers are anxious for the product to gain final approval. The prediction is that custom clothing will really fit like a glove.

Exercise 34.2: Pattern Practice

Using the patterns and examples given here, write your own sentences with dashes. Write two sentences for each pattern given.

Pattern A: At the beginning or end of the sentence for added explanation or illustration

> Those leather boots cost about $100—almost half a week's salary.

Pattern B: To mark an interruption or break in thought

> Rick is always borrowing—but not returning—everyone else's ballpoint pens.

Pattern C: To set off phrases and clauses with their own commas

> There were several exercise program—including aerobic dancing, gymnastics, and aquatic exercises in the pool—to choose from in the students' recreational program at the gymnasium.

34b Slashes (/)

I. Slashes to Mark the End of a Line of Poetry

When you quote two or three lines of poetry within a paragraph, indicate the end of each line with a slash (with a space before and after the slash). Don't use the slash mark when you indent and quote three or more lines of poetry.

Andrew Marvell's poem "To His Coy Mistress" begins by reminding the lady that life is indeed short: "Had we but world enough, and time / This coyness, lady, were no crime." And as the poem progresses, the imagery of death reinforces this reminder of our brief moment of life:

> But at my back I always hear
> Time's winged chariot hurrying near;
> And yonder all before us lie
> Deserts of vast eternity.

2. Slashes to Indicate Acceptable Alternatives

Use the forward slash mark, with no space before or afterward, to indicate that either of two terms can apply. The forward slash mark on a typewriter or computer keyboard is the slanting line /.

pass/fail   and/or   yes/no

Exercise 34.3: Proofreading Practice

Add slash marks where appropriate in the following paragraph.

I have kept a journal since I entered college. In this journal, I have recorded my favorite poems and or their significance in my life at the time I read them. I enrolled in a poetry course for fun because I was a biology major and poetry was not often recited in lab. Of course, I opted for the pass fail grading system because I feared that my scientific mind would not yield memorable poetry. I think the poem that I will remember forever is "I never saw a Moor" by Emily Dickinson. The first stanza is familiar to almost everyone:

I never saw a Moor—
I never saw the Sea—
Yet know I how the Heather looks
And what a Billow be.

I have heard these lines again and again since taking the college poetry course. It is the second stanza that is less familiar. The first two lines of the second stanza contain the theme of the poem: "I never spoke with God, Nor visited in Heaven—" These are the two lines I wrote about in my journal. In fact, the journal is filled with lines from the poetry of Emily Dickinson.

Exercise 34.4: Pattern Practice

Using the patterns and examples given here, write your own sentences with slashes. Write one sentence for each pattern given.

Pattern A: With poetry quoted within a sentence

Whenever she was asked to discuss her ability to cope with great difficulties, she quoted John Milton: "The mind is its own place, and in itself / Can make a Heaven of Hell, a Hell of Heaven."

Pattern B: With two terms when either is acceptable

Because the reading list for History 227 was so long, he decided to register for it on a pass/fail option.

34c Parentheses ( )

A dash gives emphasis to an element in the sentence, whereas a pair of parentheses indicates that the element enclosed is less important. *Parentheses* is the plural form of the word and indicates both the parenthesis at the beginning and the parenthesis at the end of the enclosed element.

1. Parentheses to Set Off Supplementary Matter

Use parentheses to enclose supplementary or less important material that you include as further explanation or as added detail or examples.

That added material does not need to be part of the grammatical structure of the sentence. If the material is inside the sentence, any punctuation needed for the rest of the sentence is outside the closing parenthesis. If a whole sentence is enclosed with parentheses, put the end punctuation for that sentence inside.

The officers of the fraternity (the ones elected last month) called a meeting just before the dance to remind everyone of the new alcohol regulations.

2. Parentheses to Enclose Figures or Letters

Use parentheses to enclose figures or letters that enumerate items in a series.

The three major items on the agenda were as follows: (1) the budget review, (2) the new parking permits, and (3) the evaluation procedures.

Exercise 34.5: Proofreading Practice

Add parentheses as needed to the following paragraph.

Medical doctors have announced a new finding that Alzheimer's patients are demonstrating remarkable abilities in painting. Alzheimer's also known as dementia is a degenerative brain disorder that affects the part of the brain responsible for several functions: 1. social skills, 2. verbal communication, and 3. physical orientation. Neuropathologists doctors who study brain disorders have found that this disease may not affect visual thinking. Some famous artists including Willem de Kooning and Vincent van Gogh may have suffered from Alzheimer's disease. This finding could lead to new and innovative treatments for Alzheimer's disease patients.

Exercise 34.6: Pattern Practice

Using the patterns and examples given here, write your own sentences with parentheses. Write a sentence for each pattern given.

Pattern A: To enclose less important material

The sixth-grade teacher decided to offer his class an opportunity to try out different drawing materials (such as pastel chalks and charcoal) that they hadn't used before.

Pattern B: To enclose figures and letters

The job offer included some very important fringe benefits that similar positions in other companies did not include: (a) a day-care center in the building, (b) retirement benefits for the employee's spouse, and (c) an opportunity to buy company cars after they were used for a year or so.

34d Brackets [ ]

1. Brackets to Add Comments within a Quotation

When you are quoting material and have to add your own explanation, comment, or addition within the quotation, enclose your addition within brackets [ ].

The word *sic* in brackets means that you copied the original quotation exactly as it appeared, but you think that the word just before *sic* may be an error or a questionable form.

After the town meeting, the newspaper's lead story reported the discussion: "The Town Board and the mayor met to discuss the mayor's proposal to raise parking meter rates. The discussion was long but not heated, and the exchange of views was fiendly [*sic*] despite some strong opposition."

Everyone agreed with Phil Brown's claim that "this great team [the Chicago Bears] is destined for next year's Super Bowl."

2. Brackets to Replace Parentheses within Parentheses

When you need to enclose something already within parentheses, use brackets instead of a second set of parentheses.

"Baby busters, the children born between 1965 and 1980, have more choices in the job market and better prospects for advancement than the previous 'baby boom' generation," says John Sayers in his recent study of population trends (*The Changing Face of Our Population* [New York: Merian, 1994] 18).

Exercise 34.7: Proofreading Practice

In the following paragraph, brackets are needed in several places. Rewrite the paragraph, placing brackets where they are needed and replacing any parentheses if necessary.

One Middle Ages Christian celebration was called the Feast of the Ass. According to John Smith, a Middle Ages scholar, "At one time this was a solemn celebration reenacting the flight of the Holy Family (Mary, Joseph, and Jesus) into Egypt. It ended with a Math *sic* in the church" (*Christian Celebrations* (New York: United Press, 1995): 23). The festival (started in the fourteenth century by the tribune, a group of church elders) became very popular as it transformed into a humorous parody in which the ass was led into the church and treated as an honored guest. Historians claim that the members of the congregation all brayed like asses. The Church abandoned the celebration in the fifteenth century, but it remained popular for years.

Exercise 34.8: Pattern Practice

Using the patterns and examples given here, write your own sentences with brackets. Write one sentence for each pattern given.

Pattern A: Brackets to all comments within a quotation

> The lab assistant explained that "everyone [who has finished the lab experiment] should hand in notebooks by Friday."

Pattern B: Brackets to replace parentheses within parentheses

> The new library guide (distributed by Newcomers Council [a subcommittee of the Student Government Board] at no cost to students) is intended to help first-year composition students become acquainted with resources for researching term paper topics.

Exercise 34.9: Proofreading Practice

Add slashes, parentheses, and brackets where they are needed in the following paragraph. Correct any wrong punctuation.

The last two lines of Archibald MacLeish's poem "Ars Poetica" (written in 1924 are often quoted as his theory of poetry. "A poem should not mean But be," he wrote. In his notebooks, he expanded on this statement: "The purpose of the expression of emotion in a poem is not to recreate the poet's emotion in someone else. . . . The poem itself is a finality, an end, a creation." G. T. Hardison, in his analysis of MacLeish's theory of poetry ("The Non-Meaning of Poetry," *Modern Poetics* 27 (1981): 45, explains that "when MacLeish says the poem 'is a finality, an ending *sic*,' he means that a good poem is self-sufficient; it is, it does not mean something else. One might as well ask the meaning of a friend or brother."

34e Omitted Words/Ellipsis (. . .)

Use an ellipsis (a series of three spaced periods) to indicate that you are omitting words or a part of a sentence from material you are quoting.

Original: "In 1891, when President Benjamin Harrison proclaimed the first forest reserves as government land, there were so many people opposed to the idea that his action was called undemocratic and un-American."

Some Words Omitted: "In 1891, when President Benjamin Harrison proclaimed the first forest reserves . . . his action was called undemocratic and un-American."

If you are omitting a whole sentence or paragraph, add a fourth period with no space after the last word preceding the ellipsis:

> "federal lands. . . . They were designated."

An ellipsis is not needed if the omission occurs at the beginning or end of the sentence you are quoting. But if your sentence ends with quoted words that are not the end of the original sentence, use an ellipsis mark. Add your period (the fourth one) with no space after the last word if there is no documentation included. If there is documentation, such as a page number, add the last period after the parentheses.

"the National Forest System. . . ."

"the National Forest System . . ." (Smith 27).

If you omit words immediately after a punctuation mark in the original, include that mark in your sentence.

"because of this use of forests for timbering, mining, and grazing, . . ."

In addition to indicating the omission of quoted words, three dots are also used to show hesitation or an unfinished statement.

The lawyer asked: "Did you see the defendant leave the room?"

"Ah, I'm not sure . . . but he might have left," replied the witness.

35 Capitals (caps)

> Capitalize words that name one particular thing, most often a
> person or place, rather than a general type or group of things.
> Names that need capitals can be thought of as legal titles that
> identify a specific entity. For example, you can take a course in
> history (a word not capitalized because it is a general field of
> study), but the course is offered by a particular department with
> a specific name, such as History Department or Department of
> Historical Studies. The name of that specific department is
> capitalized. However, if you take a course in French, *French* is
> capitalized because it is the name of a specific language.

Listed here are categories of words that should be capitalized. If you
are not sure about a particular word, check your dictionary.

- Persons

Vincent Baglia	Rifka Kaplan	Masuto Tatami

- Places, including geographical regions

Indianapolis	Ontario	Midwest

- Peoples and their languages

Spanish	Dutch	English

- Religions and their followers

Buddhist	Judaism	Christianity

- Members of national, political, racial, social, civic, and athletic
  groups

Democrat	African American	Chicago Bears
Danes	Friends of the Library	Olympics Committee

- Institutions and organizations

Supreme Court	Legal Aid Society	Lions Club

- Historical documents

The Declaration of Independence	Magna Carta

- Periods and events, but not century numbers

Middle Ages	Boston Tea Party	eighteenth century

- Days, months, and holidays, but not seasons

Monday	Thanksgiving	winter

- Trademarks

Coca-Cola	Kodak	Ford

- Holy books and words denoting the Supreme Being (including pronouns)

  Talmud   His creation   the Lord   the Bible

- Words and abbreviations derived from specific names, but not the names of things that have lost that specific association and now refer to the general type

  Stalinism   Freudian   NATO   CBS
  french fry   pasteurize   italics   panama hat

- Place words, such as *street, park,* and *city,* that are part of specific names

  New York City   Wall Street   Zion National Park

- Titles that precede people's names, but not titles that follow names

  Aunt Sylvia   Governor Lionel Washington   President Taft
  Sylvia, my aunt   Lionel Washington, governor   John Taft,
                                                        president

- Words that indicate family relationships when used as a substitute for a specific name

  Here is a gift for Mother.   Li Chen sent a gift to his mother.

- Titles of books, magazines, essays, movies, plays, and other works, but not articles (*a, an, the*), short prepositions (*to, by, on, in*), or short joining words (*and, but, or*) unless they are the first or last word. With hyphenated words, capitalize the first and other important words.

  The Taming of the Shrew   "The Sino-Soviet Conflict"
  A Dialog Between Soul and Body   "A Brother-in-Law's Lament"

  [For APA style, which has different rules, see 53c.]

- The pronoun *I* and the interjection *O,* but not the word *oh*

  "Sail on, sail on, O ship of state," I said as the canoe sank.

- The first word of every sentence and the first word of a comment in parentheses if the comment is a full sentence, but not for a series of questions in which the questions are not full sentences

  The American Olympic Ski Team (which receives very little government support) spent six months in training before the elimination trials while the German team trained for over two years. (Like most European nations, Germany provides financial support for all team members.)

  What did the settlers want from the natives? food? animal skins?

- The first word of directly quoted speech, but not for the second portion of interrupted direct quotations or quoted phrases or clauses integrated into the sentence

  She answered, "No one will understand."

  "No one," she answered, "will understand."

When Hemmings declined the nomination, he explained that he "would try again another year."

■ The first word in a list after a colon if each item in the list is a complete sentence

The rule books were very clear: (1) No player could continue to play after committing two fouls. (2) Substitute players would be permitted only with the consent of the other team. (3) Every eligible player had to be designated before the game.

(or)

The rule books were very clear:
1. No player could continue to play after committing two fouls.
2. Substitute players would be permitted only with the consent of the other team.
3. Every eligible player had to be designated before the game.

The rise in popularity of walking as an alternative to jogging has already led to commercial successes of various kinds: (1) new designs for walking shoes, (2) an expanding market for walking sticks, and (3) a rapid growth in the number of manufacturers selling walking shoes.

(or)

The rise in popularity of walking as an alternative to jogging has already led to commercial successes of various kinds:
1. new designs for walking shoes,
2. an expanding market for walking sticks, and
3. a rapid growth in the number of manufacturers selling walking shoes.

■ Words placed after a prefix that are normally capitalized

un-American   anti-Semitic

Exercise 35.1: Proofreading Practice

In the following paragraph, there are some errors in capitalization. Underline the first letter of any word that needs a capital, and circle the first letter of any word that should not be capitalized.

Melbourne, a City in Australia, will be the new site of the World's tallest building. The proposed Building will be 120 stories and contain offices and apartments. Construction is slated to start in the Spring of next year. The new Building will surpass petronas towers in Malaysia as the tallest Building. The Malaysian Building became the Tallest Building in 1996 when it took the title from the Sears Tower in chicago. The building will be twice the size of Melbourne's current tallest structure, but developers assure citizens that it will not look out of place. The developers' aim is to build a "Beautiful and appropriate building" for the city of Melbourne. "We will create a new landmark for our city," Says the chief developer. He also claims, "the people of the city will be proud of this accomplishment."

Exercise 35.2: Pattern Practice

For each of the capitalization patterns listed here, write a sentence of your own that uses capitals correctly.

Pattern A: A sentence with the name of a national, political, racial, social, civic, or athletic group; the name of a season of the year; and a person's name and title

> When Matthew Given, superintendent of the Monticello School Corporation, suggested a summer program for additional study, many parents vigorously supported his idea.

Pattern B: A sentence with a quotation interrupted by other words in the sentence

> "You know," said the customer to the salesclerk, "this is just what I was looking for."

Pattern C: Two place names and a holiday

> On the Fourth of July, Chicago hosts an art and food fair in Grant Park.

36 Abbreviations (ab)

In the fields of social science, science, and engineering, abbreviations are used frequently, but in other fields and in academic writing in the humanities, only a limited number of abbreviations are generally used.

36a Abbreviating Numbers

- Write out numbers that can be expressed in one or two words.

  nine   twenty-seven   135

- The dollar sign abbreviation is generally acceptable when the whole phrase will be three words or more.

  $2 million

- For temperatures, use words if only a few temperatures are cited, but use figures if temperatures are cited frequently in a paper.

  ten degrees below zero, Fahrenheit $-10°F$

36b Abbreviating Titles

- *Mr., Mrs.,* and *Ms.* are abbreviated when used as titles before the name.

  Mr. Tanato   Ms. Whitman   Mrs. Ojebwa

- *Dr.* and *St.* ("Saint") are abbreviated only when they immediately precede a name; they are written out when they appear after the name.

  Dr. Marlen Chaf   (but)   Marlen Chaf, doctor of internal medicine

■ *Prof., Sen., Gen., Capt.,* and similar abbreviated titles can be used when they appear in front of a full name or before initials and a last name but are not abbreviated when they appear before the last name only.

Gen. R. G. Fuller   (but)   General Fuller

■ *Sr., Jr., J.D., Ph.D., M.F.A., C.P.A.,* and other abbreviated academic titles and professional degrees can be used after the name.

Leslie Millen, Ph.D., . . .   Charleen Phipps, C.P.A.

■ *Bros., Co.,* and similar abbreviations are used only if they are part of the exact name.

Marshall Field & Co.   Brown Bros.

36c Abbreviating Places

In general, spell out names of states, countries, continents, streets, rivers, and so on.

Here are two exceptions:

■ Use the abbreviation *D.C.* in Washington, D.C. Use *U.S.* only as an adjective, not as a noun.

U.S. training bases   training bases in the United States

■ If you include a full address in a sentence, citing the street, city, and state, you can use the postal abbreviation for the state.

For further information, write to the company at 100 Peachtree Street, Atlanta, GA 30300 for a copy of their free catalog.

The company's headquarters in Atlanta, Georgia, will soon be moved.

36d Abbreviating Measurements

Spell out units of measurement, such as *acre, meter, foot,* and *percent,* but use abbreviations in tables, graphs, and figures.

36e Abbreviating Dates

Spell out months and days of the week.

With dates and times, the following are acceptable:

57 B.C. (or) 57 B.C.E.   [the abbreviations B.C. and B.C.E. (Before the Common Era) are placed after the year.]

A.D. 329   [The abbreviation A.D. is placed before the date.]

a.m., p.m.   (or)   A.M., P.M.
EST   (or)   E.S.T., est

36f Abbreviating Initials Used as Names

Use abbreviations for names of organizations, agencies, countries, and things usually referred to by their capitalized initials.

NASA	IBM	NAACP
UNICEF	USSR	VCR

If you are using the initials for a term that may not be familiar to your readers, spell it out the first time and give the initials in parentheses. From then on, you can use the initials. (See 33a.2.)

The study of children's long-term memory (LTM) has been a difficult one because of the lack of a universally accepted definition of LTM.

36g Abbreviating Latin Expressions

Some Latin expressions always appear as abbreviations.

Abbreviation	Meaning	Abbreviation	Meaning
cf.	compare	i.e.	that is
e.g.	for example	n.b.	note carefully
et al.	and others	vs. (or) v.	versus
etc.	and so forth		

36h Abbreviating Documentation

Because the format for abbreviations may vary from one style manual to another, use the abbreviations listed in the particular style manual you are following. (See Chapters 52–54).

Abbreviation	Meaning
abr.	abridged
anon.	anonymous
b.	born
c. (or) ©	copyright
c. (or) ca.	about—used with dates
ch. (or) chap.	chapter
col., cols.	column, columns
d.	died
ed., eds.	editor, editors
esp.	especially
f., ff.	and the following page, pages
illus.	illustrated by
ms., mss.	manuscript, manuscripts
no.	number
n.d.	no date of publication given
n.p.	no place of publication given
n. pag.	no page number given
p., pp.	page, pages
trans. (or) tr.	translated by
vol., vols.	volume, volumes

Exercise 36.1: Proofreading Practice

Proofread the following paragraph, and correct the errors in use or omission of abbreviations and symbols. Underline whatever you change.

The fluctuations in the stock market affect investors and job hunters alike. Business school graduates will find that the MBA does not guarantee a job after graduation. The volatile stock market has caused downsizing in investment firms such as Merrill Lynch, Prudential, and Morgan Stanley. Recent graduates had no problem landing a position starting at 64,500 dollars on average. The recruitment process has changed at prestigious schools such as Georgetown University in Washington, D.C.. However, students from the top schools will most likely obtain positions but at a lower salary than previously offered. Students in less prestigious schools in the US are more worried about finding a position. There are now two or three positions to fill in a company where there used to be ten or twelve positions. Worried students are networking to find internships that may lead to positions. An unpredictable market is a sign that MBA students can no longer expect a lucrative job.

Exercise 36.2: Pattern Practice

Using the patterns listed here, write a sentence of your own that correctly uses abbreviations.

Pattern A: A sentence that contains a number that can be written as one or two words, a name with a degree after it, and the names of a city and state

When Cleon Martin, C.P.A., looked for office space in Rochester, New York, he found a somewhat expensive but convenient office on the thirty-sixth floor of a new high-rise office building near his home.

Pattern B: A sentence with the abbreviation for the United States used correctly and the names of a month and a day of the week.

Because of recent changes in the U.S. Post Office, many local post offices are now open on Saturday mornings, especially in December.

Pattern C: A sentence with a unit of measurement and a specific dollar amount

The luxurious boat, more than sixty feet long, was purchased for $555,000.

37 Numbers (num)

Style manuals for different fields and companies vary. The suggestions for writing numbers given here are generally useful as a guide for academic writing.

■ Spell out numbers that can be expressed in one or two words, and use figures for other numbers.

Words	Figures
two pounds	126 days
six dollars	$31.50
thirty-one years	6,381 bushels
eighty-three people	4.78 liters

■ Use a combination of figures and words for numbers when such a combination will keep your writing clear.

The club celebrated the birthdays of six 90-year-olds who were born in the city.

1. Use figures for the following:

■ Days and years

December 12, 1963	(or)	12 December 1963
A.D. 1066		
in 1971–1972	(or)	in 1971–72
the 1980s	(or)	the 1980's

■ Time of day

8:00 A.M. (or) a.m.	(or)	eight o'clock in the morning
4:30 P.M. (or) p.m.	(or)	half past four in the afternoon

■ Addresses

15 Tenth Street
350 West 114 Street   (or)   350 West 114th Street
Prescott, AZ 86301

■ Identification numbers

Room 8	Channel 18
Interstate 65	Henry VIII

■ Page and division of books and plays

page 30		Book I
act 3, scene 2	(or)	Act III, Scene ii

■ Decimals and percentages

2.7 average	13 1/2 percent
0.037 metric ton	

■ Numbers in series and statistics

two apples, six oranges, and three bananas
115 feet by 90 feet

Be consistent, whichever form you choose.

■ Large round numbers

$4 billion	(or)	four billion dollars
16.5 million	(or)	16,500,000

■ Repeated numbers (in legal or commercial writing)

The bill will not exceed one hundred (100) dollars.

2. Do not use figures for the following:

- Numbers that can be expressed in one or two words

  in his twenties   the twentieth century

- Dates when the year is omitted

  June sixth

- Numbers beginning sentences

  Ten percent of the year's crop was harvested.

Exercise 37.1: Proofreading Practice

Proofread the following paragraph and correct any numbers that are written incorrectly. Underline any corrections that you make.

As the 21st century begins, many historians are reflecting on the events that shaped the latter half of the 20th century. The center of many important events of this century has been Sixteen Hundred Pennsylvania Avenue, Washington, D.C. Baby boomers remember President John F. Kennedy, who was assassinated in the year nineteen hundred and sixty-three. Another former resident of the White House, Richard M. Nixon, will be remembered for the Watergate hearings that dominated television programming for a long, hot 70's summer. Many people recall turning on Channel 2, 4, 5, 7, or 11 and finding Watergate on every station. Ronald Reagan brought the country "Reaganomics" and a new sense of patriotism. George Bush promised a "kinder, gentler nation" and promised not to raise taxes. Then came William Jefferson Clinton. Like those before him, the 42nd President of the United States gives historians much to argue about as they try to evaluate his accomplishments.

Exercise 37.2: Pattern Practice

For each of the sentences given here, compose a sentence of your own using that model for writing numbers. The first sentence is done as an example.

1. There was a 7.2 percent decrease in sales of cigarettes after the Surgeon General's speech.

   The study showed that 16.7 percent of the population in the country did not have running water.

2. The plane was due at 4:15 P.M. but arrived at 5:10 P.M.
3. That book was volume 23 in the series.
4. The astronomer calculated that the star is 18 million light-years from our planet.
5. In the sixties, during the height of the antiwar movement, the senator's political actions were not popular, but by the time of the 1972 election, more people agreed with him.
6. The television commercial warned buyers that there were only 123 days until Christmas.

38 Underlining/Italics (under)

When you are typing or writing by hand, use underlining (a printer's mark to indicate words to be set in italics). When you have italic lettering on a computer, you can use italics instead.

38a Underlining for Titles

Use underlining (or italics) for titles and names of books, magazines, newspapers, pamphlets, works of art, long works such as plays with three or more acts, movies, long musical works (operas, concertos, etc.), radio and television programs, and long poems. (For the use of quotation marks for titles of minor works and parts of whole works, see 31b.)

Do not use underlining, italics, or quotation marks for references to the Bible or legal documents.

Underlining	(or)	Italics
Catcher in the Rye		*Catcher in the Rye*
U.S. News and World Report		*U.S. News and World Report*
New York Times		*New York Times*

38b Other Uses of Underlining

1. Use underlining or italics for the following:

   - Names of ships, airplanes, and trains

     Queen Mary   Concorde   Orient Express

   - Foreign words and phrases and scientific names of plants and animals

     in vino veritas   Canis lupus

   - Words used as words, or letters, numbers, and symbols used as examples or terms

     Some words, such as Kleenex, are brand names for products.

     In English the letters ph and f often have the same sound.

     The keys for 9 and & on that typewriter are broken.

   - Words being emphasized

     It never snows here at this time of year.

     Use italics or underlining for emphasis only sparingly.

2. Do not use underlining or italics for the following:

   - Words of foreign origin that are now part of English

alumni	cliché	karate
rouge	genre	hacienda

■ Titles of your own papers

Exercise 38.1 Proofreading Practice

Add underlining where it is needed in the following paragraph, and delete any incorrect underlining or quotation marks.

The <u>Internet</u> can now be considered a mass medium, according to articles in magazines like "Time" and "Newsweek." In recent elections, the <u>Internet</u> was used as a new <u>genre</u> to lasso voters as candidates established <u>Web</u> sites. A poll of voters for the television show "Dateline" revealed that 67 percent of voters regularly use a computer at home or work. The New York Times reported that California was the first state to use the <u>Internet</u> for political purposes and was quickly imitated by "Florida," "Texas," "South Dakota," and "Wisconsin." The sites include information on a candidate, photos from the campaign trail, and a list of campaign contributors. Voters can obtain addresses for the sites from campaign literature and television commercials. While some political experts predict that this will be the best campaign method of the future, others think that having to access a site is a deterrent. The fact remains that print and television advertisements reach more voters and will never be replaced by the <u>Internet</u>. One political consultant observed, "There are more people watching Good Morning America and listening to the radio on the way to the office than visiting political <u>Web</u> sites." Voters feel the <u>Internet</u> provides options. A voter interviewed about the sites stated, "Vive la différence!"

Exercise 38.2: Pattern Practice

Using the patterns and examples given here, write your own correctly italicized (or underlined) sentences. Write two sentences for each pattern given.

Pattern A: Italics (or underlining) with titles of books, magazines, newspapers, and long works of art.

> After surveying its recently checked out materials, the library concluded that the most popular items on the shelves were murder mysteries, such as Blodgen's <u>The Dead Hero</u>; current big-city newspapers, such as the <u>New York Times</u>; and videotapes of old movies, such as <u>North by Northwest</u> and <u>Gone with the Wind</u>.

Pattern B: Italics (or underlining) with names of ships, airplanes, and trains

> When the old <u>Queen Mary</u> was no longer fit for sailing, it became a floating hotel.

Pattern C: Italics (or underlining) with foreign words or phrases and scientific names.

> Dr. Galland diagnosed the cause of his illness: infection with a combination of <u>Candida albicans</u> and <u>Giardia lamblia</u>.

Pattern D: Italics (or underlining) with words used as words or figures used as examples.

> If she would stop overusing empty words such as <u>great</u> or <u>nice</u> in her composition class papers, she would probably be able to get an <u>A</u>.

Pattern E: Italics (or underlining) for emphasis.

> When Mike woke up, he couldn't believe that he felt so refreshed even though he had been asleep for <u>only</u> ten minutes.

39 Spelling (sp)

English spelling can be difficult because many words have been imported from other languages that have different spelling conventions. But despite the difficulty, it is important to spell correctly. Some misspelled words can cause confusion in the reader's mind, but any misspelled word can signal the reader that the writer is careless and not very knowledgeable. Since no writer wants to lose credibility, correct spelling is necessary. So it is wise to spend some time on spelling, doing one or more of the following:

- **Learn some spelling rules.**
- **Make up your own memory aids.**
- **Make up some rules or letter associations** that will help you remember particularly troublesome words. Example: If you have trouble choosing between *e's* and *a's* in *separate*, it may help to remember that there's a *pa* in se*pa*rate.
- **Learn your own misspelling patterns.**
- **Learn how to proofread.**

39a Proofreading

Proofreading means reading your final written work slowly and carefully to catch misspellings and typographical errors. Proofreading is best done after you are finished writing and are preparing to turn your paper over to your readers. Some useful proofreading strategies:

- **Slow down.** Proofreading requires slowing down your reading rate so you will see all the letters in each word. In normal reading, your eyes skip across the line and you notice only groups of words.
- **Focus on each word.** One way to slow yourself down is to point a pencil or pen at each word as you say it aloud or to yourself.
- **Read backward.** Don't read left to right as you would normally do, or you will soon slip back into a more rapid reading rate. Instead,

move backward through each line from right to left. In this way, you won't be listening for meaning or checking for grammatical correctness.

■ **Cover up any distractions.** To focus on each word, hold a sheet of paper or a notecard under the line being read. This way you won't be distracted by other words on the page.

■ **Watch for your patterns of misspellings.** Remember to look for those groups or patterns of misspellings that occur most frequently in your writing.

■ **Read forward.** End-to-beginning proofreading will not catch problems with omitted words or sound-alike words. To check for those, do a second proofreading moving forward, from left to right, so that you can watch the meaning of your sentences. Listen for each word as you read aloud or to yourself.

Exercise 39.1: Proofreading Practice

Practice the proofreading strategies described in 39a by proofreading the following paragraph, which has a number of typos, misspellings, and omitted words. Underline each word that is spelled incorrectly, and correct the spelling. Write any word or words that are missing.

Turkish people do'nt think of St. Nicholas as having reindeer or elfs, living at North Pole, or climbing down chimneys with gifts on Christmass Eve. Accept for a twist of history, Santa Claus might well speak Turkish, ride a camel, dress for a warmmer climate, bring gifts of oranges and tomatoes, and appear on December 5 instead of Christmas Eve. According to the story of the Turkish church about his backround, Nicholas was the frist bishop of Myra, on the coast Turkey. Turkish scholars say he was known far and wide for his peity and charity. He was killed around A.D. 245, and after his martyrdom, on December 6, tails of his good deeds lived on. His faime was so great that in the eleventh centruy, when the Italian branch of the Catholic church began a drive to bring to Italy the remains of the most famous saints, theives stole most of Nicholas's bones from the church tomb in Turkey and took them to a town in southren Italy. Nicholas was abbreviated to Claus, and St. Nick became Santa. Since there are no dociuments or records of the original Nicholas of Myra, some sholars doubt his existance. But others are convinced there really was a St. Nicholas, even if he didn't have reindeer or live at North Pole.

39b Using Spell Checkers

Spell checkers on computers are a useful tool, but they can't catch all spelling errors. While different spell checking programs have different capabilities, they are not foolproof, and they do make mistakes. Most spell checkers will not locate or correct the following errors:

■ **Omitted words**

■ **Sound-alike words (homonyms)** Some words sound alike but are spelled differently (see 39e). The spell checker will not flag a word if it is a correctly spelled homonym of the one you want. For example, if you meant "*They're* going to the tennis match" but write "*Their* going to the tennis match," the spell checker recognizes *Their* as a word and will not highlight it for you.

■ **Many proper nouns** Some well-known proper nouns, such as *Washington,* may be in the spell checker dictionary for your program, but many will not be there.

■ **Misspelled words for which the spell checker can't find the appropriate word** Depending on the power of the spell checker and the way a word is misspelled, the program may not be able to provide the correct spelling. For example, if you meant to write *phenomena* but instead typed *phinomina,* spell checkers will highlight the word as not matching any word in their dictionary, but many won't be able to suggest the correct spelling.

39c Some Spelling Guidelines

1. ie/ei

Write *i* before *e*
Except after *c*
Or when sounded like *ay*
As in *neighbor* and *weigh.*

This rhyme reminds you to write *ie,* except under two conditions:

■ When the two letters follow a *c*

■ When the two letters sound like *ay* (as in *day*).

Some *ie* words		Some *ei* words	
believe	niece	ceiling	eight
chief	relief	conceit	receive
field	yield	deceive	vein

The following common words are exceptions to this rule:

conscience	forfeit	seize
counterfeit	height	sheik
either	leisure	species
financier	neither	sufficient
foreign	science	weird

Exercise 39.2: Proofreading Practice

The following paragraph has several ie/ei *words. Proofread the paragraph, and correct any misspellings by circling the incorrect word and writing the correct spelling.*

Diwali is a five-day Hindu festival often referred to as the Festival of Lights. During this time, homes are cleaned from ceiling to floor and the windows are opened to recieve Laksmi, a Hindu goddess. The Hindu people beleive that Laksmi is the goddess of wealth. The cheif beleif is that wealth is not a corruptive power but is considered a reward for good deeds in a past life. The festival begins with a day set aside to worship Laksmi. On the second day, Kali, the goddess of strength, is worshipped. The third day is the last day of the year in the lunar calendar. On this day, lamps are lighted and shine brightly in every home. Participants are encouraged to remove anger, hate, and jealousy from their lives on the fourth day. On the final day of the festival, Bali, an ancient Indian king, is recalled. The focus of this day is to see the good in others.

Exercise 39.3: Pattern Practice

Use each of the following ei *words in a sentence.*

eight	vein	receive	conceit	deceive

Use each of the following ie *words in a sentence.*

relief	yield	field	believe	niece

2. Doubling Consonants

A few rules about doubling the last consonant of the base word will help you spell several thousand words correctly.

One-Syllable Words

If the word ends in a consonant preceded by a single short vowel, double that last consonant when you are adding a suffix beginning with a vowel.

drag	dragged	dragging	
flip	flipped	flipping	flipper
nap	napped	napping	
shop	shopped	shopping	shopper
slip	slipped	slipping	slipper
star	starred	starring	
tap	tapped	tapping	
wet	wetted	wetting	wettest

Two-Syllable Words

For words with two or more syllables that end with a consonant preceded by a single vowel, double the consonant when both of the following conditions apply:

1. You are adding a suffix beginning with a vowel.
2. The last syllable of the base word is accented.

begin		beginning	beginner
occur	occurred	occurring	occurrence
omit	omitted	omitting	
prefer	preferred	preferring	
refer	referred	referring	
regret	regretted	regretting	regrettable
submit	submitted	submitting	
unwrap	unwrapped	unwrapping	

Exercise 39.4: Proofreading Practice

Underline the words that are misspelled in the following paragraph, and write the correct spelling.

Last week Michael planed to have his bicycle repaired, though he admitted that he was hopping he had stopped the leak in the front tire with a patch. Even though he concealled the patch with some heavy tape, he found that he had to keep tapping the patch back on the tire. Yesterday, when Michael looked at the bicycle on the way to his first class, he could see that the front tire had become flatter than it should be because it was lossing air. With no time to spare, he joged off to class, resolved that he would take the bicycle to a shop that afternoon.

Exercise 39.5: Pattern Practice

Use each of the following words in a sentence. Add -ed or -ing to each word. Remember, if a word ends in a consonant preceded by a single short vowel, double that last consonant when you are adding a suffix beginning with a vowel.

Example: drag   He dragged his backpack across the room.

flip   star   tap   shop   nap

Now add -ed or -ing to the following words and use each in a sentence. Remember, when a word has two or more syllables that end with a consonant preceded by a single vowel, double the consonant when you are adding a suffix beginning with a vowel and the last syllable of the base word is accented.

Example: begin   She is beginning to learn Latin.

occur   prefer   omit   unwrap   regret

3. Prefixes and Suffixes

A **prefix** is a group of letters added at the beginning of a base word. A **suffix** is a group of letters added to the end of the word.

The following prefixes are used in many English words:

Prefix	Meaning	Examples
ante-	before	anteroom
anti-	against	antidote
auto-	self	automobile
bene-	good	benefit
bi-	two, twice	bicycle, biweekly
bio-	life	biography, biology
de-	away, down	depress
dis-	not, no longer, away	disappear
ex-	out, no longer	exclude, expel, ex-wife
inter-	between, among	interact, interstate
intra-	within, between members of the same group	intramural, intrastate

mis-	wrong, bad	misspell, misdeed
per-	entirely, through	perfect, pertain
post-	after	postgame, postdate
pre-	before	pregame, prefix
pro-	for, take place of	prohibit, pro-American, proclaim
re-	again, back	retell, redo, readmit
semi-	half, partially	semicircle, semiautomatic
un-	not, contrary to	unhappy, unable

The -ly Suffix

If a word ends in -l, don't drop the -l when adding the suffix -ly. But if the word already ends with two -l's, add only the -y.

chill	chilly
formal	formally
hill	hilly
real	really
usual	usually

Suffixes with Words Ending in -ic

When a word ends in -ic, add a -k before suffixes starting with -i, -e, or -y. Some words that end in -ic add the suffix *ally*, not -ly.

logic	logically
picnic	picnicking
politic	politicking
traffic	trafficking
tragic	tragically

Exercise 39.6: Pattern Practice

Using your dictionary, look up three examples of words that include the prefixes listed here.

1. ante-	7. dis-	13. post-
2. anti-	8. ex-	14. pre-
3. auto-	9. inter-	15. pro-
4. bene-	10. intra-	16. re-
5. bio-	11. mis-	17. semi-
6. de-	12. per-	18. un-

Exercise 39.7: Pattern Practice

Using your dictionary to check the correct spelling, add the suffixes to the words listed here.

1. -ing	rise, guide, come
2. -ly	like, sure, true
3. -ful	care, use, stress
4. -ous	continue, courage, nerve
5. -able	desire, notice, knowledge

4. y to i

When adding a suffix to words ending with -y, change the -y to an -i.
But to avoid a double i in a word, keep the -y before the -ing suffix.

apply	applies, applied	(but)	applying
carry	carries, carried	(but)	carrying
study	studies, studied	(but)	studying
apology	apologies		
beauty	beautiful		
ceremony	ceremonious		
busy	busied, business		
easy	easily, easiness		
happy	happily, happiness		

Exception: If there is a vowel before the final -y, keep the -y before
adding -s or -ed:

stay	stays, stayed
enjoy	enjoys, enjoyed
day	days
attorney	attorneys
key	keys

Exercise 39.8: Pattern Practice

Using your dictionary to check the correct spelling, add the suffixes in paren-
theses to the words listed here.

1. tray + (-s)
2. apology + (-s)
3. ally + (-ed)
4. steady + (-ing)
5. accompany + (-ing)
6. study + (-ing)

7. mercy + (-ful)
8. funny + (-er)
9. monkey + (-s)
10. bury + (-al)
11. likely + (-er)
12. story + (-s)

13. lonely + (-ness)
14. vary + (-ed)
15. ninety + (-eth)
16. study + (-ous)
17. pretty + (-ness)
18. employ + (-er)

39d Plurals

- Most plurals are formed by adding -s. Add -es when words end in
  -s, -sh, -ch, -x, or -z because another syllable is needed.

one apple	two apples
one box	two boxes
a brush	many brushes
a buzz	six buzzes
the card	all those cards
the church	several churches
a loss	some losses
one wall	three walls

- With phrases and hyphenated words, pluralize the last word
  unless another word is more important.

one videocassette recorder   two videocassette recorders

one systems analyst   two systems analysts
one sister-in-law   two sisters-in-law

■ For some words that end in *-f* or *-fe*, change the *f* to *ve* and add *-s*. For other words that end in *-f*, add *-s* without any change in the base word.

one thief	six thieves
a leaf	some leaves
a roof	two roofs
his belief	their beliefs
the chief	two chiefs

■ For words ending in a consonant plus *-y*, change the *y* to *i* and add *-es*. For words ending in a vowel plus *-y*, add an *-s*.

one boy	several boys
one company	four companies
one candy	some candies
a monkey	two monkeys

■ For words ending in a vowel plus *-o*, add an *-s*. For words ending in a consonant plus *-o*, add an *-s*, *-es*, or either *-s* or *-es*.

a radio	some radios
one patio	two patios
the auto	some autos
his hero	their heroes
one potato	bag of potatoes
one zero	two zeros (or) zeroes
the cargo	boats' cargos (or) cargoes

■ For some words, the plural is formed by changing the base word.

one child	several children
one woman	two women
one goose	nine geese
one mouse	some mice

■ Some words have the same form for both singular and plural.

deer   sheep   pliers

■ Some words from other languages keep their original plural endings.

for men: one alumnus	some alumni
for women: one alumna	several alumnae
one antenna	two antennae
an appendix	three appendices
a basis	some bases
a criterion	some criteria
a crisis	two crises
one datum	several pieces of data
a medium	all the media
one memorandum	two memoranda
a phenomenon	some phenomena
one radius	two radii
a thesis	several theses

But some of these words are beginning to acquire an English plural, such as *antennas, appendixes,* and *memorandums.*

Exercise 39.9: Proofreading Practice

Which of the following words is an incorrectly spelled plural? Use your dictionary if needed.

1. foxs	6. stereos	11. womans
2. papers	7. tariffs	12. freshmans
3. companys	8. brother-in-laws	13. passer-bys
4. latchs	9. bushes	14. heroes
5. analyses	10. windows	15. attorneys

39e Sound-Alike Words (Homonyms)

English has a number of words that sound alike but are spelled differently and have different meanings. These are called **homonyms.**

accept/except
accept (a verb meaning "to agree," "to receive"): She accepted the gift.
except (a preposition meaning "other than"): Everyone danced except Tom.

affect/effect
affect (a verb meaning "to influence"): Lack of sleep affects his performance.
effect (a noun meaning "result," used in phrases such as *in effect, take effect,* and *to that effect,*): What effect does that medicine have?
effect (a verb meaning "to accomplish"): to effect a cure

all ready/already
all ready (an adjective expressing readiness): Finally, the family was all ready to leave.
already (an adverb expressing time): Everyone had already left.

all together/altogether
all together (an adverb meaning "in a group"): The students were all together in the cafeteria.
altogether (an adverb meaning "thoroughly"): Her actions were altogether unnecessary.

any more/anymore
any more (a phrase referring to one or more items): Are there any more potato chips?
anymore (an adverb meaning "now," "henceforth"): I don't want to see her anymore.

any one/anyone
any one (a phrase referring to a specific person or thing): Any one of those newspapers will have the story.

anyone (a pronoun meaning any person at all): Can anyone hear me?

a while/awhile

a while (an article and a noun meaning "a period of time"): It will take a while to finish this.

awhile (an adverb meaning "for a short while"): I can stay awhile.

desert/dessert

desert (a noun meaning "dry," "arid place"; a verb meaning "to abandon"): While exploring the Mojave Desert, they deserted their friends when danger appeared.

dessert (a noun meaning "sweet course at the end of a meal"): They ordered cherry pie for dessert.

hear/here

hear (a verb): Did you hear that?

here (indicates a place): Come over here.

its/it's

its (shows possession): We checked its oil and gas.

it's (a contraction = "it is"): It's hard to do that.

quiet/quit/quite

quiet (an adjective meaning "no sound or noise"): Mornings are a quiet time.

quit (a verb meaning "to give up," "abandon"): He quit working on it.

quite (an adverb meaning "very," "entirely"): That painting is quite nice.

than/then

than (a word used in comparisons): She is richer than I.

then (a time word): Then he went home.

their/there/they're

their (shows possession): They paid for their books.

there (indicates a place): Look over there.

they're (a contraction = "they are"): They're going to paint that house.

to/too

to (a preposition): Take this to the office.

too (adverb meaning "also," "very"): It is too bad that she is too tired to join us.

were/we're/where

were (verb): They were singing.

we're (contraction = "we are"): We are about to leave here.

where (in what place): Where is he?

who's/whose

who's (contraction = "who is"): Who's going to the game?

whose (shows possession): Whose book is this?

your/you're

your (shows possession): Your grades have improved.

you're (a contraction = "you are"): You're part of that group.

Exercise 39.10: Proofreading Practice

Select the correctly spelled word for each of the following sentences.

1. The weather always (affects, effects) my moods.
2. She was (to, too) tired to join in.
3. It was a (quite, quiet) summer evening.
4. Would (anyone, any one) of these shirts be acceptable?
5. I need another (envelop, envelope) for these letters.
6. Her tardiness was an (every day, everyday) occurrence.
7. The coach offered some useful (advice, advise).
8. It seemed that (any way, anyway) he threw the hoop, it landed on the rung.
9. It is always cooler in the woods (than, then) in the city.
10. I often drive (by, buy) the Smiths' house.
11. When (it's, its) snowing, the street sounds seem muffled.
12. The table remained (stationary, stationery) when the wind shook the room.
13. When the teacher asked a question, the students answered (all together, altogether).
14. The dictionary (maybe, may be) helpful in deciding which word you want.
15. Whenever the train (passed, past) the station, the conductor waved to the stationmaster.
16. The salesclerk asked his supervisor for some (assistants, assistance) with the computer.
17. The committee agreed that it was (alright, all right) to table the motion being discussed.
18. The football game was nearing the end of the (forth, fourth) quarter.
19. The teacher asked everyone to (sight, cite, site) all the sources used in the term paper.
20. What does (there, their, they're) car horn sound like?

40 Sexist Language (sxt)

In order to avoid language that either favors the male noun or pronoun or excludes females, consider the following guidelines and suggestions.

40a Alternatives to *Man*

Man originally referred in a general way to both males and females, but the word has become closely associated with adult males only. To avoid this use of *man*, use alternative terms.

Man	Alternative
man	person, individual
mankind	people, human beings, humanity
man-made	machine-made, synthetic, artificial
the common man	the average (or ordinary) person
to man	to operate

40b Alternative Job Titles

Many terms for jobs suggest that only men hold or can hold those jobs. To avoid this, try an alternative term.

Man	Alternative
chairman	chairperson, chair, coordinator
mailman	letter carrier, postal worker
policeman	police officer
steward, stewardess	flight attendant
congressman	congressional representative
Dear Sir:	Dear Editor: Dear Service Representative:

40c Alternatives to the Masculine Pronoun

Use an alternative term when you want to convey a general meaning or refer to both sexes instead of using the masculine pronoun *he*.

■ Use the plural instead.

Give the customer his receipt with the change.

Revised: Give customers their receipts with the change.

■ Eliminate the male pronoun or reword to avoid unnecessary problems.

The average citizen worries about his retirement benefits.

Revised: The average citizen worries about retirement benefits.

If the taxpayer has questions about the new form, he can call a government representative.

Revised: The taxpayer with questions about the new form can call a government representative.

■ Replace the male pronoun with *one, you, he or she,* or an article (*a, an, the*).

The pet owner who can afford it takes his pet to a veterinarian.

Revised: The pet owner who can afford it takes his or her pet to a veterinarian.

(or)

The pet owner who can afford it takes the pet to a veterinarian.

■ Repeat a title rather than using a male pronoun.

See your doctor first, and he will explain the prescription.

Revised: See your doctor first, and the doctor will explain the prescription.

■ Alternate male and female examples. (But be careful not to confuse your reader.)

A young child is often persuaded by advertisements to buy what he sees on television. When a child goes shopping with a parent, she sees the product on the shelf, remembers it, and asks to have it.

■ Address the reader directly in the second person.

The applicant must mail his form by Thursday.

Revised: Mail your form by Thursday.

For the indefinite pronouns *everybody, anybody, everyone,* and *anyone,* some people prefer to continue using the male pronoun (*everyone . . . he*). But the plural pronoun has also become acceptable (*everyone . . . they*).

Exercise 40.1: Proofreading Practice

In the following paragraph, there is some language that could be deemed sexist. Revise the paragraph so that nonsexist language is used consistently.

In the curricula of most business schools, the study of failure has not yet become an accepted subject. Yet the average business student needs to know what he should do when a business strategy fails and how he can learn from his mistakes. Even the chairman of one Fortune 500 company says that the average businessman can learn more from his mistakes than from his successes. Yet the concept of studying failure has been slow in catching on. However, a few business schools and even engineering management majors at one university in California now confront the question of how anyone can recover from his mistakes. Student papers analyze how a typical failed entrepreneur might have better managed his problems. Sometimes, a perceptive student can even relate the lessons to his own behavior. One of the typical problems that is studied is that of escalating commitment, the tendency of a manager to throw more and more of his financial resources and manpower into a project that is failing. Another is the tendency of the hapless executive not to see that his idea is a bomb. For this reason, computers are being enlisted to help him—and his superiors—make decisions about whether he should bail out or stay in. The study of failure clearly promises to breed success, at least for future businessmen now enrolled in business schools.

Exercise 40.2: Pattern Practice

Using the suggestions for avoiding sexist language offered in 40c, write a short paragraph about people in a particular profession or group. To gain practice in using various options for using nonsexist language, try to include a variety of suggestions from this section.

41 Unnecessary Words

41a Conciseness (con)

Be concise when writing because you will be communicating to your reader more clearly and are more likely to keep your reader's interest. Many readers also don't have time for excess words. To keep your paper concise, eliminate what your readers do not need to know, what they already know, and whatever doesn't further the purpose of your paper. That often means resisting the impulse to include everything you know about a subject. Suggestions for eliminating unnecessary words:

- Avoid repetition. Some phrases, such as the following, say the same thing twice:

first beginning	6 P.M. in the evening
final completion	beautiful and lovely
circular in shape	true facts
green in color	prove conclusively
really and truly	each and every
positive benefits	connected together

- Avoid fillers. Some phrases, such as the following, say little or nothing:

there is (or) that there is	there are
in view of the fact that	I am going to explain
I am going to discuss	

                                        is
He said ~~that there is~~ a storm ˄approaching.

                              because
The mayor said that ~~in view of the fact that~~ the budget was overspent, no more projects could be started.

It
~~It seems to me that it~~ is getting dark out.

Artificial
~~I am going to discuss artificial~~ intelligence,~~/which~~ is an exciting new field of research.

■ Combine sentences. When the same nouns or pronouns appear in two sentences, combine the two sentences into one.

and
The data will be entered into the reports,~~/It will also be~~ included in the graphs.

■ Eliminate *who, which,* and *that.*

The book ~~that was~~ lying on the piano belongs to her.

■ Turn phrases and clauses into adjectives and adverbs.

the player who was very tired	=	the tired player
all applicants who are interested	=	all interested applicants
touched in a hesitant manner	=	touched hesitantly
the piano built out of mahogany	=	the mahogany piano

■ Turn prepositional phrases into adjectives.

an employee with ambition	=	an ambitious employee
the entrance to the station	=	the station entrance

■ Use active rather than passive.

research department   the figures.
The ~~figures were~~ checked ~~by the research department.~~

■ Remove excess nouns and change to verbs whenever possible.

He ~~made the statement that he~~ agreed ~~with the concept~~ that inflation could be controlled.

stores
The ~~function of the~~ box ~~is the storage of~~ excess wire connectors.

■ Replace jargon with clearer, shorter words.

Avoid	Use
advantageous	beneficial
implement	carry out
procure	acquire
utilize	use
effectuate	carry out
ascertain	find out

Exercise 41.1: Proofreading Practice

The following paragraph is very wordy. Eliminate as many words as you can without losing clarity. You may need to add a few words, too.

It has recently been noted by researchers that there is a growing concern among psychologists that as more parents who are working entrust the responsibility for caring for their infants of a very young age to day-care centers, some of these babies may face harm of a psychological nature. The research findings of the researchers in this field focus on children who are younger than eighteen months of age who are left in day-care centers more than twenty hours a week. For children who are at that most formative age, say the researchers, day care seems to increase the feeling of insecurity. One of the foremost leading researchers in this field says that he isn't sure how the increase in the feeling of insecurity happens, but it is his guess that the stress that a child undergoes each and every day as a result of the separation from the parent can be a contributing causal factor here. Studies of the infants who are in day care for long periods of time each week have shown that more of these infants exhibit feelings of anxiousness and also hyperactivity. These findings definitely and strongly challenge the older view that day care does not harm or hurt a young child.

Exercise 41.2: Pattern Practice

Listed here are some patterns for eliminating unnecessary words. Following the patterns and examples given here, make up a wordy sentence and then a more concise revision.

Pattern A: Reducing a *who, which,* or *what* clause

Wordy: The cook who was flipping hamburgers . . .

Revised: The cook flipping hamburgers . . .

Pattern B: Eliminating fillers

Wordy: It is important that we agree that . . .

Revised: We must agree that . . .

Pattern C: Changing a passive verb to active

Wordy: The car was started by the driver.

Revised: The driver started the car.

Pattern D: Combining sentences

Wordy: The cereal box was decorated with pictures of famous athletes on one side. The box had recipes for candy and snacks on the other side.

Revised: The cereal box was decorated with pictures of famous athletes on one side and recipes for candy and snacks on the other side.

Pattern E: Turning a phrase or clause into an adjective or adverb

Wordy: The salesperson who sold used cars starred in the TV commercial.

Revised: The used-car salesperson starred in the TV commercial.

Pattern F: Eliminating repetition

Wordy: When she was first beginning to drive her car, she never drove more than thirty miles per hour.

Revised: When she began to drive her car, she never drove more than thirty miles per hour.

Pattern F: Turning a prepositional phrase into an adjective

Wordy: Use the paper with the red lines.

Revised: Use the red-lined paper.

41b   Clichés (cl)

Clichés are overused, tired expressions that have lost their ability to communicate effectively.

When you read phrases such as *busy as a beaver* or *a crying shame,* you are not likely to think about a beaver busily working or someone actually crying in shame. Avoid expressions such as the following, which are worn out from too much repetition and are no longer vivid:

white as snow	rat race
beat around the bush	have a screw loose
suits me to a tee	add insult to injury
in a nutshell	calm before the storm
crack of dawn	better late than never
clear as mud	green with envy
playing with fire	stubborn as a mule
at the drop of a hat	sell like hotcakes

Exercise 41.3: Proofreading Practice

Underline the clichés in the following paragraph.

The Ford Motor Company has developed a new method of testing automobiles for different age groups. In a nutshell, Ford has designed a suit that makes the crash tester feel as old as the day is long. In order for the tester to experience empathy for aging customers, the suit dims vision, weakens muscles and makes the tester feel stiff as a board. One tester states, "I'm thirty-two years old, but this gear suits me to a tee because it helps me do my job." Testers wear the suit while getting in and out of vehicles, buckling the seat belt, and driving in reverse. Ford hopes that vehicles designed for aging consumers will sell like hot cakes. Many senior citizens feel that they are ignored in the competitive market of automobile sales. One senior says, "We are virtually ignored in the car market, so it is good to see cars designed for senior citizens. It's better late than never." With the success of Ford's designing techniques, many other motor companies will be jumping on the bandwagon.

Exercise 41.4: Revision Practice

Revise the paragraph in Exercise 41.3 by using more precise language in place of the clichés.

41c Pretentious Language (wc)

Pretentious language is language that is too showy; it calls attention to itself by the use of overly complex sentences and ornate, polysyllabic words used for their own sake.

The following sentence is an example of overblown, pompous language that makes the writer sound pretentious and affected. Plain English that communicates clearly is far better than such attempts at showing off.

Pretentious: The lucidity with which she formulated her questions as she interrogated the indigenous population of the rustic isle drew gasps of admiration from her cohorts.

Revised: Her friends admired her ability to clearly phrase the questions she asked the island's inhabitants.

42 Appropriate Words (wds)

Choosing among words is a matter of selecting the correct word, the word that is right in any writing situation. For example, whether an essay is formal or informal, you should always write "between you and *me*" (not "between you and *I*"). But other word choices are not so clear-cut. Instead, it is a question of which word is appropriate for the subject, audience, and purpose of a particular piece of writing.

42a Standard English

Standard English is the generally accepted language of educated people. It is "standard" because it conforms to established rules of grammar, sentence structure, punctuation, and spelling.

Standard English, the language used in magazines, newspapers, and books read by educated people, is the language you are expected to use in academic writing. If you are not sure a particular word is standard, check the dictionary. Nonstandard words such as *ain't* are labeled to indicate that they are not acceptable for standard usage.

42b Colloquialisms, Slang, and Regionalisms

Colloquial words are the language of casual conversation and informal writing.

kids (instead of *children*)
sci-fi (instead of *science fiction*)
flunk (instead of *fail*)

Slang words are terms that are made up (such as *ditz* or *zonked out*) or are given new definitions (such as *gig* for musician's engagement or *pig* for police officer) in order to be novel or unconventional. (Distinguishing between colloquialisms and slang is often difficult, and experts who are consulted when dictionaries are compiled do not always agree.)

to dis (to show disrespect)   blow off
classic (in the sense of very good) in your face
chill (in the sense of calm down)   hit on

Regional words (also called *localisms* or *provincialisms*) are words and phrases more commonly used in one geographic area than in another.

pail   (or) bucket
bag   (or) sack   (or) poke   (or) tote
porch   (or) verandah
seesaw   (or) teeter-totter (or) teeterboard

Although colloquialisms, slang, and regionalisms are not substandard or illiterate, most readers consider them inappropriate for formal academic writing. Colloquial language is acceptable for informal writing and dialogue, but slang may be unfamiliar to some readers. Slang terms are appropriate for very informal conversations among a group familiar with the current meanings of the terms. After a period of usage, many slang terms become outdated and disappear (for example, *the cat's pajamas, twenty-three skiddoo,* or *a real cool cat*), but some, such as *mob, dropout, fan, job,* and *phone,* have become accepted as standard usage.

Some writers are able to make use of an occasional colloquialism or slang term for effect when the writing is not highly formal.

The arts and humanities should be paid for by the private sector, not by government grants. Freedom of artistic expression is in danger when government has its paws where they should not be.

The National Park Service is fighting back at people who say it doesn't know beans about keeping up the ecological health of our national parks. To stand up for its recent actions, the service has sent out some reports that show its policies have had beneficial effects.

Exercise 42.1: Dictionary Practice

Look up the following colloquialisms and slang terms in two or three different dictionaries. What labels and usage suggestions are given for these terms?

1. yo (meaning: "a greeting")
2. cheesy (meaning: "something of poor quality")
3. chill (meaning: "relax")
4. diss (meaning: "put a person down verbally")
5. nerd (meaning: "a person who is not popular")
6. flaky (meaning: "eccentric, strange")
7. boss (meaning: "something of high quality")

8. rip off (meaning: "something overpriced")
9. dude (meaning: "guy")
10. airhead (meaning: "someone lacking common sense")

Exercise 42.2: Writing Practice

List five slang words that you know. Use the words in sentences, and then rewrite the sentence using a standard word with the same definition.

Example: gross out

Slang: He was so grossed out by the biology experiment that he was unable to finish.

Revised: He was so disgusted by the biology experiment that he was unable to finish.

42c Levels of Formality

The level of formality is the **tone** in writing; it reflects the attitude of the writer toward the subject and audience. The tone may be highly formal or very informal or somewhere in between.

Informal tone uses words and sentence constructions close to ordinary speech and may include slang, colloquialisms, and regionalisms. Like everyday speech, informal writing tends not to have the most precise word choices. It uses contractions; it uses first and second person pronouns such as *I* and *you* (see 18b); it uses verbs such as *get, is,* and *have;* and it may include sentence fragments for effect. An informal tone is used by speakers and writers for everyday communication and is appropriate in informal writing.

Informal: He was *sort of* irritated because he couldn't find his car keys and didn't have *a whole lot of* time to get to his office.

Medium tone is not too casual, not too scholarly. It uses standard vocabulary, conventional sentence structures, and few or no contractions, and it is often the level you'll be expected to use for papers.

Medium: He was *somewhat* irritated because he could *not* find his car keys and did *not* have *much* time to get to his office.

Formal tone is scholarly and uses sophisticated, multisyllabic words in complex sentence structures not likely to be used when speaking. It often uses the third person pronouns *he or she* or *one* (see 18b) instead of *I* or *you.* Formal writing is preferred by some readers, but others find that it is not as easy to read or understand. Many businesses as well as government and other public offices encourage employees to maintain a medium level of formality.

Formal: Unable to locate his car keys and lacking sufficient time to find alternative transportation to his office, he was agitated.

In the following example the same information is presented at several levels of formality:

Informal: Someone who wants to have a bill passed in this state should start the process by getting it presented in the General Assembly or the Senate. The next thing that happens is that there's a committee that looks at it. The committee meets to decide on changing, accepting, or killing the bill. Usually, there's a lot of discussion when the bill comes back to the General Assembly and Senate. Both places have to okay the bill. If they don't like it, then a committee gets together with people from both the General Assembly and the Senate. They pound out a version that will make both houses happy. When the bill gets passed in both houses, it gets to move on to the governor. If the governor signs the bill or just doesn't do anything, it becomes a law. If the governor says no, it either dies or goes back to the Senate and General Assembly. It's got to get a two-thirds vote in both houses to become a law.

Medium: For a bill to become a law in this state, the first step is to have it introduced in the General Assembly or the Senate. Next, the bill is sent to a committee that holds hearings to change, approve, or kill the bill. When the bill returns to the General Assembly and Senate, there is often a great deal of debate before a vote is taken. If both houses do not pass the bill, a joint committee is appointed, with representatives from both the General Assembly and the Senate. This committee then draws up a bill that is acceptable to both houses. When both houses approve and pass the bill, it moves to the governor's office. For the bill to become a law, the governor can either sign it or take no action. The governor may, however, veto the bill. In this case, it either dies or goes back to both houses where it must pass with a two-thirds majority. If so, it then becomes a law, despite the governor's veto.

Formal: The procedure for passage of legislation in this state originates in either the General Assembly or the Senate. From here the bill is forwarded to a committee where hearings are initiated to determine whether the bill will be endorsed, altered, or terminated. From there, the bill returns to the General Assembly and Senate where extensive debate occurs before voting is completed. If the bill fails to pass both houses, a joint committee is charged with formulating a compromise bill acceptable to both the Senate and General Assembly. Approval by both houses results in advancing the bill to the governor; the bill will then become law with the governor's signature or with no action being taken in the governor's office. Should the governor reject the bill with a veto, it is either no longer viable or can be resuscitated through a two-thirds favorable vote in both houses, which then constitutes passage into law.

Once you set the level of formality in an essay, keep it consistent. Mixing levels can be distracting and indicates that the writer doesn't have adequate control (see 11c).

The economist offered the business executives a lengthy explanation for
the recent fluctuation in the stock market. But it was ~~pretty~~ *quite* obvious from
their questions afterward that they ~~didn't get~~ *did not understand* it.

For an example of a paragraph with an inconsistent level of formality,
see Exercise 42.3.

Exercise 42.3: Proofreading Practice

*The following paragraph is intended to be written in a medium to formal tone,
but the writer lost control and slipped into some inappropriate choices of informal words and phrases. Rewrite the paragraph so that the wording is consistently at a medium to formal level.*

A new technology called MP3 could change the way consumers buy
their favorite music. Musicians can use this thing to market their songs
directly to consumers, bypassing agents, recording companies, and dis-
tributors. We could then use a special recording device to download the
best stuff off the computer. Consumers will even be able to copy and
store CD's on home computers and transfer them to a music player.
Music industry bosses are sweating this out. These guys are afraid they
won't get their cut. The Recording Industry of America Association
warns that many illegal copies of an artist's work will be floating around.
The RIAA is concerned for the artists and the royalties they may lose
because of this new technology. The artists, consumers, and record
companies can all get a pretty good deal from this new technology if
they cool it at the get-go.

Exercise 42.4: Pattern Practice

*The tone of the following sentences can be altered by changing some of the key
terms. If the sentence is informal, change it to a more formal tone. Similarly, if
the sentence is formal, change it to a more informal tone. A sample sentence
has been changed from formal to informal.*

Original: Scientists are issuing warnings that one procedure for alleviat-
ing the menace of global warming is to reduce carbon dioxide
emissions.

Informal Tone: Scientists warn that one way to reduce the threat of
global warming is to cut down on carbon dioxide
exhaust.

1. A step in the right direction would be to lean on automobile
makers and make them raise the fuel efficiency of the gas-
guzzling cars they are turning out.
2. But an even quicker way to drop fuel use would be to hike the
gas tax.
3. Environmentalists are also requesting stricter limitations on
smokestack emissions of sulfur dioxide, a major contributor to
acid rain.

4. But states now producing high-sulfur coal aren't happy about the damage this will do to their economies.

42d Jargon and Technical Terms

Jargon (also called *technical terms*) is the specialized language of various trades, professions, and groups, such as lawyers, plumbers, electricians, biologists, horse racers, and pharmacists. These terms are used by specialists within a group to communicate with each other in a concise way when referring to various complex concepts, objects, techniques, and so on. Jargon is also a negative term that refers to the use of unnecessarily inflated expressions, including *euphemisms*, which are terms used to disguise unpleasant realities.

Specialized Language: subcutaneous hemorrhage, metabolic disorders, carburetors, fuel injectors, exhaust manifolds

Inflated Expressions: learning facilitator (teacher)
monetary remuneration (pay)

Euphemisms: revenue enhancement (taxes)
pre-owned (used)
nonmilitary collateral damage (dead citizens)

When you are writing about a specialized subject for a general audience and need to use a technical term, define the term in easily understandable language the first time it is used. You can then use the word later on and not lose the reader.

One of the great challenges for the future is the development of superconductors, metallic ceramics that when cooled below a certain critical temperature offer no resistance to the flow of an electric current. Presently, research on superconductors has not resulted in any major breakthroughs.

Unnecessary jargon indicates the writer's inability to write clearly. Note the wordiness and pompous tone of this example:

Original: Utilize this receptacle, which functions as a repository for matter to be disposed of.

Revised: Deposit litter here.

42e General and Specific Words

General words refer to whole categories or large classes of items. **Specific words** identify items in a group.

Tree is more general than *maple,* and *maple* is more general than *sugar maple,* a particular kind of maple tree.

General	Specific	More specific
animal	dog	cocker spaniel
plant	flower	rose
clothing	shoes	loafers

Sometimes, a general word is adequate or appropriate for the occasion. For example, *car* is a more general word than *Ford*, and it is more appropriate in the following brief account of a trip:

> This year we visited several parts of the country that we had not seen before. Last fall, we flew to New Mexico for a week, and during spring vacation we traveled by car from New York to Chicago.

General terms are appropriate in some contexts, but specific words are often better choices because they are more precise and vivid and can help the reader's imagination in seeing, hearing, feeling, and smelling what is described (if that is the writer's purpose). Compare these examples.

General: He walked across the street to see the merchandise in the store window.

More Specific: He ambled across Lexington Avenue to see the velvet ties in the window at Bloomingdale's.

General: To help our economy, America needs to sell more products on the world market.

More Specific: To decrease our trade deficit, American industries should develop their best high-tech products, such as high-resolution television and communications satellites, to sell to growing markets in China and Europe.

Some general words are too vague to convey a writer's meaning.

bad child   [Is the child rude? evil? ungrateful?]

bad food   [Is the food contaminated? tasteless? unhealthy?]

Exercise 42.5: Pattern Practice

Listed next are some general terms. What are more specific words that could be used instead?

General	Specific	More specific
food	vegetable	carrot
1. music	**5.** field of study	**9.** place of business
2. book	**6.** machine	**10.** athlete
3. animal	**7.** car	
4. clothes	**8.** food	

42f   Concrete and Abstract Words

Concrete words refer to people and things that can be perceived by the senses. We are able to form images in our minds of concrete terms: *the thick white foam in the glass, dog, garden gate, smoke.*

Abstract words refer to qualities, concepts, conditions, and ideas: *truth, economics, slow, happy, ethical.*

We need both abstract terms to communicate complex ideas and concrete words to convey what we see, hear, taste, touch, and feel. However, dull writing tends to be unnecessarily abstract and overuses words such as *aspects, factors,* and *means.*

Abstract: Rain forest trees constitute more than 20 percent of the industrial world's consumption of wood. The harvest from rain forest trees is a valuable crop because of the trees' resistance to disease and insect infestations. In addition, because wood from these trees has special properties, they are useful for particular types of structures. Their characteristic colors and growth patterns make rain forest trees well suited for use in furniture and other wooden products in which color is a prized commodity. Thus, in recent years, global demand for tropical hardwoods has increased dramatically.

Concrete: More than 20 percent of the wood used throughout the world is cut from rain forests. The trees from these forests are valued for their ability to resist termites, fungi, and other common diseases of wood. In addition, rain forest hardwoods have qualities that make them especially useful for certain purposes. For example, teak resists water damage, so it is used on sailboats. The dark reddish color and interesting grain of rosewood are particularly attractive when made into chairs, tables, and beds; dark brown or black ebony wood is used in billiard balls and for the black keys of pianos. Thus, in the last five years, countries throughout the world have ordered and imported more tropical wood than they used in the preceding fifty years.

Exercise 42.6: Revision Practice

The following description in a travel magazine has some abstract and general terms that could be revised to be more specific and concrete. Rewrite the paragraph so that it is more specific and concrete.

Traveling to the Bahamas, a group of islands fifty miles across the water from the United States, is an easy trip for private boats. Since gambling is a popular sport, people go on weekends to gamble and to enjoy other sports. Tourism is the nation's leading industry, and Bahamian planners predict a sharp rise in the future. Because of this expectation, developers are building more housing of different types. Nassau, which has suffered from increased crime, is no longer the primary location for tourist development, but boats continue to stop there to let people look around.

42g Denotation and Connotation

The **denotation** of a word is the dictionary meaning, the definition.

> The **connotation** is the group of ideas implied but not directly indicated by the word. The connotation conveys attitudes and emotional overtones, either positive or negative, beyond the direct definition. Although connotations may vary among individuals, there is also a large group of shared connotations.

A pig is an animal (the denotation), but there are also negative connotations of sloppiness, dirt, and fat associated with pigs. *Elected official* and *politician* have similar denotative meanings, but *politician* has a negative connotation, whereas *elected official* connotes a more positive quality. While *fat, plump,* and *obese* describe the same condition, *fat* has a more negative connotation than *plump,* and *obese,* a medical term, is generally considered to be a more neutral term.

Exercise 42.7: Pattern Practice

The following groups of words have similar denotative meanings, but their connotations differ. Arrange each group so that the words go from most positive to most negative.

Most Positive	Neutral	Most Negative
slender	lean	scrawny

1. canine, mutt, puppy
2. law-enforcement officer, police officer, cop
3. cheap, inexpensive, economical
4. ornate, embellished, garish
5. counterfeit, replica, copy
6. scholar, egghead, intellectual
7. determined, stubborn, uncompromising
8. scared, apprehensive, paranoid
9. explanation, excuse, reason
10. gabby, talkative, chatty

43 Finding a Topic (top)

Finding a topic for a research paper is a four-step process:

1. **Find** a general topic that interests you.
2. **Narrow** that topic to fit the assignment.
3. **Formulate** a research question about your topic.
4. **Formulate** a thesis statement that answers your research question.

43a Finding a General Topic

If you are not assigned a specific topic for a research paper, you can begin by looking for information about any subject that interests you. This can be an opportunity to learn about some aspect of your major field, about future careers, or about another subject that interests you. Do some explorative thinking about your hobbies, about the world around you, about interesting topics that have come up in conversation, or about something you're studying in a course. For example, have you recently heard something interesting about organic food? teaching animals to communicate? the rapid growth of the electronics industry? the history of jazz? earthquake predictions? the future of car design? the technology boom? the confusing options in health care insurance? pollution in the ocean? America's changing preferences in sports? fossil findings? What news items do you read or hear on television that you'd like more background on?

One way to locate an interesting subject is to browse through any book or catalog of subject headings. For example, the *Library of Congress Subject Headings* or the *Reader's Guide to Periodical Literature* are thick volumes of headings and subheadings. Another way to locate a fresh subject is to skim through the table of contents of a magazine you read regularly or a magazine in your library's collection.

43b Narrowing the Topic

Once you've identified a general subject, you will need to narrow it into a topic that is more specific and manageable. How much time will you have to do the research? How long will the paper be? The answers to these questions will determine how much you have to narrow your topic. A topic you can spend six to eight weeks researching can be larger or more complex than one you only have two weeks to investigate. Similarly, if you are expected to write a twenty-page paper, you will be able to cover more about a topic than if you are expected to write an eight-page paper.

To narrow your topic, begin by thinking of it as a tree with many branches or a blanket covering many subtopics or smaller aspects. What are some of those subtopics? Choose one and think of some of the aspects of that subtopic that might be topics in themselves. For example, suppose you had decided on the topic of changing preferences in sports in America. That topic could branch into sports that have declined in popularity as well as other sports that are becoming national pastimes. If you chose sports that have become more popular, you could focus on one of these sports, such as soccer. Now, if you needed to narrow your topic even further, you might subdivide it into categories, such as the growing popularity of soccer as a school sport or as a national spectator sport in America, and choose only one of those. As you search for information, you may find the need to narrow even further.

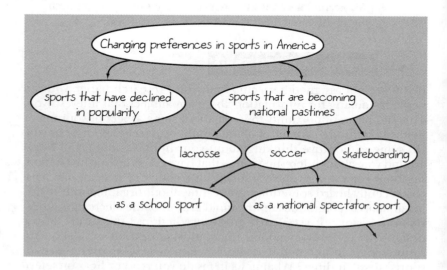

43c Formulating a Research Question

After you have located a general topic and narrowed it sufficiently, you need to formulate a question your research is going to answer. This process will lead to your thesis, but before you formulate a thesis, collect your information and see what you find. The research question will help you decide what information is relevant. Suppose you are writing about the benefits to your community for recycling paper, glass, and aluminum. What will your research question be? Are you interested in knowing whether the local government saves money by recycling? Or are you interested in the effect recycling might have on the cost of dumping garbage? Or are you interested in the community's support for this program? You can also ask yourself the reporter's *who, what, why, how,* and *when* questions. It may help to formulate a thesis, a statement that you think might be true but that might also change as you do your research.

43d Formulating a Thesis

After completing your research and reviewing your information, you will be able to formulate a tentative thesis or main point that is the result of your investigation. This main point will answer your research question and will make a statement about one aspect of the general topic you started with. It may need to be revised as you write and revise the paper. The thesis is more than a summary of the information, however. It states your position or the point that you are arguing and should synthesize and bring together the information into a unified whole that conveys what you, the knowledgeable writer, have learned.

Subject	Alternative health treatments, such as herbal therapies
Topic	Herbal medicines
Original research question (too broad and had to be narrowed)	What are herbal medicines being used for?
Revised research question	What herbal remedies are investigators learning about that fight colds?
Thesis	Investigators are finding that elderberry root shows promise of reducing or stopping the growth of flu viruses.

44 Searching for Information (info)

44a Locating Sources of Information

The two categories of information are primary and secondary sources.

- **Primary sources** are original or firsthand materials. If you read a novel or a poem by an author, you are reading the original or primary source; if you read a study or review of that writing, you are reading secondary material *about* that work of fiction or poetry, not the work itself. Primary sources include writings by the original author, such as novels or autobiographies (but not, for example, biographies *about* that person); surveys, studies, speeches, or interviews that you conduct; any creative work by the original author (poems, plays, art forms such as pictures and sculpture, etc.); and firsthand accounts of events.

  Primary sources may be more accurate because they have not been distorted by others, though they are not always available and may be difficult to access. That is, you might not be able to view an older movie no longer publicly available and may have to settle for a secondhand report of it. But the secondhand report will be filtered through someone else's mind or viewpoint, so whenever possible, use primary sources.

- **Secondary sources** are secondhand accounts, information, or reports *about* primary sources. Typical secondary sources include reviews, biographies about a person you are studying, documentaries, encyclopedia articles, and other material interpreted or studied by others. Although reading secondary sources may save time, remember that they are interpretations or analyses that may be biased, inaccurate, or incomplete. Because real research does not depend solely on the analyses or evaluations done by others, use secondary sources to support your own thinking.

It's important to remember that the same source can be both a primary source in one field of research and a secondary source for another. For example, a biography about President Nixon would be a secondary source if you are researching some aspect of his life. But if you are researching public opinion and reactions to President Nixon, that biography would be a primary source.

HINT   **Emphasizing the Writer's Views**

While some cultures place more value on student writing that primarily brings together or collects the thoughts of great scholars or experts, readers of research papers in American institutions value the writer's own interpretations and thinking about the subject.

Finding information is an art, not a science. Just as a good angler learns where the best fishing spots are located, a skilled researcher learns where the best sources are, depending on the kinds of information being sought. Some information is best found in print sources located through the library or online, but it might be supplemented by information you gather from knowledgeable people around you. For example, if you're interested in health care for the elderly, there are a variety of articles in printed sources, but don't overlook local hospitals and nursing home administrators or local government agencies that are designed to provide such health care. Perhaps there is a faculty member at your school who does research in this area.

Start by building a working bibliography of materials to read, that is, an initial list of sources that seem promising, even though some will not turn out to be helpful and will be dropped before you put together your final list of works cited. Build the working bibliography by consulting a variety of sources in your library, by accessing online information on the Internet, by consulting resources in your own community, by communicating with people who can add to your knowledge about the topic, and by doing field research to collect firsthand information.

I. Libraries
Before you begin searching, spend some time learning about your library—what its resources are, where they are located, and how they are used. Libraries have various printed guides for users and an information desk where helpful librarians will answer your questions. Library catalogs, which list all the library's materials by author, title, and subject, may be available on cards, microfiche, or computers. Many library online catalogs are also connected to thousands of other

library catalogs so that you can locate materials in other libraries and ask for an interlibrary loan. Libraries have a variety of sources to help you begin with general or broad surveys of a topic. That will help you gain an overview and provide suggestions for further reading before you go on to more specific sources. Libraries also have collections of pamphlets and brochures, audio and video materials, and interlibrary loan services. (To document your sources, including those found on CD-ROM, videos, etc., see 52b, 53b, and Chapter 54.)

General Reference Sources

The library's reference section has encyclopedias such as *The New Encyclopedia Britannica* and the *Encyclopedia Americana,* as well as encyclopedias for specific areas of study such as the *Encyclopedia of Anthropology, Encyclopedia of Computer Science and Technology, Harvard Guide to American History,* or *The Oxford Companion to American Literature.* Librarians can show you where to locate such books and direct you to encyclopedias relevant to your topic. Other general sources include collections of biographies such as *Current Biography* or *African American Biographies,* yearbooks and almanacs such as the *World Almanac and Book of Facts,* dictionaries, atlases, and government publications such as *Statistical Abstract of the United States.*

Indexes, Catalogs, and Databases

Your library will have book indexes such as *Books in Print* and periodical indexes such as the *Reader's Guide to Periodical Literature.* If the library's catalog is computerized, you can also do online searches of the library's holdings by author, title, keyword, and subject heading. When you request a *keyword search,* the search tool will look for the word in any part of the entry in the catalog (title, subtitle, abstract, etc.), while the *subject heading* has to match word for word with the Library of Congress headings (listed in the *Library of Congress Subject Headings*). When doing a keyword search, you can also try synonyms for your topic or broader terms that might include it. For example, when searching for information about electric cars, you can also try "battery-operated cars" or "alternative energy sources" as keywords.

Library collections of CD-ROM databases permit you to search a great variety of sources. Many libraries also subscribe to one or more computerized bibliographic utilities such as *FirstSearch* (which accesses databases such as academic journals, corporations, congressional publications, and medical journals) or *Newsbank CD News* (which indexes articles from a variety of newspapers). Nexis/Lexis, a commercial service available online, has abstracts and full texts of magazines, newspapers, publications from industry and government, wire services, and other sources.

2. Online Sources

The Internet, an online network of networks, is a vast storehouse of information that can be searched in a variety of ways. Because searching online has greatly increased in popularity and complexity, you'll find detailed help with how to find information on the Internet, evaluate it, and document it in Chapters 48 through 51.

3. Community Sources

Your community has a variety of resources that can be tapped. If you are seeking public records or other local government information, your city hall or county courthouse can be a good place to search. Other sources of information are community service workers, social service agencies, schoolteachers and school administrators, community leaders, and religious leaders and religious institutions, as well as coordinators in nonprofit groups. The local newspaper is another storehouse of useful information. If there is a chamber of commerce or visitors and convention bureau nearby, their lists of local organizations may be helpful. Or you can check the phone book or the local public library for lists of community resources and people to contact. Local history can be studied at a historical museum or the local library, and the newspaper may have useful archives. Don't forget your campus as part of your community; faculty or administrators can be good sources of information.

4. Interviews and Surveys

You can do field research and seek information firsthand by interviewing people, sending e-mail messages, conducting surveys, and taking notes on your own observations. These forms of information gathering need to be undertaken thoughtfully. You need to be sure that you ask good questions and that you know how to collect information without distorting it. You should always be aware of your own filtering of material. Use these methods carefully.

44b Using Search Strategies

To search efficiently through the sources you've found, begin by drawing up a systematic plan and a schedule for finding the materials you want. Ask yourself the following questions:

- *Given the deadline I have, how much time can I devote to searching for materials?* Remember that you'll need time for reading, note taking, and organizing your material as well as for writing drafts of the paper. Allow for delays in getting resources, especially if you are requesting materials through interlibrary loan.

- *How current do the materials need to be?* Periodicals have more current materials than books do.

- *Does the assignment specify how many or what types of sources I should consult?*

I. Starting a Working Bibliography

Build a working bibliography, a list of all the sources you will read. Since you may not use all of these sources in your paper, the final list of sources you used will be shorter than your working bibliography. Use the suggestions in Chapter 45 to help evaluate the sources as you decide which you will read.

Consider making each bibliographic entry on a separate 3" × 5" card so that you can easily insert new entries in alphabetical order. Or, if you are using a computer, construct your list in a separate file from the paper. You can use the printout when you are not near your computer, and you won't need to retype your list of works cited, though you'll need to delete the entries that didn't provide material for the paper.

In each entry, include all the information you'll need in your references list (see 52c and 53c and Chapter 54) to locate the source. You'll save time later by determining now what documentation style you will be using (for example, MLA or APA) and putting all your working bibliography references in that style.

For books:

- Library call number (or other information needed to locate the entry)
- Names of authors, editors, translators
- Title and subtitle of the book
- Edition
- Publishing information (city, publishing company name, date)

329.54
Re7
1989
(library call number)

Marbell, Jaime. <u>Route 66</u>: <u>The First American Transcontinental Highway</u>.
(author)   *(title and subtitle)*

Rev. ed. San Francisco: Berham, 1989.
(edition)   *(publishing information)*

Sample bibliography card in MLA documentation style for a book

For articles:

- Names of author(s)
- Title and subtitle of the article
- Title of magazine, journal, newspaper
- Volume and issue numbers, if needed
- Date and page numbers

Yang, James, Thomas Uderwek, and Kulma Mahtar.
(authors)

"Credit Card Security Systems for the Internet." <u>Business Week</u>
(article title)   *(magazine title)*

14 Feb. 1995: 90–96.
(date and page numbers)

Sample bibliography card in MLA documentation style for an article

2. Finding Useful Terms

The subject headings in the *Library of Congress Subject Headings* can be useful in suggesting terms or keywords to use as well as additional terms that might not have occurred to you. Under most entries are alternative terms listed as BT (broader topic), RT (related topic), and NT (narrower topic). For example, if you look up global warming, you will find as a broader topic "global temperature changes" and as related topics "greenhouse effect, atmospheric changes." These are alternative terms you can use as you search for sources. Also, many databases have a thesaurus of keywords, and you can consult a print thesaurus for other options. As you read your sources, other synonyms or relevant keywords may occur to you.

3. Using Search Engines

Computer searches for library catalogs, online databases, and Internet search engines vary in the way you can use them. Some permit only the entry of keywords or terms, but in others you can indicate logical relationships between terms, using words such as *and, or,* and *not* to help you either broaden or narrow the search. The following examples in parentheses assume you are looking for material on teen alcoholism but not its relationship to teen crime:

AND	Use this to get listings that include two items.	
	A **AND** B	[alcoholism *and* teens]
OR	Use this to find items containing either term.	
	A **OR** B	[teens *or* juveniles]
NOT	Use this to eliminate irrelevant items.	
	A **NOT** B	[alcoholism *not* crime]
AND NOT	Use this to combine some related topics and eliminate others.	
	A **AND** B **NOT** C	[teens *and* alcohol *not* drugs]
*	Use this to include various forms of a word.	
	*alcohol.	[listing will include alcohol, alcoholism, alcoholics, etc.]

45 Evaluating Sources

We live in an age of such vast amounts of information that we cannot know everything about a subject. All the information that comes streaming at us from newspapers, magazines, the media, books, journals, brochures, Web sites, and so on is also of very uneven quality. People want to convince us to depend on their data, buy their products, accept their viewpoints, vote for their candidates, make donations to their causes, agree with their opinions, and rely on them as experts.

We make decisions all the time about which information we will use based on how we evaluate it. Evaluating sources, then, is a skill we need all the time, and applying that skill to research papers is equally important. Listed here are some stages in the process of evaluating sources for those research papers.

For additional material on evaluating sources on the Internet, see Chapter 50.

45a Getting Started

To begin, ask yourself what kinds of information you are looking for and where you are likely to find appropriate sources for that kind of information. You want to be sure that you are headed in the right direction as you launch into your search, and this too is part of the evaluation process—evaluating where you are most likely to get the right kind of information for your purpose.

- *What kind of information are you looking for?* Do you want facts? opinions? news reports? research studies? analyses? historical accounts? personal reflections? data? public records? scholarly essays reflecting on the topic? reviews?

- *Where would you find such information?* Which sources are most likely to be useful? libraries with scholarly journals, books, and government publications? public libraries with popular magazines? the Internet? newspapers? community records? someone on your campus?

If, for example, you are searching for information on some current event, a reliable newspaper such as the *New York Times* will be a useful source, and it is likely to be available in a university or public library and on the Web. If you need some statistics on the U.S. population, government census documents in libraries and on the Internet will be appropriate places to search. But if you want to do research into local history, the archives of local government offices and the local newspaper are better places to start. Consider whether there are organizations designed to gather and publish the kinds of information you are seeking. For example, if you are seeking information about teen drinking and driving, MADD (Mothers Against Drunk Driving) is likely to be a useful source. And be sure to ask yourself whether the organization's goal is to be objective or to gain support for its viewpoint. For example, a tobacco institute, funded by a large tobacco company, is not likely to gather as much unbiased information as possible about the harmfulness of cigarettes.

45b Evaluating Bibliographic Citations

Before you spend time hunting for a source or reading it, look at the following information in the citation to evaluate whether it's worth your time.

1. Author

Credentials

How reputable is the person (or organization) listed as the author?

■ What is the author's educational background? Is it appropriate for the kind of expertise you want?

■ What has the author written in the past about this topic? If this is the author's first publication in this area, perhaps the author is not yet an expert.

■ Why is this person considered an expert or a reliable authority? Who considers this person to be an expert? Would they be likely to have any bias?

You can learn more about the author by checking the Library of Congress catalog to see what else this person has written, and the *Book Review Index* and *Book Review Digest* may lead you to reviews of other books by this author. Your library may have citation indexes in the field that will lead you to other articles and short pieces by this person that have been cited by others.

For biographical information you can read *Who's Who in America* or the *Biography Index*. There may also be information about the person in the publication, such as a listing of previous writings, awards, and notes about the author. Your goal is to get some sense of who this person is and why it's worth reading what he or she wrote before you plunge in and begin reading. That may be important as you write the paper and build your case. For example, if you are citing a source to show the spread of AIDS in Africa, which of these sentences strengthens your argument?

> Dr. John Smith notes that the incidence of AIDS in Africa has more than doubled in the last five years.

> (or)

> Dr. John Smith, head of the World Health Organization committee studying AIDS in African countries, notes that the incidence of AIDS in Africa has more than doubled in the last five years.

References

■ Did a teacher or librarian or some other person who is knowledgeable about the topic mention this person?

■ Did you see the person listed in other sources that you've already determined to be trustworthy?

When someone is an authority, you may find other references to this person. Decide whether this person's viewpoint or knowledge of the topic is important to read.

Institution or Affiliation

■ What organization, institution, or company is the author associated with? If the name is not easily identified, perhaps the group is less than reliable.

■ What are the goals of this group? Is there a bias or reason for the group to slant the truth in any way?

- Does the group monitor or review what is published under its name?

- Why might this group be trying to sell you something or convince you to accept its views? Do its members conduct disinterested research? Are they trying to be sensational or attention-getting to enhance their own popularity or ratings?

2. Timeliness

- When was the source published? (For Web sites, look at the "last revised" date at the end of the page.)

- Is that date current enough to be useful, or might there be out-dated material?

- Is the source a revision of an earlier edition? If so, it is likely to be more current, and a revision indicates that the source is sufficiently valuable to revise. Check a library catalog or *Books in Print* to see whether you have the latest edition.

3. Publisher/Producer

- Who published or produced the material?

- Is that publisher reputable? For example, a university press or a government agency is likely to be a reputable source that reviews what it publishes.

- Is the group recognized as being an authority?

- Is the publisher or group an appropriate one for this topic?

- Might the publisher be likely to have a particular bias? (For example, a brochure printed by a right-to-life group is not going to argue for abortion.)

- Is there any review process or fact checking? (If a pharmaceutical company publishes data on a new drug it is developing, is there evidence of outside review of the data?)

4. Audience

- Can you tell who the intended audience is? Is that audience appropriate for your purposes?

- Is the material too specialized or too popular or brief to be useful? (A three-volume study of gene splitting is more than you need for a five-page paper on some genetically transmitted disease. But a half-page article on a visit to the Antarctica won't tell you much about research into ozone depletion going on there.)

45c Evaluating Content

When you have decided to find the source and have it in hand, you can evaluate the content by keeping in mind the following important criteria:

- **Accuracy** What reasons do you have to think that the facts are accurate? Do they agree with other information you've read? Are there sources for the data given?

- **Comprehensiveness** Is the topic covered in adequate depth? Or is it too superficial or limited to only one aspect that therefore overemphasizes only one part of the topic?

- **Credibility** Is the source of the material generally considered trustworthy? Does the source have a review process or do fact checking? Is the author an expert? What are the author's credentials for writing about this topic? Is the article about personal perceptions of how bad this season's flu epidemic is, or is it a report by the government's Center for Disease Control and Prevention?

- **Fairness** If the author has a particular viewpoint, are differing views presented with some sense of fairness? Or are opposing views presented as irrational or stupid?

- **Objectivity** Is the language objective or emotional? Does the author acknowledge differing viewpoints? Are the various perspectives fairly presented? If you are reading an article in a magazine, do other articles in that source promote a particular viewpoint?

- **Relevance** How closely related is the material to your topic? Is it really relevant or merely related? Is it too general or too specific? too technical?

- **Timeliness** Is the information current enough to be useful? How necessary is timeliness for your topic?

To help you determine the degree to which the criteria listed above are present in the source, follow these suggestions:

- Read the preface. What does the author want to accomplish?

- Browse through the table of contents and the index. Is the topic covered in enough depth to be helpful?

- Is there a list of references to show that the author has consulted other sources? Can the sources lead you to useful material?

- Are you the intended audience? Consider the tone, style, level of information, and assumptions the author makes about the reader. Are they appropriate to your needs?

- Is the content of the source fact, opinion, or propaganda? If the material is presented as factual, are the sources of the facts clearly indicated? Do you think enough evidence is offered? Is the coverage comprehensive? (As you learn more about the topic, answering these questions will become easier.) Is the language emotional or objective?

- Are there broad, sweeping generalizations that overstate or simplify the matter?

- Does the author use a mix of primary and secondary sources?

- To determine accuracy, consider whether the source is outdated. Do some cross-checking. Do you find some of the same information elsewhere?

- Are there arguments that are one-sided with no acknowledgement of other viewpoints?

46 Taking Notes (note)

46a Writing Notecards

When you've decided a source is likely to be useful, you can record information on notecards, using either 3" × 5" or 4" × 6" cards, to summarize (see 46b), paraphrase (see 46c), or record a quotation (see 46d). Use parentheses to include your own comments on the significance of a source and to record your thoughts as to how you can use this source in your paper. It is best to limit each notecard to one short aspect of a topic so that you can reorder the cards later as you organize the whole project. One way is to decide what the heading or subheading for this notecard will be. You can use the headings and subheadings of your outline, and as you take more notes, new subheadings may occur to you.

For each notecard, record the last name of the author in the upper right-hand corner with a shortened form of the title. The heading for the card's topic can be written in the upper left-hand corner. As you write information on the card, include the exact page reference. If the note refers to more than one page in your source, indicate where the new page starts. For quotations, be sure that you've copied the original exactly. For short research projects, you can photocopy some material and highlight or write notes in the margin. Or you can type notes into a computer as you read and then print out your notes for reordering.

For information on how to document your sources for summaries, paraphrases, and quotations, see Chapters 52 through 54.

46b Summarizing

A **summary** is a brief restatement of the main ideas in a source, using your own words. As you write, include summaries of other people's writing when you refer to the main idea but do not wish to quote that person. Good reasons for using summaries are that the source has unnecessary detail, that the writer's phrasing is not particularly memorable or worth quoting, or that you want to keep your writing concise. When you include a summary, you need to cite the source to give credit to the writer. (See Chapters 52, 53, and 54 for information on how to cite your sources and 47c on avoiding plagiarism.) Unlike paraphrases (see 46c), summaries are shorter than the original source. They include only the main points and do not follow the organization of the source.

> **HINT** **Characteristics of Summaries**
>
> - Summaries are written in your own words, not copied from your source.
>
> - Summaries include only the main points, omitting details, facts, examples, illustrations, direct quotations, and other specifics.
>
> - Summaries use fewer words than the source being summarized.
>
> - Summaries do not follow the organization of the source.
>
> - Summaries are objective and do not include your own interpretation or reflect your slant on the material.

To write a summary, follow these steps:

- Read the original source carefully and thoughtfully.

- After the first reading, ask yourself what the author's major point is.

- Go back and reread the source, making a few notes in the margin.

- Look away from your source, and then, like a newscaster, panelist, or speaker reporting to a group, finish the sentence: "This person is saying that. . . ."

- Write down what you've just said.

- Go back and reread both the source and your notes in the margins to check that you've correctly remembered and included the main points.

- Revise your summary as needed.

Original Source:
As human beings have populated the lands of the earth, we have pushed out other forms of life. It seemed to some that our impact must stop at the ocean's edge, but that has not proved to be so. By overharvesting the living bounty of the sea and by flushing the wastes and by-products of our societies from the land into the ocean, we have managed to impoverish, if not destroy, living ecosystems there as well.

(Thorne-Miller, Boyce, and John G. Catena. *The Living Ocean: Understanding and Protecting Marine Biodiversity*. Washington: Island, 1991. 3–4.)

> Thorne-Miller, "Living Ocean"
> People have destroyed numerous forms of life on land and are now doing the same with the oceans. Overfishing and dumping waste products into the waters have brought about the destruction of various forms of ocean life. (pp. 3–4)

Summary on a notecard

46c Paraphrasing

A **paraphrase** restates information from a source, using your own words.

HINT   Characteristics of Paraphrases

- Paraphrases have approximately the same number of words as the source. (A summary, conversely, is much shorter.)

- Paraphrases use your own words, not those of the source.

- Paraphrases keep the same organization as the source.

- Paraphrases are more detailed than a summary.

- Paraphrases are objective and do not include your own interpretation or slant on the material.

Unlike summaries (see 46b), paraphrases are approximately the same length as the source. They keep the same organization and are more detailed than a summary.

To write a paraphrase, follow these steps:

- Read the original passage as many times as is needed to understand its full meaning.

- As you read, take notes, using your own words, if that helps.

- Put the original source aside and write a draft of your paraphrase, using your notes if needed.

- Check your version against the original source by rereading the original to be sure you've included all the ideas and followed the same organization as the source.

- If you find a phrase worth quoting in your own writing, use quotation marks in the paraphrase to identify your borrowing, and note the page number.

Original Source:

The automobile once promised a dazzling world of speed, freedom, and convenience, magically conveying people wherever the road would take them. Given these alluring qualities, it is not surprising that people around the world enthusiastically embraced the dream of car ownership. But societies that have built their transport systems around the automobile are now waking up to a much harsher reality. The problems created by overreliance on the car are outweighing its benefits.

(Lowe, Marcia D. "Rethinking Urban Transport." *State of the World 1991.* New York: Norton, 1991. 56.)

> Lowe, "Rethinking"
>
> Automobiles, which offered swift, easy, and independent transportation, allowed people to travel wherever there were roads. Owning a car became everyone's dream, a result that is not surprising, given the benefits of car travel. Nations built their transportation systems on the car, but despite its advantages, societies that rely heavily on cars are beginning to recognize that they cause severe problems as well. Heavy dependence on automobiles creates problems that offset their advantages. (p. 56)

Paraphrase on a notecard

Exercise 46.1: Writing Practice

A. To practice summarizing and paraphrasing, rewrite both of the following quotations, first as a summary of the contents and then as a paraphrase. These quotations are not from any real source, but when you cite them in the second part of the exercise, create a fictitious source to cite.

1. The National Rifle Association (NRA), which was founded in 1871 to teach safety and marksmanship to gun owners, has become the nation's most powerful lobbying group in the bitter fight against gun-control laws. Arguing that the Second Amendment to the Constitution guarantees the rights of citizens to own guns, the NRA promotes people's right to protect themselves and their property. Most gun owners, claims the NRA, are law-abiding people who use guns for sport or for self-defense. While the NRA acknowledges the widespread use of guns by criminals and the ever-increasing numbers of innocent children killed by guns, NRA officials also point out that criminals are the ones who kill, not guns. Stricter laws and law enforcement, argues the NRA, can reduce crime, not gun-control laws. No matter how strict the laws become for the purchase of guns, those bent on illegally owning a gun can find ways to get one if they have the money.

2. Gun-control supporters, who lobby for stricter ownership laws and against the National Rifle Association (NRA), argue that guns are not useful for self-defense and do not inhibit crime. Various groups calling for stronger legislation against gun ownership point out that guns promote killing. When a gun is present, they note, the level of violence can increase rapidly. Research shows that a gun kept for protection is far more likely to be used to kill someone the gun owner knows than to be used to kill a thief. Moreover, guns in the home result in accidents in which children are killed. Opponents of the NRA answer the charge that they are ignoring the Second Amendment by citing the First Amendment, which guarantees the right to hold public meetings and parades. Although Americans have the right to hold parades, they point out, people have to get a permit to do so, and gun permits are no more of an infringement on the rights of Americans than are parade permits.

B. To practice incorporating summaries and paraphrases into your own writing, write a paragraph either for or against stronger gun-control laws, and make use of the sources you have just summarized and paraphrased. Remember to cite the made-up source you create. For help with citing sources, see Chapters 52 through 54.

46d Quoting

A **quotation** is the record of the exact words of a written or spoken source and is set off by quotation marks. All quotations should have an accompanying citation to the source of the quotation.

I. When to Quote

Follow these guidelines for using quotations effectively:

- Use quotations as evidence, as support, or as further explanation of what you have written. Quotations are not substitutes for stating your point in your own words.

- Use quotations sparingly. Too many quotations strung together with very little of your own writing makes a paper look like a scrapbook of pasted-together sources, not a thoughtful integration of what is known about a subject. (See 47a on integrating your sources into your writing.)

- Use quotations that illustrate the author's own viewpoint or style, or quote excerpts that would not be as effective if rewritten in different words. Effective quotations are succinct or particularly well phrased.

- Introduce quotations with words that signal the relationship of the quotation to the rest of your discussion (see 47b).

HINT **When to Use Quotations**

- Quote when the writer's words are especially vivid, memorable, or expressive.

- Quote when an expert explains so clearly and concisely that a paraphrase would be less clear and would contain more words.

- Quote when the words the source uses are important to the discussion.

Original Source 1:
When asked to comment on the recent investigations of government fraud, Senator Smith said to a *New York Times* reporter, "Their ability to undermine our economy is exceeded only by their stupidity in thinking that they wouldn't get caught."

("Fraud Hearings." *New York Times* 18 Nov. 1998, late ed.: A4.)

[This statement is worth quoting because restating it in different words would probably take more words and have less punch.]

Original Source 2:
When asked in a television interview to comment on the recent investigations of government fraud, Senator Smith said, "These huge payments for materials that should have cost less will now cost the government money because they will increase our budget deficit more than we anticipated."

(Smith, Saul. Interview with Nina Totenberg. *Nightline*. ABC. WILI, Chicago. 23 Nov. 1998.)

[This statement is a good candidate for paraphrasing, with a reference to Senator Smith, because the statement is not particularly concise, well phrased, or characteristic of a particular person's way of saying something.]

Paraphrase of Source 2 (using the same source):
During a televised interview Senator Smith responded to a question about investigations of government fraud by noting that overpayments on materials will cause an unexpected increase in the budget deficit.

2. Types of Quotations

Quoting Prose

■ **Short Quotations** If your quotation is no more than four lines (either handwritten or typed), include the quotation in your paragraph and use quotation marks (see 31a).

During the summer of 1974, at a crucial stage of development in the Apollo program, national interest in NASA was sharply diverted by the Watergate affair. As Joseph Trento, an investigative reporter, explains in his book on the Apollo program: "The nation was sitting on the edge of its collective seat wondering if Richard Nixon would leave us in peace or pull the whole system down with him" (142).

(Trento, Joseph. *Prescription for Disaster*. New York: Crown, 1987.)

■ **Long Quotations** If the quotation is more than four handwritten or typed lines, set it off by indenting ten spaces from the left margin. Double-space the quotation, and do not use quotation marks. If the first line of the quotation is the beginning of the paragraph in the source, indent that line an additional five spaces.

In his book on the Apollo and space shuttle programs, Joseph Trento reports on the final mission in the Apollo program:

> The last mission involving the Apollo hardware nearly ended in tragedy for the American crew. After reentry the crew opened a pressure release valve to equalize the command module atmosphere with the earth's atmosphere. But the reaction control rockets failed to shut down and deadly nitrogen tetroxide

oxydizer gas entered the cabin's breathing air. The crew survived the incident, but some at Houston and in Washington wondered if the layoff from manned flight hadn't put the crew at risk. (144)

(Trento, Joseph. *Prescription for Disaster.* New York: Crown, 1987.)

Quoting Poetry

If you are quoting a line of poetry, see 31a.2.

Quoting Dialogue

If you are quoting the speech of two or more people who are talking, see 31a.3.

3. Capitalization of Quotations

Capitalize the first word of directly quoted speech in the following situations:

- When the first quoted word begins a sentence

  She said, "He likes to talk about football, especially when the Super Bowl is coming up."

- When the first word in the dialogue is a fragment

  "He likes to talk about football," she said. "Especially when the Super Bowl is coming up."

Do not capitalize quoted speech in the following situations:

- When the first quoted word is not the beginning of a sentence

  She said that he likes talking about football, "especially when the Super Bowl is coming up."

- When the quotation is interrupted and then continues on in the same sentence

  "He likes to talk about football," she said, "especially when the Super Bowl is coming up."

4. Punctuation of Quotations

Commas

When you introduce quotations, use the comma to set off less formal expressions such as *he said, she asked,* or *Brady stated.*

  As R. F. Notel explains, "The gestures people use to greet each other differ greatly from one culture to another."

But when the quotation follows *that,* do not use a comma and do not capitalize the first letter of the first word in the quotation.

  The public relations director noted that "newsletters to alumni are the best source of good publicity—and donations."

Colon

Use the colon to introduce formal quotations and quotations that have two or more sentences.

> The selection of juries has become a very complex and closely researched process: "In addition to employing social scientists, some lawyers now practice beforehand with 'shadow juries,' groups of twelve people demographically similar to an actual jury."

End Punctuation

Put periods before the second quotation mark. If the quotation has an exclamation mark or question mark, include that before the second quotation mark. But if the exclamation mark or question mark is part of the sentence but not the quotation, put the mark after the second quotation mark.

> Matt explained, "I didn't mean to upset her."

> The stage director issued his usual command to the actor: "Work with me!"

> Did she really say "I quit"?

Brackets

Occasionally, you may need to add some information within a quotation, insert words to make the quotation fit your sentence, or indicate with *sic* that you are quoting your source exactly even though you recognize an error there. When you insert any words within the quotation, set off your words with brackets. (See 34d for more on brackets.)

> "During President Carter's administration, Press [Frank Press, Carter's science adviser] indicated his strong bias against funding applied research."

Ellipsis (for omitted words)

When you omit words from a quotation, use an ellipsis (three spaced dots) to indicate that material has been left out. (See 34e for more information on ellipsis.)

> **Original Source:**
> Contributing editors are people whose names are listed on the masthead of a magazine, but who are usually not on the staff. Basically, they're freelance writers with a good track record of producing ideas and articles prolifically.

> **Use of Quotation:**
> Not all the names listed on the masthead of a magazine are regular staff members. Some are "freelance writers [who have] . . . a good track record of producing ideas and articles prolifically."

Single Quotation Marks

When you are enclosing a quotation within a quotation, use a single quotation mark (the apostrophe mark on a keyboard).

In his book on the history of the atomic bomb, Richard Rhodes describes Enrico Fermi, one of the creators of the first atomic bomb, as he stood at his window in the physics tower at Columbia University and gazed out over New York City: "He cupped his hands as if he were holding a ball. 'A little bomb like that,' he said simply, for once not lightly, 'and it would all disappear' " (275).

(Rhodes, Richard. *The Making of the Atomic Bomb.* New York, Simon, 1986.)

(For more information on the use of punctuation with quotation marks, see 31d.)

47 Using Sources

47a Integrating Sources

When you refer to your sources of information by summarizing, paraphrasing, or quoting from them, your goal is to integrate the material smoothly and seamlessly. Otherwise, readers feel a choppy bump when the writing moves from the writer's words to those of the source material, and even worse, the writer loses control of the paper if the sources seem to dominate the paper. To create smooth transitions and to use sources effectively, consider the following suggestions.

- **Explain how the source material is connected to the rest of the paragraph.** Always show your readers the connection between the reference and the point you are making. Introduce the material by showing a logical link, or add a follow-up comment that integrates a quotation into your paragraph.

  Although most experts predict that high-definition television will not replace the current system in the near future, one spokesperson for the electronics industry says that global competition will force this sooner than most people anticipate: "American consumers aren't going to settle for the old technology when they travel abroad and see the brilliant clarity of high definition television now available in other countries." (Marklen 7).

- **Use the name of the source and, if it's appropriate, that person's credentials for being an authority.**

  The treatment of osteoporosis usually includes medications to improve bone density, but Dr. Matthew Benjamin, head of the Department of Osteoporosis Research at the University of Ottawa, warns that the most commonly prescribed medications also have potentially dangerous side effects that have not been adequately studied.

- **Use signal words and phrases with quotations.** When you are quoting from sources, use words and phrases that prepare your reader for the quotation that will follow and that add smooth transitions from your words to the quotation. For examples of signal words and phrases, see 47b.

■ **Limit the use of quotations.** When a paragraph has a string of quotations and references to source material connected by a few words from the writer, the writer has lost control of the paper and given it over to the collection of quotations. The result often seems like a cut-and-paste scrapbook of materials from other people. A few good quotations, used sparingly, will be much more effective.

■ **Be sure to include the names of the sources.** When you include quotations, summaries, and paraphrases, check to see that you've indicated the name so that readers can find the source in your list at the end of the paper.

47b Using Signal Words and Phrases

Signal phrases let the reader know that a quotation will follow.

Signal Phrases

It is often effective to use the author's name in that phrase. The phrase helps to explain how the quotation will fit into the discussion.

As the film critic, Leon Baberman, has noted, ". . ." (43).

Maya Moon answers her critics when she says, ". . ." (9).

Dr. Rahmo Milwoicz clarifies this point succinctly when he writes, ". . ." (108).

". . ." as Luanne Yah explains, ". . ." (36).

According to J. S. Locanno, an expert in restoring prairie land, ". . ." (27).

Signal Words

To add variety to the verbs you use, consider these common signal words:

acknowledges	condemns	observes
adds	considers	points out
admits	contends	predicts
advises	denies	proposes
agrees	describes	rejects
argues	disagrees	reports
as (name) explains	emphasizes	responds
asks	explains	reveals
asserts	finds	says
believes	has found that	shows
claims	holds that	speculates
comments	illustrates	suggests
complains	insists	thinks
concedes	maintains	warns
concludes	notes	writes

Examples:
Although it is hard to predict the future of the toy industry, Robert Lillo, a senior analyst at the American Economics Institute, warns that "the bottom may fall out of the electronic game industry as CD-ROMs gobble up that market with cheaper, more elaborate products with better graphics" (21).

(Lillo, Robert. "The Electronic Industry Braces for Hard Times." *Business Weekly* 14 Feb. 1996: 18–23.)

In 1990 when the United Nations International Human Rights Commission predicted "there will be an outburst of major violations of human rights in Yugoslavia within the next few years" (14), few people in Europe or the United States paid attention to the warning.

(United Nations. International Human Rights Commission. *The Future of Human Rights in Eastern Europe.* New York: United Nations, 1990.)

Quotation not integrated into the paragraph:
Modern farming techniques are different from those used twenty years ago. John Hession, an Iowa soybean grower, says, "Without a computer program to plan my crop allotments or to record my expenses, I'd be back in the dark ages of guessing what to do." New computer software programs are being developed commercially and are selling well.

(Hession, John. Personal interview. 27 July 1998.)

[The quotation here is abruptly dropped into the paragraph, without an introduction and without a clear indication from the writer as to how Mr. Hession's statement fits into the ideas being discussed.]

Revised:
Modern farming techniques differ from those of twenty years ago, particularly in the use of computer programs for planning and budgeting. John Hession, an Iowa soybean grower who relies heavily on computers, explains, "Without a computer program to plan my crop allotments or to record my expenses, I'd be back in the dark ages of guessing what to do." Commercial software programs such as those used by Mr. Hession, for crop allotments and budgeting, are being developed and are selling well.

[This revision explains how Mr. Hession's statement confirms the point being made.]

Exercise 47.1: Writing Practice

Assume that you are writing a paper on the topics listed here and want to quote from the source given for each topic. Using the information in 46d, write a paragraph that quotes the source directly. Include some summarizing and paraphrasing (see 46b and 46c).

1. Possible topics: Causes of school violence, effects of school violence, safety in schools

   Not all school violence is caused by students. Outsiders (students from other schools, students who have been expelled, or adults) go into schools to rob, attack, kidnap, rape, or murder students or staff members. This can occur when an outsider wants to harm a specific individual. For example, a gang member may seek revenge on someone who happens to be a student and attack him or her at school. Or violence can occur when one person attacks another at random on school grounds. For example, a drug addict may enter a school to rob or steal and may assault a teacher or student.

It is important to remember that school crime affects more than just the victim and the perpetrator. It affects the whole school. Students may become fearful, angry, and frustrated. They may feel guilty that they were not able to prevent the incident, and they may even suffer long-term psychological problems. Like an adult whose home has been burglarized, students may feel violated. Their sense of security may be damaged, possibly never to be fully repaired (12).

(Day, Nancy. *Violence in Schools: Learning in Fear.* Springfield: Enslow, 1996.)

2. Possible topics: Prenatal care, substance abuse during pregnancy, the effects of drugs on a fetus and/or newborn

Heavy exposure before birth to alcohol, tobacco, or narcotic drugs can cause a great variety of problems. In particular, exposure to these substances can lead not only to a decrease in the number of brain cells due to interference with cellular replication in critical periods of growth but also to damage to the connections between parts of the brain. A smaller brain can result. Cocaine and crack raise the blood pressure, close off small capillaries, and damage brain substance in developing areas of the brain. In addition, an addicted mother tends to eat poorly, and malnutrition in the developing fetus adds to its vulnerability. If an addicted person continues to ingest these toxins toward the latter part of the pregnancy, the baby is likely to have mild or major interference in the transmission of messages from one part of the brain to another.

At birth, the baby's behavior will reflect these disorders in neurotransmission through slowness to respond to stimuli, unreachableness, and apparent attempts to maintain a sleep state. They can be so volatile that they appear to have no state in which they can take in information from the environment, digest it, and respond appropriately. These babies can be at high risk for abuse or neglect. They are not only unrewarding to their already depressed, addicted mothers, but they give back only negative or disorganized responses. They are extremely difficult to feed and to organize for sleep. Their potential for failing to thrive is enormous (14).

(Brazelton, T. Berry. *Touchpoints: Your Child's Emotional and Behavioral Development.* New York: Addison Wesley Longman, 1992.)

3. Possible topics: Coping at college, verbal self-defense

Sometimes, in spite of all your best intentions, you find yourself in a situation where you have really fouled it up. You are 100 percent in the wrong, you have no excuse for what you've done, and disaster approaches. Let us say, for example, that you enrolled in a class, went to it three or four times, did none of the work, forgot to drop it before the deadline, and are going to flunk. Or let's say that you challenged an instructor on some information and got nowhere trying to convince him or her that you were right; then you talked to a counselor, who got nowhere trying to convince you that you were wrong; next you spent quite a lot of time doing your duty to the other students in the class by telling them individually that the instructor is completely confused; and how, much too late, you have discovered that it is you who are in error. Either of these will do as a standard example of impending academic doom.

In such a case, there's only one thing you can do, and you're not going to like it. Go to the instructor's office hour, sit down, and level. Say that you are there because you've done whatever ridiculous thing you have done, that you already know you have no excuse for it, and that you have come in to clear it up as best you can. Do not rationalize; do not talk about how this would never have happened if it hadn't been for some other instructor's behavior; do not mention something the instructor you are talking to should have done to ward this off; do not, in other words, try to spread your guilt around. Level and be done with it (260–61).

(Elgin, Suzette Haden. *The Gentle Art of Verbal Self-Defense.* New York: Dorset, 1988.)

47c Avoiding Plagiarism

Plagiarism results when writers fail to document a source so that the words and ideas of someone else are presented as the writer's own work.

1. Information that Requires Documentation

When we use the ideas, findings, data, conclusions, arguments, and words of others, we need to acknowledge that we are borrowing their work and inserting it in our own by documenting it. Consciously or unconsciously passing off the work of others as our own results in the very serious form of stealing known as plagiarism, an act that can cause the writer to fail a course or even be expelled from a school. Summarizing or paraphrasing that follows the wording of a source too closely is one form of unconscious plagiarism; depending too heavily on quotations from a source is another form of plagiarism.

HINT   Importance of Citing Sources

In some cultures educated writers are expected to know and incorporate the thinking of great scholars, and it may be considered an insult to the reader to mention the names of scholars, implying that the reader is not acquainted with these scholarly works. However, in American writing this is not the case, and writers are always expected to acknowledge their sources and give public credit to the appropriate person or group.

2. Information that Does Not Require Documentation

Common knowledge, that body of general ideas we share with our readers, does not have to be documented. Common knowledge consists of standard information on a subject that people know, information that is widely shared and can be found in numerous sources without reference to any source. For example, if your audience is American educators, it is common knowledge among this group that American schoolchildren are not well acquainted with geography. However, if you cite test results proving the extent of the problem or use the words and ideas of a knowledgeable person about the causes of the problem, that is not common knowledge and needs documentation. Similarly, it is common knowledge among most Americans aware of current energy problems that solar power is one answer to future energy needs. But forecasts about how widely solar power may be used twenty years from now would be the work of some person or group studying the subject, and documentation would be needed. Common knowledge also consists of facts widely available in a variety of standard reference books. Field research you conduct also does not need to be documented, though you should indicate that you are reporting your own findings.

 Avoiding Plagiarism

To avoid plagiarism, read over your paper and ask yourself whether your readers can properly identify which ideas and words are yours and which are from the sources you cite. If that is clear, if you have not let your paper become merely a string of quotations from sources, and if the paper predominantly reflects your words, phrases, and integration of ideas, then you are not plagiarizing.

Original Source:

One of the most obvious—and most important—approaches to saving rainforests is to protect them in national parks, the same way that industrialized nations such as the United States and Canada safeguard their tropical wonders. Yet so far fewer than 5% of the world's tropical forests are included in parks or other kinds of protected areas. Most of the developing countries that house these forests simply do not have enough money to buy land and set up park systems. And many of the nations that do establish parks are then unable to pay park rangers to protect the land. These unprotected parks routinely are invaded by poor, local people who desperately need the forest's wood, food, land, or products to sell. The areas are often called "paper parks" because they exist on paper but not in reality (105–106).

(Tangley, Laura. *The Rainforest: Earth at Risk.* New York: Chelsea, 1992.)

Accidental Plagiarism:

[In this paragraph the words, phrases, and ideas from the original source are underlined. Note how much of this paraphrase comes from the original source and how the author has neglected to signal to the reader that this material comes from another source.]

The problem of saving the world's rainforests has become a matter of great public concern. There are a number of solutions being offered, <u>but the most obvious and most important approach is to protect them in national parks.</u> This is <u>the same way that industrialized nations such as the United States and Canada safeguard their natural wonders.</u> In poorer nations this does not work because they <u>do not have enough money to buy land and set up park systems.</u> What happens is that when they don't have money, <u>they are unable to pay park rangers to protect the land.</u> Without any protection from rangers, poor people come in and invade because they <u>desperately need the forest's wood, food, land, or products to sell.</u> These parks then don't really exist as parks.

Acceptable Paraphrase:
The problem of saving the world's rain forests has become a matter of great public concern. Of the approaches being considered, Laura Tangley, in *The Rainforest,* considers one of the most important solutions to be turning rainforests into national parks. Tangley points out, however, that this is a solution only for industrialized nations such as the United States and Canada because they have the funding to keep national parks protected from poachers. In developing nations that cannot afford park rangers, the local populations are not prevented from taking wood, food, land, or forest products that they can sell. Tangley states that such forests, because they are not protected from human destruction, "exist on paper but not in reality" (105–06).

Exercise 47.2: Writing Practice

To practice citing sources and avoiding plagiarism, add citations in MLA format to the following paragraph, which incorporates material from the two sources listed here. For information on parenthetical citations and references in MLA format, see Chapter 52.

A. The quotations included here are from the following source:

Lowe, Marcia D. "Rethinking Urban Transport." *State of the World 1991.* New York: Norton, 1991.

- "Cities with streets designed for cars instead of people are increasing unlivable" (56).

- "Traffic congestion, now a fact of life in major cities, has stretched rush hours to 12 hours or longer in Seoul and 14 in Rio de Janeiro. In 1989, London traffic broke a record with a 53-kilometer backup of cars at a near standstill" (57).

- "Roaring engines and blaring horns cause distress and hypertension, as in downtown Cairo, where noise levels are 10 times the limit set by health and safety standards" (57).

B. The quotations here are from the following source:

Lipperman, Irwin, *Planning for a Livable Tomorrow.* New York: Nathanson, 1992.

- "City space is rapidly being eaten up by automobiles. Parking in a city center can use up to 20 or 30% of the available space, and suburban malls often have parking lots bigger than the malls themselves" (99).

- "Automobile pollutants in the air inhaled by urbanites increase the likelihood of lung disorders and make bronchial problems more severe, especially among the elderly" (108).

The following paragraph is part of a research paper on the topic of city planning.

Another important concern in city planning is to formulate proposals to eliminate or reduce problems caused by automobiles. Cities with streets designed for cars instead of people are increasingly unlivable, for cars cause congestion, pollution, and noise. Providing more public transportation can reduce these problems, but it is not likely that city dwellers will give up owning cars. Therefore, solutions are needed for parking, which already uses up as much as 20 to 30 percent of the space available in downtown areas, and for rush hour traffic, which now extends to more than twelve hours in Seoul and to fourteen hours in Rio de Janeiro. Pollution, another urban problem caused partly by cars, needs to be controlled. Automobile emissions cause lung disorders and aggravate bronchial problems. In addition, noise from automobiles must be curbed. Noise has already become a health problem in cities such as Cairo, where noise levels are already ten times the acceptable standard for human health.

48 Research Online

Searching for information online can be very fruitful because the Internet connects you to late-breaking news, the most current resources, material that is available only online, and resources in distant places. You can access all this quickly and easily. But it's important to have a clear sense of which kinds of information are available online and which are better searched for in libraries or obtained from other sources such as the community or your campus.

48a What Is Available on the Internet?

The Internet is particularly useful when searching for the kinds of information listed here. For specific sites, see Chapter 49.

■ **Government sources** The federal government maintains numerous sites on the Internet with large quantities of information produced by various bureaus and agencies, in addition to that which is produced by legislative action. You can also check for references to appropriate government publications that your library may have on the shelves.

■ **Library catalogs online** You can search many libraries online to find other materials on your topic, and your library may be able to borrow these for you. You can also read titles and abstracts to get a sense of what's available on the topic. Online catalogs are especially useful for compiling a working bibliography to start your search. Some of the major libraries online also have searchable databases and lists of resources in various areas that may be useful.

■ **Search engines** There are search engines that will find materials from a vast variety of resources, search engines that will find discussions of your topic on newsgroups, and even search engines that search other ones to give you a composite report of what different search engines found. To learn how to use these effectively, see 48c.

■ **Related materials gathered by category** Most search engines have materials arranged by categories (such as "arts," "business," "education," "entertainment," and "health") and within each category and subcategory you can find a collection of numerous related sites. These can be very helpful to browse through when you are looking for a topic for a paper. The categories are also helpful when you don't yet have specific information on a topic you are just learning about. For example, suppose you want to look into the effects of El Niño, but you aren't sure which government agency site will have information you can use. One of the categories in the *Yahoo* search engine is titled "science." Within "science" are numerous subcategories, including "oceanography." Under "oceanography" is a list of related sites, one of which is

"El Niño." Here you will find several dozen links to sites, including some on research done by the agency you were searching for, the National Oceanic and Atmospheric Administration.

■ **Current news and publications** Many newspapers (such as the *New York Times*), television networks (such as CNN, ABC, CBS, and NBC), and print publications (such as *Time, Byte, The New Republic,* and some scholarly journals) maintain online databases of information that include excerpts from current articles and news stories from their print sources or television programs.

■ **Some older books** There are several projects, such as Project Bartleby at Columbia University, the English Server at Carnegie Mellon University, and Project Gutenberg, dedicated to making available online older books whose copyrights have expired. Other projects are dedicated to making rare or hard-to-find older resources available online.

In addition, you'll find sites maintained by public interest groups (such as environmental groups or consumer safety organizations) and non-profit organizations (such as museums and universities) with information about their areas of interest; newsgroups (many with archives and answers to Frequently Asked Questions, usually referred to as FAQ files) in which people trade information about a particular topic; databases and reference books; directories that help you locate companies and people; company sites with information about their products; city and state sites that offer information of local concern; and foreign government sites that offer information about their countries.

48b Finding Information on the Internet

When you begin your search, you'll need to refine your topic, formulate research questions, and follow other general research strategies as explained in Chapters 43 and 44. You will also need to evaluate your sources: the lack of control or monitoring on the Internet means that although much valuable information is available, a great deal of what you find will be worthless or simply wrong. (See Chapter 50 on evaluating Internet sources.) Because the Web is constantly changing, there is also a lot of transient information. What is available one day when you surf the Net may be different or gone when you return.

Different Types of Search Tools

Just as we need different types of tools (hammers, saws, screwdrivers, etc.) to construct or fix things, we also need different types of search tools online for various projects.

■ **Search engines** Search engines work by searching among the contents of public sites on the Internet for key terms that you indicate. The search engine returns a list of sites that include the key terms. Some sites also have their own search engines to help you find information on various parts of that site. Since various search engines work differently, each will turn up some different results. Be sure to read any help files the search engine site offers so that you use it effectively. Metasearch engines such as Meta-Crawler or Dogpile simultaneously search with numerous search engines. See 48c for more information on search engines and terms to use when you enter your key terms; see Chapter 49 for search engine addresses.

- **Subject categories or directories** These indexes or directories organize Web resources by categories such as "health," "entertainment," and "business." The "reference" category often contains a group of useful references conveniently gathered together. Most have subdirectories under the main headings. These lists are particularly useful when your subject is broad (horror films, AIDS research, the economy) and when you are looking for suggestions for a topic, for a quick look at the types of information available on that topic, or for ways to phrase key terms for searches. Categories are especially useful when you have a well-known topic but don't yet have specific information on where to start or on what aspect of the topic you might want to research.

- **Newsgroups and listservs** Newsgroups are open forums on the Usenet network where anyone can post a message on the topic of the forum. Listservs are e-mail discussion groups in which participants have to subscribe to the list. Any message from any member of the listserv goes to all the subscribers. The list owner may or may not moderate what appears by controlling which message gets through to the list. Many newsgroups and listservs have very useful FAQs that may answer your questions, and some have archives of past discussions.

- **Web sites with collections of information** In Chapter 49 you will find addresses for Web sites that compile large quantities of information in a particular area, and the Prentice Hall Web site for this book has additional addresses at www.prenhall.com/harris.

Different Ways to Search

Use your detective skills to think about different ways to start and which leads to follow. When you use some creative thinking, you'll find that you begin to think of a variety of sites besides the ordinary or expected ones.

Suppose your assignment is to research your major, and you want to learn more about job opportunities related to that major. Here are some different ways to approach your search:

- Go to general job search sites to see what they list.

- Try the resource lists and directories in that academic field (see Chapter 49). These Web sites may list relevant job opportunities.

- Go to college and university Web sites. You may find that departments in your field list job opportunities.

- Look at U.S. census reports to see employment data. Other federal government sites look at prospects for various fields.

- Try Web sites of large companies in your field to see what they list as job openings. (Some online search engines list company Web addresses in addition to street and city locations.)

- Tune in to listservs and newsgroups of people in your area of work to see what they are discussing.

- Use a few search engines to see what they turn up. (There will be some similarities in their listings, but there will also be different ones in each. But be prepared to find that the search engine turns up more items than you want to read.)

48c Using Search Engines on the Web

Search engines differ in the way they search, the documents they search, and the options for searching they offer. Some have basic and advanced searches, and you will need to decide how you want to start. Search engines also differ in the way they suggest using search terms such as AND and NOT. So, before using any search engine, read the help file or explanations offered on the site. That will give you a better idea of how to use that search engine effectively. A list of many of the most often used search engines is in Chapter 49.

As you will notice when you read various guidelines, *Alta Vista* permits you to select the language to search in: *HotBot* permits you to specify the date, medium, and so on to search through; and *Infoseek* permits you to ask questions. *Deja News* searches newsgroup postings.

Boolean Search Terms

To narrow your search, you can define the topic and reduce the number of irrelevant results by using various search terms in combination with the words in your topic. Knowing how to use these search terms (Boolean terms) will save you time.

AND	AND is the most useful and most important term. It tells the search engine to find your first word *and* your second word or term. However, AND can cause problems if you use it with two terms that are likely to appear together in several contexts.

For example, suppose you'd like some information about the Chicago Bulls, the basketball team. If you type in "Chicago AND Bulls," you will get many references to Chicago and to bulls. Since Chicago is the center of a large meatpacking industry, many of the references returned by the search engine will be about the meatpacking industry in Chicago.

OR	OR is not always a helpful term because you may find too many combinations with OR.

If you type in "American OR economy," you will get thousands of references to documents containing the word *American* or the word *economy*. Use OR when a key term may appear in two different ways. For example, if you want information on sudden infant death syndrome, try "sudden infant death syndrome OR SIDS."

NEAR   NEAR is a useful term that appears only on some search engines. It tells the search engine to find documents in which both words appear near each other, usually within a few words.

If you were looking for information on mobile homes, you'd have a problem because almost every site has a button labeled "Click here to return to the home page." The search engine would find thousands of those sites that also have the word "mobile" in them. Using NEAR would help to solve that problem.

NOT   NOT tells the search engine to find a reference that contains one term but not the other.

For example, if you want information about the life of Martin Luther King, Jr., but not his assassination (as that would be too much to cover in your paper), you would type "Martin Luther King, Jr. NOT assassination."

Searching the Web Effectively

- Use phrases instead of single words to define your search more specifically.

- Put quotation marks around the phrase to indicate the whole term is the object of the search.

- Use metasearch engines such as *Dogpile* and *MetaCrawler* to query many search engines at once.

- When you find a useful site, look for links that connect you to related sites.

- Be sure your terms are spelled correctly.

49 Web Resources

In addition to the following addresses of useful Web sites, check the Prentice Hall Web site for this book at www.prenhall.com/harris.

- **Writer's Resources**

    Inkspot   www.inkspot.com

- **Writing Guides**

    Strunk and White, *Elements of Style*
             www.columbia.edu/acis/bartleby/strunk

- **Writing Lab OWLs (Online Writing Labs)**

    National Writing Centers Association OWLs
             departments.colgate.edu/diw/NWCAOWLS.html

Purdue University
>owl.english.purdue.edu

■ References

Bartlett's Familiar Quotations
>www.columbia.edu/acis/bartleby/bartlett

Biographical Dictionary
>s9.com/biography

Merriam Webster Dictionary
>www.m-w.com/dictionary

Online Dictionaries
>www.bucknell.edu/~rbeard/diction.html

Roget's Thesaurus
>humanities.uchicago.edu/form_unrest/ROGET.html

■ Search Engines

Alta Vista   www.altavista.digital.com

Deja News   www.dejanews.com

Dogpile   www.dogpile.com

Excite   www.excite.com

HotBot   www.hotbot.com

Infoseek   www.infoseek.com

Lycos   www.lycos.com

MetaCrawler
>www.metacrawler.com

Northern Lights
>www.nlsearch.com

Starting Point
>www.stpt.com

WebCrawler   www.webcrawler.com

Yahoo   www.yahoo.com

■ General Subject Directories

Argus Clearinghouse for Subject-Oriented
Internet Resource Guides
>www.clearinghouse.net

Awesome List
>www.clark.net/pub/journalism/awesome.html

Internet Public Library
>www.ipl.org

WWW Virtual Library
>vlib.stanford.edu/Overview.html

■ **Books**

Electronic Texts and Publishing Resources
        lcweb.loc.gov/global/etext/etext.html

Project Bartleby
        www.cc.columbia.edu/acis/bartleby

Project Gutenberg
        promo.net/pg

■ **Electronic Listservs and Newsgroups**

Tile.net   tile.net/lists

■ **Journals and Periodicals**

Journals   eserver.org/journals

■ **Newspapers, News Services, and Magazines**

Ecola Newsstand
        www.ecola.com

Electronic Newsstand
        enews.com

Electronic Journals
        www.library.ubc.ca/ejour

New York Times
        nytimes.com

WWW Virtual Library Electronic Journals
        www.edoc.com/ejournals

■ **Universities in the United States**

American Universities
        www.clas.ufl.edu/CLAS/american-universities.html

■ **Fields of Study**

Academic Information Index
        www.academicinfo.net/table.html

■ **Government**

Bureau of the Census
        www.census.gov

Central Intelligence Agency
        www.odci.gov/cia/ciahome.html

Fedworld   www.fedworld.gov

National Institutes of Health

        www.nih.gov

Nonprofit   www.nonprofit.gov

Statistics   www.stat-usa.gov/stat-usa.html

Thomas   thomas.loc.gov

Links to Government Servers and Information
        www.eff.org/govt.html

White House
        www.whitehouse.gov

World Health Organization
        www.who.ch

■ **Libraries**

American Library Association
        www/ala.org

Internet Public Library
        www.ipl.gov

LIBCAT   www.metronet.lib.mn.us/lc/lcl.html

Library of Congress
        lcweb.loc.gov

50 Evaluating Internet Sources

Evaluating Internet sources is particularly difficult because anyone can put anything he or she wants on the Internet. There is no outside monitor or fact checking, though there are some site ratings you can consult. For a discussion of companies that review Internet sites, see <http://www.tiac.net/users/hope/findqual.html>. Consider the criteria below as you read Internet sources.

Authorship

■ **Is an author or organization clearly listed?** If so, review the questions about authorship listed in 45b. Can the author be contacted? If an e-mail address is given, you may be able to learn the person's name by entering the e-mail address as a search term in the following search engines: Alta Vista, Deja News, or Excite.

■ **What can you find out about the author?** If there is no information on the site, use a search engine or search Usenet. You may find the author's home page or other documents that mention this person. Or look up the person on the Internet Directory of Published Writers at <http://www.writers.net>. If the person is associated with a university, look at the university Web site.

■ **What can you learn about an organization sponsoring a page?** You can search the site by following links to the home page or going back a previous level on the site by deleting the last part of the address, after the various slash marks. Another way to find the organization is to go to the "View" menu at the top of your Web browser and open the document information window, where the owner of the document is listed.

Does the organization take responsibility for what's on the site? Does it monitor or review what's there? Look at the address. If it ends in *.edu,* that indicates it's an educational institution. If it ends in *.gov,* whatever you find should be fairly objective government-sponsored material. Addresses with *.org* are usually nonprofit organizations or advocacy groups. For example, the Sierra Club at <http://www.sierra.org> is an advocacy group whose postings conform to the goal of environmental protection. Information posted by advocacy groups may be accurate but not entirely objective. If the site has a *.com* address, it's most likely a commercial site promoting or selling something.

Accuracy of Information

■ Is there documentation to indicate the source of the information? There may be a link to the original source.

■ Can you tell how well researched the information is?

■ Are criteria for including information offered?

■ Is there a bibliography, or are there links to other useful sites? Has the author incorporated information from those sites or considered viewpoints represented there?

■ Is the information current? When was it updated? (Check at the bottom of the page for a "last revised" date.) If there are numerous dead links, that's a clue that the page has not been updated recently.

■ Is there an indication of bias on the site?

■ Does the site have any credentials? Is it rated by a reputable rating group? If you see a high rating, is that because of the reliability of the content or the quality of the graphics? (The attractiveness of a page is not a reason for accepting its information as reliable.)

Goals of the Site

■ What is the purpose of the site? to advertise? to persuade? to provide information? to provide disinformation? Some political groups intent on helping their candidates get elected put up sites that emphasize the opponents' weaknesses or ridicule the opponents. Some sites are owned by hate groups that manage to disguise their real purpose.

■ Are the goals of the site clearly indicated?

■ Who is the intended audience?

■ Does the site display a lot of flash and color and gimmicks to attract attention? Is all the glitter masking a lack of sound information or attempting to get you to buy or do something?

Access

■ How did you find the site? Were there links from reputable sites? from ads? Finding a site through a search engine means only that the site has the keywords in your topic prominently placed or used with great frequency. Finding a site by browsing through a subject directory may mean only that someone at that site registered it with that directory.

Internet Resources on Evaluation

Many Web sites post essays on evaluating sources and links to other useful sites.

Alexander, Jan, and Marsha Tate. "Teaching Critical Evaluation Skills for the World Wide Web." <http://www.science.widener.edu/~withers/webeval.htm>

Grassian, Esther. "Thinking Critically About World Wide Web Resources." <http://www.library.ucla.edu/libraries/college/instruct/critical.htm>

Kirk, Elizabeth. "Evaluating Information Found on the Internet." <http://milton.mse.jhu.edu:8001/research/education/net.html>

Ormondroyd, J., M. Engle, and T. Cosgrave. "How to Critically Analyze Information Sources." <http://www.library.cornell.edu/okuref/research/skill26.htm>

Patterson, Shawn, Alan Wendt, and Robert Schroeder. "Evaluating and Citing Internet Resources." <http://www.udmercy.edu/html/Academics/library/webpage>

51 Citing Internet Sources

Because the Internet is so new and is constantly expanding and changing, the standard bibliographic citation formats may not always be entirely adequate or appropriate for a source you want to cite. The guiding principle, however, is still the same—to provide your readers with enough information to find that source themselves. Also, because the Internet does change so rapidly, with sites that change their content, you need to include the date you accessed the site to indicate when your information was available.

51a MLA Online Citation

The Internet and Online Databases

In 52c, on citing sources in the format recommended by the Modern Language Association (MLA), you will find formats for citing CD-ROMs and other portable databases. These are available commercially and in libraries. But when you are citing information from the Internet or from online databases, you are using databases that are not bought in stores or carried around. Access to the Internet is free, but services such as America Online or online databases such as Lexis-Nexis charge a fee. Thus, some additional elements to be included in the citation are the publication medium (that is, *Online*), the name of the computer service or computer network through which the database is accessed, and the date of access.

Material Accessed Through a Computer Service or Network Such as the World Wide Web

There are two groups of such materials:

1. **Materials with a Print Source** For materials that were or are still available in print, list information on both the print and online versions, including the date the online version was accessed.

   ```
   Meharry, William. "Beta-Carotene May Be Dangerous
       to Your Health." New York Times 24 January
       1996, late ed.: B3. New York Times Online.
       Lexis-Nexis. 15 August 1996.
   ```

2. **Materials with No Print Source** For materials that do not have a print source, include as much information as is available.

   ```
   Sapir, Mortimer. "Dangers of Anesthesia." American
       Medical Encyclopedia. Online. Prodigy. 9 Aug.
       1995.
   ```

3. **In-Text Citations** The MLA has not specified a format for how to document Internet sources, so follow the guidelines MLA offers for all in-text citations (see 52a):

   - References to sources in your paper should be clear and should allow your reader to find that source in your Works Cited section. Usually, this means indicating the author or the first item for that entry in your Works Cited list.

   - If possible, indicate where the specific information being cited is located in the source. For many Web sites, however, this is not possible.

Words Cited: Citing Sources from the World Wide Web

The MLA has posted authorized guidelines on its Web site at <http://www.mla.org/set_stl.htm>. The MLA guidelines, recognizing that online sources may lack some of the standard information included in citations, recommend that you include as many items from the following list as you can.

1. **Name** Include the name of the author, editor, compiler, or translator, in reversed order, followed by an abbreviation such as *ed.* or *trans.*

2. **Title** List the title of the work (poem, short story, article, and so on) within a scholarly project, database, or periodical, in quotation marks; or the title of a posting (found in the subject line) to a discussion list or forum, in quotation marks, followed by the description *Online posting*.

3. **Title of book (underlined)**

4. **Name of editor, compiler, etc.** If it is not already cited as the first entry (see item 1 above), include the name of the editor, compiler, or translator of the text, preceded by an abbreviation such as *Ed.* or *Trans.*

5. **Publication information for any print version of the source**

6. **Title of project or site** List the title of the scholarly project, database, periodical, or professional or personal site (underlined); or, for a professional or personal site with no title, include a description such as *Home page* (neither underlined nor in quotation marks).

7. **Name of editor** List the name of the editor of the scholarly project or database, if available.

8. **Version number of the source** If it is not listed as part of the title, include the version number of the source or, for a journal, give the volume number, issue number, or other identifying number.

9. **Date** List the date of electronic publication, the latest update, or the posting.

10. **List or forum name** For a posting to a discussion list or forum, include the name of the list or forum.

11. **Numbers** Give the total number of pages, paragraphs, or other sections, if numbered.

12. **Organization or institution name** Identify the sponsoring organization or institution.

13. **Date of access** Give the date you accessed the source.

14. **Electronic address** Place the electronic address, or URL, in angle brackets: < >. If you have to divide the address so that it starts on one line and continues on to the next, break the address before a period or after a slash mark. Never add hyphens or permit your word processing software to add hyphens.

Scholarly Project

> Smith, Terry Donovan, and Katie Johnson. "Domestic
> Life in 19th Century English Drama." The 19th
> Century London Stage: An Exploration. Eds.
> Jack Wolcott and Joan Robertson. University
> of Washington School of Drama. 4 Feb. 1998

<http://artsci.washington.edu/drama-phd/
19title.html>.

Professional Site

Women's Studies Program. Ed. Chun-Hui Sophie Ho.
June 1997. Purdue U. 5 Feb. 1998
<http://www.sla.purdue.edu/academic/idis/
womens-studies/main.html>

Personal Site

Kaplan, Hannah. Home page. 9 Feb. 1998
<http://www.mcs.com/~dkaplan/hannah.html>.

Book

Yonge, Charlotte. Henrietta's Wish; or, Domineering:
A Tale. 2nd ed. London, 1853. Ed. Perry
Willett. 4 Feb. 1998. Indiana U. 9 Feb. 1998
<http://www.indiana.edu/~letrs/vwwp/yonge/
henrietta.html>.

Poem

Eliot, T. S. "Whispers of Immortality." Poems. New
York. 1920. Project Bartleby Archive. 1994.
Columbia U. 6 Feb. 1998 <http://www.columbia
.edu/acis/bartleby/eliot/22.html>.

Article in a Reference Database

"Kennedy, John Fitzgerald." Encyclopedia.com. 1998.
Electric Library. 5 Feb. 1998 <www.encyclopedia
.com/articles/06898.html>.

Article in a Journal

Materassi, Mario. "The Forest and the Trees: Some
Notes on the Study of Multiculturalism in Italy."
American Quarterly 48.1 (1996): 110-120. 6 Feb.
1998 <http://direct.press.jhu.edu/journals/
american_quarterly/v048/48.1materassi.html>.

Article in an Online Periodical

Palmentier, Marianne. "Today's Children." Parents
Online 4.7 (1998): 18 pars. 21 Nov. 1998
<http://www.parentstoday.com/issue4.7html>.

Article in a Newspaper or Online Newswire

"Microsoft Testimony Continues." <u>AP Online</u> 3 Dec.

1998. 3 Dec. 1998 <http://www.nytimes.com/

aponline/e/AP-Carter.html>.

Article in a Magazine

Surowiecki, James. "The Taming of the Barbarians."

<u>Slate</u> 5 Feb. 1998. 6 Feb. 1998 <http://www

.slate.com/motleyfool/98-02-05/motleyfool.asp>.

Posting to an E-mail Discussion List

Maxon, Don. "Blending ESL and Bilingual Education."

Online posting. 5 Jan. 1998. Dave Sperling

Presents ESL Discussion Center Forum for

Teachers: Bilingual Education. 6 Feb. 1998

<http://www.eslcafe.com/discussion/ds/index

.cgi?read=2>.

E-mail Communication

Harris, David. "Madeleine Albright's Statement."

E-mail to the author. 5 Dec. 1998.

Synchronous Communication
(an online forum such as a MUD or MOO)

Garlenum, Karl. Online discussion of peer tutoring

WRITE-C/MOO. 27 Nov. 1998 <telnet://write-c

.udel.edu:2341>.

51b APA Online Citation

Electronic Sources

In addition to the guidelines in the most recent *Publication Manual of the American Psychological Association* (4th edition), guidelines are posted on the APA Web site at <http://www.apa.org/journals/webref.html> about how to cite information from the Internet and the World Wide Web. The goal of references remains the same—to credit the author and to help your reader find the material. Electronic correspondence (e-mail, electronic discussion groups, and so on) is cited as personal communication in your text but does not need to be included in your reference list.

All references begin with the same information (or as much as possible) that is included for a print source. World Wide Web information is placed at the end of the reference. Use "Retrieved from" and the date of retrieval because documents can be changed, revised, or removed from the site. For databases and CD-ROM materials, see 53c. For in-text citations of electronic sources in APA format, see 53a.

The Internet and the World Wide Web

Examples here are from the World Wide Web, and a similar format can be used to cite gopher or ftp sources with the medium and path adequately identified.

Journal

> Klein, D. F. (1997). Control groups in pharmaco-
> therapy and psychotherapy evaluations. Treatment, 1.
> Retrieved February 9, 1998 from the World Wide Web:
> http://journals.apa.org/treatment/vol1/97_a1.html

Newspaper Article

> Freiberg, P. (1998, February). We know how to
> stop the spread of AIDS: So why can't we? Psycholo-
> gists point to a need for more work in the policy
> arena. APA Monitor [Newspaper, selected stories on
> line.] Retrieved February 9, 1998 from the World
> Wide Web: http://www.apa.org/monitor/aids.html

Abstract

> McCutchen, A., Francis, M. & Kerr, S. (1997).
> Revising for meaning: Effects of knowledge and
> strategy [Abstract]. Journal of Educational
> Psychology, 89, 667-676. Retrieved February 9, 1998
> from the World Wide Web: http://www.apa.org/
> journals/edu/1297ab.html#8

Online Abstract

> Brindelstein, C. & Chen, S. (1993). The social
> interaction of small children in task differentiated
> groups. [On-line]. Childhood Socializing, 14, 234-241.
> Abstract from: DIALOG File: PyscINFO Item: 46-12144.

Online Journal, Subscriber-Based

> Cross-Cultural Speech Interference Study Group.
> (1995, October 21). Signaling affirmation in informal
> conversation: Contrasting behaviors of Hispanics and

African-Americans [720 paragraphs]. <u>Online Journal</u>
<u>of Contrastive Cultural Behaviors</u> [On-line serial].
Available: Doc. No. 99

E-mail and Listserv Discussions These sources are listed only as personal communication in the paper and are not listed in References lists.

51c Other Formats for Citing Online Sources

Chicago Manual Style

For information on citing electronic sources in *Chicago Manual* style, see 54a.

Council of Biology Editors (CBE)

For information on citing electronic sources in CBE style, see 54b.

Other Styles

■ CIC Electronic Journals Collections: <http://ejournals.cic.net>

The CIC (Committee on Institutional Cooperation, a group of major Midwestern universities) sponsors this site, which lists and connects to electronic journals in many fields. Some of those journals offer electronic citation information in their guidelines for submission of essays. Or you can read the online issues to see how bibliographies in recent articles are formatted.

■ IFLA (International Federation of Library Associations and Institutions): <http://www.ifla.org/I/training/citation/citing.htm>

This site lists style guides and resources on the Internet, along with books, software, and e-mail notes about electronic citation.

■ Internet Public Library, "Citing Electronic Resources": <http://www.ipl.org/ref/QUE/FARQ/netciteFARQ.html>

This site lists books and other sites on the Web (including the *Yahoo* category "Internet Citation") that offer information on electronic citation.

■ National Library of Canada, "Citing Electronic Sources: A Bibliography": <http://www.nlc-bnc.ca/services/eciting.htm>

This site lists Internet sites and articles with information on citing electronic sources. It also includes an annotated bibliography on style guides in print format, separated into (1) publications that focus on citing electronic information and (2) publications that include sections on citing electronic publications.

52 Documenting in MLA Style (MLA)

Modern Language Association (MLA) format is used to document papers in the arts and humanities. As you research your topic, you will be building on the work of others. Your work can, in turn, contribute to the pool of knowledge about the topic for others who will read and depend on your research. The process of documentation requires that you acknowledge those whose work you have summarized, paraphrased, and quoted in your research paper so that readers of your work can find the sources you have used.

Documentation formats can vary, depending on the field of study. For research papers in the arts and humanities, use the format of the Modern Language Association (MLA). The most current style manuals published by MLA are the following:

Gibaldi, Joseph. *MLA Handbook for Writers of Research Papers.* 5th ed. New York: MLA, 1999.

Gibaldi, Joseph. *MLA Style Manual and Guide to Scholarly Publishing.* 2nd ed. New York: MLA, 1998.

MLA style is explained here; American Psychological Association (APA) format is explained in Chapter 53; and your library will have manuals for other fields as well. For information on some of those other styles, including the *Chicago Manual* style (used in history), Council of Biology Editors (CBE) style, and others, see Chapter 54. Newspapers and other publishing companies, businesses, and large organizations often have their own formats, which are explained in their own style manuals.

Some of the major features of MLA style are as follows:

- In in-text citations give the author's last name and the page number of the source, preferably within the sentence rather than after it.

- Use full first and last names and middle initials of authors.

- Capitalize all major words in titles, and underline titles or put them in italics. Enclose article titles in quotation marks.

- In a list of works cited at the end of the paper, give full publication information, alphabetized by author.

When you document sources using MLA format, there are three aspects to consider:

- **In-text citations** In your paper you need parenthetical references to your sources to acknowledge wherever you use the words, ideas, and facts you've taken from your sources.

- **Endnotes** If you need to add material that would disrupt your paper if it were included in the text, include such notes at the end of the paper.

■ **Works cited** At the end of your paper, include a list of the sources from which you have quoted, summarized, or paraphrased.

52a In-Text Citations

The purpose of in-text citations is to help your reader find the appropriate reference in the list of works cited at the end of the paper. You may have previously used footnotes to indicate each source as you used it, but the current MLA format recommends parenthetical citations, depending on how much information you include in your sentence or in your introduction to a quotation. Try to be brief, but not at the expense of clarity, and remember to use signal words and phrases (see 47b).

EXAMPLES OF MLA IN-TEXT CITATIONS

1. Author's Name Not Given in the Text
2. Author's Name Given in the Text
3. Two or More Works by the Same Author
4. Two or Three Authors
5. More than Three Authors
6. Unknown Author
7. Corporate Author or Government Document
8. An Entire Work
9. A Literary Work
10. A Multivolume Work
11. Indirect Source
12. Two or More Sources
13. A Work Listed by Title
14. An Electronic Source

1. Author's Name Not Given in the Text If the author's name is not in your sentence, put the last name in parentheses, leave a space with no punctuation, and then put the page number.

```
Recent research on sleep and dreaming indicates that
dreams move backward in time as the night progresses
(Dement 72).
```

2. Author's Name Given in the Text If you include the author's name in the sentence, only the page number is needed in parentheses.

```
Freud states that "a dream is the fulfillment of a
wish" (154).
```

3. Two or More Works by the Same Author If you used two or more different sources by the same author, put a comma after the author's last name and include a shortened version of the title and the page reference. If the author's name is in the text, include only the title and page reference.

One current theory emphasizes the principle that dreams
express "profound aspects of personality" (Foulkes,
Sleep 144).

Foulkes' investigation shows that young children's
dreams are "rather simple and unemotional" (Children's
Dreams 90).

4. Two or Three Authors If your source has two or three authors,
either name them in your sentence or include the names in
parentheses.

Jeffrey and Milanovitch argue that the recently
reported statistics for teen pregnancies are
inaccurate (112).

The recently reported statistics for teen pregnancies
are said to be inaccurate (Jeffrey and Milanovitch 112).

5. More than Three Authors If your source has more than three
authors, either use the first author's last name followed by *et al.*
(which means "and others") or list all the last names.

The conclusion drawn from a survey on the growth of
the Internet, conducted by Martin et al., is that
global usage will double within two years (36).

Recent figures on the growth of the Internet indicate
that global usage will double within two years (Martin,
Ober, Mancuso, and Blum 36).

6. Unknown Author If the author is unknown, use a shortened form
of the title in your citation.

More detailed nutritional information in food labels
is proving to be a great advantage to diabetics ("New
Labeling Laws" 3).

7. Corporate Author or Government Document Use the name of
the corporation or government agency, shortened or in full. Try to
include long names in your sentence to avoid extending the parenthetical reference.

The United Nations Regional Flood Containment Commission has been studying weather patterns that contribute
to flooding in Africa (4).

8. An Entire Work If you cite an entire work, it is preferable to include the author's name in the text.

Lafmun was the first to argue that small infants

respond to music.

9. A Literary Work If you refer to classic prose works, such as novels or plays, that are available in several editions, it is helpful to provide more information than just a page reference to the edition you used. A chapter number, for example, might help readers locate the reference in any copy they find. In such a reference, give the page number first, add a semicolon, and then give other identifying information.

In The Prince, Machiavelli reminds us that while some

manage to jump from humble origins to great power, such

people find their greatest challenge to be staying in

power: "Those who rise from private citizens to be

princes merely by fortune have little trouble in rising

but very much trouble in maintaining their position"

(23; ch. 7).

For verse plays and poems, omit page numbers and use act, scene, canto, and line numbers separated by periods. For lines, use the word *line* or *lines* in the first reference, and then afterward give only the numbers.

Eliot again reminds us of society's superficiality in

"The Love Song of J. Alfred Prufrock": "There will be

time, there will be time / To prepare a face to meet

the faces that you meet" (lines 26-27).

10. A Multivolume Work When you cite a volume number as well as a page reference for a multivolume work, separate the two by a colon and a space. Do not use the word *volume* or *page*.

In his History of the Civil War, Jimmersen traces the

economic influences that contributed to the decisions

of several states to stay in the Union (3: 798-823).

11. Indirect Source If you have to rely on a secondhand source in which someone's quoted words appear in a source written by someone else, start the citation with the abbreviation *qtd. in.*

Although Newman has established a high degree of accu-

racy for such tests, he reminds us that "no test like

this is ever completely and totally accurate" (qtd. in

Mazor 33).

12. Two or More Sources If you refer to more than one work in your parenthetical citation, separate the references by a semicolon.

```
Recent attempts to control the rapid destruction of the

rain forests in Central America have met with little

success (Costanza 22; Kinderman 94).
```

13. A Work Listed by Title For sources listed by title in your list of works cited, use the title in your sentence or in the parenthetical citation. If you shorten the title because it is long, use a shortened form that begins with the word by which it is alphabetized in your Works Cited list.

```
The video excerpts shown on Sixty Minutes revealed

sophisticated techniques unknown in the early science

fiction movies ("Making Today's Sci-fi Flicks").
```

14. An Electronic Source For electronic sources, start with the word by which the source is alphabetized in your Works Cited list (see 51a).

```
The World Wide Web is a helpful source for community

groups seeking information on how to protest projects

that damage the local environment ("Environmental

Activism").
```

52b Endnotes

When you have additional comments or information that would disrupt the paper, cite the information in endnotes numbered consecutively through the paper. Put the number at the end of the phrase, clause, or sentence containing the material you are referring to, after the punctuation. Raise the number above the line, with no punctuation. Leave no extra space before the number.

```
The treasure hunt for sixteenth-century pirate loot

buried in Nova Scotia began in 1927,³ but hunting was

discontinued when the treasure seekers found the site

flooded at high tide.⁴
```

At the end of your paper, begin a new sheet with the heading "Notes," but do not underline or put the heading in quotation marks. Leave a one-inch margin at the top, center the heading, double-space, and then begin listing your notes. For each note, indent five spaces, raise the number above the line, and begin the note. Double-space, and if the note continues on the next line, begin that line at the left-hand margin. The format is slightly different from that used in the Works Cited section in that the author's name appears in normal order, followed by a comma, the title, the publisher, the date in parentheses, and a page reference.

³ Some historians argue that this widely accepted date is inaccurate. See Jerome Flynn, <u>Buried Treasures</u> (New York: Newport, 1978): 29-43.

⁴ Avery Jones and Jessica Lund, "The Nova Scotia Mystery Treasure," <u>Contemporary History</u> 9 (1985): 81-83.

If you are asked to use footnotes instead of endnotes, place them at the bottoms of pages, beginning four lines (two double spaces) below the text. Single-space footnotes, but double-space between them. Number them consecutively through the paper.

52c Works Cited List

The list of works cited lists all the sources you cite in your paper. Do not include other materials you read but didn't refer to in your paper. Arrange the list alphabetically by the last name of the author; if there is no author, alphabetize by the first word of the title (but not the articles *a, an,* or *the*).

For the Works Cited section, begin a new sheet of paper, leave a one-inch margin at the top, center the heading "Works Cited" (with no underlining or quotation marks), and then double-space before the first entry. For each entry, begin at the left-hand margin for the first line, and indent five spaces (or one-half inch) for additional lines in the entry. Double-space throughout. Place the Works Cited list at the end of your paper after the notes, if you have any.

There are three parts to each reference: (1) author, (2) title, and (3) publishing information. Each part is followed by a period and one space.

Books

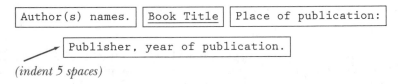

| Author(s) names. | Book Title | Place of publication: |

| Publisher, year of publication. |

(indent 5 spaces)

Articles in Periodicals

Periodicals are published regularly on a fixed schedule. Some, like newspapers and magazines usually appear daily, weekly, or monthly, but scholarly journals are typically published less often. Some publications, such as *Time* or *Wired,* are easily recognized as magazines, and others, such as *Scientific American,* are cited as magazines but are closer to scholarly journals in their content.

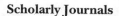

Scholarly Journals

| Author(s) names. | "Title of Article." | Journal Title |

| volume number (year of publication): |

| page number(s). |

(indent 5 spaces)

Magazines

| Author(s) names. | "Title of Article." | Magazine Name |

| day Month year: page number(s). |

(indent 5 spaces)

Newspapers

| Author(s) names. | "Title of Article." | Newspaper Name |

| day Month year, edition: page number(s). |

(indent 5 spaces)

Electronic Sources

For electronic sources (portable databases, online databases, and Internet and Web sources), include as many items from the lists in entry 36 as are relevant and as are found in the source. (For more information, see 51a.)

| Author(s) names. | Title of Project or Database. |

| Name of editor. | Electronic publication |

| information, including date of creation or |

| latest update and sponsoring organization. |

| Date of access and <electronic address>. |

(indent 5 spaces)

EXAMPLES OF MLA WORKS CITED

Books

1. One Author
2. Two or Three Authors
3. More than Three Authors
4. More than One Work by the Same Author
5. A Work that Names an Editor
6. A Work with an Author and an Editor
7. A Work that Names a Translator
8. A Work by a Corporate Author

(continued on next page)

EXAMPLES OF MLA WORKS CITED *(continued from previous page)*

9. A Work by an Unknown Author
10. A Work that Has More than One Volume
11. A Work in an Anthology
12. Two or More Works in the Same Anthology
13. An Article in a Reference Book
14. Introduction, Foreword, Preface, or Afterword
15. A Work with a Title Within a Title
16. Second or Later Edition
17. Modern Reprint
18. A Work in a Series
19. A Work with a Publisher's Imprint
20. Government Publication
21. Proceedings of a Conference

Articles in Periodicals

22. Scholarly Journal with Continuous Paging
23. Scholarly Journal that Pages Each Issue Separately
24. Monthly or Bimonthly Magazine Article
25. Weekly or Biweekly Magazine Article
26. Newspaper Article
27. Unsigned Article
28. Editorial or Letter to the Editor
29. Review of a Work
30. Article in Microform Collection of Articles

Electronic Sources

CD-ROMs and Other Portable Databases
31. Material Accessed from a Periodically Published Database on CD-ROM
32. Publication on CD-ROM
33. Publication on Diskette
34. Publication on Magnetic Tape
35. Work in More than One Published Medium

Online Databases and the Internet
36. Material Accessed Through a Computer Service or Network

Other Sources

37. Computer Software
38. Television or Radio Program
39. Record, Tape Cassette, or CD
40. Film or Video Recording
41. Live Performance of a Play
42. Musical Composition
43. Work of Art
44. Letter, Memo, or E-mail Communication
45. Personal Interview
46. Published Interview

47. Radio or Television Interview
48. Map or Chart
49. Cartoon
50. Advertisement
51. Lecture, Speech, or Address
52. Pamphlet
53. Published Dissertation
54. Abstract of a Dissertation
55. Unpublished Dissertation

Books

1. One Author

Joos, Martin. The Five Clocks. New York: Harcourt,

Brace, and World, 1962.

2. Two or Three Authors Reverse name of first author only.

Duggan, Stephen, and Betty Drury. The Rescue of Science

and Learning. New York: Macmillan, 1948.

Mellerman, Sidney, John Scarcini, and Leslie Karlin.

Human Development: An Introduction to Cognitive

Growth. New York: Harper, 1981.

3. More than Three Authors For more than three authors, you may name only the first and add *et al.* (for "and others") or you may give all names in full in the order in which they appear on the title page.

Spiller, Robert, et al. Literary History of the United

States. New York: Macmillan, 1960.

(or)

Spiller, Robert, Harlan Minton, Michael Upta, and

Gretchen Kielstra. Literary History of the United

States. New York: Macmillan, 1960.

4. More than One Work by the Same Author Use the author's name in the first entry only. From then on, type three hyphens and a period and then begin the next title. Alphabetize by title. If the person edited or translated another work in your list, use a comma and *ed.* or *trans.* after the three hyphens.

Newman, Edwin. A Civil Tongue. Indianapolis: Bobbs-

Merrill, 1966.

---. Strictly Speaking. New York: Warner Books, 1974.

5. A Work that Names an Editor Use the abbreviation *ed.* for one editor and *eds.* for more than one editor.

Kinkead, Joyce A., and Jeanette Harris, eds. Writing

Centers in Context: Twelve Case Studies. Urbana:

NCTE, 1993.

6. A Work with an Author and an Editor If there is an editor in addition to an author, give the editor's name after the title. Before the editor's name, put the abbreviation *Ed.* (for "Edited by").

Frankfurter, Felix. The Diaries of Felix Frankfurter.

Ed. Thomas Sayres. Boston: Norton, 1975.

7. A Work that Names a Translator Use the abbreviation *Trans.* (for "Translated by").

Sastre, Alfonso. Sad Are the Eyes of William Tell.

Trans. Leonard Pronko. Ed. George Wellwarth. New

York: New York UP, 1970.

8. A Work by a Corporate Author

United States Capitol Society. We, the People: The

Story of the United States Capitol. Washington,

Natl. Geographic Soc., 1964.

9. A Work by an Unknown Author

Report of the Commission on Tests. New York: College

Entrance Examination Board, 1970.

10. A Work that Has More than One Volume If you are citing two or more volumes of a work in your paper, put references to volume and page numbers in the parenthetical citations. If you are citing only one of the volumes in your paper, state the number of that volume in the Works Cited list and give publication information for that volume alone.

Esler, Anthony. The Human Venture. 3rd ed. Vol. 1.

Upper Saddle River, NJ: Prentice Hall, 1996.

Rutherford, Ernest. The Collected Papers. 3 vols.

Philadelphia: Allen, 1962.

11. A Work in an Anthology State the author and title of the work first, and then give the title and other information about the anthology, including page numbers on which the selection appears. Use the abbreviation *Comp.* (for "Compiled by"). If a selection has been published before, give that information, then use *Rpt.* (for "Reprinted in") with the anthology information.

Dymvok, George E., Jr. "Vengeance." Poetry in the

Modern Age. Comp. and ed. Jason Metier. San

Francisco: New Horizons. 1994. 54.

```
Licouktis, Michelle. "From Slavery to Freedom." New

     South Quarterly 29 (1962): 87-98. Rpt. in Voices

     of the Sixties: Selected Essays. Ed. Myrabelle

     McConn. Atlanta: Horizons, 1995. 12-19.
```

12. Two or More Works in the Same Anthology If you cite two or more works from the same collection and wish to avoid unnecessary repetition, you may include a complete entry for the collection and then cross-reference the works to that collection. In the cross-reference include the author and title of the work, the last name of the editor of the collection, and the page numbers.

```
Batu, Marda, and Hillary Matthews, eds. Voices of

     American Women. New York: Littlefield, 1995.

Jamba, Shawleen. "My Mother's Not Going Home." Batu

     and Matthews 423-31.

Little River, Lillian. "Listening to the World."

     Batu and Matthews 234-45.
```

13. An Article in a Reference Book Treat an encyclopedia article or a dictionary entry like a piece in an anthology, but do not cite the editor of the reference work. If the article is signed, give the author first. If it is unsigned, give the title first. If articles are arranged alphabetically, omit volume and page numbers. When citing familiar reference books, list only the edition and year of publication.

```
"Bioluminescence." The Concise Columbia Encyclopedia.

     1983 ed.
```

14. Introduction, Foreword, Preface, or Afterword Start the entry with the author of the part you are citing. Then add the information about the book, followed by the page numbers where that part appears. If the author of the part is not the author of the book, use the word *By* and give the book author's full name. If the author of the part and the book are the same, use *By* and the author's last name only.

```
Asimov, Isaac. Foreword. Isaac Asimov's Book of Facts.

     By Asimov. New York: Bell, 1979. vii.

Bruner, Jerome. Introduction. Thought and Language.

     By Lev Vygotsky. Cambridge: MITP, 1962. v-xiii.
```

15. A Work with a Title within a Title If a title that is normally underlined appears within another title, do not underline it or put it inside quotation marks.

```
Lillo, Alphonso. Re-Reading Shakespeare's Hamlet from

     the Outside. Boston: Martinson, 1995.
```

16. Second or Later Edition

> Ornstein, Robert E. The Psychology of Consciousness.
>
> 2nd ed. New York: Harcourt, 1977.

17. Modern Reprint State the original publication date after the title of the book. In the publication information that follows, put the date of publication for the reprint.

> Weston, Jessie L. From Ritual to Romance. 1920. Garden
>
> City: Anchor-Doubleday, 1957.

18. A Work in a Series If the title page or preceding page of the book you are citing indicates that it is part of a series, include the series name, without underlining or quotation marks, and the series number, followed by a period, before the publication information. Use common abbreviations for words in the series name.

> Waldheim, Isaac. Revisiting the Bill of Rights. Studies
>
> of Amer. Constitutional Hist. 18. New York:
>
> Waterman, 1991.

19. A Work with a Publisher's Imprint Publishers sometimes put some of their books under imprints or special names that usually appear with the publisher's name on the title page. Include the imprint name, a hyphen, and the name of the publisher.

> Tamataru, Ishiko. Sunlight and Strength. New York:
>
> Anchor-Doubleday, 1992.

20. Government Publication Use the abbreviation *GPO* for publications from the Government Printing Office.

> United States. Office of Education. Tutor-Trainer's
>
> Resource Handbook. Washington: GPO, 1973.

21. Proceedings of a Conference If the proceedings of a conference are published, treat the entry like a book and add information about the conference if such information isn't included in the title.

> Esquino, Luis. Second Language Acquisition in the
>
> Classroom. Proc. of the Soc. for Second Language
>
> Acquisition Conference, Nov. 1994, U of Texas.
>
> Dallas: Midlands, 1995.
>
> Standino, Alexander, ed. Proceedings of the Fifteenth
>
> Annual Meeting of the Native American Folklore
>
> Society, March 15-17, 1991. Albuquerque: Native
>
> American Folklore Soc., 1991.

Articles in Periodicals

22. Scholarly Journal with Continuous Paging Most scholarly journals have continuous pagination throughout the whole volume for the year. Then, at the end of the year, all issues in that volume are bound together and ordered on shelves by the year of the volume. To find a particular issue on the shelf, you need only the volume number and the page, not the issue number.

> Delbrück, Max. "Mind from Matter." <u>American Scholar</u>
> 47 (1978): 339-53.

23. Scholarly Journal that Pages Each Issue Separately If each issue of the journal starts with page 1, then include the issue number.

> Barthla, Frederick, and Joseph Murphy. "Alcoholism
> in Fiction." <u>Kansas Quarterly</u> 17.2 (1981): 77-80.

24. Monthly or Bimonthly Magazine Article If the article is not printed on consecutive pages, give only the first page number followed by a plus sign.

> Diamond, Jared. "The Worst Mistake in Human History."
> <u>Discover</u> May 1987: 64+.

> Lillio, Debra. "New Cures for Migraine Headaches."
> <u>Health Digest</u> Oct. 1995: 14, 18.

25. Weekly or Biweekly Magazine Article For a magazine published every week or every two weeks, give the complete date, beginning with the day and abbreviating the month. Do not give the volume and issue numbers even if they are listed.

> Isaacson, Walter. "Will the Cold War Fade Away?" <u>Time</u>
> 27 Feb. 1987: 40-45.

26. Newspaper Article Provide the author's name and the title of the article, then the name of the newspaper as it appears on the masthead, omitting any introductory article such as *The*. If the city of publication is not included in the name, add the city in square brackets after the name: *Journal-Courier* [Trenton]. If the paper is nationally published, such as the *Wall Street Journal*, do not add the city of publication. Abbreviate all months except for May, June, and July. Give any information about edition, and follow it with a colon and page numbers.

> Strout, Richard L. "Another Bicentennial." <u>New York</u>
> <u>Times</u> 10 Nov. 1994, late ed.: A9+.

27. Unsigned Article

> "Trading Lives." <u>Newsweek</u> 21 Apr. 1993: 87-89.

28. Editorial or Letter to the Editor If you are citing an editorial, add the word *Editorial* after the title of the editorial. Use the word *Letter* after the author of a letter to the editor.

"Watching Hillary's Defense Team at Play." Editorial.

Washington Times 5 Jan. 1996, late ed.: A18.

Berwitz, Ken. Letter. New York Times 14 Feb. 1996,

late ed.: A20.

29. Review of a Work Include the reviewer's name and title of the review, if any, followed by the words *Rev. of* (for "Review of"), the title of the work being reviewed, a comma, the word *by,* and then the author's name. If the work has no title and is not signed, begin the entry with *Rev. of* and in your list of works cited alphabetize under the title of the work being reviewed.

Kauffmann, Stanley. "Cast of Character." Rev. of Nixon,

dir. Oliver Stone. New Republic 22 Jan. 1996: 26-27.

Rev. of The Beak of the Finch, by Jonathan Weiner.

Science Weekly 12 Dec. 1995: 36.

30. Article in Microform Collection of Articles

Gilman, Elias. "New Programs for School Reform."

Charleston Herald 18 Jan. 1991: 14. Newsbank:

School Reform 14 (1991): fiche 1, grids A7-12.

Electronic Sources

CD-ROMs and Other Portable Databases

Sources in electronic form that are stored on CD-ROMs, diskettes, and magnetic tapes and have to be read on computers are portable databases (that is, they can be carried around, unlike online databases, which are explained in entry 36). When citing these sources, state the medium of publication (such as CD-ROM or diskette), the vendor's name, and the date of electronic publication.

31. Material Accessed from a Periodically Published Database on CD-ROM If no printed source is indicated, include author, title of material (in quotation marks), date of material (if given), title of database (underlined), publication medium, name of vendor, and electronic publication date.

Anstor, Marylee. "Nutrition for Pregnant Women." New

York Times 12 Apr. 1994, late ed.: C1. New York

Times Ondisc. CD-ROM. UMI-Proquest. Oct. 1994.

Institute for Virus Research. "Coenzyme-Cell Wall

Interaction." 14 Feb. 1995. Institutes for

Health Research. CD-ROM. Health Studies Source

Search. June 1995.

32. Publication on CD-ROM Many CD-ROM publications are published, like books, without updates or regular revisions. Cite these like books, but add a description of the medium of publication.

Mattmer, Tobias. "Discovering Jane Austen." Discovering

Authors. Vers. 1.0. CD-ROM. Detroit: Gale, 1992.

All-Movie Guide. CD-ROM. Ottawa: Corel, 1996.

33. Publication on Diskette Diskette publications are cited like books, with an added description of the medium of publication.

Lehmo, Jarred. Ethnicity in Dance. Diskette. Chicago:

U of Chicago P, 1995.

34. Publication on Magnetic Tape Magnetic tape publications are cited like books, with an added description of the medium of publication.

"Television Advertising." Encyclopedia of Modern

Advertising. Magnetic tape. Detroit: Giley, 1994.

35. Work in More than One Published Medium Some electronic publications appear as packages of materials in different publication media. For example, a CD-ROM may be packaged with a diskette. Cite such publication packages as you would a CD-ROM product (see entry 32), specifying the media in the package.

History of Stage Costuming in Europe. CD-ROM,

videodisc. Philadelphia: Michelson, 1995.

Online Databases and the Internet

Online databases are those that are not bought in stores and cannot be carried around. They can be accessed only online and may be continually updated or revised. Some additional elements to be included in the citation are the publication medium (that is, *Online*), the name of the computer service or computer network through which the database is accessed, and the date of access.

36. Material Accessed Through a Computer Service There are two groups of such materials:

1. **Materials with a Print Source** For materials that were or are still available in print. The citation includes information both on the print version and on how and when the material was accessed online.

Meharry, William. "Beta-Carotene May Be Dangerous to

Your Health." New York Times 24 Jan. 1996, late

ed.: B3. New York Times Online. Online. Lexis-

Nexis. 15 Aug. 1996.

2. **Materials with No Print Source** These are materials that do not indicate a printed source, and the citation includes as

much information as is available. See the items listed below for the World Wide Web.

Sapir, Mortimer. "Dangers of Anesthesia." <u>American</u>
        <u>Medical Encyclopedia</u>. Online. Prodigy. 9 Aug. 1995.

Citing Sources from the World Wide Web and the Internet

The World Wide Web is one way to gain access to information on the Internet and requires a browser such as *Netscape Navigator* or *Internet Explorer.* Electronic mail and discussion forums transmitted through the Internet are other sources of online information. For more complete information on citing electronic sources, see 51a.

World Wide Web Site

Salvatore, Steve, Dr. "Ethicists, Doctors Debate Multiple
        Births." <u>CNN Interactive</u> 22 Dec. 1998 <http://cnn
        .com/HEALTH/9812/22/reproductive.ethics/index.html>.

Posting to a Discussion List

Sellars, Ann. "Video vs. CD-ROM." Online posting. 20
        Nov. 1998. Dave Sperling Presents the ESL Discus-
        sion Forum for Teachers. 28 Dec. 1998 <http://www
        .eslcafe.com/discussion/dz3/index.cgi?read=105>.

E-mail

Marsten, Thomas. "Re: Child Safety Belt Research."
        E-mail to the author. 18 Nov. 1998.

Other Sources

37. Computer Software References to computer software are similar to references to CD-ROM or diskette materials (see entries 32 and 33).

<u>McProof</u>. Vers. 3.2.1. Diskette. Salt Lake City:
        Lexpertise, 1987.

38. Television or Radio Program Include the title of the episode (in quotation marks), the title of the program (underlined), the title of the series (with no underlining or quotation marks), the name of the network, the call letters and city of the local station, and the broadcast date. If pertinent, add information such as the names of the performers, director, or narrator.

"Tall Tales from the West." <u>American Folklore</u>. Narr.
        Hugh McKenna. Writ. Carl Tannenberg. PBS. WFYI,
        Indianapolis. 14 Mar. 1995.

39. Record, Tape Cassette, or CD Depending on which you want to emphasize, cite the composer, conductor, or performer first. Then list the title (underlined); artist, medium, if not a compact disc (no underlining or quotation marks); manufacturer; and year of issue (if unknown, include *n.d.* for "no date"). Place a comma between manufacturer and date, with periods following all other items.

```
Perlman, Itzhak. Mozart Violin Concertos Nos. 3 & 5.

    Weiner Philarmoniker Orch. Cond. James Levine.

    Deutsche Grammophon, 1983.

Schiff, Heinrich. Five Cello Concertos. By Antonio

    Vivaldi. Academy of St. Martin-in-the-Fields.

    Dir. Iona Brown. Audiocassette. Philips, 1984.
```

40. Film or Video Recording Begin a reference to a film with the title (underlined), and include the director, distributor, and year. You also may include the names of the writer, performers, and producer. Treat a videocassette, videodisc, slide program, or filmstrip like a film, and give the original release date and the medium before the name of the distributor.

```
Richard III. By William Shakespeare. Dir. Ian McKellen

    and Richard Loncrain. Perf. Ian McKellen, Annette

    Bening, Jim Broadbent, and Robert Downey, Jr.

    MGM/UA, 1995.

Renoir, Jean, dir. The Rules of the Game [Le Regle du

    Jeu]. Perf. Marcel Dalio and Nora Gregor. 1937.

    Videocassette. Video Images, 1981.
```

41. Live Performance of a Play Like a reference to a film (see entry 40), references to performances usually begin with the title and include similar information. Include the theater and city where the performance was given, separated by a comma and followed by a period, and the date of the performance.

```
Inherit the Wind. By Jerome Lawrence and Robert E. Lee.

    Dir. John Tillinger. Perf. George C. Scott and

    Charles Durning. Royale Theatre, New York. 23

    January 1996.
```

42. Musical Composition Begin with the composer's name. Underline the title of an opera, a ballet, or a piece of music with a name, and put quotation marks around the name of a song. If the composition is known only by number, form, or key, do not underline or use quotation marks. If the score is published, cite it like a book and capitalize abbreviations such as *no.* and *op.* You may include the date after the title.

```
Bach, Johann Sebastian. Brandenburg Concertos.
```

```
Bach, Johann Sebastian. Orchestral Suite no. 1 in

    C major.
```

43. Work of Art Begin with the artist's name; underline the title of the work; and include the institution that houses the work or the person who owns it, followed by a comma and the city. If you include the date the work was created, add that after the title. If you use a photograph of the work, include the publication information for your source, citing the page, slide, figure, or plate number.

```
Manet, Edouard. The Balcony. Jeu de Paume, Paris.

Monet, Claude. Rouen Cathedral. Metropolitan Museum of

    Art, New York. Masterpieces of Fifty Centuries.

    New York: Dutton, 1970. 316.
```

44. Letter, Memo, E-mail Communication

```
Blumen, Lado. Letter to Lui Han. 14 Oct. 1998. Lado

    Blumen Papers. Minneapolis Museum of Art Lib.,

    Minneapolis.

Milan, Theresa. "Greetings." E-mail to Simon Mahr.

    18 Sept. 1998.
```

45. Personal Interview

```
Kochem, Prof. Alexander. Personal interview. 18 Apr. 1995.
```

46. Published Interview

```
Goran, Nadya. "A Poet's Reflections on the End of the

    Cold War." By Leonid Tuzman. International Liter-

    ary Times 18 Nov. 1995: 41-44.
```

47. Radio or Television Interview

```
Netanyahu, Benjamin. Interview with Ted Koppel.

    Nightline. ABC. WABC, New York. 18 Aug. 1995.
```

48. Map or Chart Treat a map or chart like a book without an author (see entry 9), but add the descriptive label (*Map* or *Chart*).

```
New York. Map. Chicago: Rand, 1995.
```

49. Cartoon Begin with the cartoonist's name, followed by the title of the cartoon (if any) in quotation marks and the descriptive label *Cartoon,* and conclude with the usual publication information.

```
Adams, Scott. "Dilbert." Cartoon. Journal and Courier

    [Lafayette] 20 Jan. 1996: B7.
```

50. Advertisement Begin with the name of the product, company, or institution that is the subject of the advertisement, followed by the descriptive label *Advertisement,* and conclude with the usual publication information.

Apple Computer. Advertisement. <u>GQ</u>, Dec. 1998: 145-46.

51. Lecture, Speech, or Address Begin with the speaker's name, the title of the presentation in quotation marks, the meeting and sponsoring organization, location, and date. Use a descriptive label such as *Address* or *Reading* if there is no title.

Lihandro, Alexandra. "Writing to Learn." Conf. on Coll.

Composition and Communication Convention. Palmer

House, Chicago. 23 Mar. 1990.

Trapun, Millicent. Address. Loeb Theater. Indianapolis.

16 Mar. 1995.

52. Pamphlet Cite a pamphlet like a book.

<u>Thirty Foods for Your Health</u>. New York: Consumers

Health Soc., 1996.

53. Published Dissertation Treat a published dissertation like a book, but include dissertation information before the publication information. You may add the University Microfilms International (UMI) order number after the date if UMI published the work.

Blalock, Mary Jo. <u>Consumer Awareness of Food Additives</u>

<u>in Products Offered as Organic</u>. Diss. U Plain-

field, 1994. Ann Arbor: UMI, 1995. 10325891.

54. Abstract of a Dissertation Begin with the publication information for the original work, and then add the information for the journal in which the abstract appears.

McGuy, Timothy. "Campaign Rhetoric of Conservatives

in the 1994 Congressional Elections." Diss. Johns

Hopkins U, 1995. <u>DAI</u> 56 (1996): 1402A.

55. Unpublished Dissertation Put the title of an unpublished dissertation in quotation marks and include the descriptive label *Diss.*, followed by the name of the university granting the degree, a comma, and the year.

Tibbur, Matthew. "Computer-Mediated Intervention

in Early Childhood Stuttering." Diss. Stan-

ford U, 1991.

52d Sample MLA-Style Research Paper

Included here is a research paper with a title page, a first page for a paper that does not have a title page, and a Works Cited list. Research papers that follow MLA style generally do not need a title page, but if you are asked to include one, follow the format shown here.

I. Title Page Following MLA Style

A Miracle Drug to Keep Us Young   *center title*
or Another False Hope?   *one-third*
down page

Michael G. Mitun   *name*

Professor Jomale   *instructor*
English 102, Section 59   *course*
19 April 1999   *date*

(Proportions shown in margins of paper are not actual but are adjusted to fit space limitations of this book. Follow actual dimensions shown in margins and your instructor's directions.)

2. Research Paper Following MLA Style

↑ *1 inch*

↑ *½ inch*
Mitun 1

Michael G. Mitun

Professor Jomale

} *double-space*

English 102

19 April 1999

} *double-space*

A Miracle Drug to Keep Us Young

or Another False Hope? } *double-space*

Even before Ponce de Leon landed in
Florida in 1513, searching for a fountain of
youth, people looked for ways to resist the
aging process. But now modern medicine is opening the door to new therapies that might work,
pills based on hormones that our bodies produce
when we're young but that decrease as we grow
old. At the moment, one of the most promising
of these hormones is DHEA, the subject of magazine and newspaper articles ("Nature's"; Oppenheim), a television newsmagazine program (Eye
to Eye), and medical research (Ames; Garcia,
"Effects"; Li; Rosch). As medical evidence continues to appear, the number of believers is
increasing. But most physicians are unwilling
to prescribe DHEA for their patients, and the
U.S. Food and Drug Administration has not
approved its sale in the United States. At the
present time, DHEA shows promise but is not yet
the miraculous fountain of youth people have
been waiting for.

1 inch (left margin) *1 inch* (right margin)

↑ *1 inch*

(continued on next page)

(continued from previous page)

↓ *1 inch*

↓ *½ inch*
Mitun 2

At a conference hosted by the New York Academy of Sciences, titled "Dehydroepiandrosterone (DHEA) and Aging," medical researchers reported on their studies of DHEA. Burkhard Bilger, one of the people attending that conference, heard vivid testimonials about this compound, which he describes as "the most plentiful steroid hormone in the human body-- and the most poorly understood" (26). But research has confirmed that the highest concentration of DHEA in our bodies is reached during puberty, and then production begins to decline after about age twenty or so (Health and Aging). Dr. Ray Shelian, in DHEA: A Practical Guide, explains that DHEA is a hormone produced by the adrenal glands and is used throughout our bodies:

> After DHEA is made, it goes into the bloodstream, and from then on it travels all over the body and goes into our cells, where it is converted into male hormones, known as androgens, or female hormones, known as estrogens. (45)

Advertising hype, especially prevalent on the World Wide Web, where dozens of companies have sites selling their vitamins and health

supplements, claims that DHEA slows aging,
burns fat, builds muscle, enhances sex drive,
and wards off such diseases as Type II dia-
betes, Alzheimer's disease, and Parkinson's
disease. DHEA may also decrease the incidence
of osteoporosis and decrease the rate of heart
disease by lowering cholesterol and acting as
a blood thinner. Dr. C. Norman Shealy also
notes that it plays a major role in the immune
system and determines general levels of well-
being and mood. But Dr.Shelian cautions that
most studies of the effects of DHEA supplemen-
tation on aging have been performed only on
rodents; therefore, similar effects on humans
are unknown (108).

Although there is the promise of potential
benefits of taking DHEA as a supplement that
might indeed offer us a new fountain of youth
(Rabin), Dr. Anna McCormick, the chief of
biology at the National Institute on Aging,
warns that there are also potential harmful
effects (Jaroff). Dr. Susan Hoch expresses
caution when she notes that she would be "quite
concerned about someone randomly taking DHEA
for several reasons." She notes several studies
suggesting that women blood donors who were
later found to have breast cancer had higher

(continued on next page)

(continued from previous page)

↓ *1 inch*

↓ *½ inch*
Mitun 4

levels of DHEA than normal, and similarly women
with ovarian cancer were also found to have
high levels of DHEA. In the <u>Mayo Clinic Health
Letter</u> ("What About . . . ?") Mayo physicians
have similarly advised against taking DHEA as
supplements because most studies to date have
involved only animal research or very limited
human clinical trials and because no one knows
for sure what supplemental DHEA does, how it
works, how it may interact with other drugs,
and what the long-term effects may be. In addition, DHEA deficiency is not known to cause any
disease, and no medical uses for the supplements have been approved by the U.S. Food and
Drug Administration (FDA).

Because the FDA has banned sales of DHEA,
it is now sold as a "dietary supplement," which
does not require FDA approval. Given the medical community's warnings about possible dangers and the lack of long-term research to
prove conclusively that DHEA can ward off diseases that we are prone to as we age, DHEA may
not be the fountain of youth we are all looking
for. The only certainty is that it results in
huge profits for the companies who peddle it to
willing believers.

3. Works Cited Page Following MLA Style

1 inch ↓   ↑ *½ inch*
Mitun 5

Works Cited

Ames, Donna Spahn. "The Effects of Chronic
Endurance Training on DHEA and DHEA-S Lev-
els in Middle-Aged Men." Diss. U of New
Hampshire, 1997.

Bilger, Burkhard. "Forever Young." The Sciences
Sept./Oct. 1998: 26-30.

Eye to Eye. CBS. WCBS, New York. 15 June 1998.

Garcia, Homer. "Effects of Dehydroepiandrosterone (DHEA) on Brain Tissue."
DHEA Transformations in Target Tissue.
Ed. Milan Zucheffa. London: Binn,
1994: 36-45.

---, "Estrogens in Target Tissues." Endo-
crinology 136 (1995): 3247-56.

Hoch, Susan. "Post re DHEA." Online posting.
22 Oct. 97. Menopause and Beyond.
21 Dec. 1998 <http://www.oxford.net/
~tishy/dhea.html>.

Jaroff, Leon. "New Age Therapy." Time 23 Jan.
1996: 52.

Health and Aging. Prod. Hormone Therapy
Project, Middleton Medical School. Videodisc. Middleton, Ohio: Coronet, 1994.

1 inch

(continued on next page)

(continued from previous page)

↓ *1 inch*   ↓ *½ inch*
                                                  Mitun 6

Li, Min Zhen, ed. The Biologic Role of Dehydro-
    epiandrosterone (DHEA). Berlin: de
    Gruyter, 1990.

"Nature's Other Time-Stopper." Newsweek 7 Aug.
    1995: 49.

Oppenheim, Edgar. "DHEA Offers Promise."
    Springfield Courier 22 June 1995, late
    ed.: B1. Current News Ondisc. CD-ROM. New
    York: Qube, 1995.

Rabin, Prof. Jonathan. Personal interview.
    21 Oct. 1998.

Rosch, Paul J. "DHEA, Electrical Stimulation,
    and the Fountain of Youth." Stress
    Medicine 11.4 (1995): 211-27.

Shealy, C. Norman. DHEA: The Youth and Health
    Hormone. New York: Keats, 1996.

Shelian, Ray. DHEA: A Practical Guide.
    Philadelphia: Cowan, 1997.

"What About . . . ?" Mayo Clinic Health
    Letter. 4 Mar. 1997. 18 Dec. 1998
    <http://www.mayohealth.org/mayo/9704/
    html/2nd-op1.htm>.

53 Documenting in APA Style (APA)

American Psychological Association (APA) format is used to document papers in the behavioral and social sciences. If you are asked to use APA format, consult the *Publication Manual of the American Psychological Association* (4th ed., Washington, D.C.: American Psychological Association, 1994).

APA style is like MLA style (see Chapter 52) in that you have parenthetical citations in your paper to refer readers to the list at the end of the paper; numbered notes that are to be used only to include information that would disrupt the writing if included there; and at the end of the paper, a References list of works cited.* References in this list include only the sources used in the research and preparation of your paper. However, because of the greater emphasis in the social sciences on how current the source is, APA style includes the date of publication in parenthetical citations, and the date appears after the author's name in the reference list. In addition, authors' first and middle names are indicated by initials only. Capitalization and use of quotation marks and underlines also differ in APA style.

Some features of APA style are as follows:

- In in-text citations, give the author's last name and the publication year of the source.

- In quotations, put signal words (see 47b) in past tense (such as "Smith reported") or present perfect tense (such as "as Smith has reported").

- Use full last names and initials of first and middle names of authors.

- Capitalize only the first word and proper names in book and article titles, but capitalize all major words in journal titles. Underline titles of books and journals; do not put article titles in quotation marks.

- In your References list at the end of the paper, give full publication information, alphabetized by author.

53a In-Text Citations

When you use APA format and refer to sources in your text, include the author's name and date of publication. For direct quotations, include the page number also.

*Ask your instructor which of APA's two recommended formats you should use for References list entries: (1) first line indented five spaces, subsequent lines full measure (as shown in this book), or (2) first line full measure, subsequent lines indented five spaces.

EXAMPLES OF APA IN-TEXT CITATIONS	
1. Direct Quotations	**7.** Authors with the Same Last Name
2. Author's Name Given in the Text	**8.** Two or More Works in the Same Parentheses
3. Author's Name Not Given in the Text	**9.** Classical Works
4. Work by Multiple Authors	**10.** Specific Parts of a Source
5. Group as Author	**11.** Personal Communications
6. Work with Unknown Author	**12.** World Wide Web

1. Direct Quotations When you quote a source, end with quotation marks and give the author, year, and page number in parentheses.

```
Many others agree with the assessment that "this is a

seriously flawed study" (Methasa, 1994, p. 22) and do

not include its data in their own work.
```

2. Author's Name Given in the Text Cite only the year of publication in parentheses. If the year also appears in the sentence, do not add parenthetical information. If you refer to the same study again in the paragraph, with the source's name, you do not have to cite the year again if it is clear that the same study is being referred to.

```
When Millard (1970) compared reaction times among the

participants, he noticed an increase in errors.

In 1994 Pradha found improvement in short-term memory

with accompanying practice.
```

3. Author's Name Not Given in the Text Cite the name and year, separated by a comma.

```
In a recent study of reaction times (Millard, 1970) no

change was noticed.
```

4. Work by Multiple Authors For two authors, cite both names every time you refer to the source. Use *and* in the text, but use an ampersand (&) in parenthetical material, tables, captions, and the References list.

```
When Glick and Metah (1991) reported on their findings,

they were unaware of a similar study (Grimm & Tolman,

1991) with contradictory data.
```

For three, four, or five authors, include all authors (and date) the first time you cite the source. For additional references, include only the first author's name and *et al.* (for "and others"), with no underlining or italics.

```
Ellison, Mayer, Brunerd, and Keif (1987) studied

supervisors who were given no training. Later, when

Ellison et al. (1987) continued to study these same

supervisors, they added a one-week training program.
```

For six or more authors, cite only the first author and *et al.* and the year for all references.

```
Mokach et al. (1989) noted no improvement in norms for

participant scores.
```

5. Group as Author The name of the group that serves as the author (for example, a government agency or a corporation) is usually spelled out every time it appears in a citation. If the name is long but easily identified by its abbreviation and you want to switch to the abbreviation, give the abbreviation in parentheses when the entire name first appears.

```
In 1992 when the National Institute of Mental Health

(NIMH) prepared its report, no field data on this

epidemic were available. However, NIMH agreed that

future reports would correct this deficiency.
```

6. Work with Unknown Author When a work has no author, cite the first few words of the reference list entry and the year.

```
One newspaper article ("When South Americans," 1987)

indicated the rapid growth of this phenomenon.
```

7. Authors with the Same Last Name If two or more authors who appear in your reference list have the same last name, include their initials in all text citations.

```
Until T. A. Wilman (1994) studied the initial survey

(M. R. Wilman, 1993), no reports were issued.
```

8. Two or More Works in the Same Parentheses When two or more works are cited within the same parentheses, arrange them in the order they appear in the References list, and separate them with semicolons.

```
Several studies (Canin, 1989; Duniere, 1987; Pferman & Chu,

1991) reported similar behavior patterns in such cases.
```

9. Classical Works Reference entries are not necessary for major classical works such as ancient Greek and Roman works and the Bible, but identify the version you used in the first citation in your text. If appropriate, in each citation, include the part (book, chapter, lines).

```
This was known (Aristotle, trans. 1931) to be prevalent

among young men with these symptoms.
```

10. Specific Parts of a Source To cite a specific part of a source, include the page, chapter, figure, or table, and use the abbreviations *p.* (for "page") and *chap.* (for "chapter").

```
No work was done on interaction of long-term memory and
computer programming (Sitwa & Shiu, 1993, p. 224), but
recently (Takamuru, 1996, chap. 6) reported studies
that have considered this interaction.
```

11. Personal Communications Personal communications include letters, memos, telephone conversations, and electronic communications such as e-mail, discussion groups, and messages on electronic bulletin boards. Because the data cannot be recovered, these are included only in the text and not in the References list. Include the initials and last name of the communicator and as exact a date as possible. (For electronic sources that can be documented, see 51b).

```
According to I. M. Boza (personal communication, June
18, 1995), no population studies of the problem were
done before 1993.
```

12. World Wide Web To cite a Web site in the text (but not a specific document), include the Web address. See 51b for more information.

```
The Web site for the American Psychological Association
(http://www.apa.org) has listed an update on how to
cite information found on the World Wide Web.
```

53b Footnotes

In the paper you may need footnotes for content and for copyright permission. Content footnotes add important information that cannot be integrated into the text, but they are distracting and should be used only if they strengthen the discussion. Copyright permission footnotes acknowledge the source of quotations that are copyrighted. Number the footnotes consecutively with superscript arabic numerals and include the footnotes on a separate page after the References list.

53c References List

Arrange all entries in alphabetical order by the author's last name, and for several works by one author, arrange by year of publication with the earliest one first. For authors' names, give all surnames first and then the initials. Use commas to separate a list of two or more names, and use an ampersand (&) before the last name in the list. Capitalize only the first word of the title and the subtitle (and any proper names) of a book or article, but capitalize the name of the journal. Underline (or italicize) book titles, names of journals, and the volume number of the journal.

EXAMPLES OF APA REFERENCES
Books

1. One Author
2. Two or More Works by the Same Author
3. Two or More Authors
4. Group or Corporate Author
5. Unknown Author
6. Edited Volume
7. Translation
8. Article or Chapter in an Edited Book
9. Article in a Reference Book
10. Revised Edition
11. Multivolume Work
12. Technical and Research Report
13. Report from a University

Articles in Periodicals

14. Article in a Journal Paged Continuously
15. Article in a Journal Paged Separately by Issue
16. Article in a Magazine
17. Article in a Newspaper
18. Unsigned Article
19. Monograph
20. Review of a Book, Film, or Video

Electronic Sources

21. Internet and the World Wide Web
22. Online Abstract
23. Online Journal, Subscriber Based
24. Electronic Database
25. CD-ROM
26. Computer Program or Software

Other Sources

27. Information Service
28. Dissertation Abstract
29. Government Document
30. Conference Proceedings
31. Interview
32. Film, Videotape, Performance, or Artwork
33. Recording
34. Cassette Recording
35. Television Broadcast, Series, and Single Episode from a Series
36. Unpublished Paper Presented at a Meeting

Start the reference list on a new page, with the word *References* centered at the top of the page, and double-space all entries. Indent the first line of each entry five to seven spaces, the same as a paragraph in the text. (The APA manual also permits a hanging indent in which the first line begins at the left margin and all subsequent lines are indented five spaces. Ask your instructor which to use.)

Books

1. One Author

Rico, G. L. (1983). <u>Writing the natural way.</u>
Los Angeles: Tarcher.

2. Two or More Works by the Same Author

Include the author's name in all references and arrange by year of publication, the earliest first.

Kilmonto, R. J. (1983). <u>Culture and ethnicity.</u>
Washington, DC: American Psychiatric Press.

Kilmonto, R. J. (1989). Comparisons of cultural
adaptations. <u>Modern Cultural Studies, 27,</u> 237-243.

3. Two or More Authors

Strunk, W., Jr., & White, E. B. (1979). <u>The</u>
<u>elements of style</u> (3rd ed.). New York: Macmillan.

4. Group or Corporate Author

If the publication is a brochure, list this in brackets.

Mental Health Technical Training Support Center.
(1994). <u>Guidelines for mental health nonprofit agency</u>
<u>staffs</u> (2nd ed.) [Brochure]. Manhattan, KS: Author.

5. Unknown Author

<u>Americana collegiate dictionary</u> (4th ed.).
(1995). Indianapolis: Huntsfield.

6. Edited Volume

Griffith, J.W., & Frey, C.H. (Eds.). (1996).
<u>Classics of children's literature</u> (4th ed.). Upper
Saddle River, NJ: Prentice Hall.

7. Translation

Lefranc, J. R. (1976). <u>A Treatise on</u>
<u>probability</u> (R. W. Mateau & D. Trilling, Trans.).
New York: Macmillan. (Original work published 1952)

8. Article or Chapter in an Edited Book

Riesen, A. H. (1991). Sensory deprivation.
In E. Stellar & J. M. Sprague (Eds.), <u>Progress in</u>
<u>physiological psychology</u> (pp. 24-54). New York:
Academic Press.

9. Article in a Reference Book

Terusami, H. T. (1993). Relativity. In The new handbook of science (Vol. 12, pp. 247-249). Chicago: Modern Science Encyclopedia.

10. Revised Edition

Telphafi, J. (1989). Diagnostic techniques (Rev. ed.). Newbury Park, CA: Pine.

11. Multivolume Work

Donovan, W. (Ed.). (1979-1986). Social sciences: A history (Vols. 1-5). New York: Hollins.

12. Technical and Research Report

Birney, A. F., & Hall, M. M. (1981). Early identification of children with written language disabilities (Report No. 81-502). Washington, DC: National Education Association.

13. Report from a University

Lundersen, P. S., McIver, R. L., & Yepperman, B. B. (1990). Sexual harassment policies and the law (Tech. Rep. No. 9). Springfield, IN: University of Central Indiana, Faculty Affairs Research Center.

Articles in Periodicals

14. Article in a Journal Paged Continuously

Schaubroeck, J., Sime, W. E., & Mayes, B. T. (1991). The nomological validity of the type A personality. Journal of Applied Psychology, 76, 143-168.

15. Article in a Journal Paged Separately by Issue

Timmo, L. A., & Kikovio, R. (1994). Young children's attempts at deception. Research in Early Childhood Learning, 53(2), 49-67.

16. Article in a Magazine

Simmons, H. (1995, November 29). Changing our buying habits. American Consumer, 21, 29-36.

17. Article in a Newspaper For newspaper articles, use *p.* or *pp.* before the page numbers.

> Leftlow, B. S. (1993, December 18). Corporate
>
> take-overs confuse stock market predictions. Wall
>
> Street Journal, pp. A1, A14.

18. Unsigned Article

> New study promises age-defying pills. (1995,
>
> July 27). The Washington Post, p. B21.

19. Monograph

> Rotter, P. B., & Stolz, G. (1966). Generalized
>
> expectancies of early childhood speech patterns.
>
> Monographs of the Childhood Education Society, 36
>
> (2, Serial No. 181).

20. Review of a Book, Film, or Video If the review is untitled, use the material in brackets as the title and indicate whether the review is of a book, film, or video; the brackets indicate the material is a description of form and content, not a title.

> Carmody, T. P. (1982). A new look at medicine
>
> from the social perspective [Review of the book
>
> Social contexts of health, illness, and patient
>
> care]. Contemporary Psychology, 27, 208-209.

Electronic Sources

The American Psychological Association has posted guidelines on the Web at http://www.apa.org/journals/webref.html on how to cite information from the Internet and the World Wide Web. The goal of references is to credit the author and to help your reader find the material. Electronic correspondence (e-mail messages, electronic discussion groups, and so on) is cited as personal communication in your text but does not need to be included in your reference list (see 51b).

All references begin with the same information (or as much as is possible) that is included for a print source. World Wide Web information is placed at the end of a reference, and "Retrieved from" and the date of retrieval are used because the content of documents can be changed, revised, or removed from the site.

21. Internet and the World Wide Web A similar format can be used to cite gopher or ftp sources with the medium and path adequately identified.

McCutchen, A., Francis, M. & Kerr, S. (1997). Revising for meaning: Effects of knowledge and strategy [Abstract]. Journal of Educational Psychology 89, 667-676. Retrieved February 9, 1998 from the World Wide Web: http://www.apa.org/journals/edu/1297ab.html#8

22. Online Abstract

Brindelstein, C., & Chen, S. (1993). The social interaction of small children in task-differentiated groups. [On-line]. Childhood Socializing, 14, 234-241. Abstract from: DIALOG File: PsycINFO Item: 46-12144

23. Online Journal, Subscriber Based

Cross-Cultural Speech Interference Study Group. (1995, October 21). Signaling affirmation in informal conversation: Contrasting behaviors of Hispanics and African-Americans [720 paragraphs]. Online Journal of Contrastive Cultural Behaviors [On-line serial]. Available: Doc. No. 99

24. Electronic Database

Survey of Public Response to Terrorism Abroad: 1992-93. [Electronic database]. (1994). Washington, DC: Center for Public Policy Study [Producer and Distributor].

25. CD-ROM

Culrose, P., Trimmer, N., & Debruikker, K. (1996). Gender differentiation in fear responses [CD-ROM]. Emotion and Behavior, 27, 914-937. Abstract from: FirstSearch: PsycLIT Item: 900312

26. Computer Program or Software

Gangnopahdhav, A. (1994). Data analyzer for E-mail usage [Computer software]. Princeton, NJ: MasterMinders.

Other Sources

27. Information Service

> Mead, J. V. (1992). Looking at old photographs:
> Investigating the teacher tales that novice teachers
> bring with them (Report No. NCRTL-RR-92-4). East
> Lansing, MI: National Center for Research on Teacher
> Learning. (ERIC Document Reproduction Service No. ED
> 346 082)

28. Dissertation Abstract

> Rosen, P. R. (1994). Learning to cope with
> family crises through counsellor mediation (Doctoral
> dissertation, Claremont University, 1994). Disser-
> tation Abstracts International, 53, Z6812.

29. Government Document

> United States Bureau of Statistics. (1994)
> Population density in the contiguous United States
> (No. A1994-2306). Washington, DC: U.S. Government
> Printing Office.

30. Conference Proceedings

> Cordulla, F. M., Teitelman, P. J., & Preba, E. E.
> (1995). Bio-feedback in muscle relaxation.
> Proceedings of the National Academy of Biological
> Sciences, USA, 96, 1271-1342.

31. Interview Personal interviews are not included in the References list. Instead use a parenthetical citation in the text. List published interviews under the interviewer's name.

> Daly, C. C. (1995, July 14). [Interview with Mal-
> colm Forbes]. International Business Weekly, 37, 34-35.

32. Film, Videotape, Performance, or Artwork Start with the name and, in parentheses, functions of the originators or primary contributors. Put the medium, such as film, videotape, slides, and so on, in brackets after the title. Give the name and location of the distributor, and if the company is not well known, include the address.

Weiss, I. (Producer), & Terris, A. (Director).
(1992). Infant babbling and speech production [Film].
(Available from Childhood Research Foundation, 125
Marchmont Avenue, Suite 224, New York, NY 10022)

33. Recording

Totonn, R. (1993). When I wander [Recorded by
A. Lopper, T. Seagrim, & E. Post]. On Songs of our
age [CD]. Wilmington, ME: Folk Heritage Records.

34. Cassette Recording

Trussler, R.W., Jr. (Speaker). (1989). Validity
of mental measurements with young children (Cassette
Recording No. 21-47B). Washington, DC: American
Psychological Measurements Society.

35. Television Broadcast, Series, and Single Episode from a Series

Widener, I. (Executive Producer). (1995,
October 21). Window on the world. New York: Public
Policy Broadcasting.

Biaccio, R. (Producer). (1994). The mind of
man. New York: WNET.

Nostanci, L. (1994). The human sense of
curiosity (R. Mindlin, Director). In R. Biaccio
(Producer), The mind of man. New York: WNET.

36. Unpublished Paper Presented at a Meeting

Lillestein, M.A. (1994, January). Notes on
inter-racial conflict in college settings. Paper
presented at the meeting of the American Cultural
Studies Society, San Antonio, TX.

53d Sample APA-Style Research Paper

If you are using APA style and are asked to include a title page, follow
the format shown here. Included also are a sample paper that does
not also have a title page and a References list. For all pages, leave a
margin of at least one inch on all sides.

I. Title Page Following APA Style

↑ *½ inch*
Selecting Options   1
abbreviated title and page number

centered and Selecting Options in American   *title*
double-spaced Forest Management Policies

Aviva Lipkin   *writer*

Prof. Fujiyamu   *instructor*

Humanities 207   *course*

October 12, 1998   *date*

(Proportions shown in margins of paper are not actual but are adjusted to fit space
limitations of this book. Follow actual dimensions shown in margins and your
instructor's directions.)

2. Research Paper Following APA Style

1 inch | ↓ *½ inch*
Selecting Options 2

Selecting Options in American Forest
Management Policies

As Americans become more aware of the damage done to the environment by logging, they are increasing their support to halt timber harvesting. However, like most Americans, these people also like wooden furniture, wood stoves, and redwood decks and continue to use vast amounts of wood products. Presently, we consume more than 500 million cubic meters of wood and wood products a year, an amount projected to increase to close to 600 million cubic meters in less than ten years (Haynes, Adams, & Mills, 1993). To visualize that amount, picture a train of 2 million fully loaded boxcars encircling the Earth at the equator (Dekker-Robertson & Libby, 1998). What policies should we adopt to deal with the need to protect our environment without eliminating the tree harvesting that will meet America's needs?

Reduce Demand and Encourage Recycling

It is difficult to see how Americans can reduce our need for wood when it is a major commercial product. For example, Home Depot, the world's largest retailer of products that come from old-growth forests, controls over 30% of the home improvement market and boasts sales of over $24 billion. As it has expanded from North American into Chile and Brazil and

↓ *1 inch*

(continued on next page)

(continued from previous page)

1 inch

½ inch

expects to nearly double its number of stores in several years, Home Depot has continued to sell old-growth wood, despite its claims that it does not, and will be increasing its sales as the company grows. The Rainforest Action Network (1998) thus claims that "Home Depot is also a major force in the destruction of the world's remaining old growth forests." Another problem with reducing consumption of wood is that the world will continue to need more wood as Earth's population grows. Jacques Cousteau noted in his address to the world's leaders at the Rio de Janeiro Summit, "Every six months, the equivalent of France [50 million people] is added. Every ten years, there is a new China born in the poorest regions of our Earth" (p. 4). If the rest of the world's rapidly increasing number of people continues to consume wood in larger amounts, the prices will rise. American lumber companies will find it difficult to resist the lure of ever more profitable wood sales, especially since the U.S. Forest Service has a long history of opposing environmentalists and signing contracts with timber companies to cut trees for a fraction of their market value (Satchell, 1996). Recycling may be a more viable way to reduce wood consumption, but as wood products are recycled, new wood fiber has to be added. However, recycling does reduce landfills.

↕ *1 inch*

↕ *½ inch*
Selecting Options   4

Substitute Other Materials for Wood

To halt declining wood supplies, it has been suggested that manufacturers could turn to other plant products such as straw and bagasse, which are by-products of sugar and grain, or kenaf (Bielski, 1996). One concern with this solution, however, is that sugarcane, kenaf, and other annual crops damage the environment more than tree plantations do (Maclaren, 1996). While tree plantations do not provide the kinds of biodiversity that sustains wildlife that natural forests do, capable forestry management organizations claim that they can encourage diversity of wildlife and habitats (New England Forestry Foundation, 1997).

Import More Wood

America can increase its imports of wood, but we are already the world's largest importer of wood products (Food and Agriculture Organization, 1995), and we will continue to import even more wood from Canada, our largest source of wood imports. But Canadian provinces such as British Columbia face the same environmental problems as Washington, Oregon, and Northern California. Greenpeace, founded in Vancouver, is only one of the vocal Canadian groups pressuring the Canadian provinces to protect their forests even as their tree harvesting continues to decline.

Grow More Timber in America

Yet another option is to grow more and better

(continued on next page)

(continued from previous page)

1 inch   *½ inch*
                        Selecting Options 5

trees in the United States on land presently used
for such purposes. With genetically improved tree
species and more intensive cultivation, we can
increase our tree harvests and meet more of our
own demand. A model for this option is New
Zealand, which meets 100% of its net domestic
needs from plantations; approximately 30% of its
original native forest is now in protected
reserves (Maclaren, 1996). There are already
intensive programs in the United States, such as
loblolly pine plantations in the Southeast where
productivity has risen 12% in one generation of
trees. Jess Daniels, a forest geneticist, supports such efforts: "The bottom line is this: If
we are going to continue using more and more
wood, then we have a moral responsibility to grow
more wood to meet that demand" (p. 11).

Conclusion

With our forests becoming depleted and
environmental activists continuing their
efforts to decrease the lands available for
logging, Americans will have to explore options
for our wood-hungry population. We can decrease
the amount of wood we use, recycle what we do
use, substitute other products in place of
wood, import more wood from other countries, or
cultivate our tree plantations to be more productive. None of these options is without problems, but we will have to find policies that
will not harm our environment or our economy.

1 inch | ↕ ½ inch
Selecting Options   6

References

Bielski, V. (1996, July/August). Shopper, spare that tree! Sierra 38, 64-66.

Cousteau, J.-Y. (1992). Convince to conquer. Address to the United Nations Conference on Environment and Development. 5 June 1992, Rio de Janeiro, Brazil.

Daniels, J. D. (1993). Forest genetics and you: What's the connection? Forests Today & Forever, 7, 4-5, 11.

Dekker-Robertson, D. L., & Libby, W. J. (1998) "American forest policy--global ethics tradeoffs." BioScience 48(6), 471.

Food and Agriculture Organization of the United Nations. (1995). Forestry statistics for tomorrow. Rome: FAO Forestry Planning and Statistics Branch.

Haynes, R. W., Adams, D. M., & Mills, J. R. (1993). The 1993 RPA Timber Assessment Update. Fort Collins, CO: USDA Forest Service.

Maclaren, J. P. (1996). Environmental effects of planted forests. Rotorua, New Zealand: New Zealand Forest Research Institute. (FRI Bulletin No. 198).

New England Forestry Foundation. (1997). Retrieved December 23, 1998 from the World Wide Web: http://www.neforestry.org

↕ 1 inch

(continued on next page)

(continued from previous page)

1 inch | ½ inch
Selecting Options 7

Rainforest Action Network. (1998). "Fueling the chain saws: How Home Depot supports old growth forest destruction." <u>San Diego Earth Times,</u> Dec. 1998. Retrieved December 27, 1998 from the World Wide Web: http://www.sdearthtimes .com/et1298/et1298s3.html

Satchell, M. (1996, September 18). At war in an ancient forest. <u>US News & World Report.</u> Retrieved December 26, 1998 from the World Wide Web: www.usnews.com/usnews/23fore.htm

54 Documenting in Other Styles

54a Chicago Manual of Style

In disciplines such as history and other humanities, the preferred style is the *Chicago Manual*. The most recent guide for this is *The Chicago Manual of Style* (14th ed., 1993). A shorter volume, for student writers, is the following:

> Turabian, Kate L. *A Manual for Writers of Term Papers, Theses, and Dissertations*. 6th ed. Rev. John Grossman and Alice Bennett. Chicago: U of Chicago P, 1996.

When you use *Chicago Manual* style, include (1) notes or endnotes to cite references in the text and (2) a bibliography at the end of the paper to list those works referred to in the notes.

Notes in Chicago Style

- **Numbering in the text** Number citations consecutively with superscript ([1]) for publication information or for explanations and additional material that would interrupt the main text if inserted there. Put the note number at the end of the citation following the sentence punctuation with no space between the last letter or punctuation mark.

```
The violence in the Raj at that time was more pro-
nounced than it had been in the previous conflict.⁴
But, as has been noted by Peter Holman, "the military
police were at a loss to stem the tide of bloodshed."⁵
```

- **Placing notes** List notes at the bottom of the page as footnotes or at the end of the essay as endnotes.

- **Spacing notes** Single-space individual notes, with the first line indented five spaces. Double-space between notes.

- **Ordering the parts of notes** Begin with the author's first and last names, add the title(s), and then include the publishing information and page numbers.

- **Punctuating, capitalizing, and abbreviating**

  Use commas between elements, and put publishing information within parentheses.
  Include the page number, but omit the abbreviation *p* or *pp*.
  Underline or italicize titles of books and periodicals.
  Capitalize titles of articles, books, and journals.
  Use quotation marks around parts of books or articles in periodicals.
  Do not abbreviate the name of the publisher.

Later Notes

- The first time a source is cited, all the relevant information is included. Later citations for that source are shortened.

- For most cases, note the author's last name, insert a comma, and then list the page(s) cited, but omit *p* or *pp*.

- If you cite more than one work by the same author, use a shortened form of the title.

- If you wish, use *ibid.* to refer to the work in the previous note or, if the page is different, use *ibid.* followed by a comma and the page number.

```
        6. Peter Holman, The History of the Raj:
Nineteenth and Twentieth Centuries (New York: Dorset
Press, 1996), 18.

        7. Holman, 34-36.

        8. Ibid., 72.
```

Bibliography in Chicago Style

- There are some differences between the notes and the bibliography. While notes have names in natural order (first name, then last name), the bibliography inverts the first author's name, with last name first. Elements in the bibliography are separated by periods, not commas and parentheses.

```
Holman, Peter. The History of the Raj: Nineteenth and
        Twentieth Centuries. New York: Dorset Press, 1996.
```

- Use the title "Bibliography," "Select Bibliography," "Works Cited," or "References."

- Start with the first line at the left margin and indent other lines in the entry. Double-space throughout.

- Include all the elements that were in the first note for that source, but do not put parentheses around the publishing information.

- Underline or italicize titles of books and periodicals.

- Use quotation marks around parts of books or articles in periodicals.

- Do not abbreviate the name of the publisher.

Parts of the Bibliography Entry

Information appears in the order given here.

- `Author` Give the full names of author(s), editor(s), and translator(s).

- `Title` Give the full title, including subtitle.

- `Editor, compiler, or translator` List these if any and if in addition to the author.

■ Volume   Give the total number of volumes if the work is referred to as a whole.

■ Volume number   If a single volume in the whole work is cited, list only that number.

■ Title of individual volume   List the volume title if applicable.

■ Facts of publication   Include the city, the publisher's full name, and the date of publication.

■ Page number(s)   Give volume and page numbers if the work includes them.

EXAMPLES OF CHICAGO-STYLE NOTES AND BIBLIOGRAPHY

Books

1. One Author
2. Two or Three Authors
3. Four or More Authors
4. Unknown Author
5. Editor or Translator
6. Edition Other than the First One
7. Selection or Book Chapter in an Anthology
8. Multivolume Book
9. Reference Book
10. Biblical or Other Scriptural Reference

Periodicals

11. Article in a Journal Paginated by Volume
12. Article in a Journal Paginated by Issue
13. Article in a Magazine
14. Article in a Newspaper
15. Book Review

Electronic Sources

16. Information Service
17. Online Database
18. Electronic Documents
19. Computer Software

Other Sources

20. Government Publication
21. Unpublished Dissertation
22. Interview
23. Personal Communication
24. Film or Videotape
25. Sound Recording
26. Source Quoted from Another Source

Books

1. One Author

N:*   1. George Abbot, <u>Israel in Europe</u> (New York: Humanities Press, 1972), 18.

*N=Note; B=Bibliography

B: Abbot, George. *Israel in Europe.* New York:
      Humanities Press, 1972.

2. Two or Three Authors

N: 2. A. Y. Yodfat and Y. Arnon-Channa, *P.L.O.*
Strategy and Tactics (London: Croom Helm, 1981), 45.

B: Yodfat, A. Y., and Y. Arnon-Channa. *P.L.O. Strategy*
      and Tactics. London: Croom Helm, 1981.

3. Four or More Authors

N: 3. John K. Fairbank, Edwin O. Reischauer,
      George Allen, and Albert Craig, *East Asia:*
      Tradition and Transformation (Boston: Houghton
      Mifflin, 1973), 274-5.

Chicago Style also permits giving the name of the first author followed by *et al.* or *and others* with no intervening punctuation.

B: Fairbank, John K., Edwin O. Reischauer, George Allen,
      and Albert Craig. *East Asia: Tradition and*
      Transformation. Boston: Houghton Mifflin, 1973.

4. Unknown Author

N: 4. *The Chicago Manual of Style.* 14th ed.
      (Chicago: University of Chicago Press, 1993). 420.

B: *The Chicago Manual of Style,* 14th ed. Chicago:
      University of Chicago Press, 1993.

5. Editor or Translator

N: 5. Dan Caspi, Abraham Diskin, and Emmanuel
      Gutmann, eds., *The Roots of Begin's Success* (New
      York: St. Martin's Press, 1984), 36.

B: Caspi, Dan, Abraham Diskin, and Emmanuel Gutmann,
      eds. *The Roots of Begin's Success.* New York:
      St. Martin's Press, 1984.

6. Edition Other than the First One

N: 6. John Joseph Mathews, *The Osages: Children*
      of the Middle Waters, 2nd ed. (Norman: University
      of Oklahoma Press, 1963), 145-47.

B: Mathews, John Joseph. *The Osages: Children of the*
      Middle Waters. 2nd ed. Norman: University of
      Oklahoma Press, 1963.

7. Selection or Book Chapter in an Anthology

N: 7. Emmanuel Anati, "The Prehistory of the
      Holy Land (Until 3200 BC)," in *A History of the*
      Holy Land, ed. Michael Avi-Yonah (Jerusalem:
      Jerusalem Publishing House, 1969), 33-41.

B: Anati, Emmanuel. "The Prehistory of the Holy Land
      (Until 3200 BC)." In *A History of the Holy*
      Land, edited by Michael Avi-Yonah. Jerusalem:
      Jerusalem Publishing House, 1969.

8. Multivolume Book

N: 8. Cao Xuequin, The Story of Stone, trans. David Hawkes (Harmondsworth: Penguin Books, 1977), 2:150-51.

B: Xuequin, Cao. The Story of Stone. Translated by David Hawkes. Vol. 2. Harmondsworth: Penguin Books, 1977.

9. Reference Book

N: 9. Encyclopedia Britannica, 15th ed., s.v. "Henry Clay."

Do not include the volume or page number. Instead, cite the term in the reference book under which the information is contained. Use the abbreviation *s.v.* for *sub verbo,* meaning "under the word." Well-known reference books are not usually listed in the bibliography.

10. Biblical or Other Scriptural Reference

N: 10. Gen. 21:14-18.

Include the book, abbreviated with no underline or italics, chapter, and verse, but no page number. Scriptural references are usually cited only in the notes.

Periodicals

11. Article in a Journal Paginated by Volume

N: 11. Russell Reid, "Journals of the Atkinson-O'Fallon Expedition," North Dakota Historical Quarterly 4 (1929): 5-56.

B: Reid, Russell. "Journals of the Atkinson-O'Fallon Expedition." North Dakota Historical Quarterly 4 (1929): 5-56.

12. Article in a Journal Paginated by Issue

N: 12. Carl Coke Rister, "The Significance of the Destruction of the Buffalo in the Southwest," Southwestern Historical Society 33, no. 1 (1929): 44.

B: Rister, Carl Coke. "The Significance of the Destruction of the Buffalo in the Southwest." Southwestern Historical Society 33, no. 1 (1929): 44-57.

13. Article in a Magazine

N: 13. Jacob Schlesinger, "Sundown," The New Republic, 3 August 1998, 12.

B: Schlesinger, Jacob. "Sundown," The New Republic, 3 August 1998, 12.

14. Article in a Newspaper

N: 14. Barbara Crossette, "New U.N. Push to Urge Iraq to Cooperate with Inspectors," New York Times, 8 August 1998, sec. A.

B: Crossette, Barbara. "New U.N. Push to Urge Iraq to
    Cooperate with Inspectors." New York Times,
    8 August 1998, sec. A.

15. Book Review

N: 15. Bernard Lewis, review of Autumn of Fury:
    The Assassination of Anwar Sadat, by Mohamed Heikal,
    New York Review of Books, 31 May 1984, 25-27.

B: Lewis, Bernard. Review of Autumn of Fury: The
    Assassination of Anwar Sadat, by Mohamed
    Heikal. New York Review of Books, 31 May
    1984, 25-27.

Electronic Sources

The Chicago Manual of Style recommends following the latest documentation system of the International Standards Organization (ISO). The ISO is constructing and continues to modify a uniform system of citing electronic documents.

16. Information Service

N: 16. Linda Flower, "Diagnoses in Revision: The
    Experts' Option," Communications Design Center
    Technical Report No. 27 (Pittsburgh: Carnegie Mellon
    University, 1986), OVID, ERIC ED 266 464.

B: Flower, Linda. "Diagnoses in Revision: The
    Experts' Option." Communications Design
    Center Technical Report No. 27. Pittsburgh:
    Carnegie Mellon University, 1986. OVID,
    ERIC ED 266 464

17. Online Database

N: 17. Pennti, Aalto, "Swells of the Mongol-
    Storm Around the Baltic." Acta Orientalia 36
    (Budapest, 1982): 5-15, in Bibliography of Asian
    Studies [database online] [cited 24 August 1998];
    available from OVID Information Services, Inc.,
    Murray, Utah, identifier no. 19980218.232.

B: Aalto, Pennti. "Swells of the Mongol-Storm Around
    the Baltic." Acta Orientalia 36 (Budapest,
    1982): 5-15. In Bibliography of Asian Studies
    [database online] [cited 24 August 1998].
    Murray, UT: OVID Information Services, Inc.
    Identifier no. 19980218.232.

18. Electronic documents

Listserv

N: 18. John Murray, "Economic Historians in the
    News," in EH.T [electronic bulletin board] [cited
    12 March 1998]; available from EH.T@cs.muohio
    .edu;Internet.

B: Murray, John. "Economic Historians in the News."
                In EH.T [electronic bulletin board] [cited 12
                March 1998]. Available from EH.T@cs
                .muohio.edu; Internet.

Electronic Journal

N: 18. Lucia Sommer, "Simon Penny's Electronic
                Critique: Notes on the Politicization of Art Against
                the Aestheticization of Politics," Cultronix 1
                [electronic journal] [Pittsburgh: Carnegie Mellon
                University, 1994 [cited 27 August 1998]); available
                from http://eserver.org/cultronix/sommer.

B: Sommer, Lucia. "Simon Penny's Electronic Critique:
                Notes on the Politicization of Art Against
                the Aestheticization of Politics." Cultronix
                1 [electronic journal]. Pittsburgh: Carnegie
                Mellon University, 1994 [cited 27 August
                1998]. Available from http://eserver.org/
                cultronix/sommer.

19. Computer Software
N: 19. CensusCounts, Ver. 2.1, Decisionmark
        Corporation, Cedar Rapids, Iowa.

B: CensusCounts, Ver. 2.1. Decisionmark Corporation,
                Cedar Rapids, Iowa.

Other Sources

20. Government Publication
N: 20. William Lilley, The State Atlas of
        Political and Cultural Diversity (Washington,
        D.C.: Congressional Quarterly, 1997), 31-45.

B: Lilley, William. The State Atlas of Political and
                Cultural Diversity. Washington, D.C.:
                Congressional Quarterly, 1997.

21. Unpublished Dissertation
N: 21. Arnold Mayniew, "Historical Perceptions
        of Royal Prerogative" (Ph.D. diss., University of
        Illinois, 1991), 32-37.

B: Mayniew, Arnold. "Historical Perceptions of Royal
                Prerogative." Ph.D. diss., University of
                Illinois, 1991.

22. Interview
N: 22. David Gergen, interview by Ted Koppell,
        Nightline, American Broadcasting Company, 18
        August 1998.

B: Gergen, David. Interview by Ted Koppell.
                Nightline. American Broadcasting Company, 18
                August 1998.

23. Personal Communication (including e-mail)

N: 23. Maynard Jimmerson, telephone interview by author, 27 July 1998.

     24. Daniel Kaplan, e-mail to author, 15 September 1998.

Personal communications are not usually included in the bibliography.

24. Film or Videotape

N: 25. The Luttrell Psalter: Everyday Life in Medieval England, prod. and dir. Martin Schuman, 1 hr. 22 min., Films for the Humanities & Sciences, 1996, videocassette.

B: The Luttrell Psalter: Everyday Life in Medieval England. Produced and directed by Martin Schuman. 1 hr. 22 min. Films for the Humanities & Sciences, 1996. Videocassette.

25. Sound Recording

N: 26. J. S. Bach, Four Concerti for Various Instruments, Orchestra of St. Luke's, Michael Feldman, Musical Heritage Society, compact disk 512268T.

B: Bach, J. S. Four Concerti for Various Instruments. Orchestra of St. Luke's. Michael Feldman. Musical Heritage Society, compact disk 512268T.

26. Source Quoted from Another Source

N: 27. H. H. Dubs, "An Ancient Chinese Mystery Cult," Harvard Theological Review, 35 (1942): 223, quoted in Susan Naquin, Millenarian Rebellion in China: The Eight Trigrams Uprising of 1813 (New Haven: Yale University Press, 1976), 288.

B: Dubs, H. H. "An Ancient Chinese Mystery Cult." Harvard Theological Review, 35 (1942): 223. Quoted in Susan Naquin, Millenarian Rebellion in China: The Eight Trigrams Uprising of 1813 (New Haven: Yale University Press, 1976), 288.

54b CBE (Council of Biology Editors)

Writers in the physical and life sciences follow the documentation style developed by the Council of Biology Editors (CBE) and found in *Scientific Style and Format: The CBE Manual for Authors, Editors, and Publishers* (6th ed., New York: Cambridge UP, 1994). Mathematicians also use this style. (See 54c for a list of style manuals for other scientific fields.)

The CBE Manual offers two documentation styles. You can ask your instructor which one is preferred for your papers, or you can check a current journal in the field. The two styles are *name-date* and *numbered notes*.

Author's Names and Publication Dates

Authors' names and publication dates are included in parenthetical citations in the text, closely resembling the APA style (see 53a).

In-Text Citation

```
The earlier studies done on this virus (Fong and Townes
1992; Mindlin 1994) reported similar results. However, one
of these studies (Mindlin 1994) noted a mutated strain.
```

In the References list at the end, the names are listed alphabetically with the date after the name.

References List

```
    Fong L, Townes HC. (1992). Viral longevity.
        Biological Reports 27: 129-45.
```

In-Text Numbered References

In CBE format, references are listed with in-text superscript numbers (numbers set above the line, such as [1] and [2]) that refer to a list of numbered references at the end. The references are numbered according to the order in which they are used in the text, and later references to the same work use the original number. When you have two or more sources cited at once, put the numbers in sequence and separate them with commas but no spaces.

In-Text Citation

```
Earlier studies on this virus[1,4,9] reported similar
results. However, one of these studies[4] noted a
mutated strain.
```

In the References list, list the entries in the order in which they are cited in the paper, not alphabetically.

References List

```
    1. Fong L, Townes H. Viral longevity. Biological
        Reports 1992; 27: 129-45.
```

CBE References List

At the end of the paper, include a list titled "References" or "Cited References." The placement of the date will differ depending on which format you use.

■ Name and Publication Date Format

Put the date after the author's name.
Arrange the list alphabetically by last names.
Do not indent any lines in the entries.

■ **In-Text Numbered References**

For books, put the date after the publisher's name.
For references to periodicals, put the date after the periodical name.
Arrange the list by number.
Put the number at the left margin, followed by the authors' last names. For the second and following lines, align beneath the first letter of the line above.

1. XXXXXXXXXXXXXXXXXX

   XXXXXXXXXX

2. XXXXXXXXXXXXXXXXXX

   XXXX

References in CBE Style

Use periods between major divisions of the entry.

■ `Author's name` Start with the last name first, no comma, and initials without periods for first and middle names. Separate authors' names with commas. End the list of authors' names with a period.

■ `Title` For books and article titles, capitalize only for the first word and proper nouns. Do not underline, italicize, or use quotation marks. For journals, abbreviate titles and capitalize all major words.

■ `Place of publication (colon): publisher (semicolon); and publication date (period).` Include a space between the full name of the publisher and date. Use a semicolon with no space between the date and volume number of the journal. Abbreviate months.

■ `Number of pages` For books, include the total number of pages, with *p.* after the number. End the entry with a period. For journal articles, show the page numbers (for example, *122–7, 49–51, 131–8, 200–9*). End with a period.

EXAMPLES OF CBE FORMAT FOR REFERENCES LIST

1. Books with One Author
2. Books with More than One Author
3. Books with an Editor
4. Organization as Author
5. Section of a Book
6. Articles in a Scholarly Journal
7. Newspaper or Magazine Article
8. Article with No Author
9. Editorial
10. Audiovisual Materials
11. Electronic Journal Articles
12. Web Sources

1. Book with One Author

1. Glenn EP. Encyclopedia of environmental biology. San Diego: Academic Press; 1995. 1289 p.

2. Book with More than One Author

2. Rouse Ball WW, Coxeter HSM. Mathematical recreations and essays. 13th ed. Mineola, NY: Dover Publications; 1987. 381 p.

3. Book with an Editor

3. Estes JW, Smith BG, editors. A melancholy scene of devastation: the public response to the 1793 Philadelphia yellow fever epidemic. Philadelphia: Science History Publications/USA; 1997. 436 p.

4. Organization as Author

4. Council of Biology Editors. Scientific style and format: the CBE manual for authors, editors, and publishers. 6th ed. New York: Cambridge UP; 1994. 704 p.

5. Section of a Book

5. Saari JC. Retinoids in photosensitive systems. In: Sporn MB, editor, The retinoids. 2nd ed. New York: Raven Press; 1994. p 351-78.

6. Article in a Scholarly Journal

6. Adleman LM. Molecular computation of solutions to combinatorial problems. Science 1994;266:1021-4.

7. Newspaper or Magazine Article

7. Allen A. Mighty mice: the perils of patenting genes. The New Republic 1998 Aug 10:16-8.

8. Article with No Author

Begin the entry with "[Anonymous]."

9. Editorial

After the title, add "[editorial]."

10. Audiovisual Materials

The CBE Manual does not have guidelines for CD-ROM sources, but the format shown here is a suggested model to follow.

8. Recent developments in DNA models [videocassette]. Miletius T, editor. DistanceED Productions, producer. [San Diego]: Media Forum; 1997. 3 videocassettes: 315 min, sound, color, 1/2 in (Genetics laboratories; Nr 9). Accompanied by: 3 guides. Available from: Boston National Visual Instruction Library, Boston, MA.

11. Electronic Journal Articles

9. Arlinghaus SL, Drake WD, Nystuen, JD. Animaps. Solstice: an electronic journal of geography and mathematics 1998;9(1): Available from: http://www-personal.umich.edu/~sarhaus/image/ animaps.html. Accessed 1998 Aug 16.

12. Web Sources

The CBE Manual does not have guidelines for citing Web sources. The following suggested format follows the journal article format and includes the date of Internet publication, the Web address, and your date of access.

10. Finn R. DNA vaccines generate excitement as human trials begin. The Scientist 1998 Mar.16; 12(16): http://www.the-scientist.library.upenn.edu/yr1998/ mar/research_980316.html. Accessed 1998 Aug. 16.

54c Style Manuals for Various Fields

Anthropology
Chicago Manual of Style (see 54a) and *Webster's 10th New Collegiate Dictionary.* On its Web site at <http://www.ameranthassn.org/ aaastyle.htm#1> the American Anthropological Association offers a brief "AAA Style Guide."

Astronomy
See entry for Physics and Astronomy.

Biology
Council of Biology Editors. *Scientific Style and Format: The CBE Manual for Authors, Editors, and Publishers.* 6th ed. New York: Cambridge UP, 1994.

Chemistry
Dodd, Janet S., ed. *The ACS Style Guide: A Manual for Authors and Editors.* 2nd ed. Washington: Amer. Chemical Soc., 1997.

Education
APA (see Chapter 53) and MLA (Chapter 52) styles.

English
Gibaldi, Joseph, and Walter S. Achert. *MLA Handbook for Writers of Research Papers.* 5th ed. New York: Modern Language Association of America, 1999. (See Chapter 52).

History
The Chicago Manual of Style, 14th edition. Chicago: U of Chicago P, 1993. (See 54a.)

Journalism
Goldstein, Norm, et al. *Associated Press Style Book and Libel Manual.* Rev. and updated ed. Portland: Perseus Press, 1998.
Lewis, Jordan, ed. *New York Times Manual of Style and Usage.* New York: Times Books, 1982.

Mathematics
American Mathematical Society. *The AMS Author Handbook: General Instructions for Preparing Manuscripts.* Providence: AMS, 1997.

Medicine
Iverson, Cheryl, et al. *American Medical Association Manual of Style.* 9th ed. Baltimore: Williams and Wilkins, 1997.

Music
Holoman, D. Kern, ed. *Writing About Music: A Style Sheet from the Editors of* 19th-Century Music. Berkeley: U of California P, 1988.

Philosophy
Guidebook for Publishing in Philosophy. Newark, DE: American Philosophy Association, 1997.

Physics and Astronomy
American Institute of Physics. *AIP Style Manual.* 4th ed. College Park, MD: AIP, 1990.

Political Science
American Political Science Association. *Style Manual for Political Science.* Washington: Amer. Political Science Assn., 1984.

Psychology
American Psychology Association. *Publication Manual of the American Psychological Association.* 4th ed. Washington: APA, 1994. (See Chapter 53.)

55 American Style in Writing

If your first language is not English, you may have writing style preferences that are different from American style and also questions about English grammar and usage. Some of these matters are discussed here. If you are a student at an institution with a writing center, talk with a tutor in the writing center.

Your style preferences and customs will depend on what language(s) you are more familiar with, but in general, consider the following differences between the language(s) you know and academic style in American English:

- **Conciseness** In some languages, writers strive for a type of eloquence marked by a profusion of words and phrases that elaborate on the same topic. Effective academic style in American English, however, is concise, eliminating extra or unnecessary words.

- **Clearly announced topic at the beginning of the paper** In some languages, the topic is delayed or not immediately announced. Instead, there are suggestions that will lead readers to formulate the main ideas for themselves. In American English, there is a strong preference for announcing the topic in the opening paragraph or near the beginning of the paper.

- **Tight organization** Although digressions into side topics or related matters can be interesting and are expected in writing in some languages, American academic writing stays on topic and does not digress.

- **Sources clearly cited** In some languages, there is less attention to citing sources of information, ideas, or the exact words used by others. In American academic writing, however, writers are expected to cite all sources for information that is not generally known by most people. Otherwise, the writer is in danger of being viewed as plagiarizing. (See 47c.)

56 Verbs

Verbs are very important parts of English sentences because they indicate time and person as well as other information explained in Chapter 17. This chapter provides additional information needed by writers learning English as an additional language.

56a Helping Verbs with Main Verbs

Helping (or **auxiliary**) **verbs** combine with other verbs to form all the tenses except the simple present and simple past. The following table shows the forms of major helping verbs:

FORMS OF HELPING VERBS		
be	be am is are was were	
	+ -*ing* form:	I am going.
	with model first:	I may be going.
	passive (with past participle):	I was given the title.
have	have has had	I have started.
		He had started.
do	do does did + base form	Did she buy that?

I. Modals

Modal verbs are helping verbs with a variety of meanings. After a modal, use the base form.

can	may	must	should	would
could	might	shall	will	ought to

Permission: May I take this? [Is it all right if I take this?]

Advisability: I ought to take this. [It's a good idea to take this.]

Necessity: Must I take this? [Am I required to take this?]

Ability: Can I take this? [Am I able to take this?]

Uncertainty: Should I take this?

[I'm not certain whether I should take this.]

Possibility: Even an expert can make mistakes.
Even an expert might make a mistake.

[It is possible for experts to make a mistake.]

2. Conditionals

In conditional sentences, clauses after *if, when,* and *unless* show whether the result is possible or real, depending on other circumstances.

■ **Prediction** Predicts something based on some condition.

Present	Future (Usually Modal + Base Form)
If you eat more fresh fruit,	you will be healthier.
Unless she arrives soon,	we will be late for the concert.

■ **Fact** Something usually happens when something else happens.

Present	Present
When that dog barks at night,	he wakes us up.

Past	Past

When that dog barked at night, he woke us up.

- **Not real** Use *would* in the result clause to show that the result is impossible, did not happen, or is unlikely to happen.

Past	Would + Base Form

If she drove more slowly, she would get fewer speeding tickets.

To show that something is not reality, use *were* instead of *was*.

If I were rich, I would have traveled to Tahiti.

- **Speculative** To show that something is possible but unlikely, use *were* instead of *was*.

Past	Would, Could, Might + Base Form

If he had a car, he could drive us to the restaurant.
If you were prepared, you might understand the problem.

HINT   **Using *would*, *could*, and *might***

When *would*, *could*, and *might* are used with the base form, *-s* is not added to the base form for third person singular present.

                drive
If he had a car, he could ~~drives~~ us to the restaurant.

56b Two-Word (Phrasal) Verbs

Two-word (phrasal) verbs have two (or sometimes three) words (particles) following the verb that help to indicate the meaning. Because the additional word or words often change the meaning, these verbs are idioms (see Chapter 62).

look over (examine)   She looked over the terms of the contract.
look up (search)   I need to look up that phone number.

In some cases, a noun or pronoun can be inserted so that the verb is separated from its additional word or words. In other cases, there can be no separation.

Separable: count in (include)

Manuel told the team to count **him** in.
          (inserted pronoun)

Inseparable: count on (rely)

The team could count on **him** to help.
          (pronoun not inserted)

Some Common Two-Word Verbs

If the second word can be separated from the verb, a pronoun is included in parentheses.

add (it) up	cut (it) up	look like
back out of	drop (it) off	look out for
bring (it) on	fall behind	pass out
bring (it) up	get around	put (it) off
burn (it) down	get by	put (it) on
burn (it) up	get out of	run across
call for	get through	run into
call (it) off	give (it) away	show off
call (her) up	go over	show up
carry (it) out	hand (it) in	stay up
clean (it) up	keep on	take (it) off
come across	keep (it) up	take (it) up
cross (it) out	leave (it) out	try (it) out
cut (it) off	look ahead	turn up
cut (it) out	look into	use (it) up

56c Verbs with *-ing* and *to* + Verb Forms

Some verbs combine only with the *-ing* form of the verb (gerund); some combine only with the *to* + verb form (infinitive); some verbs can be followed by either form.

■ Verbs followed only by *-ing* forms (gerunds):

admit	enjoy	practice
appreciate	finish	recall
avoid	keep	risk
consider	keep on	stop
deny	postpone	suggest

He <u>admits spending</u> that money.
  (verb) + (gerund)

reading
I recall ~~to read~~ that book.

■ Verbs followed only by *to* + verb forms (infinitives):

agree	have	offer
ask	hope	plan
claim	manage	promise
decide	mean	wait
expect	need	want

We <u>agree to send</u> an answer soon.
(verb) + (infinitive)

to go
They planned ~~going~~ on vacation.

■ Verbs that can be followed by either form:

begin	intend	prefer
continue	like	start
hate	love	try

They begin to sing.   (or)   They begin singing.

Some verbs that can be followed by either form change meaning:

| forget | remember | stop | try |

She stopped talking. [She ceased and did not talk.]

She stopped to talk. [She paused while going somewhere in order to talk.]

Exercise 56.1: Proofreading Practice

In the following paragraph, there are some errors in the verbs. Underline the errors, and write your corrections above the words underlined.

(1) When people from other countries will visit the United States, they find a bewildering variety of words that can be used for the same thing. (2) In some parts of the United States, a salesperson will asked the customer if she would want the item in a "sack." (3) In other places, the salesperson might ask, "Did you wanted this in a 'bag'?" (4) It is hard for tourists who don't understand to bring up it when they don't know whether there is a difference. (5) Or a tourist may ask, "May I take this metro to First Avenue?" in a city where the underground train is called "the subway." (6) If I was one of those tourists, I could always keep a dictionary in my pocket to use when the situation calls it for.

Exercise 56.2: Pattern Practice

In the following paragraph, there are choices between verb forms. Underline the correct form of the verb that is needed.

In schools in the United States, teachers hope (1. to encourage, encouraging) students to ask questions. They think that if students (2. talk, will talk) about a subject and ask questions, they (3. will learn, learn) more about the subject. In some other countries, students avoid (4. to ask, asking) questions because that may be a sign of rudeness in their country. The culture of the country has a very important influence on how teachers want (5. talking, to talk) to the class and how the class continues (6. to respond, responding) to the teacher. In the United States, some teachers like (7. to have, having) their students call them by their first name. This often surprises students from other countries where they (8. might be, must be) very formal with their teachers in order to show respect.

Exercise 56.3: Pattern Practice

Use the following verb forms in sentences of your own.

1. may + verb	5. look like	9. begin + verb
2. can + verb	6. hope + verb	10. do + verb
3. If she were	7. try (it) out	11. could + verb
4. hand (it) in	8. forget + verb	12. have + verb

57 Omitted Words

57a Verbs

Verbs are necessary parts of English sentences and must be included. Verbs such as *is/are* or other helping verbs can be omitted in other languages, but not in English.

    is
Liu ʌ studying to be a computer programmer.

    has
She ʌ been studying ancient Mayan ruins in Mexico for many summers.

might
It ʌ be a good idea to bring some water when we hike.

57b Subjects and *There/It*

In some languages the subject can be omitted, but in English the subject is left out only when expressing a command (*Put that box here, please.*)

            they
All the children laughed when ʌ were watching the cartoon.

        who
The hockey player ʌ was guarding the goal got hurt in the game.

Particularly troublesome are *there* and *it* as subjects. Even when *there* is the subject word and the real subject is elsewhere in the sentence, *there* must be included. *It* is sometimes needed as a subject in sentences about the weather, distance, time, and other aspects of the world around us.

     there
Certainly, ʌ are many confusing rules in English spelling.

    it
I think ʌ is about ten miles from here to the shopping mall.

58 Repeated Words

58a Subjects

In some languages, the subject can be repeated as a pronoun before the verb. In English, the subject is included only once.

Bones in the body ~~they~~ become brittle when people grow older.

[In this sentence both *bones* and *they* are the subject of the verb *brittle*.]

The plane that was ready for takeoff ~~it~~ stopped on the runway.

[In this sentence both *plane* and *it* are the subject of the verb *stopped*.]

58b Pronouns and Adverbs

When relative pronouns such as *who, which,* and *that* or relative adverbs such as *where* or *when* introduce clauses (see Chapter 24), they are the object of the verb or prepositional phrase, so no additional word is needed.

The woman tried on the hat that I left ~~it~~ on the seat.

[*That* is the object of the verb *left*, and *it* is unnecessary repetition.]

The city where I live ~~there~~ has two soccer fields.

[*Where* is the object of the verb *live*, and *there* is unnecessary repetition.]

Exercise 58.1: Proofreading Practice

The following paragraph has omitted words. Add the missing words. Where words are unnecessarily repeated, draw a line through them.

(1) When students looking for part-time work, one difficulty is that they want the job to be after class hours. (2) Another difficulty for students is that want the job to be near their school so that don't have far to travel. (3) But that means are many students who want to work at the same time and in the same area of town. (4) The competition for the jobs that exist it causes too many students to be unable to find work. (5) Some counselors they tell their students to try looking for jobs that have flexible hours or for work that it can be done at home. (6) Is also worth trying to look farther away from the campus.

59 Count and Noncount Nouns

Nouns are either proper nouns that name specific things and begin with capital letters or common nouns (see Chapter 35). There are two kinds of common nouns, count and noncount nouns.

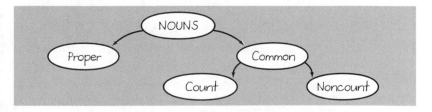

A **count noun** names something that can be counted because it can be divided into separate and distinct units. Count nouns have plurals (see 18a) and usually refer to things that can be seen, heard, touched, tasted, or smelled.

A **noncount noun** names something that cannot be counted because it is an abstraction (a substance that is thought of as a whole) or something that cannot be cut into parts. Noncount nouns do not have plurals and may have a collective meaning.

Count Nouns

apple	(one apple, two apples)
chair	(a chair, several chairs)
child	(the child, six children)

Noncount Nouns

air	humor	oil
furniture	milk	weather

The names of many foods are noncount nouns.

bread	corn	spinach
coffee	spaghetti	tofu

To indicate the amount for a noncount noun, use a count noun first.

a pound of coffee	a loaf of bread
an ear of corn	a gallon of oil

Nouns that Can Be Both Count and Noncount Nouns

Some nouns in English have both a count and a noncount meaning, depending on the context in which the noun is used. The count meaning is specific, and the noncount meaning is abstract.

Count:　The **exercises** were difficult to do.
Noncount: **Exercise** is good for our health.

Count:　There were bright **lights** in the sky.
Noncount: Those plants need more **light.**

Count:　She ate five **chocolates** from the box.
Noncount: **Chocolate** is fattening.

 HINT　**Identifying Count and Noncount Nouns**

Knowing whether a noun is a count or noncount noun is important in determining whether or not to use *a, an,* or *the* (see 60c).

Singular count nouns need an article.	She returned **the** book.
Noncount nouns usually do not need an article.	Plants enjoy water.

Exercise 59.1: Proofreading Practice

In the parentheses in the following paragraph, underline the correct choice between count and noncount nouns.

(1. American, Americans) love browsing and shopping for consumer (2. good, goods). In our (3. society, societies), a shopper has choices that

include shopping in (4. mall, malls), (5. outlet, outlets), department (6. store, stores), or wholesale (7. club, clubs). A (8. consumer, consumers) must know prices and return (9. policy, policies) to get the best deal. For shoppers in a (10. mall, malls), the prices and return policies will be standard. Malls have mostly chain (11. store, stores) that can be overpriced unless items are on sale. Most stores in a mall will allow customers to return an item with the (12. receipt, receipts). An outlet store offers reduced (13. price, prices) on discontinued and irregular items. However, (14. shopper, shoppers) must know that most items are "final sale" and cannot be returned in outlet (15. store, stores). Department stores offer a large variety of items and have weekly sales. Returning items is usually not a problem, but some stores require that the item be returned within a (16. week, weeks) of purchase. If an item is a gift, a shopper can receive store (17. credit, credits) so that the shopper can select another item of equal value. Wholesale clubs are a newer addition to the (18. United State, United States). Wholesale clubs look like warehouses and carry large quantities of (19. item, items) for reduced prices. The shopper must know prices to get the best bargain. Many items appear to be discounted but are really less expensive to purchase in a regular (20. supermarket, supermarkets). Wholesale clubs will allow returns within thirty days of purchase as long as the customer has a receipt. Consumers should always check prices and policies before purchasing items.

Exercise 59.2: Pattern Practice

Make up sentences of your own, using the underlined count and noncount nouns in the following sentences:

1. The insect had four <u>wings</u>.
2. They walked down many <u>streets</u> to the river.
3. Some <u>bones</u> in the skeleton were broken, but the museum had no <u>bone</u> to use in repairing the exhibit.
4. The coat was made of <u>cotton</u>.
5. She picked some <u>roses</u> from the garden.
6. He knew six <u>languages</u> and wanted to learn another one because <u>language</u> is a fascinating thing to study.
7. She likes to eat <u>rice</u> with a lot of <u>sugar</u> on it.
8. The <u>rain</u> caused some <u>mud</u> to splash on my car.
9. The <u>clothing</u> was on sale in the store.
10. After the <u>snow</u> melted and froze again, the street was like a sheet of <u>ice</u>.

60 Adjectives and Adverbs

60a Placement

The ordering of adjectives and adverbs in English is as follows:

Adverb	→	Adjective	→	Noun
very		large		gate

Adverbs are placed first because they describe adjectives. Then, adjectives are placed next because they describe nouns.

Adverbs that describe verbs can move around in the sentence and appear in the following places:

- At the beginning of the sentence

  <u>Sometimes</u>, Noah can find great bargains.

- At the end of the sentence

  Noah can find great bargains <u>sometimes</u>.

- Before the verb

  Noah <u>sometimes</u> can find great bargains.

- After the verb

  Jana types <u>quickly</u> on her laptop computer.

- Between the helping and main verb

  Noah can <u>sometimes</u> find great bargains.

  Do not place adverbs between verbs and objects.

  Wrong: She picks quickly the fruit.

  Revised: She quickly picks the fruit.

60b Order

Putting adjectives in the accepted English order can be confusing to speakers of other languages. Follow the order of these categories, but it is best not to pile up more than two or three adjectives between the article (or other determiner) and the noun.

ORDER OF ADJECTIVES

Determiner	Evaluation or Opinion	Physical Description				Nationality	Religion	Material	Noun
		Size	Shape	Age	Color				
a, three, her	lovely	big	round	old	green	English	Catholic	silk	purse

the quiet Japanese rock garden
a square blue cotton handkerchief
my lazy old Siamese cat

six excellent new movies
many difficult physics problems
every big green plant

Exercise 60.1: Pattern Practice

Reorder the adjectives and nouns in these clusters, and write your own sentences.

1. old   famous   six   sports stars

2. Hispanic   favorite   her   song   old
3. steel   German   new   a   knife
4. square   small   strange   a   box
5. large   nine   balls   yellow

60c A/An/The

A and *an* identify nouns in a general or indefinite way and refer to any member of a group. *A* and *an*, which mean "one among many," are generally used with singular count nouns. (See Chapter 59 on count nouns.)

She likes to read **a** book before going to sleep.

[This sentence does not specify which book, just any book. *Book* is a singular count noun.]

The identifies a particular or specific noun in a group or a noun already identified in a previous phrase or sentence. *The* may be used with singular or plural nouns.

She read **the** book. [This sentence identifies a specific book.]

Give the coins to **the** boys. [This sentence identifies a specific group.]

A new model of computer was introduced yesterday. **The** model will cost much less than **the** older model.

[*A* introduces the noun the first time it is mentioned, and then *the* is used afterwards whenever the noun is mentioned.]

A, An, and *The* with Proper Nouns

- **Singular:** Usually no article   Mrs. Samosa
- **Plural:** Usually use *the*   **the** United States

A, An, and *The* with Common Nouns

- **Count nouns**

  Singular: Use an article or pronoun for singular count nouns.

  a tree, **her** wrist

  Plural: Use *the* when naming a specific representative of a category.

  the committee

  Do not use *the* when the meaning is "all" or "in general."

  Chairs were provided.   People are creatures of habit.

- **Noncount nouns** Never use *a* or *an* with noncount nouns.

Other Uses of *The*

- Use *the* when an essential phrase or clause follows the noun (see Chapter 25).

  The man who is standing at the door is my cousin.

■ Use *the* when the noun refers to a class as a whole.

The ferret is a popular pet.

■ Use *the* with names composed partly of common nouns.

the British Commonwealth   **the** Sahara Desert

■ Use *the* with names composed of common nouns plus proper names.

the Province of Quebec   **the** University of Illinois

■ Use *the* when names are plurals.

the Netherlands   **the** Balkans

■ Use *the* with names that refer to rivers, oceans, seas, points on the globe, deserts, forests, gulfs, and peninsulas.

the Nile   **the** Pacific Ocean   **the** Persian Gulf

■ Use *the* when points of the compass are used as names.

the South   **the** Midwest

■ Use *the* when points of time are indicated.

the beginning   **the** present   **the** afternoon

■ Use *the* with superlatives.

the best reporter   **the** most expensive car

■ Use *the* with adjectives used as nouns.

The homeless are in need of health care.

■ Use *the* with gerunds or abstract nouns followed by *of* phrases.

The meaning of that word is not clear.

No Articles

Articles are not used with names of streets, cities, states, countries, continents, lakes, parks, mountains, names of languages, sports, holidays, universities and colleges without *of* in the name, and academic subjects.

He traveled to Africa.   She is studying Chinese.
That shop is on Fifth Avenue.   Pollution in Lake Erie has been reduced.
He prefers to watch volleyball. My major is political science.
They celebrated Thanksgiving.   She applied to Brandeis University.

The following table summarizes the most frequent uses of *a, an,* and *the:*

Uses of *a, an,* and *the*

A/An
   ■ Unspecified singular count nouns

   A computer is **a** useful tool.

The

- Particular or specific singular count nouns and specific plural count nouns

  I ate **the** pizza, but she wanted **the** pretzels.

- Noncount nouns that are specific members of a general group

  The sunlight in the late afternoon sky cast interesting shadows.

- Plural proper nouns

  They sailed to **the** Virgin Islands.

No articles

- Singular proper nouns

  He moved to Salt Lake City.

- Unspecified plural count nouns meaning "all" or "in general"

  Bats are night feeders.

- Noncount nouns

  Trina does not like beer.

Exercise 60.2: Proofreading Practice

In the following paragraph, add a, an, *or* the *where needed.*

One of most interesting physicists of this century was Richard Feynman. He wrote best-selling book about his own life, but he became even more famous on television as man who was member of team that investigated after accident happened to *Challenger,* space shuttle that crashed in 1986. People watched on television as he demonstrated that faulty part in space shuttle probably caused accident. Feynman's greatest achievement in science was theory of quantum electrodynamics, which described behavior of subatomic particles, atoms, light, electricity, and magnetism. Field of computer science also owes much to work of Feynman. Many scientists consider Feynman to be one of geniuses of twentieth century.

60d *Some/Any, Much/Many, Little/Few, Less/Fewer, Enough, No*

Some/Any/Enough/No

- These words modify count and noncount nouns (see Chapter 59).

  She brought **some** fresh flowers.   There is **some** water on the floor.

  Do you have **any** erasers?   Do you have **any** food?

  I have **enough** glasses for everyone.   There is **enough** money to buy a car.

  There are **no** squirrels in the park.   There is **no** time to finish now.

- *Some* is used in positive statements.

  They ate **some** fruit.

- *Any* is used in negative statements and in questions.

  They did not eat **any** fruit.   Did they eat **any** fruit?

With Noncount Nouns	With Count Nouns
(not) much	(not) many
little	few
less	fewer

They have **much** money in the bank.   **Many** Americans travel to Europe.
He had **little** food in the house.   There are a **few** doctors here.
Use **less** oil in the mixture.   We ordered **fewer** books.

---

61 Prepositions

For a list of idiomatic prepositions, see 21a. The following guide will help you choose among *on, at, in, of,* and *for* to indicate time, place, and logical relationships.

Prepositions of Time

On   Use with days (**on** Monday).

At   Use with hours of the day (**at** 9 P.M.) and with noon, night, midnight, and dawn (**at** midnight).

In   Use with other parts of the day: morning, afternoon, evening (**in** the morning); use with months, years, seasons (**in** the winter).

They are getting married **on** Sunday **at** four o'clock **in** the afternoon.

Prepositions of Place

On   Indicates a surface on which something rests.

The car is **on** the street.
She put curtains **on** the windows.

At   Indicates a point in relation to another object.

My sister is **at** home.
I'll meet you **at** Second Avenue and Main Street.

In   Indicates an object is inside the boundaries of an area or volume.

The sample is **in** the bottle.
She is **in** the bank.

Prepositions to Show Logical Relationships

Of   Shows relationship between a part (or parts) and the whole.

One **of** her teachers gave a quiz.

Shows material or content.

They gave me a basket **of** food.

For Shows purpose.

We bought a new hose **for** our garden.

Exercise 61.1: Proofreading Practice

In the following paragraph, there are some errors in the use of prepositions in, on, *and* at *and some errors in the use of* some/any/much/many/little/ few. *Underline the errors, and write your corrections near the words.*

(1) Table Tennis used to be a minor pastime at America, but a little years ago it began to develop into an important sport. (2) Newcomers to the United States from countries such as Nigeria, Korea, and China, where table tennis is a major sport, have helped the United States become a respectable contender at world competition. (3) Much new residents who are very good in this sport have brought their skills to this country. (4) Now there are specialized table tennis parlors where players play in tables with special hard surfaces. (5) Players no longer use some sandpaper paddles. (6) Instead, much paddles are made of carbon fiber and have special coatings in the hitting surface. (7) At the past, America was often on last place in international competitions. (8) But now, with many strong players, often born at China, the United States is beginning to win.

Exercise 61.2: Pattern Practice

Make up sentences of your own that use the following words.

1. some
2. any
3. few
4. less
5. many
6. in (with a time expression)
7. on (a place)
8. in (a place)
9. of (showing a relationship)
10. at (a place)

62 Idioms

An **idiom** is an expression that means something beyond the simple definition or literal translation into another language. An idiom such as *kick the bucket* (meaning "die") is not understandable from the meanings of the individual words. Many idioms are classified as colloquial, indicating that they are normally used only in informal English.

Most dictionaries indicate the meanings of idioms and label as "collo-quial" or "informal" those that are considered appropriate only for informal writing or speaking. You can also consult dictionaries of idioms. Listed here are some typical idioms:

bottom line
the last figure on a financial balance sheet; the result or final out-come or ultimate truth: The bottom line is that he will not admit his mistake.

eager beaver
someone who is very enthusiastic or works hard: The team's new coach is an eager beaver and ready to start spring training.

hand over fist
very rapidly, with rapid progress: Mina made money on that invest-ment hand over fist.

hold water
adequate to be proved, be correct: The excuse she gave did not hold water with her instructor.

on one's toes
eager, alert: The new computer system keeps us on our toes.

on the table
open for discussion: Put that plan on the table and see if anyone objects.

see the light
understand something clearly at last, realize one's mistake: After working on the homework problem for several hours, he finally saw the light and answered the question correctly.

throw one's hat in the ring
announce that one is a candidate, take up a challenge: Before the election, three people announced they would throw their hats in the ring.

toe the line
do what is expected or required, follow the rules, especially unwillingly or under pressure: The new rules were designed to see whether the employees would toe the line.

For a list of idiomatic prepositions that follow certain words, see 21a. Because the meaning of two-word (phrasal) verbs (see 56b) is not the same as the literal meaning of each of the words, these verbs are also idioms.

A Document Design (doc)

A1 Titles

An essay's title serves several purposes. It indicates to readers what they can expect as to the topic and the author's perspective in the essay. Some titles state in a straightforward manner what the essay will be about; for example, the title "Nutritional Benefits of High-Fiber Foods" is a clear indication of the content and the author's intention to address it directly, in a formal manner. Other titles, particularly of personal essays, may offer the reader only a hint about the topic—a hint that becomes clearer after reading the essay. "At Sea over the Ocean" might be the title for an essay describing a frightening trip in a hot-air balloon or a humorous experience in an airplane.

Choosing a Title

A title helps the writer organize a topic and select the emphasis for a particular essay. Writers who select the title before or during the early stages of writing may need to check at a later stage to see that the title still relates to the essay as it evolves and develops.

- **Good titles are clear and specific.** An example of an overly general title for a short essay would be "Divorce" because it does not indicate what aspect of divorce will be discussed. Even a title such as "Recent Trends in Automotive Design" is too general for a short essay because so much material could be discussed under this heading.

- **Good titles are brief.** Most titles are no more than six or seven words.

A title should stand alone. The title should not be part of the first sentence, and it should not be referred to by a pronoun in the first sentence. For example, in a research paper titled "The Influence of Television Advertisements in Presidential Elections," the first sentence should not read as follows:

Incorrect Opening Sentence: This is a topic of great concern both to politicians and to those who think that these elections have become popularity contests.

Revised: The degree to which television advertisements influence voters' choices in presidential elections worries politicians and others who think that national elections have become popularity contests.

Capitalizing a Title

Capitalize the first and last words of a title, plus all other words except articles (*a, an, the*), short prepositions (*by, for, in, to, on,* etc.), and short joining words (*but, and, or,* etc.). Capitalize both words of a hyphenated word and the first word of a subtitle that appears after a colon. (For more on capitalization, see Chapter 35.)

Choosing a Career in Retailing	Short but Sweet
A History of Anti-Imperialism	Myths Through the Ages
My Childhood: The Plight of Growing Up Black	The Last Straw

Punctuating a Title

For your own essays, do not put the title in quotation marks, and do not use a period after the title. (For more information on using quotations marks and underlining, see Chapters 31 and 38.)

Spacing a Title on the Page

- **For word-processed or typed pages** If you have a cover page for research papers and reports and are using MLA format, see the sample paper in 52d. For APA format, see the sample paper in 53d. If you do not have a cover page, leave a one-inch margin at the top and then put your name, your instructor's name, the course and section number, and date submitted at the left-hand margin. Double-space this information. Then double-space and type the title, centered on the page. If you need more than one line for the title, double-space between these lines. Then double-space between the title and the first line of text.

- **For handwritten papers** Follow the format for typed papers by leaving a one-inch margin at the top and writing your name, your instructor's name, the course and section number, and date submitted at the left-hand margin. Put the title on the first ruled line of the page, skip a line, and then begin writing your paper, skipping every other ruled line.

A2 Headings and Subheadings

Headings are the short titles that define sections and subsections in long reports and papers. Headings provide visual emphasis by breaking the paper into manageable portions that are easily seen and identified. Headings with numbers also indicate relationships because the numbers tell the reader which parts are segments of a larger part, which are equal, and which are of less importance. Subheadings are the headings of less importance within a series of headings. While headings and subheadings don't substitute for the transitions you provide for your readers, they help your readers see the organization of the paper and locate material more easily.

Headings for tables of contents, outlines, and most reports are numbered, either in the decimal system or with Roman numerals. While the decimal system is used more often in technical and professional fields than Roman numerals, some of these fields still follow traditional use of Roman numerals. Decimals can also be combined with letters.

Decimal numbers	Roman numerals
1.0	I.
1.1 (or) 1.a. (or) 1a	A.
1.2 (or) 1.b. (or) 1b	1.
1.2.1 (or) 1.a.1.	2.
1.2.2 (or) 1.a.2.	B.
1.2.2.1	I.
2.0	a.
2.1 (or) 2.a	1)
	a)
	2.
	II.

For all headings and subheadings, be sure to use the same grammatical form to start each phrase. (See Chapter 10 on parallelism.)

Not Parallel

A. For Preliminary Planning
B. The Rough Draft
C. Polishing the Draft

Revised

A. Planning the Paper	A. The Preliminary Draft
B. Writing the Rough Draft (or)	B. The Rough Draft
C. Polishing the Draft	C. The Polished Draft

A3 Page Preparation

- **Paper** Use 8½" × 11" white, unlined paper for typing and printing, and use lined sheets for handwritten papers. Do not use thin or erasable paper. For handwritten, typed, and printed papers, use only one side of each sheet. For computer printout on continuous-sheet paper, tear off the edging of the paper, and separate the sheets.

- **Line spacing** Double-space typewritten and printed papers, and write on every other line for handwritten papers, including quotations, notes, and the list of works cited. Writing on every other line allows you room for making corrections and gives your instructor space in which to write comments.

- **Ink** Use black ribbon for typewritten papers and black or blue ink for handwritten papers. Do not use pencil.

- **Margins** Except for page numbers, leave margins of one inch at top and bottom and at both sides of the page.

- **Indentations** Indent the first word of each paragraph one-half inch or five spaces from the left-hand margin. For long quotations within paragraphs, indent one inch or ten spaces from the left-hand margin.

- **Page numbers** Use Arabic numerals (1, 2, 3, and so on), and place them in the upper right-hand corner, one-half inch from the top of the page and flush with the right-hand margin. Include your last name before the page number (to prevent confusion if pages are misplaced), and do not use the abbreviation *p.* before the page number. Do not use any punctuation in page numbers.

A4 Spacing for Punctuation

■ **End punctuation (. ? !)** Leave no space before the end punctuation. Leave one space before the next sentence.

. . . next year. After the term of . . .

■ **Periods after abbreviations (.)** Leave no space before the period and one space after. When a sentence ends with an abbreviation, use only one period to indicate both the abbreviation and the period that ends the sentence.

Dr. Smith was noted for . . .   . . . at 8 A.M. The next day . . .

■ **Commas, semicolons, colons (, ; :)** Leave no space before the mark and one space after.

happy, healthy child   John, a musician; Josh, a doctor; and . . .

■ **Apostrophes (')** Leave no space within a word. At the end of a word, leave no space before the apostrophe, with one space after.

don't   boy's hat   boxes' lids

■ **Quotation marks (" " ' ')** Leave no space between the quotation marks and what they enclose, no space between double and single quotation marks, and one space afterward in the middle of a sentence.

"No way" was his favorite expression.

"'Battle Hymn of the Republic' should be the last song on the program," she explained.

■ **Hyphen (-)** Leave no space before or after. If the hyphen shows the connection of two prefixes to one root word, put one space after the first hyphen.

a six-page report   the pre- and post-test scores

■ **Dash (-- —)** In a typewritten paper, type two hyphens, with no space before or after. For handwritten papers, write a longer line than the hyphen, leaving no space before or after. For papers written on a computer, there may be a dash mark to use.

Not one of us--Tobias, Matthew, or Nick--thought it mattered.

Not one of us—Tobias, Matthew, or Nick—thought it mattered.

■ **Slash (/)** Leave no space before or after except for marking lines of poetry, when one space is left before and after.

and/or

He read his favorite two lines from the poem, "slipping, sliding on his tongue / the sound of music in his soul."

- **Brackets, parentheses [ ] ( )** Leave no space before or after the material being enclosed.

  "When [the fund-raising group] presented its report (not previously published), the press covered the event."

- **Ellipsis (. . .)** Leave one space before each period, one space between, and one space after. If you are using four dots to indicate that you are omitting one or more sentences, treat the first dot like a period, with no space after the last word, and then space evenly.

  No one . . . noticed the error.

  Every worker signed the contract. . . . No one opposed the new guidelines for health care.

- **Underlining (<u>abcdef</u>) or italics (*abcdef*)** When using a typewriter or writing by hand, you can use underlining with or without breaks between words, but be consistent once you choose to use or not use breaks. If your computer has italic type, ask your instructor whether italics or underlining is preferred.

  <u>Wind in the Willows</u>   Wind <u>in the</u> Willows

  <u>Wind in the Willows</u>   *Wind in the Willows*

A5 Document Design

The visual appeal of your pages is important because readers react to what they see as well as to what they read. When you see an overcrowded page with too little white space and long, unbroken sections of text, you are likely to react negatively. You are also missing helpful visual cues that sort out sections of the paper. To add visual appeal to your pages, especially with memos, reports, and résumés, consider the following guidelines:

- **Use white space to open up the page visually.** White space, well used, invites the reader into the page and offers some relief from the heaviness of blocks of text. White space also helps to indicate sections or segments of the text.

- **Use lists whenever possible.** Instead of writing long paragraphs with many items, consider listing key points with bullets or dashes. This strategy also helps add white space to the page.

  The major parts of a proposal are the following:

  - Problem statement
  - Proposed project and purpose
  - Plan
  - Evaluation

- **Use headings and subheadings to indicate sections.** For longer essays and reports, use words and phrases to announce new topics or segments of a topic (see A2).

- **Use visuals such as tables and charts.** Visuals convey information easily and succinctly. Tables present information in columns and rows and can include numbers or words. Figures, including pie charts, graphs, and drawings, are useful for indicating relationships. If you include a visual, refer to it in your text before it appears, and explain the main point it conveys.

B Résumés

An effective résumé focuses on the organization to which you are applying, so select the details that display your particular skills and achievements for that job. When you are applying for positions in different companies or for different jobs, you will need to tailor your résumé to fit each one. If readers take only a short time to look at your résumé, they need to see the information easily and quickly. They won't search for your strong points. Keep in mind the following:

- The overall format should be visually appealing and uncluttered.

- Don't overload the résumé with too much information.

- Use headings and bullets for emphasis and clarity.

- Use only one or, if needed, two pages.

- Use action verbs and keep lists in parallel structure. (See the table of action verbs in B1.)

- Check very carefully for misspellings or typos.

(For information on scannable résumés, see B4.)

B1 Sections of the Résumé

The order of the sections will depend on what is most appropriate to the job you are seeking. The name of the section might vary according to the content. For example, if you haven't had much work experience but have other experience you want to highlight, such as being treasurer of a campus organization or doing publicity work for a local group, use "Experience" rather than "Work Experience." If you submit a résumé through the World Wide Web, section names may be set by the company or job listing service.

Name

Generally, you should use your full name rather than initials or a nickname.

Address

Include your college and permanent addresses if they are different so that your prospective employer can contact you at either place. Include phone numbers, dates that you will be at both addresses, and other contact information such as a fax number or e-mail address.

MARK DANIEL KANE

College Address	Permanent Address
521 Cary Quadrangle	1523 Elmwood Drive
West Lafayette, IN 47906	Nobleton, IN 46623
(765) 555-0224	(765) 555-8789; fax (765) 555-4527
markkane@purdue.edu	mkane@aol.com
(Until May 15, 2000)	(After May 15, 2000)

Career Objective

This very important section, which can be labeled "Career Objective," "Objective," "Professional Objective," and so on, is placed immediately below your name and address. It contains one to three lines of text describing the position you are applying for and summarizing your main qualifications. Some writers choose sentence format; others use descriptive phrases with minimal punctuation. Follow these guidelines:

- Relate this section directly to the job you want, and tie in the skills you have acquired, your education, and your activities.

- Include the job title you seek and the skills you want to use. The rest of your résumé proves that you have the necessary skills, education, and experience.

- Do not emphasize what you want from the job ("to learn" or "to gain experience"). Instead emphasize what you can do for the company.

- Be specific. The most common problem is being too vague or too general.

  Too general: A position utilizing my skills and experience in different areas

  More specific: A position as a support specialist allowing me to use my skills in management information and experience as a computer lab manager

Education

This is a major section for most students. Include the following:

- Name of college(s) attended

- Degree(s) and graduation date (month and year)

- Major, minor, or specialization

- Grade point average (optional). Include your GPA first, then a slash mark, and then the highest possible GPA at the school. Or you can include your GPA in your major, then a slash mark, and then your overall GPA, as follows

  GPA (Major): 3.8/4.0

Put these in the order of whichever aspect you want to emphasize, the degree or the college.

Purdue University
Bachelor of Science, May 2001
Major: Chemical Engineering: GPA: 3.7/4.0
(or)
Bachelor of Science in Chemical Engineering, May 2001, Purdue University
GPA: 3.7/4.0

You may want to list some upper-level courses you've taken that are particularly significant to the job you are applying for, or you might list special courses that are different from those everyone in your major must take. Use a specific heading such as "Public Relations Courses" rather than a vague "Significant Courses." If appropriate, indicate programming languages you know and software you can use.

Under the heading "Special Projects," you can highlight unique features of your education that make you stand out from other applicants. Describe special projects you have completed, reports you have written, or conferences you have attended. Briefly give the most important details.

Work Experience or Experience

Before deciding how to arrange and present this information, make a list of the following items:

- Job titles, places worked, locations, and dates. Include part-time, temporary, and volunteer work as well as cooperative programs and internships.

- Duties you performed and skills you acquired.

You can organize this information as a functional or chronological résumé. Use action verbs in this section. (See B2 on résumé styles.)

Research Analyst
Kellogg Co.; Montack, Michigan; Summer 1999
- Supervised 9 assistants gathering information on cows' eating habits.
- Researched most recent information on cows' nutritional needs.
- Analyzed data to determine how to reduce number of feeding hours while maintaining nutritional quality.

Skills

Not all résumés include a skills section, but this is a useful way to emphasize skills you acquired from various jobs and activities. List the following:

- Jobs, club activities, projects, special offices or responsibilities.

- Skills you have developed from these experiences. For example, as president of a club, you led meetings, delegated responsibilities, coordinated activities, and so on.

Group the skills under three to five categories that relate to the job you are seeking, as described in your goal or career statement, and use those categories as your headings.

Management
- Chaired a committee to prepare and institute new election procedures for Student Union Board.
- Evaluated employees' work progress for monthly reports.
Communication
- Wrote weekly advertisements for student government entertainment activities.
- Represented sorority in negotiations with university administrators.
- Spoke to potential funding groups for student-organized charity events.

Programming
- Analyzed and designed a program to record and average student grades for a faculty member.
- Designed a program to record and update items of sorority's $90,000 annual budget.

HINT   Action Verbs to Use in Your Résumé

To help the prospective employer see you as an active worker, use action verbs such as the following:

act	generate	persuade
adapt	get	plan
administer	govern	prepare
advise	guide	present
analyze	handle	process
assess	head	produce
build	hire	program
calculate	implement	promote
catalog	improve	provide
compile	increase	raise
complete	initiate	recommend
conduct	install	recruit
coordinate	integrate	reorganize
create	maintain	represent
decide	manage	revise
define	market	schedule
demonstrate	modify	select
design	monitor	sell
develop	motivate	send
direct	negotiate	speak
distribute	obtain	supervise
edit	operate	survey
establish	order	train
evaluate	organize	transmit
examine	oversee	update
forecast	perform	write

Activities or College Activities

This section demonstrates your leadership and involvement and can include college activities, honors, and official positions or responsibilities you have had. You may need to explain in a phrase or two what various organizations are because prospective employers will probably not be familiar with the fact that the Tomahawk Club is an honorary service organization on your campus or that Alpha Gamma Alpha is a first-year honors council at your school.

References

You can include three or four references on your résumé, but if, like many job applicants, you prefer to be selective about who gets a copy of the list, include the following statement instead:

References available on request.

List the names of your references on a separate sheet, with addresses (including e-mail) and phone numbers. Add a sentence or two that explain your connection with that person. You can mail the list if the potential employer asks for it. Be sure that you have first asked each person whether he or she will serve as a reference.

B2 Résumé Styles

The two basic types of résumés can be combined. You might begin with skills and then include employment and educational history. Examples of both are included here.

- **Reverse chronological résumé** Presents your educational background, starting with the most recent degree, followed by work experience, beginning with the most recent job. List address (city and state) of the employer and dates of employment, and include a description of your duties, responsibilities, and acquired skills. This type of résumé highlights your current job and employer. Many writers combine this type with the functional résumé by beginning with skills and then listing employment and educational history.

- **Functional résumé** Emphasizes your skills and abilities gained through jobs, experiences, and activities, and allows you to relate them to the job you want. Arrange the skills from the most to the least relevant. If appropriate, include the name and location of companies and dates of employment. This approach is particularly appropriate when the skills you've acquired are more impressive than the jobs you've had or when you want to highlight a significant skill acquired from different experiences and jobs.

 Résumé Checklist

- **Organization** Put the most important sections first. For example, is your work experience more important than your education? Are your college activities more important than your past jobs?

- **Visual appeal** Use white space and lists to make your résumé visually appealing and easy to read. Highlight your headings with different kinds of type, underlining, boldface, capital letters, and indenting to show your organizing abilities. But don't clutter by using too many different fonts or types of headings.

- **Parallel headings** Be sure that your headings and lists are in parallel form.

- **Length** Many companies prefer one-page résumés, but length may vary according to your field and career objective.

- **Uniqueness** Your goal is not to make your résumé like all the others in the pile; instead highlight your unique capabilities.

ALETHA WATMAN

UNTIL May 15, 2000
210 Waldron Drive
University City, IA 71213
(712) 555-3123
aletha@carlman.edu

AFTER May 15, 2000
12955 Bleekman Street
Pontosa, OK 85337
(834) 555-9001

PROFESSIONAL OBJECTIVE
A career in personnel management which would involve coordinating, communicating, and training

EDUCATION
Carlman College; expected graduation, May 2000
Bachelor of Arts degree in Organizational Psychology
    Minor: General Management

GPA (6.0 scale): Major and Minor 5.9; Overall 5.6

Major-Related Courses:
    Personnel Management, Interviewing, Labor Relations, Industrial
    Psychology, Organizational Communications, Persuasion, Public
    Relations, Psychological Testing, Business Writing, Marketing

SKILLS
Coordinating
— Planned and organized campaign for Homecoming Queen
    candidate
— Supervised dining room preparation at the Sheraton Plaza Hotel
Communicating
— Underwent 150 hours of training to learn peer counseling
    techniques
— Developed and delivered a seminar on peer counseling
    for the American Personnel Guidance Convention,
    Washington, D.C., 1998
— Handled customer complaints
Training
— Supervised peer counseling program in college dormitory
— Instructed other employees in proper food and beverage service

WORK EXPERIENCE (paid for 100% of college expenses)
Food Server, Carlman Memorial Union; Fall 1996 to present
Salesperson, University Book Store, Carlman College;
    Fall 1997, Spring 1998
Food Server, Sheraton Plaza Hotel, University City, Louisiana;
    Summer 1996

ACTIVITIES AND HONORS
Peer Counselor (Student Dormitory)
Campaign Manager for Homecoming Queen Candidate
Member of Psi Chi (Psychology Honor Society)
Dean's List (8 semesters)

REFERENCES
Available on request

Example of a skills résumé

NOAH ALLAN MARMOR

6545 Country Inn Lane
Fort Worth, TX 30101
    phone: (314) 991-2387
    fax: (314) 991-2380
    e-mail: marmor@emet.com

PROFESSIONAL OBJECTIVE
An engineering career in aircraft structural analysis or structural dynamics

EDUCATION
Milman Polytechnic Institute, Oshkego, New York
Bachelor of Science in Aeronautical Engineering,
December 1992
    Structures and Materials Major/ Dynamics and Control Minor

Significant Courses
Advanced Matrix Methods, Mechanics of Composite Materials, Elasticity in Aerospace Engineering, Flight Mechanics, Aircraft Design I and II, Jet Propulsion Power Plants

Special Projects
— Proposed and performed wind tunnel test of composite laminates to study aeroelastic divergence
— Worked on a team designing a supersonic fighter aircraft with short takeoff and landing capabilities
— Learned to use computer program to analyze aeroelastic stability of a wing

WORK EXPERIENCE
Bell Helicopter Textron, Fort Worth, Texas:
September 1998 to present
— Use flight dynamics simulation computer programs such as DNAW06 and C81
— Evaluate rotors and rotor-fuselage combinations
Prisler and Associates, Dallas, Texas:
December 1995 to September 1998
— Drafted rotor parts for research and flight test programs
Hughes Aircraft, Los Angeles, California (Engineering Co-op):
January 1993 to December 1996
— Tested composite specimens to verify materials specifications
— Fabricated composite structures for research programs

ACTIVITIES
Hillel Foundation Coordinator
Alpha Omicron (Engineering Honorary Society)
AIPAC Public Relations Chairperson

REFERENCES: Available on request

Example of a chronological résumé

B3 Cover Letters

When you submit a résumé, you should always have a cover letter that introduces you, states the job you are applying for, and adds depth and explanation to the qualifications on your résumé. Consider this letter as presenting an argument—that is, showing your readers why you are an outstanding candidate for the position. The goal of the letter is to get an interview.

Even if you are generally a modest person, sell yourself to the reader. Show why that company would benefit from hiring you, and indicate how you have all the qualifications and requirements for the job. Don't overlook any of those qualifications mentioned in the job listing. They are the keys to what the employer is looking for.

It is critically important to proofread your letter carefully. Recruiting teams say that grammatical and mechanical mistakes in letters help them weed out candidates.

Opening Section of the Letter

- If you have had personal contact with someone in the company or if you have been invited to apply, mention that in the opening sentence or two.

- Indicate the specific job title you are applying for and the source of your information. Did you see the job listed on your campus recruitment board or in the newspaper?

- Identify yourself in terms of your qualifications by summarizing what you can offer this company.

Middle Section of the Letter

- Make strong connections between your qualifications and those listed in the job description.

- Refer the reader to your enclosed résumé.

- Expand on your experience, education, and qualifications, and add background that enhances your appeal as an employee but that isn't evident in the résumé. For example, if leadership or supervision skills are important and you list an elected office in the student government, note that you won by a wide majority in a large field of candidates. This fact shows that you're liked by people, you're seen as a leader, and you stand out in a crowd.

Closing Section of the Letter

- Conclude with an action step. What do you want your reader to do, contact you? If so, how can you be contacted? Are you available to come for an interview? When?

- Thank the reader for considering your résumé.

- Indicated below your signature that the résumé is enclosed. At the left border, under your name, note an enclosure:

Enclosure: Résumé

Additional Letters

If you haven't heard from the employer in a week or two, you can write a follow-up letter to see if your letter was received. If you have an interview, write a letter of thanks afterwards, again reminding the interviewer of your qualifications and your interest in working for that company. The final step after you have decided to accept or reject the job offer is to write a letter indicating your decision. Acceptance letters can repeat the conditions of employment, to be sure that you and your future employer agree on matters such as salary, starting date, title, responsibilities, and so on. If you reject the offer, you can politely note that while you are unable to accept the job, you were pleased to be offered the position by a company you admire.

---

25 Oregon Way
Austin, TX 34221
April 19, 1999

Ms. Margaret Whitmore
Bankers Trust
John Hancock Building, Suite 45B
138 Trujillo Way
Darleton, Texas 32219

Dear Ms. Whitmore:

At the suggestion of Jim Mendez, one of your colleagues in the Human Resources Department, I am applying for the position of bank teller listed in the *Darleton Times* last week. My skills in accounting, my previous summer experience working as a customer service assistant in the bank in my hometown of Monroe, Mississippi, and my college courses in financial computing will allow me to be a productive employee at Bankers Trust.

As you will see from the enclosed résumé, I am about to graduate from the University of Texas at Austin with a B.A. in Finance. My courses in financial computing have been particularly useful in learning how bank records are kept and how to use the software involved. In addition to my extracurricular campus activities that allowed me to further develop my communication skills, I served as the treasurer for my fraternity, keeping accurate records of our $150,000 annual budget.

I am available for an interview any time after May 15, and I can meet with you in your office in Darleton. I will telephone in about ten days to see if that is a convenient time and to learn whether you need any additional information. You can call me at (466) 555-1212 or e-mail a message to blalock@tu.edu to arrange a time.

I am looking forward to meeting you and talking with you.

Sincerely,

William Blalock

William Blalock

Enclosure: Résumé

Sample cover letter

B4 Electronic Job Search

If you are job hunting on the Internet, there are a number of sites you can access to check on jobs or to post your résumé. If your local newspaper or newspapers from locations where you want to look for a job have Web sites, you can check the classified advertisements online. You can also check sites listing online newspapers, and you can post your résumé in online databases. Your college may also maintain a Web site so students can post résumés.

Online Sites for Job Seekers

■ Major newspapers with classified ads online

New York Times	www.nytimes.com/classified
Wall Street Journal Careers	careers.wsj.com
Washington Post	www.washingtonpost.com
CareerPost	www.washingtonpost.com/wpadv/
	classifieds/careerpost/front.htm
USA Today Career Center	usatoday.com/careers/careers.htm

  The *USA Today* site has a job search database, a place to sign up and have job openings e-mailed to you, lists of companies hiring through the Career Center, and job-seeking tips.

■ Other online newspapers

EcolaNewsstand	www.ecola.com

  This site permits you to browse for newspapers by country. Use any of the search engines listed in Chapter 49 to find specific newspapers.

■ Sites listing jobs

America's Job Bank	www.ajb.dni.us
Career City	www.careercity.com

  Lists specific companies, regions, salary ranges, etc.

Career Magazine	www.careermag.com
Career Mosaic	www.careermosaic.com/cm/jobs.html

  Searches for you by job description, place, etc., and sends your résumé to the prospective employer.

Career Path	www.careerpath.com

  Lists job fairs: allows you to post your résumé.

Federal Jobs Digest	www.jobsfed.com

  Comprehensive listing of federal jobs.

Monster Board	www.monster.com
NationJob Online Job Band	www.nationjob.com
Yahoo Classified	classifieds.yahoo.com

Scannable Résumés

Some employers ask for résumés that can be scanned into databases so they can do keyword searches. A prospective employer may put an e-mailed résumé into a database to scan. You will therefore need to keep in mind that you should include key terms that will cause the software to select your résumé for review.

On way to be sure the software selects your résumé is to have a section labeled "Keyword Summary" at the beginning (just below your name and address, instead of a career objective). Instead of verbs, use nouns as your strong words: instead of *supervised, managed,* or *taught,* use *supervisor, manager,* and *instructor.* Be sure that the rest of the résumé is strong and convincing; after the software selects it for review, someone will read and evaluate it.

If the employer has asked that you print and send a paper résumé that is scannable, avoid features that will not scan well. Since you don't know the quality of the scanner that will be used, assume that it might have difficulties with dark-colored paper; faint or light print; words that are crowded together; complex font types, italics, or underlining; and small font sizes.

GLOSSARY OF USAGE

This list includes words and phrases you may be uncertain about when writing. If you have questions about words not included here, try the index to this book to see whether the word is discussed elsewhere. You can also check a recently published dictionary. (The dictionary used here as a source of information is the *Oxford American Dictionary*, Oxford University Press, 1980.

A, An: Use *a* before words that begin with a consonant (for example, *a* cat, *a* house) and before words beginning with a vowel that sounds like a consonant (for example, *a* one-way street, *a* union). Use *an* before words that begin with a vowel (for example, *an* egg, *an* ice cube) and before words with a silent *h* (for example, *an* hour). See 20b.

Accept, Except: *Accept*, a verb, means "to agree to," "to believe," or "to receive."

> The detective **accepted** his account of the event and did not hold him as a suspect in the case.

Except, a verb, means "to exclude" or "to leave out," and *except*, a preposition, means "leaving out."

> Because he did not know any of the answers, he was **excepted** from the list of contestants and asked to leave.
> **Except** for brussels sprouts, which I hate, I eat most vegetables.

Advice, Advise: *Advice* is a noun, and *advise* is a verb.

> She always offers too much **advice.**
> Would you **advise** me about choosing the right course?

Affect, Effect: Most frequently, *affect*, which means "to influence," is used as a verb, and *effect*, which means "a result," is used as a noun.

> The weather **affects** my ability to study.
> What **effect** does too much coffee have on your concentration?

However, *effect*, meaning "to cause" or "to bring about," is also used as a verb.

> The new traffic enforcement laws **effected** a change in people's driving habits.

Common phrases with *effect* include the following:

> in effect   to that effect

Ain't: This is a nonstandard way of saying *am not, is not, has not, have not,* etc.

All ready, Already: *All ready* means "prepared"; *already* means "before" or "by this time."

> The courses for the meal are **all ready** to be served.
> When I got home, she was **already** there.

All Right, Alright: *All right* is two words, not one. *Alright* is an incorrect form.

All Together, Altogether: *All together* means "in a group," and *altogether* means "entirely," "totally."

> We were **all together** again after having separate vacations.
> He was not **altogether** happy about the outcome of the test.

Alot, A Lot: *Alot* is an incorrect form of *a lot.*

a.m., p.m. (or) A.M., P.M.: Use these with numbers, not as substitutes for the words *morning* or *evening.*

> morning at 9 A.M.
> We meet every ~~A.M.~~ for an exercise class.

Among, Between: Use *among* when referring to three or more things and *between* when referring to two things.

> The decision was discussed **among** all the members of the committee.
> I had to decide **between** the chocolate mousse pie and the almond ice cream.

Amount, Number: Use *amount* for things or ideas that are general or abstract and cannot be counted. For example, furniture is a general term and cannot be counted. That is, we cannot say "one furniture" or "two furnitures." Use *number* for things that can be counted, as, for example, four chairs or three tables.

> He had a huge **amount** of work to finish before the deadline.
> There were a **number** of people who saw the accident.

An: See the entry for *a, an.*

And: While some people discourage the use of *and* as the first word in a sentence, it is an acceptable word with which to begin a sentence.

And Etc.: Adding *and* is redundant because *et* means "and" in Latin. See the entry for *etc.*

Anybody, Any Body: See the entry for *anyone, any one.*

Anyone, Any One: *Anyone* means "any person at all." *Any one* refers to a specific person or thing in a group. There are similar distinctions for other words ending in *-body* and *-one* (for example, *everybody, every body; anybody, any body;* and *someone, some one*).

> The teacher asked if **anyone** knew the answer.

Any one of those children could have taken the ball.

Anyways, Anywheres: These are nonstandard forms for *anyway* and *anywhere.*

As, As If, As Though, Like: Use *as* in a comparison (not *like*) when there is an equality intended or when the meaning is "in the function of."

Celia acted **as** (not *like*) the leader when the group was getting organized.   [Celia = leader]

Use *as if* or *as though* for the subjunctive.

He spent his money **as if** [or **as though**] he were rich.

Use *like* in a comparison (not *as*) when the meaning is "in the manner of" or "to the same degree as."

The boy swam **like** a fish.

Don't use *like* as the opening word in a clause in formal writing.

Informal: Like I thought, he was unable to predict the weather.
Formal: As I thought, he was unable to predict the weather.

Assure, Ensure, Insure: *Assure* means "to declare" or "to promise," *ensure* means "to make safe or certain," and *insure* means "to protect with a contract of insurance."

I **assure** you that I am trying to find your lost package.
Some people claim that eating properly **ensures** good health.
This insurance policy also **insures** my car against theft.

Awful, Awfully: *Awful* is an adjective meaning "inspiring awe" or "extremely unpleasant."

He was involved in an **awful** accident.

Awfully is an adverb used in informal writing to mean "very." It should be avoided in formal writing.

Informal: The dog was **awfully** dirty.

Awhile, A While: *Awhile* is an adverb meaning "a short time" and modifies a verb:

He talked **awhile** and then left.

A *while* is an article with the noun *while* and means "a period of time:"

I'll be there in **a while.**

Bad, Badly: *Bad* is an adjective and is used after linking verbs. *Badly* is an adverb.

The wheat crop looked **bad** [not *badly*] because of lack of rain.
There was a **bad** flood last summer.
The building was **badly** constructed and unable to withstand the strong winds.

Beside, Besides: *Beside* is a preposition meaning "at the side of," "compared with," or "having nothing to do with." *Besides* is a preposition meaning "in addition to" or "other than." *Besides* as an adverb means "also" or "moreover." Don't confuse *beside* with *besides*.

> That is **beside** the point.
> **Besides** the radio, they had no other means of contact with the outside world.
> **Besides,** I enjoyed the concert.

Between, Among: See the entry for *among, between.*

Breath, Breathe: *Breath* is a noun, and *breathe* is a verb.

> She held her **breath** when she dived into the water.
> Learn to **breathe** deeply when you swim.

But: While some people discourage the use of *but* as the first word in a sentence, it is an acceptable word with which to begin a sentence.

Can, May: *Can* is a verb that expresses ability, knowledge, or capacity.

> He **can** play both the violin and the cello.

May is a verb that expresses possibility or permission. Careful writers avoid using *can* to mean permission.

> **May** [not *can*] I sit here?

Can't Hardly: This is incorrect because it is a double negative.

> can
> She c̶a̶n̶'t̶ hardly hear normal voice levels.

Choose, Chose: *Choose* is the present tense of the verb, and *chose* is the past tense.

> Jennie always **chooses** strawberry ice cream.
> Yesterday, she even **chose** strawberry-flavored popcorn.

Cloth, Clothe: *Cloth* is a noun, and *clothe* is a verb.

> Here is some **cloth** for a new scarf.
> His paycheck helps to feed and **clothe** many people in his family.

Compared To, Compared With: Use *compared to* when showing that two things are alike. Use *compared with* when showing similarities and differences.

> The speaker **compared** the economy **to** a roller coaster because both have sudden ups and downs.
> The detective **compared** the fingerprints **with** other sets from a previous crime.

Could Of: This is incorrect. Instead use *could have.*

Data: This is the plural form of *datum.* In informal usage, *data* is used as a singular noun, with a singular verb. However, since dictionaries do not accept this, use *data* as a plural form for academic writing.

Informal: The **data** is inconclusive.
Formal: The **data** are inconclusive.

Different From, Different Than: *Different from* is always correct, but some writers use *different than* if there is a clause following this phrase.

This program is **different from** the others.
That is a **different** result **than** they predicted.

Done: The past tense forms of the verb *do* are *did* and *done*. *Did* is the simple form that needs no additional verb as a helper. *Done* is the past form that requires the helper *have*. Some writers make the mistake of interchanging *did* and *done*.

They ~~done~~ it again. (or) They done it again.
    did   *have*

Effect, Affect: See the entry for *affect, effect.*

Ensure: See the entry for *assure, ensure, insure.*

Etc.: This is an abbreviation of the Latin *et cetera,* meaning "and the rest." Because it should be used sparingly if at all in formal academic writing, substitute other phrases such as *and so forth* or *and so on.*

Everybody, Every Body: See the entry for *anyone, any one.*

Everyone, Every One: See the entry for *anyone, any one.*

Except, Accept: See the entry for *accept, except.*

Farther, Further: While some writers use these words interchangeably, dictionary definitions differentiate them. *Farther* is used when actual distance is involved, and *further* is used to mean "to a greater extent," "more."

The house is **farther** from the road than I realized.
That was **furthest** from my thoughts at the time.

Fewer, Less: *Fewer* is used for things that can be counted (*fewer* trees, *fewer* people). *Less* is used for ideas; abstractions; things that are thought of collectively, not separately (*less* trouble, *less* furniture); and things that are measured by amount, not number (*less* milk, *less* fuel).

Fun: This noun is used informally as an adjective.

Informal: They had a **fun** time.

Goes, Says: *Goes* is a nonstandard form of *says.*

Whenever I give him a book to read, he ~~goes,~~ "What's it about?"
                                       says,

Gone, Went: Past tense forms of the verb *go. Went* is the simple form that needs no additional verb as a helper. *Gone* is the past form that requires the helper *have*. Some writers make the mistake of interchanging *went* and *gone.*

They already ~~gone~~ away before I woke up.
    went **(or)** *had gone*

Good, Well: *Good* is an adjective and therefore describes only nouns. *Well* is an adverb and therefore describes adjectives, other adverbs, and verbs. The word *well* is used as an adjective only in the sense of "in good health."

The stereo works ~~good~~ *well*.   I feel ~~good~~ *well*.   She is a good driver.

Got, Have: *Got* is the past tense of *get* and should not be used in place of *have*. Similarly, *got to* should not be used as a substitute for *must*. *Have got to* is an informal substitute for *must*.

Do you ~~got~~ *have* any pennies for the meter?   I ~~got to~~ *must* go now.

Informal: You have **got to** see that movie.

Great: This adjective is overworked in its formal meaning of "very enjoyable," "good," or "wonderful" and should be reserved for its more exact meanings, such as "of remarkable ability," "intense," "high degree of," and so on.

Informal: That was a **great** movie.
More Exact Uses of *Great*: The vaccine was a **great** discovery.
The map went into **great** detail.

Have, Got: See the entry for *got, have*.

Have, Of: *Have*, not *of*, should follow verbs such as *could, might, must,* and *should*.

They should ~~of~~ *have* called by now.

Hisself: This is a nonstandard substitute for *himself*.

Hopefully: This adverb means "in a hopeful way." Many people consider the meaning "it is to be hoped" unacceptable.

Acceptable: He listened **hopefully** for the knock at the door.
Often Considered Unacceptable: Hopefully, it will not rain tonight.

I: While some people discourage the use of *I* in formal essays, it is acceptable. If you wish to eliminate the use of *I*, see 17d on passive verbs.

Imply, Infer: Some writers use these interchangeably, but careful writers maintain the distinction between the two words. *Imply* means "to suggest without stating directly," "to hint." *Infer* means "to reach an opinion from facts or reasoning."

The tone of her voice **implied** that he was stupid.
The anthropologist **inferred** that this was a burial site for prehistoric people.

Insure: See the entry for *assure, ensure, insure*.

Irregardless: This is an incorrect form of the word *regardless*.

Is When, Is Why, Is Where, Is Because: These are incorrect forms for definitions. See Chapter 12 on faulty predication.

> **Faulty Predication:** Nervousness is when my palms sweat.
> **Revised:** When I am nervous, my palms sweat.
> (or)
> Nervousness is a state of being very uneasy or agitated.

Its, It's: *Its* is a personal pronoun in the possessive case. *It's* is a contraction for *it is.*

> The kitten licked **its** paw.
> **It's** a good time for a vacation.

Kind, Sort: These two forms are singular and should be used with *this* or *that.* Use *kinds* or *sorts* with *these* or *those.*

> This **kind** of cloud often indicates that there will be heavy rain.
> These **sorts** of plants are regarded as weeds.

Lay, Lie: *Lay* is a verb that needs an object and should not be used in place of *lie,* a verb that takes no direct object.

> lie
> He should ~~lay~~ down and rest awhile.

> lay
> You can ~~lie~~ that package on the front table.

Leave, Let: *Leave* means "to go away," and *let* means "to permit." It is incorrect to use *leave* when you mean *let:*

> Let
> ~~Leave~~ me get that for you.

Less, Fewer: See the entry for *fewer, less.*

Let, Leave: See the entry for *leave, let.*

Like, As: See the entry for *as, as if, as though, like.*

Like For: The phrase "I'd like for you to do that" is incorrect. Omit *for.*

May, Can: See the entry for *can, may.*

Most: It is incorrect to use *most* as a substitute for *almost.*

Nowheres: This is an incorrect form of *nowhere.*

Number, Amount: See the entry for *amount, number.*

Of, Have: See the entry for *have, of.*

Off Of: It is incorrect to write *off of* for *off* in a phrase such as *off the table.*

O.K., Ok, Okay: These can be used informally but should not be used in formal or academic writing.

Reason . . . Because: This is redundant. Instead of *because,* use *that.*

that
The reason she dropped the course is ~~because~~ she couldn't keep up with the homework.

Less Wordy Revision: She dropped the course **because** she couldn't keep up with the homework.

Reason Why: Using *why* is redundant. Drop the word *why*.

The reason ~~why~~ I called is to remind you of your promise.

Saw, Seen: Past tense forms of the verb *see*. *Saw* is the simple form that needs no additional verb as a helper. *Seen* is the past form that requires the helper *have*. Some writers make the mistake of interchanging *saw* and *seen*.

saw   *have*
They ~~seen~~ it happen.   (or)   They seen it happen.

Set, Sit: *Set* means "to place" and is followed by a direct object. *Sit* means "to be seated." It is incorrect to substitute *set* for *sit*.

sit
Come in and ~~set~~ down.

Set
~~Sit~~ the flowers on the table.

Should of: This is incorrect. Instead use *should have*.

Sit, Set: See the entry for *set, sit*.

Somebody, Some Body: See the entry for *anyone, any one*.

Someone, Some One: See the entry for *anyone, any one*.

Sort, Kind: See the entry for *kind, sort*.

Such: This is an overworked word when used in place of *very* or *extremely*.

Sure: The use of *sure* as an adverb is informal. Careful writers use *surely* instead.

Informal: I **sure** hope you can join us.
Revised: I **surely** hope you can join us.

Than, Then: *Than* is a conjunction introducing the second element in comparison. *Then* is an adverb that means "at that time," "next," "after that," "also," or "in that case."

She is taller **than** I am.
He picked up the ticket and **then** left the house.

That There, This Here, These Here, Those There: These are incorrect forms for *that, this, these, those*.

That, Which: Use *that* for essential clauses and *which* for nonessential clauses. Some writers, however, also use *which* for essential clauses. (See 19b and Chapter 25.)

Their, There, They're: *Their* is a possessive pronoun; *there* means "in," "at," or "to that place;" and *they're* is a contraction for "they are."

Their house has been sold.
There is the parking lot.
They're both good swimmers.

Theirself, Theirselves, Themself: These are all incorrect forms for *themselves.*

Them: It is incorrect to use *them* in place of either the pronoun *these* or *those.*

> those
Look at ~~them~~ apples.

Then, Than: See the entry for *than, then.*

Thusly: This is an incorrect substitute for *thus.*

To, Too, Two: *To* is a preposition; *too* is an adverb meaning "very" or "also;" and *two* is a number.

He brought his bass guitar **to** the party.
He brought his drums **too.**
He had **two** music stands.

Toward, Towards: Both are accepted forms with the same meaning, but *toward* is preferred.

Use to: This is incorrect for the modal meaning *formerly.* Instead, use *used to.*

Want for: Omit the incorrect *for* in phrases such as "I want for you to come here."

Well, Good: See the entry for *good, well.*

Went, Gone: See the entry for *gone, went.*

Where: It is incorrect to use *where* to mean *when* or *that.*

> when
The Fourth of July is a holiday ~~where~~ the town council shoots off fireworks.

> that
I see ~~where~~ there is now a ban on shooting panthers.

Where . . . at: This is a redundant form. Omit the *at.*

This is where the picnic is ~~at~~.

Which, That: See the entry for *that, which.*

While, Awhile: See the entry for *awhile, a while.*

Who, Whom: Use *who* for the subject case; use *whom* for the object case.

He is the person **who** signs that form.
He is the person **whom** I asked for help.

Who's, Whose: *Who's* is a contraction for *who is*; *whose* is a possessive pronoun.

Who's included on that list?
Whose wristwatch is this?

Your, You're: *Your* is a possessive pronoun; *you're* is a contraction for *you are.*

Your hands are cold.
You're a great success.

GLOSSARY OF GRAMMATICAL TERMS

Absolutes: Words or phrases that modify whole sentences rather than parts of sentences or individual words. An absolute phrase, which consists of a noun and participle, can be placed anywhere in the sentence but needs to be set off from the sentence by commas.

The snow having finally stopped, the football game began.
(absolute phrase)

Abstract Nouns: Nouns that refer to ideas, qualities, generalized concepts, and conditions and that do not have plural forms. (See Chapter 59.)

happiness, pride, furniture, trouble, sincerity

Active Voice: See **voice.**

Adjectives: Words that modify nouns and pronouns. (See Chapter 20.) Descriptive adjectives (*red, clean, beautiful, offensive,* for example) have three forms.

Positive: red, clean, beautiful, offensive
Comparative (for comparing two things): redder, cleaner, more beautiful, less offensive
Superlative (for comparing more than two things): reddest, cleanest, most beautiful, least offensive

Adjective Clauses: See **dependent clauses.**

Adverbs: Modify verbs, verb forms, adjectives, and other adverbs. (See Chapter 20.) Descriptive adverbs (for example, *fast, graceful, awkward*) have three forms.

Positive: fast, graceful, awkward
Comparative (for comparing two things): faster, more graceful, less awkward
Superlative (for comparing more than two things): fastest, most graceful, least awkward

Adverb Clauses: See **dependent clauses.**

Agreement: The use of the corresponding form for related words in order to have them agree in number, person, or gender. (See Chapter 11a, and 19b.)

John runs. [Both subject and verb are singular.]

It is necessary to flush the **pipes** regularly so that **they** don't freeze.

[Both subjects, *it* and *they,* are in third person; *they* agrees in number with the antecedent, *pipes.*]

Antecedents: Words or groups of words to which pronouns refer.

When the **bell** was rung, **it** sounded very loudly.

[*Bell* is the antecedent of *it.*]

Antonyms: Words with opposite meanings.

Word	Antonym
hot	cold
fast	slow
noisy	quiet

Appositives: Nonessential phrases and clauses that follow nouns and identify or explain them. (See Chapter 25.)

My uncle, **who lives in Wyoming,** is taking windsurfing lessons in
  (appositive)

Florida.

Articles: See **noun determiners.**

Auxiliary Verbs: Verbs used with main verbs in verb phrases.

should be going   **has** taken
(auxiliary verb) *(auxiliary verb)*

Cardinal Numbers: See **noun determiners.**

Case: The form or position of a noun or pronoun that shows its use or relationship to other words in a sentence. The three cases in English are (1) *subject* (or *subjective* or *nominative*), (2) *object* (or *objective*), and (3) *possessive* (or *genitive*). (See 19a).

Clauses: Groups of related words that contain both subjects and predicates and that function either as sentences or as parts of sentences. Clauses are either *independent* (or *main*) or *dependent* (or *subordinate*). (See Chapter 24.)

Clichés: Overused or tired expressions that no longer effectively communicate. (See 41b.)

Collective Nouns: Nouns that refer to groups of people or things, such as a *committee, team,* or *jury.* When the group includes a number of members acting as a unit and is the subject of the sentence, the verb is also singular. (See 7g and 18a.)

The **jury** has made a decision.

Colloquialisms: Words or phrases used in casual conversation and writing. (See 42b.)

Comma Splices: Punctuation errors in which two or more independent clauses in compound sentences are separated only by commas and no coordinating conjunctions. (See Chapter 6.)

, but (or) ;
Jesse said he could not help, that was typical of his responses to requests.

Common Nouns: Nouns that refer to general rather than specific categories of people, places, and things and are not capitalized. (See 18a.)

basket   person   history   tractor

Comparative: The form of adjectives and adverbs used when two things are being compared. (See 20c.)

higher   more intelligent   less friendly

Complement: When linking verbs link subjects to adjectives or nouns, the adjectives or nouns are complements.

Phyllis was **tired.**   She became a **musician.**
    (complement)   *(complement)*

Complex Sentences: Sentences with at least one independent clause and at least one dependent clause arranged in any order. (See 26b.3.)

Compound Nouns: Nouns such as *swimming pool, dropout, roommate,* and *stepmother,* in which more than one word is needed.

Compound Sentences: Sentences with two or more independent clauses and no dependent clauses. (See 26b.2.)

Compound-Complex Sentences: Sentences with at least two independent clauses and at least one dependent clause arranged in any order. (See 26b.4.)

Concrete Nouns: Words that refer to people and things that can be perceived by the senses. (See 42f.)

Conjunctions: Words that connect other words, phrases, and clauses in sentences. Coordinating conjunctions connect independent clauses; subordinating conjunctions connect dependent or subordinating clauses with independent or main clauses.

Coordinating Conjunctions: and, but, for, or, nor, so, yet
Some Subordinating Conjunctions: after, although, because, if, since, until, while

Conjunctive Adverbs: Words that begin or join independent clauses. (See 24a.)

consequently   however   therefore   thus   moreover

Connotation: The attitudes and emotional overtones beyond the direct definition of a word. (See 42g.)

The words *plump* and *fat* both mean fleshy, but *plump* has a more positive connotation than *fat.*

Consistency: Maintaining the same voice with pronouns, the same tense with verbs, and the same tone, voice, or mode of discourse. (See Chapter 11.)

Coordinating Conjunctions: See **conjunctions.**

Coordination: Of equal importance. Two independent clauses in the same sentence are coordinate because they have equal importance and the same emphasis. (See 13a and 24a.)

Correlative Conjunctions: Words that work in pairs and give emphasis.

both . . . and   neither . . . nor   either . . . or   not . . . but also

Count Nouns: Nouns that name things that can be counted because they can be divided into separate and distinct units. (See Chapter 59.)

Dangling Modifiers: Phrases or clauses in which the doer of the action is not clearly indicated. (See 9a.)

Tim thought
Missing an opportunity to study, the exam seemed especially difficult.

Declarative Mood: See **mood.**

Demonstrative Pronouns: Pronouns that refer to things. (See **noun determiners** and 18b.)

this   that   these   those

Denotation: The explicit dictionary definition of a word. (See 42g.)

Dependent Clauses (Subordinate Clauses): Clauses that cannot stand alone as complete sentences. (See 24b.) There are two kinds of dependent clauses: adverb clauses and adjective clauses.

Adverb clauses begin with subordinating conjunctions such as *after, if, because, while, when,* and so on.
Adjective clauses tell more about nouns or pronouns in sentences and begin with words such as *who, which, that, whose, whom.*

Determiner: See **noun determiner.**

Diagrams: See **sentence diagrams.**

Direct Discourse: See **mode of discourse.**

Direct and Indirect Quotations: Direct quotations are the exact words said by someone or the exact words in print that are being copied. Indirect quotations are not the exact words but the rephrasing or summarizing of someone else's words. (See 31a.)

Direct Objects: Nouns or pronouns that follow a transitive verb and complete the meaning or receive the action of the verb. The direct object answers the question *what?* or *whom?*

Ellipsis: A series of three dots to indicate that words or parts of sentences are being omitted from material being quoted (See 34e.)

Essential and Nonessential Clauses and Phrases: *Essential* (also called *restrictive*) clauses and phrases appear after nouns and are necessary or essential to complete the meaning of the sentence. *Nonessential* (also called *nonrestrictive*) clauses and phrases appear after nouns and add extra information, but that information can be removed from the sentence without altering the meaning. (See Chapter 25.)

Apples **that are green** are not sweet.
   (essential clause)

Golden Delicious apples, **which are yellow,** are sweet.
   (nonessential clause)

Excessive Coordination: Occurs when too many equal clauses are strung together with coordinators into one sentence. (See 13a.)

Excessive Subordination: Occurs when too many subordinate clauses are strung together in a complex sentence. (See 13b.)

Faulty Coordination: Occurs when two clauses that either are unequal in importance or that have little or no connection to each other are combined in one sentence and written as independent clauses. (See 13a.)

Faulty Parallelism: See **nonparallel structure.**

Faulty Predication: Occurs when a predicate does not appropriately fit the subject. This happens most often after forms of the *to be* verb. (See Chapter 12.)

He

~~The reason he~~ was late ~~was~~ because he had to study.

Fragments: Groups of words punctuated as sentences that either do not have both a subject and a complete verb or are dependent clauses. (See Chapter 8.)

Whenever we wanted to pick fresh fruit while we were staying on my

, we would head for the apple orchard with buckets.
grandmother's farm.

Fused Sentences: Punctuation errors (also called *run-ons*) in which there is no punctuation between independent clauses in the sentence. (See 6b.)

;
Jennifer never learned how to ask politely she just took what she wanted.

General Words: Words that refer to whole categories or large classes of items. (See 42e.) See also **specific words.**

Gerunds: Verbal forms ending in *-ing* that function as nouns. (See **phrases, verbals,** and 17b.)

Arnon enjoys **cooking. Jogging** is another of his favorite pastimes.
   (gerund) (gerund)

Helping Verbs: See **auxiliary verbs.**

Homonyms: Words that sound alike but are spelled differently and have different meanings. (See 39e.)

hear/here   passed/past   buy/by

Idioms: Expressions meaning something beyond the simple definition or literal translation into another language. For example, idioms such as "short and sweet" or "wearing his heart on his sleeve" are expressions in English that cannot be translated literally into another language. (See Chapter 62.)

Imperative Mood: See **mood.**

Indefinite Pronouns: Pronouns that make indefinite reference to nouns. (See 18b.5 and 19b.5.)

anyone   everyone   nobody   something

Independent Clauses: Clauses that can stand alone as complete sentences because they do not depend on other clauses to complete their meanings. (See 24a.)

Indicative Mood: See **mood.**

Indirect Discourse: See **mode of discourse.**

Indirect Objects: Words that follow transitive verbs and come before direct objects. They indicate the one to whom or for whom something is given, said, or done and answer the questions *to what?* or *to whom?* Indirect objects can always be replaced by a prepositional phrase beginning with *to* or *for.* (See 19a.2.)

Alice gave **me** some money.
   (indirect object)

Alice gave some money **to me.**

Infinitives: Phrases made up of the present form of the verb preceded by *to.* Infinitives can have subjects, objects, complements, or modifiers. (See **phrases** and 17b.)

Everyone wanted **to swim** in the new pool.
   (infinitive)

Intensifiers: Modifying words used for emphasis.

She **most certainly** did fix that car!

Interjections: Words used as exclamations.

Oh, I don't think I want to know about that.

Interrogative Pronouns: Pronouns used in questions. (See 18b.)

who   whose   whom   which   that

Irregular Verbs: Verbs in which the past tense forms and/or the past participles are not formed by adding *-ed* or *-d.* (See 17c.4.)

do, did, done   begin, began, begun

Intransitive Verbs: See **verbs.**

Jargon: Words and phrases that are either the specialized language of various fields or, in a negative sense, unnecessarily technical or inflated terms. (See 42d.)

Linking Verbs: Verbs linking the subject to the subject complement. The most common linking verbs are *appear, seem, become, feel, look, taste, sound,* and *be.*

> I **feel** sleepy.　　He **became** the president.
> *(linking verb)*　　*(linking verb)*

Misplaced Modifiers: Modifiers not placed next to or close to the word(s) being modified. (See 9b.)

> on television
> We saw an advertisement for an excellent new stereo system with dual headphones ~~on television~~.

Modal Verbs: Helping verbs such as *shall, should, will, would, can, could, may, might, must, ought to,* and *used to* that express an attitude such as interest, possibility, or obligation. (See 17f and 56a.)

Mode of Discourse: Direct discourse repeats the exact words that someone says, and indirect discourse reports the words but changes some of the words. (See 11e.)

> Everett said, **"I want to become a physicist."**
> *(direct discourse)*

> Everett said **that he wants to become a physicist.**
> *(indirect discourse)*

Modifiers: Words or groups of words that describe or limit other words, phrases, and clauses. The most common modifiers are adjectives and adverbs. (See Chapter 20.)

Mood: Verbs indicate whether a sentence expresses a fact (the declarative or indicative mood), expresses some doubt or something contrary to fact or states a recommendation (the subjunctive mood), or issues a command (the imperative mood). (See 17e.)

Noncount Nouns: Nouns that name things that cannot be counted because they are abstractions or things that cannot be cut into parts. (See Chapter 59.)

Nonessential Clauses and Phrases: See **essential and nonessential clauses and phrases.**

Nonparallel Structure: Lack of parallelism that occurs when like items are not in the same grammatical form. (See 10b.)

Nonrestrictive Clauses and Phrases: See **essential and nonessential clauses and phrases.**

Nouns: Words that name people, places, things, and ideas and have plural or possessive endings. Nouns function as *subjects, direct objects, predicate nominatives, objects of prepositions,* and *indirect objects.* (See 18a.)

Noun Clauses: Subordinate clauses used as nouns.

What I see here is adequate.
(noun clause)

Noun Determiners: Words that signal that a noun is about to follow. They stand next to their nouns or can be separated by adjectives. Some noun determiners can also function as nouns. There are five types of noun determiners.

1. Articles (see 60c): *the* (definite) *a, an* (indefinite)
2. Demonstratives: *this, that, these, those*
3. Possessives: *my, our, your, his, her, its, their*
4. Cardinal numbers: *one, two, three,* and so on
5. Miscellaneous: *all, another, each, every, much,* and others

Noun Phrases: See **phrases.**

Number: The quantity expressed by a noun or pronoun, either singular (one) or plural (more than one).

Object Case of Pronouns: The case needed when the pronoun is the direct or indirect object of the verb or the object of a preposition. (See 19a.)

Singular	Plural
First person: *me*	First person: *us*
Second person: *you*	Second person: *you*
Third person: *him, her, it*	Third person: *them*

Objects: See **direct objects** and **object complements.**

Object Complements: The adjectives in predicates modifying the object of the verb (not the subject).

The enlargement makes the picture **clear.**
(object complement)

Object of the Preposition: Noun or pronoun following the preposition. The preposition, its object, and any modifiers make up the *prepositional phrase.* (See 19a.)

For **Daniel**   She knocked twice **on the big wooden door.**
(object of the   *(prepositional phrase)*
preposition for)

Parallel Construction: When two or more items are listed or compared, they must be in the same grammatical form as equal elements. When items are not in the same grammatical form, they lack parallel structure (this error is often called *faulty parallelism*). (See Chapter 10.)

She was sure that **being an apprentice in a photographer's studio** would be more useful than **being a student in photography classes.**

[The phrases in bold type are parallel because they have the same grammatical form.]

Paraphrase: Restatement of information from a source, using your own words. (See 46c.)

Parenthetical Elements: Nonessential words, phrases, and clauses set off by commas, dashes, or parentheses.

Participles: Verb forms that may be part of the complete verb or function as adjectives or adverbs. The present participle ends in *-ing*, and the past participle usually ends in *-ed, -d, -n* or *-t*. (See **phrases** and 17b.)

Present participles: *running, sleeping, digging*
She is running for mayor in this campaign.

Past participles: *walked, deleted, chosen*
The elected candidate will take office in January.

Parts of Speech: The eight classes into which words are grouped according to their function, place, meaning, and use in a sentence: *nouns, pronouns, verbs, adjectives, adverbs, prepositions, conjunctions,* and *interjections.*

Passive Voice: See **voice.**

Past Participle: See **participles.**

Perfect Progressive Tense: See **verb tenses.**

Perfect Tenses: See **verb tenses.**

Person: There are three "persons" in English. (See 19a.)

First person: the person(s) speaking (*I* or *we*)
Second person: the person(s) spoken to (*you*)
Third person: the person(s) spoken about (*he, she, it, they, anyone,* etc.)

Personal Pronouns: Refer to people or things. (See 19a.)

PERSONAL PRONOUNS	Subject	Object	Possessive
Singular			
First person	I	me	my, mine
Second person	you	you	your, yours
Third person	he, she, it	him, her, it	his, her, hers, its
Plural			
First person	we	us	our, ours
Second person	you	you	your, yours
Third person	they	them	their, theirs

Phrasal Verbs: Verbs that have two or three words following the verb that help to indicate the meaning. (See 56b.)

Phrases: Groups of related words without subjects and predicates. (See Chapter 23.)

Verb phrases function as verbs.

> She **has been eating** too much sugar.
> *(verb phrase)*

Noun phrases function as nouns.

> A **major winter storm** hit **the eastern coast of Maine.**
> *(noun phrase)*   *(noun phrase)*

Prepositional phrases usually function as modifiers.

> That book **of hers** is overdue at the library.
> *(prepositional phrase)*

Participial phrases, gerund phrases, infinitive phrases, appositive phrases, and absolute phrases function as adjectives, adverbs, or nouns.

> **Participial Phrase:** I saw people **staring at my peculiar-looking haircut.**
> **Gerund Phrase: Making copies of videotapes** can be illegal.
> **Infinitive Phrase:** He likes **to give expensive presents.**
> **Appositive Phrase:** You ought to see Dr. Elman, **a dermatologist.**
> **Absolute Phrase: The test done,** he sighed with relief.

Plagiarism: Action that results when writers fail to document a source so that the words and ideas of someone else are presented as the writer's own work. (See 47c.)

Possessive Pronouns: See **personal pronouns, noun determiners,** and 19a.

Predicate Adjectives: See **subject complement.**

Predicate Nominatives: See **subject complement.**

Predicate: Words or groups of words that express action or state of being in a sentence and consist of one or more verbs, plus any complements or modifiers.

Prefixes: Word parts added to the beginning of words. (See 39c.3.)

Prefix	Word
bio- (life)	biography
mis- (wrong, bad)	misspell

Prepositions: Link and relate their objects (usually nouns or pronouns) to some other word or words in a sentence. Prepositions usually precede their objects but may follow the objects and appear at the end of the sentence. (See Chapters 21 and 61.)

> The waiter gave the check **to my date** by mistake.
>   *(prepositional phrase)*

> I wonder **what** she is asking **for.**
> *(object of the preposition) (preposition)*

Prepositional Phrases: See **phrases.**

Progressive Tenses: See **verb tenses.**

Pronouns: Words that substitute for nouns. (See 18b.) Pronouns should refer to previously stated nouns, called antecedents.

> When **Josh** came in, **he** brought some firewood.
> *(antecedent)* *(pronoun)*

Forms of pronouns: personal, demonstrative, relative, interrogative, indefinite, possessive, reflexive, and reciprocal.

Pronoun Case: Refers to the form of the pronoun that is needed in a sentence. See **subject, direct objects, indirect objects,** and **case,** and 19a.

Pronoun Reference: The relationship between the pronoun and the noun (antecedent) for which it is substituting. (See 19b.)

Proper Nouns: Refer to specific people, places, and things. Proper nouns are always capitalized. (See Chapter 35.)

> Copenhagen   Honda   House of Representatives   Spanish

Quotation: The record of the exact words of a written or spoken source, set off by quotation marks. (See 46d.)

Reciprocal Pronouns: Pronouns that refer back to individual parts of plural terms. (See 18b.8.)

Reflexive Pronouns: Pronouns that show someone or something in the sentence is acting for itself or on itself. Because a reflexive pronoun must refer to a word in a sentence, it is not the subject or direct object. If used to show emphasis, reflexive pronouns are called *intensive pronouns.* (See 18b.7.)

Singular	Plural
First person: *myself*	First person: *ourselves*
Second person: *yourself*	Second person: *yourselves*
Third person: *himself, herself, itself*	Third person: *themselves*

> She returned the book **herself** rather than giving it to her roommate to
> *(reflexive pronoun)*
> bring back.

Relative Pronouns: Pronouns that show the relationship of a dependent clause to a noun in the sentence. Relative pronouns substitute for nouns already mentioned in sentences and introduce adjective or noun clauses. (See 18b.3.)

> **Relative pronouns:** *that, which, who, whom, whose*
>
> This was the movie **that** won the Academy Award.

Restrictive Clauses and Phrases: See **essential and nonessential clauses and phrases.**

Run-on Sentences: See **fused sentences** and 6b.

Sentences: Groups of words that have at least one independent clause (a complete unit of thought with a subject and predicate). (See Chapter 26.) Sentences can be classified by their structure as *simple, compound, complex,* and *compound-complex*.

> **Simple:** One independent clause
> **Compound:** Two or more independent clauses
> **Complex:** One or more independent clauses and one or more dependent clauses
> **Compound-complex:** Two or more independent clauses and one or more dependent clauses

Sentences can also be classified by their function as *declarative, interrogative, imperative,* and *exclamatory*.

> **Declarative:** Makes a statement.
> **Interrogative:** Asks a question.
> **Imperative:** Issues a command.
> **Exclamatory:** Makes an exclamation.

Sentence Diagrams: A method of showing relationships within a sentence.

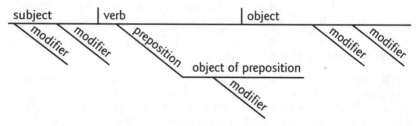

Marnie's cousin, who has no taste in food, ordered a hamburger with coleslaw at the Chinese restaurant.

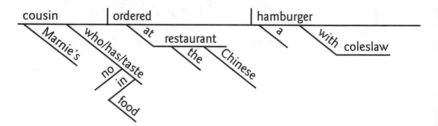

Sentence Fragment: See **fragments.**

Simple Sentence: See **sentences** and 26b.2.

Simple Tenses: See **verb tenses.**

Slang: Terms that are either invented or are given new definitions in order to be novel or unconventional. They are generally considered to be inappropriate in formal writing. (See 42b.)

Specific Words: Words that identify items in a group. (See 42e.) See also **general words.**

Split Infinitives: Phrases in which modifiers are inserted between *to* and the verb. Some people object to split infinitives, but others consider them grammatically acceptable. Some dictionaries now accept split infinitives.

to quickly turn to easily reach to forcefully enter

Standard English: Generally accepted language that conforms to established rules of grammar, sentence structure, punctuation, and spelling. (See 42a.)

Subject: The word or words in a sentence that act or are acted upon by the verb or are linked by the verb to another word or words in the sentence. The *simple subject* includes only the noun or other main word or words, and the *complete subject* includes all the modifiers with the subject. (See Chapter 22.)

Harvey objected to his roommate's alarm going off at 9 A.M.

[*Harvey* is the subject.]

Every single one of the people in the room heard her giggle.

[The simple subject is *one*; the complete subject is the whole phrase.]

Subject Complement: The noun or adjective in the predicate (*predicate noun* or *adjective*) that refers to the same entity as the subject in sentences with linking verbs, such as *is/are, feel, look, smell, sound, taste,* and *seem.*

She feels **happy.** He is a **pharmacist.**
(subject complement) *(subject complement)*

Subject Case of Pronouns: See **personal pronouns** and 19a.1.

Subject-Verb Agreement: Agreement in number and person between subjects and verb endings in sentences. (See Chapter 7.)

Subjunctive Mood: See **mood.**

Subordinating Conjunctions: Words such as *although, if, until,* and *when* that join two clauses and subordinate one to the other.

She is late. She overslept.

She is late **because** she overslept.

Subordination: The act of placing one clause in a subordinate or dependent relationship to another in a sentence because it is less important and is dependent for its meaning on the other clause. (See 13b.)

Suffix: Word part added to the end of a word. (See 39c.3.)

Suffix	Word
-ful	careful
-less	nameless

Summary: Brief restatement of the main idea in a source, using your own words. (See 46b.)

Superlative Forms of Adjectives and Adverbs: See **adjectives** and **adverbs** and 20c.

Synonyms: Words with similar meanings.

Word	Synonym
damp	moist
pretty	attractive

Tense: See **verb tense.**

Tone: The attitude or level of formality reflected in the word choices of a piece of writing. (See 11c and 42c.)

Transitions: Words in sentences that show relationships between sentences and paragraphs. (See Chapter 15.)

Transitive Verbs: See **verbs.**

Two-Word Verbs: See **phrasal verbs.**

Verbals: Words that are derived from verbs but do not act as verbs in sentences. Three types of verbals are *infinitives, participles,* and *gerunds.* (See 17b.)

> **Infinitives:** *to* + verb
>
> to wind   to say

> **Participles:** Words used as modifiers or with helping verbs. The present participle ends in -*ing,* and many past participles end in -*ed.*
>
> The dog is **panting.**   He bought only **used** clothing.
> *(present participle)*   *(past participle)*

> **Gerunds:** present participles used as nouns.
>
> **Smiling** was not a natural act for her.
> *(gerund)*

Verbs: Words or groups of words (verb phrases) in predicates that express action, show a state of being, or act as a link between the subject and the rest of the predicate. Verbs change form to show time (tense), mood, and voice and are classified as *transitive, intransitive,* and *linking verbs.* (See Chapter 17.)

■ Transitive verbs require objects to complete the predicate.

He **cut** the cardboard **box** with his knife.
(transitive verb)   *(object)*

- Intransitive verbs do not require objects.

  My ancient cat often **lies** on the porch.
  > (*intransitive verb*)

- Linking verbs link the subject to the following noun or adjective.

  The trees **are** bare.
  > (*linking verb*)

Verb Conjugations: The forms of verbs in various tenses. (See 17c.)

Regular:

Present

Simple present:

I walk	we walk
you walk	you walk
he, she, it walks	they walk

Present progressive:

I am walking	we are walking
you are walking	you are walking
he, she, it is walking	they are walking

Present perfect:

I have walked	we have walked
you have walked	you have walked
he, she, it has walked	they have walked

Present perfect progressive:

I have been walking	we have been walking
you have been walking	you have been walking
he, she, it has been walking	they have been walking

Past

Simple past:

I walked	we walked
you walked	you walked
he, she, it walked	they walked

Past progressive:

I was walking	we were walking
you were walking	you were walking
he, she, it was walking	they were walking

Past perfect:

I had walked	we had walked
you had walked	you had walked
he, she, it had walked	they had walked

Past perfect progressive:

I had been walking	we had been walking
you had been walking	you had been walking
he, she, it had been walking	they had been walking

Future

Simple future:

I will walk	we will walk
you will walk	you will walk
he, she, it will walk	they will walk

Future progressive:

I will be walking	we will be walking
you will be walking	you will be walking
he, she, it will be walking	they will be walking

Future perfect:

I will have walked	we will have walked
you will have walked	you will have walked
he, she, it will have walked	they will have walked

Future perfect progressive:

I will have been walking	we will have been walking
you will have been walking	you will have been walking
he, she, it will have been walking	they will have been walking

Irregular:

Present

Simple present:

I go	we go
you go	you go
he, she, it goes	they go

Present progressive:

I am going	we are going
you are going	you are going
he, she, it is going	they are going

Present perfect:

I have gone	we have gone
you have gone	you have gone
he, she, it has gone	they have gone

Present perfect progressive:

I have been going	we have been going
you have been going	you have been going
he, she, it has been going	they have been going

Past

Simple past:

I went	we went
you went	you went
he, she, it went	they went

Past progressive:

I was going	we were going
you were going	you were going
he, she, it was going	they were going

Past perfect:

I had gone	we had gone
you had gone	you had gone
he, she, it had gone	they had gone

Past perfect progressive:

I had been going	we had been going
you had been going	you had been going
he, she, it had been going	they had been going

Future

Simple:

I will go	we will go
you will go	you will go
he, she, it will go	they will go

Future progressive:

I will be going	we will be going
you will be going	you will be going
he, she, it will be going	they will be going

Future perfect:

I will have gone	we will have gone
you will have gone	you will have gone
he, she, it will have gone	they will have gone

Future perfect progressive:

I will have been going	we will have been going
you will have been going	you will have been going
he, she, it will have been going	they will have been going

Verb Phrases: See **verbs.**

Verb Tenses: The times indicated by the verb forms in the past, present, or future. (For the verb forms, see **verb conjugations** and 17c.)

Present

Simple present: Describes actions or situations that exist now and are habitually or generally true.

I **walk** to class every afternoon.

Present progressive: Indicates activity in progress, something not finished, or something continuing.

He **is studying** Swedish.

Present perfect: Describes single or repeated actions that were completed in the past or began in the past and lead up to and include the present.

She **has lived** in Alaska for two years.

Present perfect progressive: Indicates action that began in the past, continues to the present, and may continue into the future.

They **have been building** that parking garage for six months.

Past

Simple past: Describes completed actions or conditions in the past.

They **ate** breakfast in the cafeteria.

Past progressive: Indicates that past action that took place over a period of time.

He **was swimming** when the storm began.

Past perfect: Indicates that an action or event was completed before another event in the past.

No one **had heard** about the crisis when the newscast began.

Past perfect progressive: Indicates an ongoing condition in the past that has ended.

I **had been planning** my trip to Mexico when I heard about the earthquake.

Future

Simple future: Indicates actions or events in the future.

The store **will open** at 9 A.M.

Future progressive: Indicates future action that will continue for some time.

I **will be working** on that project next week.

Future perfect: Indicates action that will be completed by or before a specified time in the future.

Next summer, they **will have been** here for twenty years.

Future perfect progressive: Indicates ongoing actions or conditions until a specific time in the future.

By tomorrow, I **will have been waiting** for the delivery for one month.

Voice: Verbs are either in the *active* or *passive* voice. In the active voice, the subject performs the action of the verb. In the passive, the subject receives the action. (See 11d and 17d.)

The dog **bit** the boy.   The boy **was bitten** by the dog.
  (active verb)   *(passive verb)*

USING COMPARE AND CORRECT AND QUESTION AND CORRECT

When you know the terms you want to look up, you can use the table of contents or the index to this book. But when you do not know the term, there are two ways you can find the section you need.

1. Compare and Correct

On the following pages you will find examples of problems or errors that may be like those you want to correct. When you recognize a sentence with a problem similar to one in your sentence, you will be referred to the chapter in this book that will help you make the needed revision. The examples are grouped in sets as follows:

- About sentences
- About punctuation
- About mechanics and spelling
- About problems with words
- About ESL concerns

2. Question and Correct

Inside the back cover of the book is a series of questions writers often ask. When you read a question similar to the one you have in mind, you'll find a reference to the book chapter that will give you the answer. The questions are grouped in sets as follows:

- About writing
- About sentences
- About punctuation
- About mechanics and spelling
- About style and word choice
- About research and documentation
- About paper format (document design)
- About résumés

COMPARE AND CORRECT

Examples of Sentence Problems	Problem and Corresponding Section Number
1. We decided to shift to a zone defense, this gave us better coverage on Maravich. *Revised:* We decided to shift to a zone defense <u>and</u> this gave us better coverage on Maravich.	**1.** Comma splice. See **6a.**
2. Senator Levadi led the fight against salary hikes in Congress he hoped in that way to attract public favor. *Revised:* Senator Levadi led the fight against salary hikes in Congress <u>;</u> he hoped in that way to attract public favor.	**2.** Fused or run-on sentence. See **6b.**
3. Usually Tim *ride* his bike to class. *Revised:* Usually Tim <u>*rides*</u> his bike to class.	**3.** Incorrect subject-verb agreement. See **7a.**
4. Either the book or the magazines *is* a source of information on that topic. *Revised:* Either the book or the maga-zines <u>*are*</u> a source of information on that topic.	**4.** Incorrect subject-verb agreement. See **7d.**
5. One hundred miles *are* a long distance between gas stations. *Revised:* One hundred miles <u>*is*</u> a long distance between gas stations.	**5.** Incorrect subject-verb agreement. See **7h.**
6. *Living Legends sound* like a collec-tion of sport stories. *Revised:* *Living Legends <u>sounds</u>* like a collection of sport stories.	**6.** Incorrect subject-verb agreement. See **7i.**

7. There *is* so many problems with the television set that I'll return it to the store.
Revised: There *are* so many problems with the television set that I'll return it to the store.

7. Incorrect subject-verb agreement. See **7k.**

8. She is one of those teachers who *gives* you in-class quizzes every day.
Revised: She is one of those teachers who *give* you in-class quizzes every day.

8. Incorrect subject-verb agreement. See **7l.**

9. Owning a pet has many advantages. *Such as learning to care for an animal and learning responsibility.*
Revised: Owning a pet has many advantages, *such as learning to care for an animal and learning responsibility.*

9. Sentence fragment. See **8.**

10. *Being in Chem 114, it was* useful to have a calculator at all times.
Revised: *Being in Chem 114, I found it* useful to have a calculator at all times.

10. Dangling modifier. See **9a.**

11. The weather reporter announced that a tornado had been sighted *on the evening news.*
Revised: The weather reporter announced *on the evening news* that a tornado had been sighted.

11. Misplaced modifier. See **9b.**

12. In the training camp our mornings started with *6 A.M. wake-up calls and eating breakfast at 8 A.M.*
Revised: In the training camp our mornings started with *6 A.M. wake-up calls and 8 A.M. breakfasts.*

12. Faulty parallelism. See **10b.**

13. The best way to spend *one's* free time is to work on an activity *you* haven't done for a long time.
Revised: The best way to spend *your* free time is to work on an activity *you* haven't done for a long time.

13. Shift in person. See **11a.**

14. The hardest part for beginning skiers is to keep *their* skis pointed straight forward. To succeed *you* have to concentrate on the skis.
Revised: The hardest part for beginning skiers is to keep *their* skis pointed straight forward. To succeed *they* have to concentrate on the skis.

14. Shift in person. See **11a.**

15. Suddenly, as we *were driving* along, smoke or steam *starts* coming out from under our hood.
Revised: Suddenly, as we *were driving* along, smoke or steam *started* coming out from under our hood.

15. Shift in verb tense. See **11b.**

16. We *were driving* along, enjoying the scenery and not thinking about how long it had been since we stopped for gas. Suddenly, the motor *dies*.
Revised: We *were driving* along, enjoying the scenery and not thinking about how long it had been since we stopped for gas. Suddenly, the motor *died*.

16. Shift in verb tense. See **11b.**

17. It was desirable for all the candidates to have fluent speaking abilities, good social skills, and a *with-it appearance*.
Revised: It was desirable for all the candidates to have fluent speaking abilities, good social skills, and *fashionably current clothing*.

17. Shift in tone. See **11c.**

18. The boy had to stay home and do his homework, but *this was not wanted by him*.
Revised: The boy had to stay home and do his homework, but *he did not want to do this*.

18. Shift in voice. See **11d.**

19. The secretary said *that her boss was busy* and *could you* wait in the reception area.
Revised: The secretary said *that her boss was busy* and *that they could* wait in the reception area.

19. Shift in discourse. See **11e.**

20. Loneliness *is when* you have no real friend to turn to.
Revised: Loneliness *is a condition in which you find* you have no real friend to turn to.

20. Faulty predication. See **12.**

21. He drank too much on the job, *and* he was fired.
Revised: *Because* he drank too much on the job, he was fired.

21. Inappropriate coordination. See **13a.**

22. The fans objected to the referee's decision, *and* they began yelling insults, *so* the referee blew her whistle to call for quiet, *but* people didn't stop their hooting and stomping.
Revised: *When* the fans objected to the referee's decision, they began yelling insults. *As a result,* the referee blew her whistle to call for quiet. *But* people didn't stop their hooting and stomping.

22. Excessive coordination. See **13a.**

23. *When* I finally decided to major in public relations and advertising, it was a difficult decision.
Revised: I finally decided to major in public relations and advertising, *which* was a difficult decision.

23. Inappropriate subordination. See **13b.**

24. *The future is bright* for the high school vocational agriculture student *who* has training in microcomputers *because* computers are necessary on the modern farm, *which* requires planning and record keeping.
Revised: The high school vocational agriculture student *who* has training in microcomputers has a bright future. Computers are necessary on the modern farm *because* farming requires planning and record keeping.

24. Excessive subordination. See **13b.**

25. *Instead of a motorcycle helmet,* which I would have preferred, *a dictionary* was what my aunt chose for my *graduation present.*

25. Sentence moves from unknown to known. See **14a.**

Revised: For my *graduation present,* my aunt chose a *dictionary,* though I would have preferred *a motorcycle helmet.*

26. Automobile commercials that *do not* compare their brand to another one tend *not* to create as much audience interest.
Revised: Automobile commercials that compare their brand to another one tend to create more audience interest.

26. Negative language. See **14b.**

27. She *couldn't hardly* refuse the gift.
Revised: She *could hardly* refuse the gift.

27. Double negative. See **14c.**

28. *Selection* of the candidates was the next item on the committee's agenda.
Revised: The next item on the committee's agenda was *selecting* the candidates.

28. Uses a noun instead of a verb. See **14d.**

29. *It* was the wish of my parents that I would go to college.
Revised: *My parents* wished that I would go to college.

29. Sentence subject is not the intended subject. See **14e.**

30. A *mistake was made* in my sandwich order *by the waiter.*
Revised: The *waiter made a mistake* in my sandwich order.

30. Uses passive instead of active. See **14f.**

31. The tension in the arena was obvious. The crowd was not cheering noisily or tossing popcorn boxes around. We knew that without Terry our team wouldn't be able to win and go on to the semifinals. We tried to psych ourselves up anyway.
Revised: The tension in the arena was obvious. *For example,* the crowd was not cheering noisily or tossing popcorn boxes around. We knew that without Terry our team wouldn't be able to win and go on to the semi-finals. *But* we tried to psych ourselves up anyway.

31. Needs transitions. See **15.**

32. The homecoming queen waved enthusiastically to the crowd. She was teary-eyed but happy. She kept smiling at the TV camera as she rode by. It was easy to see how happy she was.
Revised: *Teary-eyed but happy*, the homecoming queen waved enthusiastically to the crowd. *As she rode by*, she kept smiling at the TV camera. It was easy to see how happy she was.

32. Monotonous sentence rhythm. See **16**.

33. He has *broke* his bike light and *need* a new one.
Revised: He has *broken* his bike light and *needs* a new one.

33. Incorrect verb form and ending. See **17c**.

34. If I *was* you, I'd be on time for that meeting.
Revised: If I *were* you, I'd be on time for that meeting.

34. Incorrect verb mood. See **17e**.

35. The library has a dozen *computer* and *printer* for students to use.
Revised: The library has a dozen *computers* and *printers* for students to use.

35. Incorrect use of plurals. See **18a**.

36. The committee had to make a choice between him and *I*.
Revised: The committee had to make a choice between him and *me*.

36. Incorrect pronoun case. See **19a**.

37. In Hollywood, *they* think that moviegoers are too conservative to appreciate really interesting background music.
Revised: In Hollywood, *composers who write music for movies* think moviegoers are too conservative to appreciate really interesting background music.

37. Vague pronoun reference. See **19b**.

38. Whenever the class does experiments with the lab assistants' measuring devices, *they* wind up leaving *their* equipment all over the lab tables.

38. Unclear pronoun reference. See **19b**.

Revised: Whenever the class does experiments with the lab assistants' measuring devices, *the students* wind up leaving *the lab assistants'* equipment all over the lab tables.

39. He learned how to play the bass guitar *real* well.
Revised: He learned how to play the bass guitar *very* well.

39. Incorrect use of adjective. See **20a.**

40. It will take *a* hour to finish this project.
Revised: It will take *an* hour to finish this project.

40. Incorrect use of *a*. See **20b.**

41. Taking the main street through town is *more quicker* than the bypass road.
Revised: Taking the main street through town is *quicker* than *taking* the bypass road.

41. Incorrect comparison. See **20c.**

42. She was bored *on* the subject of safe driving.
Revised: She was bored *with* the subject of safe driving.

42. Incorrect preposition. See **21.**

Examples of Punctuation Problems

Problem and Corresponding Section Number

43. Kari studied the catalog of summer courses and she decided to sign up for an introduction to anthropology.
Revised: Kari studied the catalog of summer courses, and she decided to sign up for an introduction to anthropology.

43. Comma needed in compound sentence. See **27a.**

44. When the sun had set the owls started to hoot.
Revised: When the sun had set, the owls started to hoot.

44. Comma needed after introductory clause. See **27b.**

45. Laura who is my cousin's daughter is coming for a visit.
Revised: Laura, who is my cousin's daughter, is coming for a visit.

45. Comma needed to set off nonessential clause. See **27c.**

46. *Jerrys* old VW is faster than my car but not *hers'*.
Revised: Jerry's old VW is faster than my car but not <u>hers</u>.

46. No apostrophe with the possessive pronoun. See **28a.**

47. The jury announced it's decision.
Revised: The jury announced <u>its</u> decision.

47. Apostrophe incorrectly used with possessive pronoun *its.* See **28a.**

48. Wade showed up on time for the meeting, however, it was the wrong day.
Revised: Wade showed up on time for the meeting; however, it was the wrong day.

48. Semicolon needed between independent clauses. See **29a.**

49. He preferred health foods, such as: whole wheat bread, organically grown vegetables, and caffeine-free drinks.
Revised: He preferred health foods, such as whole wheat bread, organically grown vegetables, and caffeine-free drinks.

49. Unnecessary colon. See **30a, 30f.**

50. Was Karl the one who said, "I'll bring the beer? "
Revised: Was Karl the one who said, "I'll bring the beer"?

50. Incorrect use of question mark with quotation. See **33b.**

51. The 6 P.M. news announced that the White House said "it would not confirm the truth of this story."
Revised: The 6 P.M. news announced that the White House said it would not confirm the truth of this story.

51. Incorrect use of quotation marks with a quotation. See **31a.**

52. "I would like to learn more about how tornadoes form," I said. "Here's a useful book," responded the librarian.
Revised:
  "I would like to learn more about how tornadoes form," I said.
  "Here's a useful book," responded the librarian.

52. Incorrect presenta-tion of dialogue. See **31a.**

53. He always writes cheers at the bottom of his e-mail notes.
Revised: He always writes "cheers" at the bottom of his e-mail notes.

53. Quotation marks needed. See **31c.**

54. They were hardly ever *a-part* after they met.
Revised: They were hardly ever *apart* after they met.

54. Incorrect word division at the end of a line. See **32a.**

55. For the six page paper, use one inch margins, not two inch margins.
Revised: For the six-page paper, use one-inch margins, not two-inch margins.

55. Incorrect hyphenation of two-word units. See **32c.**

56. The puppy returned with some black and white shreds in its mouth—my morning newspaper. I gulped—again.
Revised: The puppy returned with some black and white shreds in its mouth—my morning newspaper. I gulped, again.

56. Overuse of dashes. See **34a.**

Examples of Problems with Mechanics and Spelling

Problem and Corresponding Section Number

57. I took two *Economics* courses this semester, one English course, and one *History* course.
Revised: I took two *economics* courses this semester, one English course, and one *history* course.

57. Incorrect capitalization. See Section **35.**

58. 43 more names were added to the list.
Revised: *Forty-three* more names were added to the list.

58. Incorrect use of numbers. See **37.**

59. One of his favorite old movies, "Casablanca," was on the late show last night.
Revised: One of his favorite old movies, *Casablanca,* was on the late show last night.

59. Needs italics. See **38a.**

60. When winter comes, I always enjoy *planing* trip to warm beaches, even if don't always go.

60. Needs proofreading. See **39a.**

Revised: When winter comes,
I always enjoy *planning a* trip to
warm beaches, even if *I* don't
always go.

61. She *recieved* a B.A. in the *feild* of art
history.
Revised: She *received* a B.A. in the
field of art history.

61. Spelling error
(*ie/ei*). See **39c.**

62. She *discribed* the hill she would climb
tommorrow.
Revised: She *described* the hill she
would climb *tomorrow.*

62. Incorrect prefixes.
See **39c.**

63. Echo Bay is a *desireable* place to go
picnicing.
Revised: Echo Bay is a *desirable* place
to go *picnicking.*

63. Incorrect suffixes.
See **39c.**

64. Of all the various electronic *mediums,*
broadcasting via *radioes* is the most
popular.
Revised: Of all the various electronic
media, broadcasting via *radios* is the
most popular.

64. Spelling error
(plurals). See **39d.**

65. *There* train *past* through *to* quickly
to see much of the town *accept* the
station.
Revised: *Their* train *passed* through
too quickly to see much of the town
except the station.

65. Incorrect
sound-alike
words.
See **39e.**

Examples of Problems with Words	**Problem and Corresponding Section Number**

66. In the last ten years, the *mailman has*
had an increased workload because
of the tide of bulk mail *he* must
deliver.
Revised: In the last ten years, *mail
carriers have* had an increased workload because of the tide of bulk
mail *they* must deliver.

66. Sexist language.
See **40b.**

67. At 8 A.M. *in the morning* I *first* began
to feel ill.
Revised: At 8 A.M. I began to feel ill.

67. Unnecessary
words.
See **41a.**

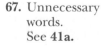

68. Tina is usually a *quick study* and can master new skills with *lightning speed.* But the computer programming course was *over her head.*
Revised: Tina is usually a *quick learner* who masters new skills *in jet-speed time.* But in the computer programming course, she *groped helplessly,* unable to cope with the material that was too advanced for her.

68. Clichés. See **41b.**

69. The legal system is intended to protect the average *guy's* rights.
Revised: The legal system is intended to protect the average *person's* rights.

69. Mixture of formal and informal language. See **42c.**

Examples of Concerns of ESL Students	**Problem and Corresponding Section Number**
70. I have *starting* my homework. *Revised:* I have *started* my homework.	**70.** Verb forms with helping verbs. See **56a.**
71. If Mr. Patel had more time, he *may* join us. *Revised:* If Mr. Patel had more time, he *would* join us.	**71.** Verbs with conditionals. See **56a.**
72. He *cut up it.* *Revised:* He *cut it up.*	**72.** Phrasal verbs. See **56b.**
73. Miranda appreciates *to join* the group. *Revised:* Miranda appreciates *joining* the group.	**73.** Verbs with *-ing* and *to* + verb. See **56c.**
74. Mussah going to visit his cousin lives in Denver. *Revised:* Mussah *is* going to visit his cousin *who* lives in Denver.	**74.** Omitted words. See **57.**
75. The book she was reading *it* was very helpful. *Revised:* The book she was reading was very helpful.	**75.** Repeated words. See **58.**
76. Sumanas was not used to the *weathers* in Minnesota. *Revised:* Sumanas was not used to the *weather* in Minnesota.	**76.** Count and noncount nouns. See **59.**

77. His favorite snack is a *red big* apple.
Revised: His favorite snack is a <u>big red</u> apple.

77. Adjective order. See **60b**.

78. Whenever Mr. Tran sees book on geography, he wants to buy it.
Revised: Whenever Mr. Tran sees <u>a</u> book on geography, he wants to buy it.

78. Articles (*a/an/the*). See **60c**.

79. He had *much* problems with his computer.
Revised: He had <u>many</u> problems with his computer.

79. Incorrect choice of *much/many*. See **60d**.

80. The meeting will be *at* Monday.
Revised: The meeting will be <u>on</u> Monday.

80. Incorrect preposition. See **61**.

INDEX

A

a, an, the, articles, 345, 385
  adjectives and, 102–3
  indefinite pronouns and, 98
  with nouns, 102–3, ESL 323–25
  sexist language and, 196
Abbreviations, 176–78
  apostrophes with, 143–44
  dates, 177
  documentation, 178
  initials as names (acronyms), 178
  Latin expressions, 178
  measurements, 177
  with numbers, 176
  periods with, 161–62
  places/geographic regions, 177
  postal addresses, 177
  time, 177
  titles with names, 176–77
Absolute phrase, 364
Absolutes, 355
Abstract nouns, 355
Abstract words, 207–8, 324
accept, except, using, 192, 345
Acronyms. *See* Initials as names
  (acronyms)
Active verbs, 337
Active voice. *See* voice
Addresses
  commas in, 137
  numbers with, 180
Adjective clauses, 355. *See also*
  Dependent clauses
Adjectives, 100–105, 380
  articles *a, an, the* with, 102–3
  commas with, 135–36
  comparisons and, 104–5
  conciseness and, 198

  definition of, 100
  -ed endings with, 100
  -er, -est endings with, 104
  forms of, 355
  order of, ESL 322
  placement of, ESL 321–22
  predicate adjective, 364
  well, using, 101
Adverb clauses, 116–17, 355. *See also*
  Dependent clauses
  marker words for, 116
  punctuation with, 117
Adverbs, 100–105
  comparisons and, 104–5
  conciseness and, 198
  coordination with, 57
  definition of, 100
  forms of, 355
  -ly endings with, 100–101
  modifying verbs with, 100–101
  order of, ESL 322
  placement of, ESL 321–22
  repeated words and, ESL 319
  so, such, too, with, 101
advice, advise, using, 345
affect, effect, using, 192, 345
Agreement, 355–56. *See also*
  Consistency (avoiding shifts);
  Subject-verb agreement
ain't, using, 346
Airplanes, underlining/italics
  with, 182
all, verb agreement, 89
all ready, already, using, 192, 346
all right, alright, 346
all together, altogether, using, 192, 346
alot, a lot, using, 346
a.m., p.m. or A.M., P.M., using, 346

Ambiguity, avoiding, 160
Ambiguous terms, 21
American Psychological Association
    (APA), 281
among, between, using, 346
amount, number, using, 346
Amounts, subject-verb agreement,
    38–39
an, using, 346
Analogy, 16–17
Analyzing, writing process and, 1
and
    beginning sentence with, 346
    as joining word, 33–34
    for transition, 66
and etc., using, 346
Antecedents, 40, 356
Antonyms, 356
any
    with nouns, ESL 325–26
    verb agreement, 38, 89
anybody, any body, 346
any more, anymore, using, 192
any one, anyone, using, 192–93, 346
anyways, anywheres, using, 347
APA. *See* American Psychological
    Association (APA)
APA-style documentation, 281–91.
        See also Citing Internet
        sources
    footnotes, 284
    in-text citations, 281–84
        books, 282–84
        personal communications, 284
        World Wide Web, 284
    list of references (*See* References
    list, APA-style)
Apostrophes, 142–44
    consistency in use, 144
    with contractions, 143
    document design, 332
    with plurals, 143–44
    with possessives, 88, 142, 381
    unnecessary use of, 144
    using, 143
Appositive phrase, 364
Appositives, 356
Appropriate coordination, 57
Appropriate subordination, 58–59

Appropriate words. *See* Word choice
Argument, 20–30
    audience, appeals to, 21–22
    claims, 24–25
    common ground and, 22–23
    credibility and, 21
    deductive/inductive reasoning, 27
    fallacies and, 27–29
    logic with, 26–27
    organizing of, 29–30
    support for, 25
    topics for, 23–24
    warrants with, 25–26
    writing/reading, 20–21
Articles, 380. *See also* Noun deter-
    miners
Articles in periodicals
    CBE-style documentation, 309
    Chicago-style documentation,
        303–4
    MLA documentation for, 267–68
    note taking from, 217
as, as if, as though, like, using, 347
assure, ensure, insure, using, 347
Attack the person *(ad hominem),* 29
Audience, 2–3
    in argument, 21–22
    revision and, 11–12
Auxiliary verbs, 356
awful, awfully, using, 347
a while, awhile, using, 193
awhile, a while, using, 347

B

bad, badly, using, 347
badly, well, using, 101
Bandwagon argument, 29
Base form of verbs, 75
because, if, when, with clauses, 116–17
Begging the question (circular
        reasoning), 28
beside, besides, using, 348
between, among, using, 348
Bibliography, working, 216–17
Biographies, 215
Books
    APA-style documentation, 282–84,
        286–87
    CBE-style documentation, 309

Books *(cont.)*
 Chicago-style documentation, 301–3
 MLA-style documentation, 251, 256–57, 263–66
 online versions, 240
 working bibliography for, 217
Boolean search terms, 242–43
Brackets
 document design, 333
 with parentheses, 170
 with quotations, 170, 230
Brainstorming, 4–5, 30
breath, breathe, using, 348
Buried subjects, agreement with, 36–37
but
 as first word in sentence, 348
 as joining word, 33–34
 for transition, 66

C
can, could, using, 85
can, may, using, 348
can't hardly, using, 348
Capitalization, 173–76, 382
 days/months/holidays, 173
 directly quoted speech, 174
 family relationships, 174
 historical documents, 173
 holy books, 174
 initials as names (acronyms), 174
 institutions/organizations, 173
 lists of sentences, 175
 members of groups, 173
 peoples/their languages, 173
 periods/events, 173
 persons, 173
 places/geographic regions, 173
 place words, 174
 prefixes, 175
 of pronoun *I* and interjection *O*, 174
 quoting information and, 229
 religions/their followers, 173
 sentence's first word, 174
 Supreme Being, 174
 titles of papers, 329–30
 titles of works, 174

 titles with names, 174
 trademarks, 173
 words following prefixes, 175
Cardinal numbers, 362
Case, 356. *See also* Possessives; Pronoun case
Catalogs, library, 214–15
 online versions, 239
Cause and effect, 16
CBE. *See* Council of Biology Editors (CBE)
CBE-style documentation, 306–10
 directory of examples, 308
 in-text citations, 307
 models for entries, 307–8
 reference list
  audiovisual materials, 309
  books, 309
  electronic sources, 309–10
  periodicals, 309
CD-ROMs, 215
 APA documentation for, 289
 CBE-style documentation for, 309–10
 MLA documentation for, 268–69
Chicago Manual of Style, 254, 299
Chicago-style documentation, 299–306
 bibliography/notes, 301–6
  books, 301–3
  electronic sources, 304–5
  film/videotape, 306
  government publications, 305
  interviews, 305
  periodicals, 303–4
  personal communications/ e-mail, 306
  quoted sources, 306
  sound recordings, 306
 directory of examples, 301
 model for entries, 300–301
 notes in, 299–300
choose, chose, using, 348
Citing Internet sources. *See also* Plagiarism
 APA style, 252–54
  abstracts, 253
  electronic sources, 252–53
  journals, 253–54
  newspaper article, 253

CBE style, 254

Chicago Manual of Style, 254

CIC style, 254

IFLA style, 254

Internet Public Library style, 254

MLA style, 248–52

   article in database, 251

   books, 251

   citing WWW sources, 249–50

   e-mail postings, 252

   in-text citations, 249

   journal/periodical articles, 251–52

   poems, 251

   professional/personal sites, 251

   scholarly projects, 250

   synchronous communications, 252

   National Library of Canada style, 254

Claims, 24–25

Clarity, sentence, 61–64

   active *vs.* passive voice, 63, 378

   double negatives, 62, 378

   intended subjects, 63, 378

   from known to unknown, 61, 377

   positives *vs.* negatives, 61–62, 378

   verbs for nouns, 62–63, 378

Classification, 17–18

Clauses, 113–17

   adjective, 116

   adverb, 116–17, 122

   agreement and, 38

   clarity and, 71–72

   conciseness and, 198

   conditional, ESL 314

   dashes with, 166

   definition of, 113, 356

   dependent clauses (*See* Dependent clauses)

   essential, 119–20

   independent (*See* Independent clauses)

   introductory, 130–31

   nonessential, 120–21

   punctuation with, 57, 117, 127–28, 130–33

   in series, 134–35

   subordinate (*See* Dependent clauses)

Clichés, 200, 356, 384

cloth, clothe, using, 348

Clustering and branching, 5

Coherence in paragraphs, 14

Collaboration, 8–10

Collective nouns, 38–39, 86, 356

Colloquialisms, 201–2, 356, ESL 328

Colons, 151–53

   document design, 332

   between elements, 152

   at end of sentence, 151–53

   meaning of, 152

   with quotation marks, 157

   with quotations, 152–53, 230

   in salutations, 152

   to separate clauses, 152

   with series/lists, 151

   unnecessary use of, 153, 381

Combining sentences, 69–70

Commands, 84, 360

   exclamation points with, 164

Commas

   in addresses, 137

   with adjectives, 135–36

   after introductory words, phrases, clauses, 130–31, 380

   avoiding confusion with, 138–39

   with complex sentences, 127

   in compound sentences, 33, 127–29, 380

   connectors with, 148

   with coordinating conjunctions, 57, 127

   with dates, 137

   document design, 332

   with essential/nonessential word groups, 132–33, 380

   in geographical names, 137

   with numbers, 137

   with opening/closings of letters, 139

   with phrases, 139

   with quotations, 139, 229

   with series/lists, 134–35

   set off questions, 139

   unnecessary use of, 140–41

Comma splices, 33–34, 357, 374

Common nouns, 86, 357

Community sources, 216

Company names, agreement and, 39

Comparative, 104, 357
compared to, compared with, using, 348
Comparison and contrast, development with, 19–20
Comparisons, 104–5, 380
    adjectives/adverbs in, 104
    completion of, 105
    double comparisons, 105
    -er/-est endings with, 104–5
    irregular forms, 104
    omissions with, 95
Complements, 39, 357
Complex sentences, 125, 357, 366
    punctuation with, 127–28
Compound-complex sentences, 125, 357, 366
Compound nouns, 357
Compound sentences, 33–34, 124, 366
    commas in, 33, 127–29
    coordinating conjunctions with, 127
    definition of, 357, 366
    pronouns in, 93–94
    punctuation in, 127
    semicolons in, 148
Compound subjects
    agreement with, 37, 97
Computers, 214. *See also* Internet
    drafting with, 31
    editing/proofreading with, 32
    note taking with, 217
    organizing with, 31
    outlining with, 32
    planning with, 30–31
    revising with, 31–32
    spell checkers, 185–86
Conclusions, paragraphs and, 14–15
Concrete nouns, 357
Concrete words, 207–8
Conditionals, ESL 314–15
Conjunctions, 57, 357
    coordinating, 57, 114, 127
    correlative, 50, 358
    subordinating, 58–59
Conjunctive adverbs, 57, 114, 357
Connectors, 148
Connotation, 208–9, 357

Consistency (avoiding shifts), 52–55, 358
    in discourse, 54–55, 376
    in number, 53
    person and, 52–53, 375–76
    in tone, 53, 376
    in verb tense, 53, 376
    in voice, 54, 376
Contractions, 62, 123, 143
Contrast and comparison, 19–20
Coordinating conjunctions, 57, 114, 127
    "fanboys" rule for, 128
Coordination, 57–58
    appropriate, 57
    conjunctions/adverbs with, 57
    excessive, 58, 377
    faulty, 359
    inappropriate, 57–58, 376
Correlative conjunctions, 50, 358
could, can, using, 85
could of, using, 348
Council of Biology Editors (CBE), 254
Count nouns, 358, ESL 319–20, ESL 323
    a/an/the with, ESL 324–25
Cover letters, 341–42

D

Dangling modifiers, 45–47, 358, 375
Dashes
    beginning/ending of sentence, 166
    document design, 332
    marking interruptions with, 166
    overuse of, 382
    with quotation marks, 157
    setting off phrases/clauses containing commas, 166
data, using, 348
Databases, 215
    APA documentation for, 289
    Chicago-style documentation for, 304
    MLA documentation for, 251, 268
Dates
    abbreviations for, 177
    commas with, 137
    numbers with, 180
Days, months, holidays, capitalization with, 173

Decimals, percentages, numbers with, 180
Declarative mood, 84
Declarative sentence, 366
Deductive reasoning, 27
Defining information, 1
Demonstrative pronouns, 88, 358
-d endings, with verbs, 75
Denotation, 208–9, 358
Dependent clauses, 115–17, 122–23
  adjective, 116
  adverb, 116–17, 122
  because/if/when with, 116–17
  in complex sentences, 125
  in compound-complex sentences, 122–23
  defined, 115, 358
  marker words signifying, 116–17, 127–28
  punctuation with, 117, 127–28
  starting sentences with, 122–23
  who/which/that with, 97–98, 116
Description, 15–16
desert, dessert, using, 193
Determiner. *See* Noun determiners
Development. *See also* Patterns of organization
  of paragraphs, 14
  revision and, 12
Diagrams. *See* Sentence diagrams
Dialogue, 155–56, 381
Dictionary, checking for capitalization, 173
different from, different than, using, 349
Direct discourse, 54–55, 358
Direct objects, 358
Direct quotations, 154–55
  brackets with, 170
  ellipses with, 171–72
Discussing, examining, 1
Document design, 329–34
  headings/subheadings, 330–31
  page preparation, 331–32
  spacing for punctuation, 332–33
  titles, 329–30
  visual appeal, 333–34
Documenting sources, 235–37. *See also* Citing Internet sources; Note taking; Plagiarism
  abbreviations for, 178

APA style (*See* APA-style documentation)
CBE style (*See* CBE-style documentation)
Chicago Manual of Style (*See* Chicago-style documentation)
MLA style (*See* MLA-style documentation)
styles for various disciplines, 310–11
Double comparisons, 105
Double negatives, 62
Doubling consonants guideline, 187
Doubt, indicating with question marks, 163
Doubt cause *(post hoc, ergo propter hoc),* 28
Drafting, 7

E

each, as indefinite, 38
-ed endings
  with adjectives, 100
  spelling rules for, 190
  with verbs, 75, 79
Editing, 12–13, 32
effect, affect, using, 349
either . . . or
  agreement and, 37–38
  parallelism and, 50
Either . . . or argument, 29
Electronic job searches, 343–44
Ellipses, 171–72, 230, 358
E-mail, 30
  Chicago-style documentation, 306
  MLA-style documentation, 252, 272
Emphasis
  dashes for, 166
  exclamation point for, 164–65
  transitions for, 65
  underlining/italics for, 182
Endnotes, MLA-style documentation, 255
End punctuation, 161–65, 332
  with quotations, 230
English as a second language (ESL), 313–28. *See also specific category headings*
  adjectives/adverbs, 321–22, 385

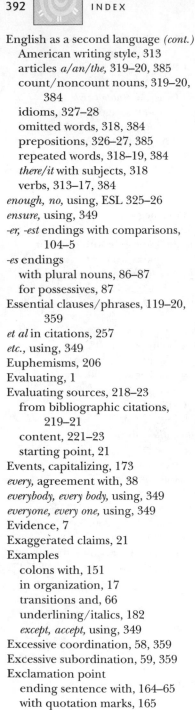

English as a second language *(cont.)*
  American writing style, 313
  articles *a/an/the,* 319–20, 385
  count/noncount nouns, 319–20,
    384
  idioms, 327–28
  omitted words, 318, 384
  prepositions, 326–27, 385
  repeated words, 318–19, 384
  there/it with subjects, 318
  verbs, 313–17, 384
enough, no, using, ESL 325–26
ensure, using, 349
-er, -est endings with comparisons,
    104–5
-es endings
  with plural nouns, 86–87
  for possessives, 87
Essential clauses/phrases, 119–20,
    359
et al in citations, 257
etc., using, 349
Euphemisms, 206
Evaluating, 1
Evaluating sources, 218–23
  from bibliographic citations,
    219–21
  content, 221–23
  starting point, 21
Events, capitalizing, 173
every, agreement with, 38
everybody, every body, using, 349
everyone, every one, using, 349
Evidence, 7
Exaggerated claims, 21
Examples
  colons with, 151
  in organization, 17
  transitions and, 66
  underlining/italics, 182
  except, accept, using, 349
Excessive coordination, 58, 359
Excessive subordination, 59, 359
Exclamation point
  ending sentence with, 164–65
  with quotation marks, 165
Exclamatory sentence, 366
Explanations
  colons with, 151
  dashes with, 166

parentheses with, 169
transitions with, 66

F

-f, -fe endings, spelling rule for, 191
Fallacies, 27–29
False analogy, 28–29
Family relationships, capitalization
    with, 174
farther, further, using, 349
Faulty coordination, 359
Faulty parallelism, 50, 359, 375
Faulty predication, 55–56, 359, 377
few, fewer, with nouns, ESL 325–26
fewer/less, using, 349
Fillers, avoiding, 197–98
Films
  APA-style documentation, 290
  Chicago-style documentation,
    306
  MLA-style documentation, 271
  underlining/italics, 182
First person, 92
Footnotes, APA documentation for,
    284
for, as joining word, 33–34
Foreign words, underlining/italics
    with, 182
Formal tone, 53, 203–5
Fractions, forming with hyphens,
    159
Fragments, 359. *See also* Sentence
    fragments
Freewriting, 4, 30
fun, using, 349
Functional résumé, 338
Fused sentences, 34, 359, 374
Future tense of verbs, 78–79, 372.
    See also Verb tense

G

General words, 206–7, 359, 367
Geographical names
  article *the* with, ESL 324
  commas with, 137
Gerund phrases, 364
Gerunds, 74–75, 359, ESL 314, ESL
    316–17, ESL 324
goes, says, using, 349
gone, went, using, 349

good, well, using, 350
got, have, using, 350
great, using, 350
Groups, capitalization of, 173

H

Handwritten papers, 154, 166, 330
has, had, with verb forms, 75–77
Hasty generalization, 28
have, got, using, 350
have, of, using, 350
Headings, subheadings, 330–31
hear, here, using, 193
Helping (auxiliary) verbs, 359, ESL 314
Higher-Order Concerns (HOCs), 11–12
hisself, using, 350
Historical documents, capitalization with, 173
Holidays, capitalization of, 173
Holy books, capitalization with, 174
Homonyms, 185–86, 360
  spelling, 192–93, 383
hopefully, using, 350
Hyphenated words, spelling rules for, 190–92
Hyphens, 158–60
  for avoiding ambiguity, 160
  dividing words with, 158–59, 382
  document design, 332
  forming compound words, 159
  joining word units, 159–60, 382
  with letters to words, 160
  with prefixes/suffixes, 160

I

I, capitalization with, 174
I, me, using, 95, 350
-ic endings, spelling and, 189
Idiomatic preposition, 108
Idioms, 360, ESL 327–28
ie, ei, spelling guidelines, 186
if, when, unless, with conditional clauses, ESL 314
Illustrations
  dashes with, 166
  organizing with, 17
Imperative mood, 84, 360
Imperative sentence, 366

imply, infer, using, 350
Inappropriate coordination, 57–58, 376
Inappropriate subordination, 59, 377
Indefinite pronouns, 89, 196, 360
Indentations
  document design, 331
  quoting sources, 228
Independent clauses, 114, 122
  colons with, 152
  commas with, 127–28
  in complex sentences, 125
  in compound-complex sentences, 125
  in compound sentences, 124
  conjunctive adverbs with, 57, 114
  coordinators with, 57, 114
  definition of, 360
  marker words with, 127
  punctuation with, 57
  semicolons with, 33–34, 127–28, 148
Indexes
  Academic Information Index, 245
  library, 215
  online versions, 241
Indicative mood, 84, 360
Indirect discourse, 54–55, 360
Indirect object, 92, 360
Indirect quotations, 154–55, 358
Inductive reasoning, 27
Infinitive phrase, 364
Infinitives (to + verb), 46, 75, 360, ESL 316–17
Inflated expressions, 206
Informal tone, 53, 203–5, ESL 328
Information. *See* Sources of information; Web resources
-ing endings, with verbs, 46, 50, 74, ESL 314, ESL 316–17
Initials as names (acronyms)
  abbreviations with, 178
  capitalization with, 174
Institutions/organizations, capitalization with, 173
insure, using, 350
Intensifiers, 360. *See also* Emphasis
Intentional fragments, 44
Interjections, 164, 360

International Federation of Library Associations and Institutions (IFLA), 254
Internet, 218, 239–43. *See also* Citing Internet sources; Web resources
  access to sites, 248
  evaluating sources, 246–47
  MLA documentation for, 269–70
  online sources, 215
  search engines and, 239
  search tools for, 240–41
  strategies for searching, 241–42
Interpreting, writing process and, 1
Interrogative pronouns, 89, 360
Interrogative sentence, 366
Interruptions, marking with dashes, 166
Interviews/surveys, 216
In-text citations
  APA style, 281–84
  CBE style, 307
  MLA style, 255–59
Intransitive verbs, 361, 369
Introductory paragraphs/clauses, 14–15, 130–31
irregardless, using, 350
Irregular verbs, 79–82, 360
  conjugated lists, 80–82, 370–71
  forms for, 79
Irrelevant proof for support *(non sequitor)*, 28
is when, is why, is where, is because, using, 351
it, agreement and, 40
Italics. *See* Underlining/italics
it is, subject placement and, 110
its, it's, using, 193, 351

J

Jargon, 198, 206, 361
Joining words, 33–34
Journal. *See* Writers notebook/journal
Journalist's (reporter's) questions, 6–7, 212
Journals
  APA online citation, 253
  MLA documentation for, 267

MLA online citation, 251
online versions, 245

K

Keyword searches, 343–44
kind, sort, using, 351

L

Languages, capitalization of, 173
Later-Order Concerns (LOCs), 12–13
Latin expressions
  abbreviations with, 178
  underling/italics with, 182
lay, lie, using, 351
leave, let, using, 351
less, fewer, using, 351, ESL 325–26
let, leave, using, 351
Letters, parentheses with, 169
Levels of formality, 203–5
Libraries, 214–15
  general reference sources, 215
  indexes/catalogs/databases, 215
  Internet Public Library, 254
  National Library of Canada, 254
Library of Congress Subject Headings, 211, 215, 218
like, as, using, 351
like for, using, 351
Linking verbs, 39, 73, 100, 112, 361
  definition of, 369
Listing, 4–5
Lists. *See* Series/lists
little, few, using, ESL 325–26
Logical fallacies, 27–29
-ly endings
  with adverbs, 100
  spelling rules and, 189

M

Magazines. *See* Periodicals
man, alternative words for, 195
Maps/charts, MLA-style documentation, 272
Marker words, 116–17. *See* Subordinating conjunctions with clauses, 127–28
Masculine pronouns, 195–96
may, can, using, 351
may, might, using, 85
may, verb agreement, 89

Measurements, abbreviations for, 177
Medium tone, 203–5
Members of groups, capitalization with, 173
Meta-search engines, 241
Microfiche, 214
might, may, using, 85
Misplaced modifiers, 47–49, 361, 375
MLA. *See* Modern Language Association (MLA)
MLA-style documentation, 217, 255–80. *See also* Citing Internet sources
  endnotes, 255, 259–60
  in-text citations, 255–59
    books, 256–57
    electronic source, 259
    indirect source, 258
    two or more sources, 259
    work listed by title, 259
  Works Cited list (*See* Works Cited, MLA style)
Modal verbs, 85, 361, ESL 314
Mode of discourse, 54–55, 361
Modern Language Association (MLA), 255
Modifiers, 45–49. *See also* Adjectives; Adverbs
  dangling, 45–47
  definition of, 361
  misplaced, 47–49
Months, capitalization of, 173
Mood, 84, 361
more, verb agreement, 89
most, using, 351
most, verb agreement, 89
Movies. *See* Films
much, many, using, 385, ESL 325–26
Musical compositions
  MLA documentation, 271–72
  underlining/italics, 182
must, ought to, using, 85

N

Narration, 15
National Library of Canada, 254
Negatives, 62
neither . . . nor
  agreement and, 37–38
  parallelism and, 50

Newsgroups/listservs, 241–42, 245
Newspapers
  APA online citation, 253
  APA-style documentation, 288
  Chicago-style documentation, 303
  MLA documentation for, 267
  MLA online citation, 252
  online access to, 240, 245
  underlining/italics, 182
no, with nouns, ESL 325
Noncount nouns, 361, ESL 319–25
none, verb agreement, 89
Nonessential clauses/phrases, 120–21, 359, 361
Nonparallel structure, 50, 361
Nonrestrictive clause/phrases, 120–21, 361
nor, as joining word, 33–34
Notebook. *See* Writers notebook/journal
Note taking. *See also* Plagiarism
  from articles, 217
  from books, 217
  cards for, 216–17
  with computers, 217
  paraphrasing information, 225–26
  punctuation with, 229–31
  quoting information, 227–28
  summarizing information, 223–24
  types of quotations, 228–29
  writing notes, 223
not only . . . but
  agreement and, 37–38
  parallelism and, 50
Noun clauses, 362
Noun determiners, 102–3, 362, 380
Noun phrases, 362, 364
Nouns
  abstract, ESL 324
  adjective modifiers with, 100
  collective, 38–39, 86
  count/noncount, 358, 361, ESL 319–20, ESL 323–25
  definition of, 362
  endings for, 87–88
  plural, 86–87
  possessive forms, 87–88, 142
  proper, 186
  singular, 86
  verbs for, 62–63, 198, 378

nowheres, using, 351
Number, 362
    avoiding shifts in, 53
    pronoun reference and, 97
number, amount, using, 351
Numbers, 179–81
    abbreviations with, 176
    addresses, 180
    commas with, 137
    dates, 180
    decimals/percentages, 180
    figure-word combination, 180
    hyphens with, 159
    for identification, 180
    large round numbers, 180
    in legal/commercial writing, 180
    pagination, 180
    parentheses with, 169
    in series/statistics, 180
    spelling out, 179–80, 382
    time of day, 180

O

O, interjection, 174
Object case, 92–93
    with *who/whom,* 94–95, 353
    with prepositions, 92–93, 362
    with pronouns, 92, 362
Object complement, 362
Objects, 360, 362
    direct objects, 358
    indirect objects, 92
    where/when, as, ESL 319
    who/which/that, as, ESL 319
of, have, using, 351
off of, using, 351
O.K., Ok, Okay, using, 351
one of . . . who, which, that, agreement
        and, 40
Online research. *See* Internet
or, as joining word, 33–34
Organizations, capitalization of, 173
Organizing, 7–8, 29–30. *See also*
        Patterns of organization
    with computers, 31
    revision and, 12
ought to, must, 85
Outlining, 6, 30
    with computers, 32

P

Pamphlets
    MLA-style documentation, 273
    underlining/italics, 182
Paragraphs, 13–20
    coherence in, 14
    development of, 14
    introductions/conclusions, 14–15
    patterns of organization
        (*See* Patterns of organization)
    in research papers, 231
    transitions between, 66–68
    unity in, 13–14
Parallel constructions, 49–51
    definition of, 362
    faulty parallelism, 50, 54
Paraphrasing information, 225–26,
        237, 363
Parentheses, 168–69
    document design, 333
    with numbers, 169
    series/lists with, 169
    with supplementary matter, 169
    using brackets with, 170
Parenthetical elements, 363
Participial phrases, 364
Participles, 80–82, 363
Parts of speech, 363. *See also specific*
        headings for
Parts of wholes, 156
Passive voice, 110, 363, 378
    sentence clarity and, 63
    shifts and, 54
    verb voice and, 83
Past participle, 363
    with irregular verbs, 80–82
Past tense of verbs, 372. *See also*
        Verb tense
Patterns of organization, 15–20
    analogy, 16–17
    classification, 17–18
    comparison and contrast, 19
    definition, 19–20
    description in, 15–16
    examples and illustration, 17
    narration, 15
    process analysis, 18–19
Peoples/their languages,
        capitalization with, 173

Perfect progressive tense, 363
Perfect tense, 363. *See also* Verb
    tense
Periodicals
  CBE-style documentation, 309
  Chicago-style documentation,
    303–4
  MLA documentation for, 267–68
  online versions, 240, 245
  underlining/italcs, 182
Periods
  with abbreviations, 161–62
  ending sentences with, 161
  with quotation marks, 156–57,
    162
  sentence fragments and, 43
Periods/events, capitalization with,
    173
Person, 363
  shifts in, 52–53
Personal pronouns, 88, 363
Persons, capitalization with, 173
Persuading, 1
Phrasal verbs, 363, ESL 315–16
Phrases, 111–12, 231, 359. *See also*
    Essential clauses/phrases;
    Nonessential clauses/phrases
  absolute phrase, 364
  appositive phrase, 364
  clarity and, 71–72
  commas with, 130, 132–33
  conciseness and, 198
  dashes with, 166
  definition of, 111, 364
  faulty parallelism and, 45
  gerund phrases, 364
  infinitive phrase, 364
  nonrestrictive, 120–21, 361
  noun phrases, 364
  participial phrases, 364
  prepositional phrases, 364
  restrictive, 119–20, 365
  in series, 134
  subject-verb agreement, 38
  for transition, 65–66
  transitional, 123
  verb, 74
Places/geographic regions
  abbreviations with, 177

  capitalization with, 173
  prepositions for, ESL 326
Place words, capitalization with, 174
Plagiarism, 235–37, 364
  accidental, 236–37
  documenting sources, 235
  paraphrasing and, 237
Planning process, 3–7
  brainstorming, 4–5
  clustering and branching, 5
  conversation/collaboration, 5
  divide and conquer, 7
  evidence, 7
  freewriting, 4
  journalist's questions, 6–7
  listing, 4–5
  manageable divisions in, 7
  outlining, 6
  reading, 6
  writers notebook/journal, 5
Plays
  APA-style documentation, 290
  MLA-style documentation, 271
  underlining/italics, 182
Plural nouns, 86–87
Plurals, 39, 379
  apostrophes with, 143–44
  -s/-es endings with, 86–88, 143–44,
    190–91
  spelling rules for, 190–92, 383
Plural subjects, agreement with, 36
Plural words, 39
Poetry
  MLA online citations, 251
  quotation marks in, 155
  quoting, 229
  slashes with, 167
  underlining/italics, 182
Possessive pronouns, 89–90, 93, 142,
    364
Possessives, 87
  apostrophes with, 142–43
Postal addresses, abbreviating, 177
Predicate adjective, 364
Predicate nominative, 364
Predicates, 55–56, 364
Prefixes, 160, 364
  capitalization with, 175
  spelling rules with, 188–89, 383

Prepositional phrases, 364
Prepositions, 107–8, 380
  definition of, 107, 364
  idiomatic forms, 108
  for logical relationships, ESL
    326–27
  object case with, 92–93
  of place, ESL 326
  for purpose, ESL 327
  of time, ESL 326
  using, 108
Present progressive tense, 363.
    See also Verb tense
Present tense of verbs, 371–72.
    See also Verb tense
Pretentious language, 201
Primary sources, 213
Process analysis, 18–19
Progressive tense, 365. *See also*
    Verb tense
Pronoun case, 91–95, 379
  chart for, 92
  in compound constructions,
    93–94
  definition of, 365
  illustrative chart, 92
  I/me with, 95
  object case, 92–93
  omissions with comparisons, 95
  possessives and, 93
  subject case, 92
  who/whom and, 94–95
Pronoun *I* and interjection *O*,
    capitalization with, 174
Pronoun reference, 96–98, 379–80
  compound subjects and, 97
  definition of, 96, 365
  indefinite pronouns and, 98
  indefinite words and, 98
  number and, 97
  who/which/that and, 97–98
Pronouns, 88–91
  definition of, 365
  demonstrative, 88, 358
  interrogative, 89
  personal, 88
  possessive, 89–90, 142
  reciprocal, 90
  reflexive, 90
  relative, 88–89
  repeated words, ESL 318–19
  as sentence subjects, 123
  as subjects, 123
  as transitions, 64–65, 66–67
Proofreading, 12–13, 32
  for fragments, 43–44
  for parallelism, 51, 382–83
  strategies for, 184–85
Proper nouns, 186, 365, ESL 323
Punctuation. *See also entries for*
    each mark
  brackets, 170, 230
  with clauses, 57, 117, 127–28,
    130–33
  with complex sentences, 127–28
  in compound sentences, 127
  dashes, 166–67, 332
  document design and, 332–33
  ellipsis, 170, 230, 358
  end punctuation, 161–65, 230,
    332
  exclamation points, 164–65
  hyphens, 158–60
  parentheses, 168–69
  periods, 161–62, 332
  question marks, 163
  quotation marks, 154–57, 230–31
  of sentences, 123–24, 127–28
  slashes, 167–68
  titles of paper, 123–24
Purpose for writing, 1

Q

Question marks, 163
  at end of sentence, 163
  indicating doubt with, 163
  with quotation marks, 157, 163,
    381
  in series/lists, 163
quiet, quit, quite, 193
Quotation marks, 154–57
  colons with, 152–53, 157
  commas with, 156–57
  dashes with, 157
  document design, 332
  exclamation point with, 165
  marking dialogue with, 155–56,
    381

with minor titles, 156
with parts of wholes, 156
periods with, 156–57
in poetry, 155
question marks with, 157, 381
for quoting prose, 154–55
semicolons with, 157
with words, 156, 382
Quotations, 152, 154–55
    APA citations for, 282
    brackets within, 170
    capitalization of, 152, 229
    definitions of, 365
    limiting use of, 232
    punctuation with, 229–31
    question marks with, 381
    types of, 228–29
Quoting prose
    note taking and, 228
    quotation marks with, 154–55

R

Radio program
    MLA documentation for, 270
    underlining/italics for, 182
Reader's Guide to Periodical Literature,
    211, 215
Reading, 6
reason . . . because, using, 351
reason why, using, 352
Reciprocal pronouns, 90, 365
References list, APA style, 286–91
    articles in periodicals, 287–88
    books, 286–87
    conference proceedings, 290
    dissertation, 290
    electronic sources, 288–89
    films/videotapes/performances/
        artwork, 290
    government document, 290
    information service, 290
    interviews, 290
    recordings, 291
    television broadcasts, 291
    unpublished presentations, 291
Reflexive pronouns, 90, 365
Regional words, 202
Regular verbs, 369–70
Relative pronouns, 88–89, 365

Religions/their followers, capitaliza-
    tion with, 173
Repeated words, ESL 318–19
Repetition, 66–67
Reporting, 1
Research paper. *See also* Plagiarism;
        Sources of information
    APA style, 291–98
        first page format, 293
        page format, 294–96
        references, 297–98
        title page, 292
    integrating sources, 231–32
    MLA-style, 273–80
        first page format, 275
        page formats, 276–78
        title page for, 274
        Works Cited pages, 279–80
    narrowing topic, 211–12
    signal words/phrases in, 232–33
    thesis formulation, 212
    topic selection, 211
Restrictive clauses/phrases, 119–20,
    365
Résumés, 334–44
    checklist for, 338
    cover letters for, 341–42
    keyword summary, 344
    online job searches, 343
    scannable, 343–44
    sections of, 334–38
    styles for, 338–40
    using active verbs, 337
Revising, 11–12
    with computers, 31–32
Run-on sentences, 34, 366, 374

S

Salutations, 139, 152
Scholarly projects, citing MLA style,
    250–51
Scientific terms, underlining/italics
    with, 182
Search engines, 218, 239–41
    meta-search engines, 241
    using on the web, 242–43
    web resources and, 244
Secondary sources, 213–14
Second person, 92

-self, -selves endings, with reflexive pronouns, 90

Semicolons, 147–48
  with complex sentences, 127–28
  with compound sentences, 127, 148
  with conjunctive adverbs, 57
  document design, 332
  with independent clauses, 33–34, 127–28, 381
  patterns for using, 147
  with quotation marks, 150, 157
  in series/lists, 149
  unnecessary use of, 150

-s endings
  agreement and, 37
  with plural nouns, 87–88
  with possessives, 142–43
  with singular verbs, 87
  spelling rules with, 190

Sentence diagrams, 366

Sentence fragments, 366, 375
  intentional, 44
  misplaced periods and, 43
  revising for, 42–43
  unintentional, 42–44

Sentences, 122–25
  capitalization of first word, 174
  clarity in (*See* Clarity, sentence)
  complex forms, 125, 127–28, 366
  compound-complex forms, 125, 366
  compound forms (*See* Compound sentences)
  dashes with, 166
  declarative sentence, 366
  end punctuation, 161–65
  exclamatory sentence, 366
  faulty predication in, 55–56
  interrogative, 366
  punctuation of, 123–24, 127–28
  purposes of, 124
  simple forms, 124, 127, 366
  variety in (*See* Variety, sentence)

Series/lists
  capitalization with, 175
  clauses in, 134–35
  colons with, 149
  commas in, 134–35
  numbers with, 180
  parentheses with, 169
  phrases in, 134
  question marks in, 163
  semicolons in, 149
  words in, 134

set, sit, using, 352

Sexist language, 195–96, 383
  alternatives to *man,* 195
  job titles and, 195
  masculine pronouns and, 195–96

shall, should, using, 85

shall, will, using, 79

Shifts, avoiding. *See* Consistency (avoiding shifts)

Ships, underling/italics with, 182

should, shall, using, 85

should of, using, 352

Signal words/phrases, 232–33

Simple sentences, 124, 127, 366

Simple tense, 76–77, 366

Singular nouns, 86

Singular subjects, agreement with, 36

sit, set, using, 352

Slang, 202, 366

Slashes, 167–68
  document design, 332
  indicating acceptable alternatives, 168
  with poetry, 167

so, as joining word, 33–34

some
  as indefinite, 38
  with nouns, ESL 325–26
  verb agreement, 89

some, any, using, ESL 325–26

somebody, some body, using, 352

someone, some one, using, 352

sort, kind, using, 352

Sources of information, 213–18. *See also* Documenting sources; Internet; Note taking
  community sources, 216
  evaluation of (*See* Evaluation of sources)
  finding useful terms, 218
  interviews/surveys, 216

libraries (*See* Libraries)
online sources, 215
primary sources, 213
secondary sources, 213–14
working bibliography for, 216–17
writer's view, 214
Spacing, document design, 330
Specialized language, 206
Specific words, 206–7, 367
Spell checkers, 185–86
Spelling, 184–94
  doubling consonants guidelines, 187
  homonyms, 192–93, 383
  ie/ei, guidelines, 186, 383
  prefixes/suffixes and, 188–89, 383
  proofreading strategies, 184–85
  rules for plurals, 190–92, 383
  spell checkers, 185–86
Split infinitives, 367
Standard English, 201, 367
Statistics, numbers with, 180
Subject case, of pronouns, 92, 367
Subject complement, 39, 367
Subjects, 109–10
  amounts as, 38–39
  buried, 36–37
  collective nouns as, 38–39
  compound, 37
  definition of, 109, 367
  either/or as, 37–38
  indefinites as, 38
  intended, 63, 378
  omitted words in, ESL 318
  plural, 36
  plural words as, 39
  sentence clarity and, 63
  singular, 36
  there/it with, ESL 318
  titles of works as, 39
  who/which/that as, 40
  words as, 39
Subject-verb agreement, 36–41, 367, 379
  amounts and, 38–39
  buried subjects and, 36–37
  clauses/phrases and, 38
  collective nouns and, 38–39
  company names and, 39
  compound subjects and, 37
  either/or and, 37–38
  indefinites and, 38
  linking verbs and, 39
  one of . . . and, 40
  plural subjects and, 36
  plural words and, 39
  singular subjects and, 36
  there is/there are/it and, 40
  titles of works and, 39
  who/which/that, 40
Subjunctive mood, 84, 367
Subordinate clauses. *See* Dependent clauses
Subordinating conjunctions, 58–59, 367
Subordination, 58–59, 367
  appropriate, 58–59
  excessive, 59, 377
  inappropriate, 59, 377
such, using, 352
Suffixes, 160, 187
  definition of, 367–68
  hyphens with, 160
  spelling rules with, 188–89, 383
Summarizing information, 1, 223–24, 368
Superlatives, 368, ESL 324
Supplementary matter, parentheses with, 169
Support for argument, 25
Supreme Being, capitalization with, 174
sure, using, 352
Synonyms, 64, 66, 368

T

Television programs
  APA-style documentation, 291
  MLA documentation for, 270
  underlining/italics for, 182
Tense, 368. *See also* Verb tense
than, then, using, 193, 352
that
  as demonstrative pronoun, 88
  with essential clauses, 120
  as relative pronoun, 88
that, which, using, 352

that there, this here, these here, those there, using, 352
their, there, they're, using, 193, 353
theirself, theirselves, themself, using, 353
them, using, 353
then, than, using, 353
there, it, with subjects, ESL 318
there is, there are
  agreement and, 40
  subject placement and, 110
these, as demonstrative pronoun, 88
Thesis
  formulation of, 212–13
  for writing, 2–3
Third person, 92
this, as demonstrative pronoun, 88
those, as demonstrative pronoun, 88
thusly, using, 353
Time of day
  abbreviations with, 177
  article *the* with, ESL 324
  numbers with, 177
  prepositions for, ESL 326
Titles, document design, 329–30
Titles, minor, 156
Titles of works
  agreement and, 39
  capitalization with, 174
Titles with names
  abbreviations for, 176–77
  capitalization with, 174
to, too, two, using, 353
to, too, using, 193
to, verb forms, 46
to be, to do, to have, verb forms, 79
Tone, 368
  levels of formality and, 203–5
  shifts in, 53–54
Topic, 1–2, 23–24
  narrowing, 211–12
  for research paper, 211
toward, towards, using, 353
Trademarks, capitalization with, 173
Trains, underlining/italics with, 182
Transitions, 64–68, 378
  for beginning sentence, 123
  definition of, 368
  between paragraphs, 66–68
  pronouns for, 64–67

repetition as, 64, 66–67
summary of, 65–66
synonyms for, 64, 66–67
words and phrases for, 65–67
Transitive verbs, 368
Two-word (phrasal) verbs, 368, ESL 315–16

U
Underlining/italics, 182–83
  document design, 333
  for emphasis, 182
  examples/terms, 182
  foreign words, 182
  ships, airplanes, trains, 182
  titles of papers, 182
  titles of works, 182, 382
Unintentional fragments, 42–44
Unity in paragraphs, 13–14
Unnecessary words, 197–201, 383
  clichés, 200, 384
  conciseness and, 197–98
  fillers as, 197–98
  pretentious language and, 201
  repetition as, 197
  strategies for avoiding, 198
use to, using, 353

V
Vague terms, 21
Variety, sentence, 379
  adding/changing words for, 70–72
  changing clauses/phrases for, 71–72
  combining sentences, 69–70
Verbals, 74–75, 359
  definition of, 368
  gerunds, 74–75, 359, ESL 314–17, ESL 324
  infinitives, 46, ESL 316–17
  participles, 80–82
Verb forms, 74–75, 379. *See also* Irregular verbs
  base form, 75
  -d/-ed endings with, 75–77
  definition of, 74
  has/had with, 75–76
  illustrative chart, 77
  -ing endings (gerunds), 74–75
  to + verb (infinitives), 75–76

Verb mood, 84, 360
Verb phrases, 74, 371, ESL 315–16
Verbs, 73–85. *See also* Verbals; Voice
  action forms, 73, 337
  conditionals, ESL 314–15
  conjugation of, 369–71
  definition of, 73, 368
  -ed endings with, 75, 79
  forms of (*See* Verb forms)
  helping (auxiliary) verbs, ESL 314
  irregular (*See* Irregular verbs)
  linking, 39
  modals with, 85
  mood of, 84
  regular, 369–70
  substituting for nouns, 62–63
Verb tense, 53, 76–82, 371. *See also*
     Irregular verbs
  forms for, 76–77
  future tense, 78–79
    future perfect, 79, 372
    future perfect progressive, 79,
      372
    future progressive, 79, 372
    simple future, 78–79, 372
  past tense, 78, 372
    past perfect, 78, 372
    past perfect progressive, 78, 372
    past progressive, 78, 372
    simple past, 78, 372
  present tense, 77–78, 371
    present perfect, 77–78, 372
    present perfect progressive, 78,
      372
    present progressive, 77, 372
    simple present, 77
Voice, 54, 63, 355
  active, 63, 83, 378
  conciseness and, 198
  passive, 83

W

want for, using, 353
Warrants, 25–26
Web resources, 243–46. *See also*
     Search engines
  books, 245
  fields of study, 245
  government sites, 245–46
  libraries, online, 246
  listservs/newsgroups, 245
  references, 244
  subject directories, 244
  university (U.S.) web sites, 245
  for writing, 243–44
Web sites, 242. *See also* Web re-
     sources
  access to, 248
well, badly, using, 100
well, good, using, 353
well, using, 101
went, gone, using, 353
were, we're, where, using, 193
what
  as interrogative pronoun, 89
  as relative pronoun, 88
when clauses, 116–17
where, using, 353
where, when, as objects, ESL 319
where . . . at, using, 353
which
  as interrogative pronoun, 89
  as relative pronoun, 88
which, that, using, 353
while, awhile, using, 353
who, which, that
  with adjective clauses, 116
  agreement and, 40
  as objects, ESL 319
  reference and, 97
who, whom
  as interrogative pronouns, 89
  pronoun case and, 94–95
  as relative pronouns, 88
  subject/object case with, 353
who's, whose, using, 193, 354
will, shall, using, 79
will, would, using, 85
Word choice, 201–9, 385. *See also*
     Unnecessary words
  adding/changing for clarity,
    70–72
  colloquial words, 201–2
  concrete/abstract words, 207–8
  connotation, 209
  denotation, 208–9
  general words/specific words,
    206–7

Word choice *(cont.)*
  jargon, 206
  levels of formality, 203–5, 384
  regional words, 202
  sexist language, 195–96, 383
  slang, 202
  Standard English, 201, 367
  technical terms, 206
Word-processor, 330
Words. *See also* Unnecessary words
  abstract words, 324
  colloquialisms, 201–2
  commas after, 130
  compound, 159
  concrete/abstract, 207–8
  dividing with hyphens, 158–59
  markers, 58–59
  omissions in comparisons, 95
  one-syllable/two-syllable, 187
  plural, 39
  regional, 202
  in series, 134
  signal, 232–33
  for transition, 65–66
Word units, 159–60
Working bibliography, 216–17
Works Cited, MLA style, 260–73
  advertisements, 272–73
  articles in periodicals, 267–68
  books, 263–66
  cartoons, 272
  computer software, 270
  dissertations, 273
  electronic sources, 268–69
  film/video recording, 271
  interviews, 272
  lecture/speech/address, 273
  letters/memos/e-mail, 272
  list of examples, 261–63
  map/chart, 272
    models for, 260–61
    online databases/Internet, 269–70
    pamphlets, 273
    performance of play, 271
    record/tape/cassette/CD, 271
    television/radio program, 270
    works of art, 272
Works of art
  APA documentation for, 290
  MLA documentation for, 272
  underlining/italics for, 182
World Wide Web (WWW). *See also*
      Internet; Web resources
  APA documentation for, 284
  job searches on, 334
would, could, might, using, ESL 315
would, will, using, 85
Writers notebook/journal, 5, 30–31
Writer's view, 214
Writing process
  purpose, 1
  thesis and, 2–3
  topic, 1–2
Writing strategies
  collaboration, 8–10
  with computers, 30–32
  drafting, 7
  editing and proofreading, 12–13
  organizing, 7–8
  planning, 3–7
  revising and, 11–12

Y

-y, -i, spelling rules for, 190
Years
  abbreviations with, 177
  numbers for, 180
yet, as joining word, 33–34
you, understood in commands, 110
your, you're, using, 193, 354

Symbol	Error Explanation	Chapter
ab	abbreviation	36
ad	adjective/adverb	20
agr	agreement	7
arg	argument	4
awk	awkward construction	10-14
ca	case	19
cap(s)	capitalization	35
comp	computers and writing	5
coord	coordination	13a
cs	comma splice	6a
dm	dangling modifier	9a
frag	sentence fragment	8
fs	fused/run-on sentence	6b
hyph	hyphenation	32
ital	italics/underlining	38
lc	use lowercase	35
log	logic	4d
mm	misplaced modifier	9b
num	number use	37
¶	new paragraph	3
//	parallelism	10
p	punctuation	27–34
para	paragraphs	3
pl	plural needed	18a
pred	predication	12
purp	purpose and audience	1
ref	reference	19b
shft	shift	11
sp	spelling	39
sub	subordination	13b
sxt	sexist language	40
t	tense	17c
trans	transition needed	15
under	underlining/italics	38
v	verb	17
var	variety needed	16
w	wordy	41
wc/wds	word choice	42
w pr	writing process	2
ww/wds	wrong word	42
x	obvious error	
∧	insert	
∩/tr	transpose	
ℓ	delete	

QUESTION AND CORRECT: SOME OF THE MOST COMMONLY ASKED QUESTIONS ABOUT WRITING

		REFER TO SECTION:

QUESTIONS ABOUT WRITING

1. How can I find a topic to write about? — 1b, 4c, 43
2. How can I think up or find things to say about a topic? — 2a, 4d, 44
3. What goes in an introduction and conclusion? — 3d
4. How can I persuade readers to accept an argument? — 4a-b
5. How can a computer help me to write? — 5

QUESTIONS ABOUT SENTENCES

6. What are comma splices, run-ons, and fused sentences? — 6a-b
7. How do I make subjects and verbs agree? — 7
8. Are there words I shouldn't start sentences with? — 26
9. How do I find the subject and verb in a sentence? — 7b, 17, 22
10. For words like *each* and *news*, is the verb *is* or *are*? — 7f-h, 18b
11. How can I tell whether a sentence is complete or a fragment? — 8a
12. What's wrong with sentences with *is when* or *is because*? — 12
13. How can I improve choppy sentences that don't flow? — 15
14. How can I make paragraphs connect to each other? — 15e
15. What is passive voice? When should I use it? — 14f, 17d
16. When should I use the different verb tenses? — 17c
17. Is it *between you and me* or *between you and I*? — 18b, 19a
18. When do you use *it's* and *its*? — 19a
19. Can you write *sure good* or *real well*? — 20a
20. When do you use *a, an,* and *the*? — 20b

QUESTIONS ABOUT PUNCTUATION

21. How do I know when to use an apostrophe? — 18a
22. When should I put a comma before *and* and *but*? — 6, 27a, 27d, 27h
23. When should I use commas before *which, that,* or *because*? — 24b, 27c
24. Is it *James' car* or *James's car*? — 28a
25. What's wrong with *yours'* or *mine*? — 19a, 28d
26. What punctuation should I use with a list? — 29d, 30a
27. Do periods go inside or outside the quotation marks? — 31a, 31d
28. How do I indicate titles? with underlining? italics? — 31b, 38a
29. How is poetry quoted in a paragraph? — 31a, 34b
30. When should I use the series of dots (. . .)? — 34e

QUESTIONS ABOUT MECHANICS AND SPELLING

31. Should I capitalize words like *winter* and *Midwest*? — 35
32. Should I write *37* or *thirty-seven*? — 36a, 37